CALIFORNIA TRAILS
NORTHERN SIERRA

CALIFORNIA TRAILS
NORTHERN SIERRA

PETER MASSEY
JEANNE WILSON
ANGELA TITUS

ADLER
PUBLISHING

Acknowledgements

Many people and organizations have made significant contributions to the research and production of this book.

Cover Design Concept: **Rudy Ramos**
Text Design and Maps: **Deborah Rust Design**
Layout: **Bob Schram**
Copyediting and Proofreading: **Sallie Greenwood and Alice Levine**

We would like to thank Scott J. Lawson, director, and staff of the Plumas County Museum; Deborah Tibbetts, district archaeologist at Lassen National Forest; Bev Way, Bill Tierney, Jami Nield, Nancy Gardner, and Gerald R. Gates of Modoc National Forest.

Staff at many offices of the U.S. Forest Service also provided us with valuable assistance.

Publisher's Note: Every effort has been taken to ensure that the information in this book is accurate at press time. Please visit our website to advise us of any changes or corrections you find. We also welcome recommendations for new 4WD trails or other suggestions to improve the information in this book.

Adler Publishing Company, Inc.
1601 Pacific Coast Highway, Suite 290
Hermosa Beach, CA 90254
Phone: 800-660-5107
Fax: 310-698-0709
4WDbooks.com

Contents

Before You Go

Why a 4WD Does It Better

The design and engineering of 4WD vehicles provide them with many advantages over normal cars when you head off the paved road:

■ improved distribution of power to all four wheels;

■ a transmission transfer case, which provides low-range gear selection for greater pulling power and for crawling over difficult terrain;

■ high ground clearance;

■ less overhang of the vehicle's body past the wheels, which provides better front- and rear-clearance when crossing gullies and ridges;

■ large-lug, wide-tread tires;

■ rugged construction (including underbody skid plates on many models).

If you plan to do off-highway touring, all of these considerations are important whether you are evaluating the capabilities of your current 4WD or are looking to buy one; each is considered in detail in this chapter.

To explore the most difficult trails described in this book, you will need a 4WD vehicle that is well rated in each of the above features. If you own a 2WD sport utility vehicle, a lighter car-type SUV, or a pickup truck, your ability to explore the more difficult trails will depend on conditions and your level of experience.

A word of caution: Whatever type of 4WD vehicle you drive, understand that it is not invincible or indestructible. Nor can it go everywhere. A 4WD has a much higher center of gravity and weighs more than a car, and so has its own consequent limitations.

Experience is the only way to learn what your vehicle can and cannot do. Therefore, if you are inexperienced, we strongly recommend that you start with trails that have lower difficulty ratings. As you develop an understanding of your vehicle and of your own taste for adventure, you can safely tackle the more challenging trails.

One way to beef up your knowledge quickly, while avoiding the costly and sometimes dangerous lessons learned from on-the-road mistakes, is to undertake a 4WD course taught by a professional. Look in the Yellow Pages for courses in your area.

Using This Book

Route Planning

The regional map on pages 24 to 27 provide a convenient overview of the trails in the Northern Sierra region of California. Each 4WD trail is shown, as are major highways and towns, helping you plan various routes by connecting a series of 4WD trails and paved roads.

As you plan your overall route, you will probably want to utilize as many 4WD trails as possible. However, check the difficulty rating and time required for each trail before finalizing your plans. You don't want to be stuck 50 miles from the highway—at sunset and without camping gear, since your trip was supposed to be over hours ago—when you discover that your vehicle can't handle a certain difficult passage.

Difficulty Ratings

We utilize a point system to rate the difficulty of each trail. Any such system is subjective, and your experience of the trails will vary depending on your skill and the road conditions at the time. Indeed, any amount of rain may make the trails much more difficult, if not completely impassable.

We have rated the 4WD trails on a scale of 1 to 10—1 being passable for a normal passenger vehicle in good conditions and 10 requiring a heavily modified vehicle and an experienced driver who expects to encounter vehicle damage. Because this book is designed for owners of unmodified 4WD vehicles—who we assume do not want to damage their vehicles—most of the trails are rated 5 or lower. A few trails are included that rate as high as 7, while those rated 8 to 10 are beyond the scope of this book.

This is not to say that the moderate-rated trails are easy. We strongly recommend that inexperienced drivers not tackle trails rated at 4 or higher until they have undertaken a number of the lower-rated ones, so that they can gauge their skill level and prepare for the difficulty of the higher-rated trails.

In assessing the trails, we have always assumed good road conditions (dry road surface, good visibility, and so on). The factors influencing our ratings are as follows:

■ obstacles such as rocks, mud, ruts, sand, slickrock, and stream crossings;

■ the stability of the road surface;

■ the width of the road and the vehicle clearance between trees or rocks;

■ the steepness of the road;

■ the margin for driver error (for example, a very high, open shelf road would be rated more difficult even if it was not very steep and had a stable surface).

The following is a guide to the ratings.

Rating 1: The trail is graded dirt but suitable for a normal passenger vehicle. It usually has gentle grades, is fairly wide, and has very shallow water crossings (if any).

Rating 2: High-clearance vehicles are preferred but not necessary. These trails are dirt roads, but they may have rocks, grades, water crossings, or ruts that make clearance a concern in a normal passenger vehicle. The trails are fairly wide, making passing possible at almost any point along the trail. Mud is not a concern under normal weather conditions.

Rating 3: High-clearance 4WDs are preferred, but any high-clearance vehicle is acceptable. Expect a rough road surface; mud and sand are possible but will be easily passable. You may encounter rocks up to 6 inches in diameter, a loose road surface, and shelf roads, though these will be wide enough for passing or will have adequate pull-offs.

Rating 4: High-clearance 4WDs are recommended, though most stock SUVs are acceptable. Expect a rough road surface with rocks larger than 6 inches, but there will be a reasonable driving line available. Patches of mud are possible but can be readily negotiated; sand may be deep and require lower tire pressures. There may be stream crossings up to 12 inches deep, substantial sections of single-lane shelf road, moderate grades, and sections of moderately loose road surface.

Rating 5: High-clearance 4WDs are required. These trails have either a rough, rutted surface, rocks up to 9 inches, mud and deep sand that may be impassable for inexperienced drivers, or stream crossings up to 18 inches deep. Certain sections may be steep enough to cause traction problems, and you may encounter very narrow shelf roads with steep drop-offs and tight clearance between rocks or trees.

Rating 6: These trails are for experienced four-wheel drivers only. They are potentially dangerous, with large rocks, ruts, or terraces that may need to be negotiated. They may also have stream crossings at least 18 inches deep, involve rapid currents, unstable stream bottoms, or difficult access; steep slopes, loose surfaces, and narrow clearances; or very narrow sections of shelf road with steep drop-offs and possibly challenging road surfaces.

Rating 7: Skilled, experienced four-wheel drivers only. These trails include very challenging sections with extremely steep grades, loose surfaces, large rocks, deep ruts, and/or tight clearances. Mud or sand may necessitate winching.

Rating 8 and above: Stock vehicles are likely to be damaged and may find the trail impassable. Highly skilled, experienced four-wheel drivers only.

Scenic Ratings

If rating the degree of difficulty is subjective, rating scenic beauty is guaranteed to lead to arguments. The Northern Sierra region of California contains a spectacular variety of scenery—from the crystal clear, sparkling waters of Lake Tahoe to the towering peaks of the Sierra Nevada. Despite the subjectivity of attempting a comparative rating of diverse scenery, we have tried to provide a guide to the relative scenic quality of the various trails. The ratings are based on a scale of 1 to 10, with 10 being the most attractive.

Remoteness Ratings

Many trails in the Northern Sierra region are in remote mountain country; sometimes the trails are seldom traveled, and the likelihood is low that another vehicle will appear within a reasonable time to assist you if you get stuck or break down. We have included a ranking for remoteness of +0 through +2. Prepare carefully before tackling the higher-rated, more remote trails (see Special Preparations for Remote Travel, page 11). For trails with a high remoteness rating, consider traveling with a second vehicle.

Estimated Driving Times

In calculating driving times, we have not allowed for stops. Your actual driving time may be considerably longer depending on the number and duration of the stops you make. Add more time if you prefer to drive more slowly than good conditions allow.

Current Road Information

All the 4WD trails described in this book may become impassable in poor weather conditions. Storms can alter roads, remove tracks, and create impassable washes. Most of the trails described, even easy 2WD trails, can quickly become impassable even to 4WD vehicles after only a small amount of rain. For each trail, we have provided a phone number for obtaining current information about conditions.

Abbreviations

The route directions for the 4WD trails use a series of abbreviations as follows:

SO	CONTINUE STRAIGHT ON
TL	TURN LEFT
TR	TURN RIGHT
BL	BEAR LEFT
BR	BEAR RIGHT
UT	U-TURN

Using Route Directions

For every trail, we describe and pinpoint (by odometer reading) nearly every significant feature along the route—such as intersec-

tions, streams, washes, gates, cattle guards, and so on—and provide directions from these landmarks. Odometer readings will vary from vehicle to vehicle, so you should allow for slight variations. Be aware that trails can change quickly. A new trail may be cut around a washout, a faint trail can be graded by the county, or a well-used trail may fall into disuse. All these factors will affect the accuracy of the given directions.

If you diverge from the route, zero your trip meter upon your return and continue along the route, making the necessary adjustment to the point-to-point odometer readings. In the directions, we regularly reset the odometer readings—at significant landmarks or popular lookouts and spur trails—so that you won't have to recalculate for too long.

Most of the trails can be started from either end, and the route directions include both directions of travel; reverse directions are printed in purple below the main directions. When traveling in reverse, read from the bottom of the table and work up.

Route directions include cross-references whenever two 4WD trails included in this book connect; these cross-references allow for an easy change of route or destination.

Each trail includes periodic latitude and longitude readings to facilitate using a global positioning system (GPS) receiver. These readings may also assist you in finding your location on the maps. The GPS coordinates are given in the format dd°mm.mm'. To save time when loading coordinates into your GPS receiver, you may wish to include only one decimal place, since in Northern California, the first decimal place equals about 150 yards and the second only about 15 yards.

Map References

We recommend that you supplement the information in this book with more-detailed maps. For each trail, we list the sheet maps and road atlases that provide the best detail for the area. Typically, the following references are given:

■ Bureau of Land Management Maps
■ U.S. Forest Service Maps

■ *California Road & Recreation Atlas,* 2nd ed. (Medford, Oregon: Benchmark Maps, 1998)—Scale 1:300,000

■ *Northern California Atlas & Gazetteer,* 5th ed. (Yarmouth, Maine: DeLorme Mapping, 2000)—Scale 1:150,000

■ Maptech-Terrain Navigator Topo Maps—Scale 1:100,000 and 1:24,000

■ *Trails Illustrated* Topo Maps; National Geographic Maps—Various scales, but all contain good detail

We recommend the *Trails Illustrated* series of maps as the best for navigating these trails. They are reliable, easy to read, and printed on nearly indestructible plastic paper. However, this series covers only a few of the 4WD trails described in this book.

The DeLorme *Northern California Atlas & Gazetteer* is useful and has the advantage of providing you with maps of the entire state at a reasonable price. Although its 4WD trail information doesn't go beyond what we provide, it is useful if you wish to explore the hundreds of side roads.

U.S. Forest Service maps lack the topographic detail of the other sheet maps and, in our experience, are occasionally out of date. They have the advantage of covering a broad area and are useful in identifying land use and travel restrictions. These maps are most useful for the longer trails.

In our opinion, the best single option by far is the Terrain Navigator series of maps published on CD-ROM by Maptech. These CD-ROMs contain an amazing level of detail because they include the entire set of 1,941 U.S. Geological Survey topographical maps of California at the 1:24,000 scale and all 71 maps at the 1:100,000 scale. These maps offer many advantages over normal maps:

■ GPS coordinates for any location can be found and loaded into your GPS receiver. Conversely, if you have your GPS coordinates, your location on the map can be pinpointed instantly.

■ Towns, rivers, passes, mountains, and many other sites are indexed by name so that they can be located quickly.

■ 4WD trails can be marked and profiled

for elevation changes and distances from point to point.

■ Customized maps can be printed out.

Maptech uses 14 CD-ROMs to cover the entire state of California; they can be purchased individually or as part of a two-state package at a heavily discounted price. The CD-ROMs can be used with a laptop computer and a GPS receiver in your vehicle to monitor your location on the map and navigate directly from the display.

All these maps should be available through good map stores. The Maptech CD-ROMs are available directly from the company (800-627-7236, or on the internet at www.maptech.com).

Backcountry Driving Rules and Permits

Four-wheel driving involves special driving techniques and road rules. This section is an introduction for 4WD beginners.

4WD Road Rules

To help ensure that these trails remain open and available for all four-wheel drivers to enjoy, it is important to minimize your impact on the environment and not be a safety risk to yourself or anyone else. Remember that the 4WD clubs in California fight a constant battle with the government and various lobby groups to retain the access that currently exists.

The fundamental rule when traversing the 4WD trails described in this book is to use common sense. In addition, special road rules for 4WD trails apply:

■ Vehicles traveling uphill have the right of way.

■ If you are moving more slowly than the vehicle behind you, pull over to let the other vehicle by.

■ Park out of the way in a safe place. Blocking a track may restrict access for emergency vehicles as well as for other recreationalists. Set the parking brake—don't rely on leaving the transmission in park. Manual transmissions should be left in the lowest gear.

Tread Lightly!

Remember the rules of the Tread Lightly! program:

■ Be informed. Obtain maps, regulations, and other information from the forest service or from other public land agencies. Learn the rules and follow them.

■ Resist the urge to pioneer a new road or trail or to cut across a switchback. Stay on constructed tracks and avoid running over young trees, shrubs, and grasses, damaging or killing them. Don't drive across alpine tundra; this fragile environment can take years to recover.

■ Stay off soft, wet roads and 4WD trails readily torn up by vehicles. Repairing the damage is expensive, and quite often authorities find it easier to close the road rather than repair it.

■ Travel around meadows, steep hillsides, stream banks, and lake shores that are easily scarred by churning wheels.

■ Stay away from wild animals that are rearing young or suffering from a food shortage. Do not camp close to the water sources of domestic or wild animals.

■ Obey gate closures and regulatory signs.

■ Preserve America's heritage by not disturbing old mining camps, ghost towns, or other historical features. Leave historic sites, Native American rock art, ruins, and artifacts in place and untouched.

■ Carry out all your trash, and even that of others.

■ Stay out of designated wilderness areas. They are closed to all vehicles. It is your responsibility to know where the boundaries are.

■ Get permission to cross private land. Leave livestock alone. Respect landowners' rights.

Report violations of these rules to help keep these 4WD trails open and to ensure that others will have the opportunity to visit these backcountry sites. Many groups are actively seeking to close these public lands to vehicles, thereby denying access to those who are unable, or perhaps merely unwilling, to hike long distances. This magnificent countryside is owned by, and should be available to, all Americans.

Special Preparations for Remote Travel

When traveling in remote areas, you should take some special precautions to ensure that you don't end up in a life-threatening situation:

■ When planning a trip into remote areas, always inform someone as to where you are going, your route, and when you expect to return. Stick to your plan.

■ Be sure your vehicle is in good condition with a sound battery, good hoses, spare tire, spare fan belts, necessary tools, and reserve gasoline and oil. Other spare parts and extra radiator water are also valuable. If traveling in pairs, share the common spares and carry a greater variety.

■ Keep an eye on the sky. Flash floods can occur in a wash any time you see thunderheads—even when it's not raining a drop where you are.

■ Test trails on foot before driving through washes and sandy areas. One minute of walking may save hours of hard work getting your vehicle unstuck.

■ If your vehicle breaks down, stay near it. Your emergency supplies are there. Your car has many other items useful in an emergency. Raise your hood and trunk lid to denote "help needed." Remember, a vehicle can be seen for miles, but a person on foot is very difficult to spot from a distance.

■ Leave a disabled vehicle only if you are positive of the route and the distance to help. Leave a note for rescuers that gives the time you left and the direction you are taking.

■ If you must walk, rest for at least 10 minutes out of each hour. If you are not normally physically active, rest up to 30 minutes out of each hour. Find shade, sit down, and prop up your feet. Adjust your shoes and socks, but do not remove your shoes—you may not be able to get them back on swollen feet.

■ If you have water, drink it. Do not ration it.

■ If water is limited, keep your mouth closed. Do not talk, eat, smoke, drink alcohol, or take salt.

■ If you are stalled or lost, set signal fires. Set smoky fires in the daytime and bright ones at night. Three fires in a triangle denote "help needed."

■ A roadway is a sign of civilization. If you find a road, stay on it.

■ When hiking in remote areas, equip each person, especially children, with a police-type whistle. It makes a distinctive noise with little effort. Three blasts denote "help needed."

■ Avoid unnecessary contact with wildlife. Put your hands or feet only where your eyes can see. Some mice in California carry the deadly Hanta virus, a pulmonary syndrome fatal in 60 to 70 percent of human cases. Fortunately the disease is very rare—as of May 2006 only 43 cases have been reported in California and 438 nationwide—but caution is still advised. Other rodents may transmit bubonic plague. the same epidemic that killed one-third of Europe's population in the 1300s. Be especially wary near sick animals and keep pets, especially cats, away from wildlife and their fleas. Another creature to watch for is the western black-legged tick, the carrier of Lyme disease. Wearing clothing that covers legs and arms, tucking pants into boots, and using insect repellent are good ways to avoid fleas and ticks.

Obtaining Permits

Backcountry permits, which usually cost a fee, are required for certain activities on public lands in California, whether the area is a national park, state park, national monument, Indian reservation, or BLM land.

Restrictions may require a permit for overnight stays, which can include backpacking and 4WD or bicycle camping. Permits may also be required for day use by vehicles, horses, hikers, or bikes in some areas.

When possible, we include information about fees and permit requirements and where permits may be obtained, but these regulations change constantly. If in doubt, check with the most likely governing agency.

Assessing Your Vehicle's Off-Road Ability

Many issues come into play when evaluating your 4WD vehicle, although most of the 4WDs on the market are suitable for even the roughest trails described in this book. Engine power will be adequate in even the least-powerful modern vehicle. However, some vehicles are less suited to off-highway driving than others, and some of the newest, carlike sport utility vehicles simply are not designed for off-highway touring. The following information should allow you to identify the good, the bad, and the ugly.

Differing 4WD Systems

All 4WD systems have one thing in common: The engine provides power to all four wheels rather than to only two, as is typical in most standard cars. However, there are a number of differences in the way power is applied to the wheels.

The other feature that distinguishes nearly all 4WDs from normal passenger vehicles is that the gearboxes have high and low ratios that effectively double the number of gears. The high range is comparable to the range on a passenger car. The low range provides lower speed and more power, which is useful when towing heavy loads, driving up steep hills, or crawling over rocks. When driving downhill, the 4WD's low range increases engine braking.

Various makes and models of SUVs offer different drive systems, but these differences center on two issues: the way power is applied to the other wheels if one or more wheels slip, and the ability to select between 2WD and 4WD.

Normal driving requires that all four wheels be able to turn at different speeds; this allows the vehicle to turn without scrubbing its tires. In a 2WD vehicle, the front wheels (or rear wheels in a front-wheel-drive vehicle) are not powered by the engine and thus are free to turn individually at any speed. The rear wheels, powered by the engine, are only able to turn at different speeds because of the differential, which applies power to the faster-turning wheel.

This standard method of applying traction has certain weaknesses. First, when power is applied to only one set of wheels, the other set cannot help the vehicle gain traction. Second, when one powered wheel loses traction, it spins, but the other powered wheel doesn't turn. This happens because the differential applies all the engine power to the faster-turning wheel and no power to the other wheels, which still have traction. All 4WD systems are designed to overcome these two weaknesses. However, different 4WDs address this common objective in different ways.

Full-Time 4WD. For a vehicle to remain in 4WD all the time without scrubbing the tires, all the wheels must be able to rotate at different speeds. A full-time 4WD system allows this to happen by using three differentials. One is located between the rear wheels, as in a normal passenger car, to allow the rear wheels to rotate at different speeds. The second is located between the front wheels in exactly the same way. The third differential is located between the front and rear wheels to allow different rotational speeds between the front and rear sets of wheels. In nearly all vehicles with full-time 4WD, the center differential operates only in high range. In low range, it is completely locked. This is not a disadvantage because when using low range the additional traction is normally desired and the deterioration of steering response will be less noticeable due to the vehicle traveling at a slower speed.

Part-Time 4WD. A part-time 4WD system does not have the center differential located between the front and rear wheels. Consequently, the front and rear drive shafts are both driven at the same speed and with the same power at all times when in 4WD.

This system provides improved traction because when one or both of the front or rear wheels slips, the engine continues to provide power to the other set. However, because such a system doesn't allow a difference in speed between the front and rear sets of wheels, the tires scrub when turning, placing additional strain on the whole drive system. Therefore, such a system can be used only in slippery conditions; otherwise, the ability to steer the vehicle will deteriorate and the tires will quickly wear out.

Some vehicles, such as Jeeps with Selectrac and Mitsubishi Monteros with Active Trac 4WD, offer both full-time and part-time 4WD in high range.

Manual Systems to Switch Between 2WD and 4WD. There are three manual systems for switching between 2WD and 4WD. The most basic requires stopping and getting out of the vehicle to lock the front hubs manually before selecting 4WD. The second requires you to stop, but you change to 4WD by merely throwing a lever inside the vehicle (the hubs lock automatically). The third allows shifting between 2WD and 4WD high range while the vehicle is moving. Any 4WD that does not offer the option of driving in 2WD must have a full-time 4WD system.

Automated Switching Between 2WD and 4WD. Advances in technology are leading to greater automation in the selection of two- or four-wheel drive. When operating in high range, these high-tech systems use sensors to monitor the rotation of each wheel. When any slippage is detected, the vehicle switches the proportion of power from the wheel(s) that is slipping to the wheels that retain grip. The proportion of power supplied to each wheel is therefore infinitely variable as opposed to the original systems where the vehicle was either in two-wheel drive or four-wheel drive.

In recent years, this process has been spurred on by many of the manufacturers of luxury vehicles entering the SUV market— Mercedes, BMW, Cadillac, Lincoln, and Lexus have joined Range Rover in this segment.

Manufacturers of these higher-priced vehicles have led the way in introducing sophisticated computer-controlled 4WD systems. Although each of the manufacturers has its own approach to this issue, all the systems automatically vary the allocation of power between the wheels within milliseconds of the sensors' detecting wheel slippage.

Limiting Wheel Slippage

All 4WDs employ various systems to limit wheel slippage and transfer power to the wheels that still have traction. These systems may completely lock the differentials or they may allow limited slippage before transferring power back to the wheels that retain traction.

Lockers completely eliminate the operation of one or more differentials. A locker on the center differential switches between full-time and part-time 4WD. Lockers on the front or rear differentials ensure that power remains equally applied to each set of wheels regardless of whether both have traction. Lockers may be controlled manually, by a switch or a lever in the vehicle, or they may be automatic.

The Toyota Land Cruiser offers the option of having manual lockers on all three differentials, while other brands such as the Mitsubishi Montero offer manual lockers on the center and rear differential. Manual lockers are the most controllable and effective devices for ensuring that power is provided to the wheels with traction. However, because they allow absolutely no slippage, they must be used only on slippery surfaces.

An alternative method for getting power to the wheels that have traction is to allow limited wheel slippage. Systems that work this way may be called limited-slip differentials, positraction systems, or in the center differential, viscous couplings. The advantage of these systems is that the limited difference they allow in rotational speed between wheels enables such systems to be used when driving on a dry surface. All full-time 4WD systems allow limited slippage in the center differential.

For off-highway use, a manually locking differential is the best of the above systems, but it is the most expensive. Limited-slip differentials are the cheapest but also the least satisfactory, as they require one wheel to be slipping at 2 to 3 mph before power is transferred to the other wheel. For the center differential, the best system combines a locking differential and, to enable full-time use, a viscous coupling.

Tires

The tires that came with your 4WD vehicle may be satisfactory, but many 4WDs are fitted with passenger-car tires. These are unlikely to be the best choice because they are less rugged and more likely to puncture on rocky trails. They are particularly prone to sidewall damage as well. Passenger vehicle tires also have a less aggressive tread pattern than specialized 4WD tires, providing less traction in mud.

For information on purchasing tires better suited to off-highway conditions, see Special 4WD Equipment below.

Clearance

Road clearances vary considerably among different 4WD vehicles—from less than 7 inches to more than 10 inches. Special vehicles may have far greater clearance. For instance, the Hummer has a 16-inch ground clearance. High ground clearance is particularly advantageous on the rockier or more rutted 4WD trails in this book.

When evaluating the ground clearance of your vehicle, you need to take into account the clearance of the bodywork between the wheels on each side of the vehicle. This is particularly relevant for crawling over larger rocks. Vehicles with sidesteps have significantly lower clearance than those without.

Another factor affecting clearance is the approach and departure angles of your vehicle—that is, the maximum angle the ground can slope without the front of the vehicle hitting the ridge on approach or the rear of the vehicle hitting on departure. Mounting a winch or tow hitch to your vehicle is likely to reduce your angle of approach or departure.

If you do a lot of driving on rocky trails, you will inevitably hit the bottom of the vehicle sooner or later. When this happens, you will be far less likely to damage vulnerable areas such as the oil pan and gas tank if your vehicle is fitted with skid plates. Most manufacturers offer skid plates as an option. They are worth every penny.

Maneuverability

When you tackle tight switchbacks, you will quickly appreciate that maneuverability is an important criterion when assessing 4WD vehicles. Where a full-size vehicle may be forced to go back and forth a number of times to get around a sharp turn, a small 4WD might go straight around. This is not only easier, it's safer.

If you have a full-size vehicle, all is not lost. We have traveled many of the trails in this book in a Chevrolet Suburban. That is not to say that some of these trails wouldn't have been easier to negotiate in a smaller vehicle! We have noted in the route descriptions if a trail is not suitable for larger vehicles.

In Summary

Using the criteria above, you can evaluate how well your 4WD will handle off-road touring, and if you haven't yet purchased your vehicle, you can use these criteria to help select one. Choosing the best 4WD system is, at least partly, subjective. It is also a matter of your budget. However, for the type of off-highway driving covered in this book, we make the following recommendations:

■ Select a 4WD system that offers low range and, at a minimum, has some form of limited slip differential on the rear axle.

■ Use light truck, all-terrain tires as the standard tires on your vehicle. For sand and slickrock, these will be the ideal choice. If conditions are likely to be muddy, or traction will be improved by a tread pattern that will give more bite, consider an additional set of mud tires.

■ For maximum clearance, select a vehicle with 16-inch wheels or at least choose the tallest tires that your vehicle can accommodate. Note that if you install tires with a diameter greater than standard, the odometer will undercalculate the distance you have traveled. Your engine braking and gear ratios will also be affected.

■ If you are going to try the rockier 4WD trails, don't install a sidestep or low-hanging front bar. If you have the option, have underbody skid plates mounted.

■ Remember that many of the obstacles you encounter on backcountry trails are more difficult to navigate in a full-size vehicle than in a compact 4WD.

Four-Wheel Driving Techniques

Safe four-wheel driving requires that you observe certain golden rules:
■ Size up the situation in advance.

■ Be careful and take your time.
■ Maintain smooth, steady power and momentum.
■ Engage 4WD and low-range gears before you get into a tight situation.
■ Steer toward high spots, trying to put the wheel over large rocks.
■ Straddle ruts.
■ Use gears and not just the brakes to hold the vehicle when driving downhill. On very steep slopes, chock the wheels if you park your vehicle.
■ Watch for logging and mining trucks and smaller recreational vehicles, such as all-terrain vehicles (ATVs).
■ Wear your seat belt and secure all luggage, especially heavy items such as tool boxes or coolers. Heavy items should be secured by ratchet tie-down straps rather than elastic-type straps, which are not strong enough to hold heavy items if the vehicle rolls.

California's 4WD trails have a number of common obstacles, and the following provides an introduction to the techniques required to surmount them.

Rocks. Tire selection is important in negotiating rocks. Select a multiple-ply, tough sidewall, light-truck tire with a large-lug tread.

As you approach a rocky stretch, get into 4WD low range to give yourself maximum slow-speed control. Speed is rarely necessary, since traction on a rocky surface is usually good. Plan ahead and select the line you wish to take. If a rock appears to be larger than the clearance of your vehicle, don't try to straddle it. Check to see that it is not higher than the frame of your vehicle once you get a wheel over it. Put a wheel up on the rock and slowly climb it, then gently drop over the other side using the brake to ensure a smooth landing. Bouncing the car over rocks increases the likelihood of damage, as the body's clearance is reduced by the suspension compressing. Running boards also significantly reduce your clearance in this respect. It is often helpful to use a "spotter" outside the vehicle to assist you with the best wheel placement.

Steep Uphill Grades. Consider walking the trail to ensure that the steep hill before you is passable, especially if it is clear that backtracking is going to be a problem.

Select 4WD low range to ensure that you have adequate power to pull up the hill. If the wheels begin to lose traction, turn the steering wheel gently from side to side to give the wheels a chance to regain traction.

If you lose momentum, but the car is not in danger of sliding, use the foot brake, switch off the ignition, leave the vehicle in gear (if manual transmission) or park (if automatic), engage the parking brake, and get out to examine the situation. See if you can remove any obstacles, and figure out the line you need to take. Reversing a couple of yards and starting again may allow you to get better traction and momentum.

If halfway up, you decide a stretch of road is impassably steep, back down the trail. Trying to turn the vehicle around on a steep hill is extremely dangerous; you will very likely cause it to roll over.

Steep Downhill Grades. Again, consider walking the trail to ensure that a steep downhill is passable, especially if it is clear that backtracking uphill is going to be a problem.

Select 4WD low range and use first gear to maximize braking assistance from the engine. If the surface is loose and you are losing traction, change up to second or third gear. Do not use the brakes if you can avoid it, but don't let the vehicle's speed get out of control. Feather (lightly pump) the brakes if you slip under braking. For vehicles fitted with ABS, apply even pressure if you start to slip; the ABS helps keep vehicles on line.

Travel very slowly over rock ledges or ruts. Attempt to tackle these diagonally, letting one wheel down at a time.

If the back of the vehicle begins to slide around, gently apply the throttle and correct the steering. If the rear of the vehicle starts to slide sideways, do not apply the brakes.

Sand. As with most off-highway situations, your tires are the key to your ability to cross sand. It is difficult to tell how well a particular tire will handle in sand just by looking at it, so be guided by the manufacturer and your dealer.

The key to driving in soft sand is floatation, which is achieved by a combination of low tire pressure and momentum. Before crossing a stretch of sand, reduce your tire pressure to between 15 and 20 pounds. If necessary, you can safely go to as low as 12 pounds. As you cross, maintain momentum so that your vehicle rides on the top of the soft sand without digging in or stalling. This may require plenty of engine power. Avoid using the brakes if possible; removing your foot from the accelerator alone is normally enough to slow or stop. Using the brakes digs the vehicle deep in the sand.

Air the tires back up as soon as you are out of the sand to avoid damage to the tires and the rims. Airing back up requires a high-quality air compressor. Even then, it is a slow process.

Slickrock. When you encounter slickrock, first assess the correct direction of the trail. It is easy to lose sight of the trail on slickrock, as there are seldom any developed edges. Often the way is marked with small cairns, which are simply rocks stacked high enough to make a landmark.

All-terrain tires with tighter tread are more suited to slickrock than the more open, luggier type tires. As with rocks, a multiple-ply sidewall is important. In dry conditions, slickrock offers pavement-type grip. In rain or snow, you will soon learn how it got its name. Even the best tires may not get an adequate grip. Walk steep sections first; if you are slipping on foot, chances are your vehicle will slip too.

Slickrock is characterized by ledges and long sections of "pavement." Follow the guidelines for travel over rocks. Refrain from speeding over flat-looking sections, as you may hit an unexpected crevice or water pocket, and vehicles bend easier than slickrock! Turns and ledges can be tight, and vehicles with smaller overhangs and better maneuverability are at a distinct advantage—hence the popularity of the compacts at the slickrock mecca of Moab, Utah.

On the steepest sections, engage low range and pick a straight line up or down the slope. Do not attempt to traverse a steep slope sideways.

Mud. Muddy trails are easily damaged, so

they should be avoided if possible. But if you must traverse a section of mud, your success will depend heavily on whether you have open-lugged mud tires or chains. Thick mud fills the tighter tread on normal tires, leaving the tire with no more grip than if it were bald. If the muddy stretch is only a few yards long, the momentum of your vehicle may allow you to get through regardless.

If the muddy track is very steep, uphill or downhill, or off camber, do not attempt it. Your vehicle is likely to skid in such conditions, and you may roll or slip off the edge of the road. Also, check to see that the mud has a reasonably firm base. Tackling deep mud is definitely not recommended unless you have a vehicle-mounted winch—and even then, be cautious, because the winch may not get you out. Finally, check to see that no ruts are too deep for the ground clearance of your vehicle.

When you decide you can get through and have selected the best route, use the following techniques to cross through the mud:

■ Avoid making detours off existing tracks to minimize environmental damage.

■ Select 4WD low range and a suitable gear; momentum is the key to success, so use a high enough gear to build up sufficient speed.

■ Avoid accelerating heavily, so as to minimize wheel spinning and to provide maximum traction.

■ Follow existing wheel ruts, unless they are too deep for the clearance of your vehicle.

■ To correct slides, turn the steering wheel in the direction that the rear wheels are skidding, but don't be too aggressive or you'll overcorrect and lose control again.

■ If the vehicle comes to a stop, don't continue to accelerate, as you will only spin your wheels and dig yourself into a rut. Try backing out and having another go.

■ Be prepared to turn back before reaching the point of no return.

Stream Crossings. By crossing a stream that is too deep, drivers risk far more than water flowing in and ruining the interior of their vehicles. Water sucked into the engine's air intake will seriously damage the engine.

Likewise, water that seeps into the air vent on the transmission or differential will mix with the lubricant and may lead to serious problems in due course.

Even worse, if the water is deep or fast flowing, it could easily carry your vehicle downstream, endangering the lives of everyone in the vehicle.

Some 4WD manuals tell you what fording depth the vehicle can negotiate safely. If your vehicle's owner's manual does not include this information, your local dealer may be able to assist. If you don't know, then avoid crossing through water that is more than a foot or so deep.

The first rule for crossing a stream is to know what you are getting into. You need to ascertain how deep the water is, whether there are any large rocks or holes, if the bottom is solid enough to avoid bogging down the vehicle, and whether the entry and exit points are negotiable. This may take some time and involve getting wet, but you take a great risk by crossing a stream without first properly assessing the situation.

The secret to water crossings is to keep moving, but not too fast. If you go too fast, you may drown the electrics, causing the vehicle to stall midstream. In shallow water (where the surface of the water is below the bumper), your primary concern is to safely negotiate the bottom of the stream, avoiding any rock damage and maintaining momentum if there is a danger of getting stuck or of slipping on the exit.

In deeper water (between 18 and 30 inches), the objective is to create a small bow wave in front of the moving vehicle. This requires a speed that is approximately walking pace. The bow wave reduces the depth of the water around the engine compartment. If the water's surface reaches your tailpipe, select a gear that will maintain moderate engine revs to avoid water backing up into the exhaust; and do not change gears midstream.

Crossing water deeper than 25 to 30 inches requires more extensive preparation of the vehicle and should be attempted only by experienced drivers.

Snow. The trails in this book that receive heavy snowfall are closed in winter. Therefore, the snow conditions that you are most likely to encounter are an occasional snowdrift that has not yet melted or fresh snow from an unexpected storm. Getting through such conditions depends on the depth of the snow, its consistency, the stability of the underlying surface, and your vehicle.

If the snow is no deeper than about 9 inches and there is solid ground beneath it, crossing the snow should not be a problem. In deeper snow that seems solid enough to support your vehicle, be extremely cautious: If you break through a drift, you are likely to be stuck, and if conditions are bad, you may have a long wait.

The tires you use for off-highway driving, with a wide tread pattern, are probably suitable for these snow conditions. Nonetheless, it is wise to carry chains (preferably for all four wheels), and if you have a vehicle-mounted winch, even better.

Vehicle Recovery Methods

If you do enough four-wheel driving, you are sure to get stuck sooner or later. The following techniques will help you get back on the go. The most suitable method will depend on the equipment available and the situation you are in—whether you are stuck in sand, mud, or snow, or are high-centered or unable to negotiate a hill.

Towing. Use a nylon yank strap of the type discussed in the Special 4WD Equipment section below. This type of strap will stretch 15 to 25 percent, and the elasticity will assist in extracting the vehicle.

Attach the strap only to a frame-mounted tow point. Ensure that the driver of the stuck vehicle is ready, take up all but about 6 feet of slack, then move the towing vehicle away at a moderate speed (in most circumstances this means using 4WD low range in second gear) so that the elasticity of the strap is employed in the way it is meant to be. Don't take off like a bat out of hell or you risk breaking the strap or damaging a vehicle.

Never join two yank straps together with a shackle. If one strap breaks, the shackle will become a lethal missile aimed at one of the vehicles (and anyone inside). For the same reason, never attach a yank strap to the tow ball on either vehicle.

Jacking. Jacking the vehicle allows you to pack under the wheel (with rocks, dirt, or logs) or use your shovel to remove an obstacle. However, the standard vehicle jack is unlikely to be of as much assistance as a high-lift jack. We highly recommend purchasing a good high-lift jack as a basic accessory if you decide that you are going to do a lot of serious, off-highway four-wheel driving. Remember a high-lift jack is of limited use if your vehicle does not have an appropriate jacking point. Some brush bars have two built-in forward jacking points.

Tire Chains. Tire chains can be of assistance in both mud and snow. Cable-type chains provide much less grip than link-type chains. There are also dedicated mud chains with larger, heavier links than on normal snow chains. It is best to have chains fitted to all four wheels.

Once you are bogged down is not the best time to try to fit the chains; if at all possible, try to predict their need and have them on the tires before trouble arises. An easy way to affix chains is to place two small cubes of wood under the center of the stretched-out chain. When you drive your tires up on the blocks of wood, it is easier to stretch the chains over the tires because the pressure is off.

Winching. Most recreational four-wheel drivers do not have a winch. But if you get serious about four-wheel driving, this is probably the first major accessory you should consider buying.

Under normal circumstances, a winch would be warranted only for the more difficult 4WD trails in this book. Having a winch is certainly comforting when you see a difficult section of road ahead and have to decide whether to risk it or turn back. Also, major obstacles can appear when you least expect them, even on trails that are otherwise easy.

Owning a winch is not a panacea to all your recovery problems. Winching depends on the availability of a good anchor point, and electric winches may not work if they are submerged in a stream. Despite these constraints, no accessory is more useful than a high-quality, powerful winch when you get into a difficult situation.

If you acquire a winch, learn to use it properly; take the time to study your owner's manual. Incorrect operation can be extremely dangerous and may cause damage to the winch or to your anchor points, which are usually trees.

Navigation by the Global Positioning System (GPS)

Although this book is designed so that each trail can be navigated simply by following the detailed directions provided, nothing makes navigation easier than a GPS receiver.

The global positioning system (GPS) consists of a network of 24 satellites, nearly 13,000 miles in space, in six different orbital paths. The satellites are constantly moving at about 8,500 miles per hour, making two complete orbits around the earth every 24 hours.

Each satellite is constantly transmitting data, including its identification number, its operational health, and the date and time. It also transmits its location and the location of every other satellite in the network.

By comparing the time the signal was transmitted to the time it is received, a GPS receiver calculates how far away each satellite is. With a sufficient number of signals, the receiver can then triangulate its location. With three or more satellites, the receiver can determine latitude and longitude coordinates. With four or more, it can calculate elevation. By constantly making these calculations, it can determine speed and direction. To facilitate these calculations, the time data broadcast by GPS is accurate to within 40 billionths of a second.

The U.S. military uses the system to provide positions accurate to within half an inch. When the system was first established, civilian receivers were deliberately fed slightly erroneous information in order to effectively deny military applications to hostile countries or terrorists—a practice called se-

lective availability (SA). However on May 1, 2000, in response to the growing importance of the system for civilian applications, the U.S. government stopped intentionally downgrading GPS data. The military gave its support to this change once new technology made it possible to selectively degrade the system within any defined geographical area on demand. This new feature of the system has made it safe to have higher-quality signals available for civilian use. Now, instead of the civilian-use signal having a margin of error being between 20 and 70 yards, it is only about one-tenth of that.

A GPS receiver offers the four-wheeler numerous benefits:

■ You can track to any point for which you know the longitude and latitude coordinates with no chance of heading in the wrong direction or getting lost. Most receivers provide an extremely easy-to-understand graphic display to keep you on track.

■ It works in all weather conditions.

■ It automatically records your route for easy backtracking.

■ You can record and name any location, so that you can relocate it with ease. This may include your campsite, a fishing spot, or even a silver mine you discover!

■ It displays your position, enabling you to pinpoint your location on a map.

■ By interfacing the GPS receiver directly to a portable computer, you can monitor and record your location as you travel (using the appropriate map software) or print the route you took.

However, remember that GPS units can fail, batteries can go flat, and tree cover and tight canyons can block the signals. Never rely entirely on GPS for navigation. Always carry a compass for backup.

Special 4WD Equipment

Tires

When 4WD touring, you will likely encounter a wide variety of terrain: rocks, mud, talus, slickrock, sand, gravel, dirt, and bitumen. The immense variety of tires on the market includes many specifically targeted at one or another of these types of terrain, as well as tires designed to adequately handle a range of terrain.

Every four-wheel driver seems to have a preference when it comes to tire selection, but most people undertaking the 4WD trails in this book will need tires that can handle all of the above types of terrain adequately.

The first requirement is to select rugged, light-truck tires rather than passenger-vehicle tires. Check the size data on the sidewall: it should have "LT" rather than "P" before the number. Among light-truck tires, you must choose between tires that are designated "all-terrain" and more-aggressive, wider-tread mud tires. Either type will be adequate, especially on rocks, gravel, talus, or dirt. Although mud tires have an advantage in muddy conditions and soft snow, all-terrain tires perform better on slickrock, in sand, and particularly on ice and paved roads.

When selecting tires, remember that they affect not just traction but also cornering ability, braking distances, fuel consumption, and noise levels. It pays to get good advice before making your decision.

Global Positioning System Receivers

GPS receivers have come down in price considerably in the past few years and are rapidly becoming indispensable navigational tools. Many higher-priced cars now offer integrated GPS receivers, and within the next few years, receivers will become available on most models.

Battery-powered, hand-held units that meet the needs of off-highway driving currently range from less than $100 to a little over $300 and continue to come down in price. Some high-end units feature maps that are incorporated in the display, either from a built-in database or from interchangeable memory cards. Currently, only a few of these maps include 4WD trails.

If you are considering purchasing a GPS unit, keep the following in mind:

■ Price. The very cheapest units are likely outdated and very limited in their display features. Expect to pay from $125 to $300.

■ The display. Compare the graphic display of one unit with another. Some are much easier to decipher or offer more alternative displays.

■ The controls. GPS receivers have many functions, and they need to have good, simple controls.

■ Vehicle mounting. To be useful, the unit needs to be placed where it can be read easily by both the driver and the navigator. Check that the unit can be conveniently located in your vehicle. Different units have different shapes and different mounting systems.

■ Map data. More and more units have map data built in. Some have the ability to download maps from a computer. Such maps are normally sold on a CD-ROM. GPS units have a finite storage capacity and having the ability to download maps covering a narrower geographical region means that the amount of data relating to that specific region can be greater.

■ The number of routes and the number of sites (or "waypoints") per route that can be stored in memory. For off-highway use, it is important to be able to store plenty of waypoints so that you do not have to load coordinates into the machine as frequently. Having plenty of memory also ensures that you can automatically store your present location without fear that the memory is full.

■ Waypoint storage. The better units store up to 500 waypoints and 20 reversible routes of up to 30 waypoints each. Also consider the number of characters a GPS receiver allows you to use to name waypoints. When you try to recall a waypoint, you may have difficulty recognizing names restricted to only a few characters.

■ Automatic route storing. Most units automatically store your route as you go along and enable you to display it in reverse to make backtracking easy.

After you have selected a unit, a number of optional extras are also worth considering:

■ A cigarette lighter electrical adapter. Despite GPS units becoming more power efficient, protracted in-vehicle use still makes this accessory a necessity.

■ A vehicle-mounted antenna, which will improve reception under difficult conditions. (The GPS unit can only "see" through the windows of your vehicle; it cannot monitor satellites through a metal roof.) Having a vehicle-mounted antenna also means that you do not have to consider reception when locating the receiver in your vehicle.

■ An in-car mounting system. If you are going to do a lot of touring using the GPS, consider attaching a bracket on the dash rather than relying on a Velcro mount.

■ A computer-link cable and digital maps. Data from your GPS receiver can be downloaded to your PC; maps and waypoints can be downloaded from your PC; or if you have a laptop computer, you can monitor your route as you go along, using one of a number of inexpensive map software products on the market.

Yank Straps

Yank straps are industrial-strength versions of the flimsy tow straps carried by the local discount store. They are 20 to 30 feet long and 2 to 3 inches wide, made of heavy nylon, rated to at least 20,000 pounds, and have looped ends.

Do not use tow straps with metal hooks in the ends (the hooks can become missiles in the event the strap breaks free). Likewise, never join two yank straps together using a shackle.

CB Radios

If you are stuck, injured, or just want to know the conditions up ahead, a citizen's band (CB) radio can be invaluable. CB radios are relatively inexpensive and do not require an FCC license. Their range is limited, especially in very hilly country, as their transmission patterns basically follow lines of sight. Range can be improved using single sideband (SSB) transmission, an option on more expensive units. Range is even better on vehicle-mounted units that have been professionally fitted to ensure that the antenna and cabling are matched appropriately.

Winches

There are three main options when it comes to winches: manual winches, removable electric winches, and vehicle-mounted electric winches.

If you have a full-size 4WD vehicle—

which can weigh in excess of 7,000 pounds when loaded—a manual winch is of limited use without a lot of effort and considerable time. However, a manual winch is a very handy and inexpensive accessory if you have a small 4WD. Typically, manual winches are rated to pull about 5,500 pounds.

Electric winches can be mounted to your vehicle's trailer hitch to enable them to be removed, relocated to the front of your vehicle (if you have a hitch installed), or moved to another vehicle. Although this is a very useful feature, a winch is heavy, so relocating one can be a two-person job. Consider that 5,000-pound-rated winches weigh only about 55 pounds, while 12,000-pound-rated models weigh around 140 pounds. Therefore, the larger models are best permanently front-mounted. Unfortunately, this position limits their ability to winch the vehicle backward.

When choosing among electric winches, be aware that they are rated for their maximum capacity on the first wind of the cable around the drum. As layers of cable wind onto the drum, they increase its diameter and thus decrease the maximum load the winch can handle. This decrease is significant: A winch rated to pull 8,000 pounds on a bare drum may only handle 6,500 pounds on the second layer, 5,750 pounds on the third layer, and 5,000 pounds on the fourth. Electric winches also draw a high level of current and may necessitate upgrading the battery in your 4WD or adding a second battery.

There is a wide range of mounting options—from a simple, body-mounted frame that holds the winch to heavy-duty winch bars that replace the original bumper and incorporate brush bars and mounts for auxiliary lights.

If you buy a winch, either electric or manual, you will also need quite a range of additional equipment so that you can operate it correctly:

■ at least one choker chain with hooks on each end,
■ winch extension straps or cables,
■ shackles,

- a receiver shackle,
- a snatch block,
- a tree protector,
- gloves.

Grill/Brush Bars and Winch Bars

Brush bars protect the front of the vehicle from scratches and minor bumps; they also provide a solid mount for auxiliary lights and often high-lift jacking points. The level of protection they provide depends on how solid they are and whether they are securely mounted onto the frame of the vehicle. Lighter models attach in front of the standard bumper, but the more substantial units replace the bumper. Prices range from about $150 to $450.

Winch bars replace the bumper and usually integrate a solid brush bar with a heavy-duty winch mount. Some have the brush bar as an optional extra to the winch bar component. Manufacturers such as Warn, ARB, and TJM offer a wide range of integrated winch bars. These are significantly more expensive, starting at about $650.

Remember that installing heavy equipment on the front of the vehicle may necessitate increasing the front suspension rating to cope with the additional weight.

Portable Air Compressors

Most portable air compressors on the market are flimsy models that plug into the cigarette lighter and are sold at the local discount store. These are of very limited use for four-wheel driving. They are very slow to inflate the large tires of a 4WD vehicle; for instance, to reinflate from 15 to 35 pounds typically takes about 10 minutes for each tire. They are also unlikely to be rated for continuous use, which means that they will overheat and cut off before completing the job. If you're lucky, they will start up again when they have cooled down, but this means that you are unlikely to reinflate your tires in less than an hour.

The easiest way to identify a useful air compressor is by the price—good ones cost $200 or more. Many of the quality units feature a Thomas-brand pump and are built to last. Another good unit is sold by ARB. All these pumps draw between 15 and 20 amps and thus should not be plugged into the cigarette lighter socket but attached to the vehicle's battery with clips. The ARB unit can be permanently mounted under the hood. Quick-Air makes a range of units including a 10-amp compressor that can be plugged into the cigarette lighter socket and performs well.

Auxiliary Driving Lights

There is a vast array of auxiliary lights on the market today, and selecting the best lights for your purpose can be a confusing process.

Auxiliary lights greatly improve visibility in adverse weather conditions. Driving lights provide a strong, moderately wide beam to supplement headlamp high beams, giving improved lighting in the distance and to the sides of the main beam. Fog lamps throw a wide-dispersion, flat beam; and spots provide a high-power, narrow beam to improve lighting range directly in front of the vehicle. Rear-mounted auxiliary lights provide greatly improved visibility for backing up.

For off-highway use, you will need quality lights with strong mounting brackets. Some high-powered off-highway lights are not approved by the U.S. Department of Transportation for use on public roads.

Roof Racks

Roof racks can be excellent for storing gear, as well as providing easy access for certain weatherproof items. However, they raise the center of gravity on the vehicle, which can substantially alter the rollover angle. A roof rack is best used for lightweight objects that are well strapped down. Heavy recovery gear and other bulky items should be packed low in the vehicle's interior to lower the center of gravity and stabilize the vehicle.

A roof rack should allow for safe and secure packing of items and be sturdy enough to withstand knocks.

Packing Checklist

Before embarking on any 4WD adventure, whether a lazy Sunday drive on an easy trail or a challenging climb over rugged terrain, be prepared. The following checklist will help you gather the items you need.

Essential

- ☐ Rain gear
- ☐ Small shovel or multipurpose ax, pick, shovel, and sledgehammer
- ☐ Heavy-duty yank strap
- ☐ Spare tire that matches the other tires on the vehicle
- ☐ Working jack and base plate for soft ground
- ☐ Maps
- ☐ Emergency medical kit, including sun protection and insect repellent
- ☐ Bottled water
- ☐ Blankets or space blankets
- ☐ Parka, gloves, and boots
- ☐ Spare vehicle key
- ☐ Jumper leads
- ☐ Heavy-duty flashlight
- ☐ Multipurpose tool, such as a Leatherman
- ☐ Emergency food—high-energy bars or similar

Worth Considering

- ☐ Global Positioning System (GPS) receiver
- ☐ Cell phone
- ☐ A set of light-truck, off-highway tires and matching spare
- ☐ High-lift jack
- ☐ Additional tool kit
- ☐ CB radio
- ☐ Portable air compressor
- ☐ Tire gauge
- ☐ Tire-sealing kit
- ☐ Tire chains
- ☐ Handsaw and ax
- ☐ Binoculars
- ☐ Firearms
- ☐ Whistle
- ☐ Flares
- ☐ Vehicle fire extinguisher
- ☐ Gasoline, engine oil, and other vehicle fluids
- ☐ Portable hand winch
- ☐ Electric cooler

If Your Credit Cards Aren't Maxed Out

- ☐ Electric, vehicle-mounted winch and associated recovery straps, shackles, and snatch blocks
- ☐ Auxiliary lights
- ☐ Locking differential(s)

Trails in the Northern Sierra Region

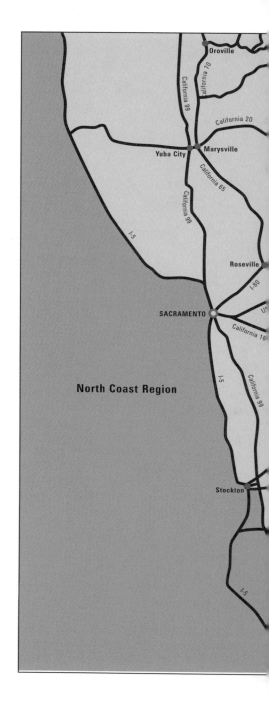

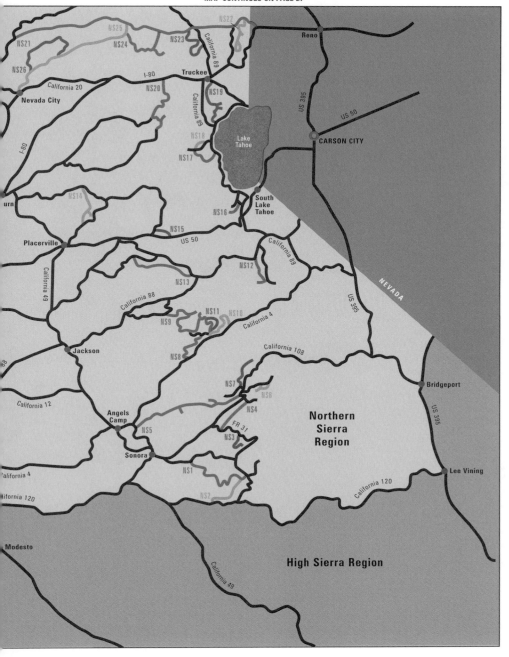

Trails in the Northern Sierra Region

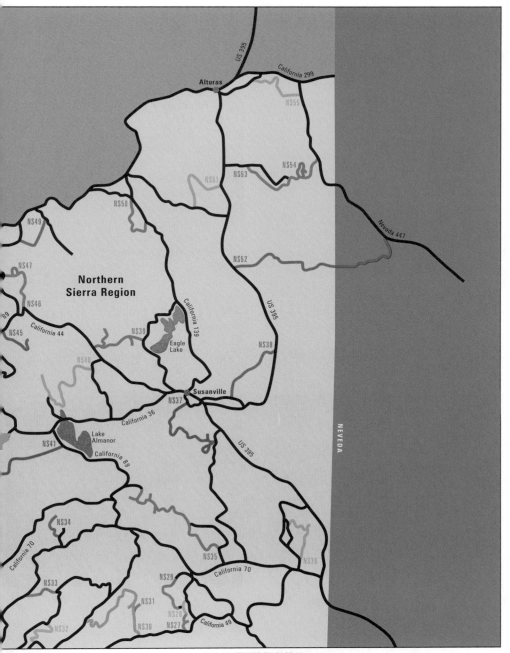

Northern Sierra Region

Alturas

NS55

NS54

NS53

NS51

NS50

NS49

NS47

NS46

NS45

California 44

NS48

NS52

NS39

California 139

Eagle Lake

NS38

US 395

Nevada 447

NS37

Susanville

California 36

NS41

Lake Almanor

California 89

US 395

NS34

California 70

NS35

NS36

NS33

NS29

California 70

NS31

NS28

NS30

NS27

California 49

NEVEDA

MAP CONTINUES ON PAGE 25

Clavey Bridge Road

STARTING POINT Buchanan Road (FR 14),
2.3 miles northeast of Tuolumne
FINISHING POINT FR 31, 0.6 miles west of
FR 17
TOTAL MILEAGE 33.7 miles
UNPAVED MILEAGE 33.7 miles
DRIVING TIME 3.5 hours
ELEVATION RANGE 2,300–4,400 feet
USUALLY OPEN April to November
BEST TIME TO TRAVEL Dry weather
DIFFICULTY RATING 3
SCENIC RATING 9
REMOTENESS RATING +1

Special Attractions

- Dramatic shelf road to the Clavey River.
- Long winding road with a network of side
  trails to explore.
- Angling for rainbow trout in the Clavey River.

History

Clavey Bridge Road begins along the North
Fork of the Tuolumne River close to the Riverside Picnic Area, former site of the Riverside
Guard Station. The ranger station's log cabin
was built in July 1911 as the Basin Ranger Station house at the West Side Lumber Company's
Camp 8, some 7 miles northeast of this location. The two-story log cabin and outbuildings
were burned down in 1968 to eradicate a sus-
pected infestation of kissing bugs. Less severe
than their South American counterparts, the
cone-nosed bugs are blood sucking by nature.
They can cause varying degrees of irritation and
illness to humans. Health departments continue to monitor any occurrence of the insect
throughout the Southwest.

William Clavey ranged cattle and sheep in
this part of Tuolumne County before the
turn of the twentieth century. In May 1897,
Jane A. Clavey patented land just north of
old Camp Clavey, farther upstream along the
West Side Lumber Company Railroad. The
camp was dismantled in 1968.

Small creek cascades across the trail

Clavey River Bridge, constructed in 1956

Clavey Bridge Road runs south of Duckwall Mountain and Duckwall Ridge. The Duckwall party of 1852 was among the many emigrant groups to endure the harsh conditions involved in crossing the Sierra Nevada. Their wagon was badly damaged as they attempted to climb out of Relief Valley, near the northern boundary of today's Emigrant Wilderness, quite some distance away and 6,000 feet higher in the mountains.

A hydroelectric plant was built downstream of the Clavey River Bridge near the confluence of the Clavey and Tuolumne Rivers. The plant supplied electricity for miners around the region. A steep road was cut into the southern face of the Tuolumne River Canyon to a bridge that crossed to the powerhouse on the north side of the river. The powerhouse was badly burned in the Cave Diggings Fire of 1928 and was destroyed by floods in 1937. Some foundations are all that remain.

Description

The trail leaves FR 14, northeast of Tuolumne, and follows a graded dirt road into Stanislaus National Forest. The Riverside Picnic Area, near the start of the trail, is a pleasant, shady place to stop along the North Fork of the Tuolumne River. The first few miles of the trail pass through parcels of private property within the national forest. Remain on the graded road, ignoring private tracks on the left and right. The long trail passes through an area burned in the Ackersop-Rogge Fire of 1997. However, the area is recovering quickly.

Past the turnoff for 1N46, the trail becomes a narrow, single-track that drops steadily down a series of switchbacks to the Clavey River. This is the most spectacular part of the trail, and the section that gives it a difficulty rating of 3. The shelf road has few passing places, and the surface is uneven. It becomes extremely greasy in wet weather and should not be attempted. The trail was closed for almost 10 years because of rockslides along this section. You will notice evidence of past rockslides and should be aware of the possibility of future slides.

The modern bridge over the Clavey River is the replacement for a bridge washed out in 1956. The foundations of the old bridge can still be seen to the north of the modern bridge. There are a couple of campsites along the river by the old bridge, but space is limited. Anglers will enjoy fishing for rainbow trout in the river. The Clavey River is designated a wild-trout stream and is not stocked. Past the bridge, the trail starts to climb steadily, zigzagging out of the Clavey River Valley to the top of a ridge, before passing through Bull Meadow. The meadow is the heart of the Jawbone mule deer herd's winter habitat. The herd migrates from the high country in Yosemite National Park to spend winters at lower elevations. The National Park Service counts the migrating deer annually. Other roads in this region are closed in winter to protect deer habitat.

A worthwhile detour is to head south along 1N09, which takes you 3 miles down an easy road to the top of Jawbone Ridge. The ridge top provides excellent views over the grassy Jawbone lava field.

The trail passes the northern end of Northern Sierra #2: Lumsden Bridge Road at the old Jawbone Station. No longer in use, the buildings stand in the middle of a small meadow. From here it is a short distance to the end of the trail on paved FR 31. The final part of the trail passes through private property. FR 17, which heads northeast to Cherry Lake, is only a short distance to the east.

Current Road Information

Stanislaus National Forest
Mi-Wok Ranger District
24695 Highway 108
Mi-Wuk Village, CA 95346
(209) 586-3234

Map References

BLM   Oakdale, Yosemite Valley
USFS Stanislaus National Forest
USGS 1:24,000 Tuolumne, Duckwall
        Mt., Cherry Lake South
        1:100,000 Oakdale, Yosemite Valley
Maptech CD-ROM: High Sierra/Yosemite
Northern California Atlas & Gazetteer,
      pp. 109, 110
California Road & Recreation Atlas, p. 72

SONORA

Known as the Queen of the Southern Mines, Sonora is on California 49 near the southern end of gold country. First settled by miners from the Mexican state of Sonora in 1848, the town was called Sonorian Camp; nearby Jamestown was then known as American Camp. The abundance of pay dirt around Sonora soon attracted a flood of Yankee miners who quickly outnumbered their Hispanic counterparts. Tensions rose between the two

Sonora, circa 1905

groups and sporadic violence hit the town. In mid-1850, following California's admission as a state, a prohibitive $20 monthly tax was imposed on all foreign residents of Sonora. Mexicans and Chileans decided to abandon the settlement, and almost overnight Sonora's population shrank from 5,000 to about 3,000. Local business suffered until the tax was repealed in 1851 and Hispanic miners began to return.

In 1850, Sonora became seat of government for Tuolumne County, one of the original 27 counties of California. The town's name was briefly changed to Stewart for Major William E. Stewart, but the change lasted only two months.

Chilean gold seekers discovered the Big Bonanza Mine, the richest pocket mine (a mine that yields a large amount of gold in a small area) in the Mother Lode. In 1871, the mine was sold cheaply to three partners. The men patiently worked the mine for several years before suddenly encountering a body of almost solid gold. The next day, they extracted $160,000 worth of the precious metal. Within a week, they had sent $500,000 of gold to the San Francisco Mint.

The Big Bonanza was not the only profitable strike near Sonora. An estimated $41 million worth of gold was removed within a two-mile radius of the town. Although its population dwindled after the gold rush, Sonora saw something of a renewal when the railroad reached town in 1898. The impressive Tuolumne County Courthouse dates from that year. Other historic buildings include the Gunn House, the oldest residence in Sonora, and the Tuolumne County Museum, the town's jail from 1865 until 1961. The oldest part of the Gunn House is an adobe, begun in 1849; it was a family home from 1851 to 1861, when it was converted into a hospital. It once again became a private residence in 1899 and is now a charming hotel, though much of the original structure has been altered. St. James Episcopal Church, built in 1859, is one of the oldest Episcopal churches in California. Nearby stands the Street-Morgan Mansion, a well-preserved Victorian home. Numerous other historic buildings in Sonora make it one of the most picturesque towns in the Mother Lode.

NORTHERN SIERRA #1: CLAVEY BRIDGE ROAD

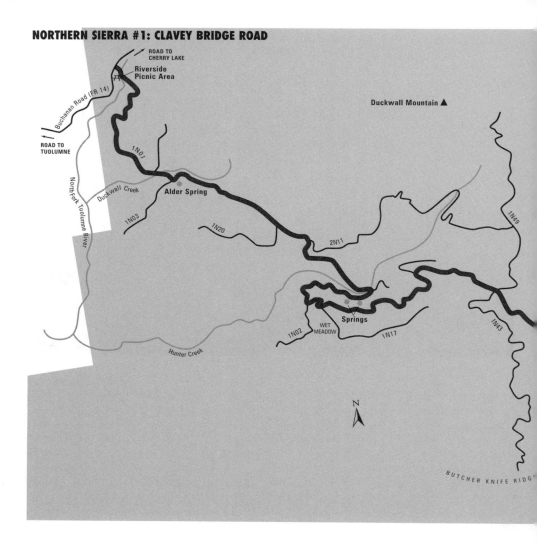

Route Directions

▼ 0.0   From Tuolumne, turn east on Buchanan Road (FR 14), following the sign for Cherry Lake. Travel 2.3 miles; then turn east on paved road immediately before the sign for Stanislaus National Forest. Zero trip meter and immediately cross over North Fork Tuolumne River on bridge. Road turns to graded dirt.

5.3 ▲   Trail ends at intersection with Buchanan Road (FR 14). Turn left for Tuolumne.
       GPS: N37°59.03′ W120°12.28′

▼ 0.1   SO   Riverside Picnic Area on right. Road is now marked 1N01.

5.2 ▲   SO   Riverside Picnic Area on left.

▼ 2.5   SO   Cattle guard.

2.8 ▲   SO   Cattle guard.

▼ 2.6   SO   Entering private property. Track on left through gate; then cross over Duckwall Creek.

2.7 ▲   SO   Cross over Duckwall Creek; then track on right through gate. Leaving private property.
       GPS: N37°57.64′ W120°11.84′

▼ 2.9   BL   Graded road on right is 1N03. Alder Spring on right.

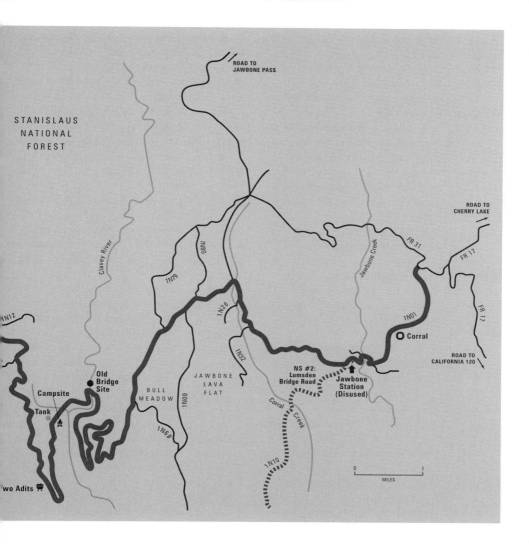

2.4 ▲   BR Alder Spring on left. Graded road on
              left is 1N03.
              GPS: N37°57.50′ W120°11.63′

▼ 4.9   SO Cattle guard; then graded road on right
              is 1N20. Continue on 1N01 and pass
              through seasonal closure gate.
0.4 ▲   SO Seasonal closure gate; then graded
              road on left is 1N20; then cattle guard.
              GPS: N37°56.67′ W120°09.95′

▼ 5.3   BR Track on left is 2N11. Remain on 1N01,
              following the sign to Hunter Creek, and
              zero trip meter.
0.0 ▲   Continue to the northwest.
              GPS: N37°56.52′ W120°09.57′

▼ 0.0   Continue to the southeast.
3.5 ▲   SO Track on right is 2N11. Remain on
              1N01, following the sign to
              Cottonwood Road, and zero trip meter.
▼ 0.8   SO Track on left.
2.7 ▲   SO Track on right.
▼ 1.3   SO Cross Hunter Creek on bridge; then
              track on left.
2.2 ▲   SO Track on right; then cross Hunter Creek
              on bridge.
▼ 1.8   SO Spring on left.
1.7 ▲   SO Spring on right.
              GPS: N37°55.67′ W120°08.87′

▼ 2.0   SO   Spring on left.
1.5 ▲   SO   Spring on right.
▼ 2.8   SO   Hiking trail on right is 17E38.
0.7 ▲   SO   Hiking trail on left is 17E38.
        GPS: N37°55.85′ W120°09.74′

▼ 3.2   BL   Track on right is 1N02 to Wet Meadow.
0.3 ▲   BR   Track on left is 1N02 to Wet Meadow.
        GPS: N37°55.60′ W120°09.68′

▼ 3.5   SO   Track on right on saddle is 1N17 to Sugarloaf Heliport. Zero trip meter and continue on 1N01.
0.0 ▲   Continue to the north.
        GPS: N37°55.66′ W120°09.44′

▼ 0.0   Continue to the south.
3.9 ▲   SO   Track on left on saddle is 1N17 to Sugarloaf Heliport. Zero trip meter and continue on 1N01.
▼ 0.3   SO   Track on right is 1N01H.
3.6 ▲   SO   Track on left is 1N01H.
▼ 0.4   SO   Spring on right.
3.5 ▲   SO   Spring on left.
▼ 2.5   SO   Track on left is 1N48B.
1.4 ▲   SO   Track on right is 1N48B.
▼ 3.9   SO   Track on right is 1N43 to Butcher Knife Ridge. Track on left is 1N49 to Duckwall Lookout and Cottonwood Road. Zero trip meter.
0.0 ▲   Continue to the northwest on 1N01. End of shelf road.
        GPS: N37°55.52′ W120°06.74′

▼ 0.0   Continue to the east on 1N01. Road becomes a formed, single-track trail and descends along a shelf road to the Clavey River.
7.8 ▲   SO   Track on left is 1N43 to Butcher Knife Ridge. Track on right is 1N49 to Duckwall Lookout and Cottonwood Road. Zero trip meter.
▼ 1.4   SO   Track on left is 1N12 and track on right. Follow the sign to Clavey River.
6.4 ▲   SO   Track on right is 1N12 and track on left. Follow the sign to Cottonwood Road.
        GPS: N37°54.92′ W120°05.74′

▼ 2.3   BL   Track on right is 1N46.

5.5 ▲   BR   Track on left is 1N46.
▼ 2.9   SO   Cross over creek.
4.9 ▲   SO   Cross over creek.
▼ 5.0   SO   Two mine adits in rock face on right.
2.8 ▲   SO   Two mine adits in rock face on left.
        GPS: N37°52.81′ W120°05.07′

▼ 6.8   SO   Tank on left and campsite on right.
1.0 ▲   SO   Tank on right and campsite on left.
▼ 7.1   SO   Cross through creek. Waterfall on left and right.
0.7 ▲   SO   Cross through creek. Waterfall on left and right.
        GPS: N37°53.75′ W120°04.67′

▼ 7.8   BR   Track on left goes 0.1 miles to the old bridge site. Zero trip meter then cross over the Clavey River Bridge.
0.0 ▲   Continue to the southwest.
        GPS: N37°53.94′ W120°04.28′

▼ 0.0   Continue to the east.
6.8 ▲   BL   Cross over the Clavey River Bridge; then zero trip meter. Track on right goes 0.1 miles to the old bridge site.
▼ 0.1   BR   Track on left to old bridge site; then seasonal closure gate.
6.7 ▲   BL   Seasonal closure gate; then track on right to old bridge site.
▼ 3.4   SO   Cross over creek.
3.4 ▲   SO   Cross over creek.
▼ 4.1   SO   Top of climb. End of shelf road.
2.7 ▲   SO   Start of shelf road. Road starts to descend.
▼ 5.0   SO   Track on right is 1N69.
1.8 ▲   BR   Track on left is 1N69.
        GPS: N37°53.78′ W120°03.57′

▼ 5.6   SO   Track on right.
1.2 ▲   SO   Track on left.
▼ 5.8   SO   Track on left is 1N28.
1.0 ▲   BL   Track on right is 1N28.
▼ 6.2   SO   Cattle guard.
0.6 ▲   SO   Cattle guard.
▼ 6.3   SO   Track on left is 1N79.
0.5 ▲   SO   Track on right is 1N79.
        GPS: N37°54.65′ W120°02.98′

▼ 6.8   SO   Track on right is 1N09, which goes through seasonal closure gate to

Clavey Bridge Road

		Jawbone Ridge. Zero trip meter.
0.0 ▲		Continue to the west.
		GPS: N37°54.87' W120°02.55'

▼ 0.0		Continue to the east.
3.7 ▲	SO	Track on left is 1N09, which goes through seasonal closure gate to Jawbone Ridge. Zero trip meter.
▼ 0.1	BR	Track on left.
3.6 ▲	BL	Track on right.
▼ 0.2	SO	Track on right.
3.5 ▲	SO	Track on left.
▼ 0.4	SO	Track on left is 1N80.
3.3 ▲	SO	Track on right is 1N80.
▼ 0.9	TR	Road continues ahead to Femmons Meadow. Turn sharp right onto small road.
2.8 ▲	TL	Turn sharp left onto small road, following the sign to Clavey River.
		GPS: N37°55.17' W120°01.76'

▼ 1.6	SO	Track on right is 1N26.
2.1 ▲	SO	Track on left is 1N26.
▼ 2.2	SO	Track on right is 1N32.
1.5 ▲	SO	Track on left is 1N32.
▼ 2.6	SO	Track on left is 1N74.
1.1 ▲	SO	Track on right is 1N74.
▼ 3.7	SO	Track on right is Northern Sierra #2: Lumsden Bridge Road (1N10), sign-posted to Groveland. Zero trip meter. Disused Jawbone USFS Station on right at the intersection.
0.0 ▲		Continue to the south.
		GPS: N37°53.97' W120°00.05'

▼ 0.0		Continue to the north.
2.7 ▲	BR	Disused Jawbone USFS station on left. Track on left is Northern Sierra #2: Lumsden Bridge Road (1N10), sign-posted to Groveland. Zero trip meter.
▼ 0.1	BR	Track on left.
2.6 ▲	BL	Track on right.
▼ 0.4	SO	Cross over Jawbone Creek.
2.3 ▲	SO	Cross over Jawbone Creek.
▼ 0.7	SO	Track on right.
2.0 ▲	SO	Track on left.
▼ 1.2	SO	Cattle guard.
1.5 ▲	SO	Cattle guard.
▼ 1.4	SO	Corral on right.
1.3 ▲	SO	Corral on left.

▼ 1.9	SO	Cattle guard.
0.8 ▲	SO	Cattle guard.
▼ 2.6	SO	Cross over creek.
0.1 ▲	SO	Cross over creek.
▼ 2.7		Seasonal closure gate; then trail ends at T-intersection with paved FR 31. Turn left for Jawbone Pass; turn right for FR 17 and Cherry Lake.
0.0 ▲		Trail commences on paved FR 31, 0.6 miles west of the intersection with FR 17, 13 miles south of Cherry Lake. Zero trip meter and turn northwest on graded dirt trail 1N01. Pass through seasonal closure gate.
		GPS: N37°55.13' W119°58.74'

NORTHERN SIERRA #2

Lumsden Bridge Road

STARTING POINT Northern Sierra #1: Clavey Bridge Road at Jawbone Station, 2.7 miles west of FR 31

FINISHING POINT Ferretti Road, 1 mile northwest of California 120

TOTAL MILEAGE 11.5 miles

UNPAVED MILEAGE 11.5 miles

DRIVING TIME 1.5 hours

ELEVATION RANGE 1,400–3,500 feet

USUALLY OPEN April to November

BEST TIME TO TRAVEL April to November

DIFFICULTY RATING 2

SCENIC RATING 9

REMOTENESS RATING +0

Special Attractions

- Easy trail that follows the Tuolumne River, a designated Wild and Scenic River.
- Popular rafting and kayaking put-ins and many angling opportunities.
- Choice of three USFS campgrounds.

History

Jawbone Station sits along Jawbone Creek at the start of Lumsden Bridge Road. The original guard station was built in 1909. Forest ranger Jack Pestoni and his faithful mule Martha assisted in transporting construction materials to the site. The cabin that replaced the original was one of many backcountry structures built by the Civilian Conservation Corps (CCC) during the Depression.

Early forest rangers in the Groveland Ranger District oversaw grazing permits for cattle, swine, sheep, and horses. In 1910, 14,245 domesticated animals ranged throughout Stanislaus National Forest. That year, a mere 1,008 sheep and goats grazed within the district. Ten years later, 14,449 sheep and goats were roaming the region.

The original Lumsden Bridge was built by the Lumsden brothers, who were employed by the Big Oak Flat–Yosemite Road Company. The bridge was part of ongoing improvements to open the region for logging, mining, grazing, and tourism.

In 1920, steel girders were added to the bridge. Tuolumne County supplied the girders and the forest service carried them in on a World War I era army truck. Transporting the girders from Sonora to Buck Meadows, south of this trail on California 120, was quite a trek for the slow-moving truck. Hauling girders down the narrow shelf road to the bridge site was even slower. Negotiating the series of tight, steep switchbacks to the bottom of the canyon took all day for the brave driver and his assistants. Many trees around the outside corners had to be cut down to make room for the overhanging girders. The large truck was forced to continually back up and go forward to negotiate the tight curves.

The bridge was well used in the 1950s when the city and county of San Francisco were involved in building the dam on Cherry Creek to the northeast. The bridge was damaged when heavy machinery passed over the aging structure. Lumsden Bridge was rebuilt in 1997, following additional damage caused by flooding.

Buck Meadows was called Hamilton Station when originally homesteaded in 1892. The station was badly burned in the 1930s and a new lodge was built alongside what is now California 120, just east of Ferretti

Lumsden Bridge Road

Road. Big Oak Lodge and Big Oak Flat Road were so named because of the presence of such fine examples of the tree. The trees have been removed over time, mostly because of their unfortunate proximity to this evolving tourist and construction route. The lodge and surrounding area enjoyed a boom time in the 1950s following construction of the Hetch Hetchy Reservoir, completed in 1934, and Cherry Lake. The lodge slowly fell into disrepair as travelers sped past it en route to Yosemite National Park. The structure was restored in 1978.

Description

This easygoing trail takes high-clearance vehicles down a gradual shelf road to the Tuolumne River. It follows the river for a while before climbing toward California 120. The trail commences on Northern Sierra #1: Clavey Bridge Road and almost immediately becomes a shelf road. The surface is rough enough that a passenger vehicle is not advised, but a high-clearance 2WD should have little trouble in dry weather. The shelf road has ample passing places.

The trail descends past oak and curl-leaf mahoganies in the shadow of Jawbone Ridge. As the views open up, you can see up and down the Tuolumne River Valley in both directions. After about 2.9 miles, a lightly used hiking trail of moderate difficulty heads down along the Tuolumne River to its confluence with the Clavey River. The start of the hiking trail can be difficult to find.

There are three forest service campgrounds around Lumsden Bridge. The first site, the Lumsden Bridge Campground, has nine shaded sites along the river. It is usually the quietest of the three because it is the farthest away from the raft put-ins. Past the bridge, the trail climbs a shelf road above the river again, before descending to the next two campgrounds—South Fork and Lumsden—and the raft put-in. Camping is permitted in campgrounds only. The trail continues along the wide shelf road to end on paved Ferretti Road, 1 mile northwest of California 120 and the Groveland Ranger Station.

The Tuolumne River is designated a Wild and Scenic River, and fishing regulations and bag and size limits apply. These regulations are posted as you enter the area from either direction. Anglers can fish for brown and rainbow trout and salmon.

The road is heavily used in rafting season, which runs from April to October. During this time you are likely to encounter large tour buses ferrying customers to raft put-ins. A permit is required to float the river between May 1 and September 30. Permits are available at the Groveland Ranger Station, near the end of the trail. There is a fee for permit reservations, but walk-in permits are free (subject to availability). Rafters are encouraged to book ahead. The ranger station is open 7 days a week in rafting season. From the put-in point, it is an 18-mile, full-day float down to Wards Ferry Bridge. The route is one of the most challenging river runs in California, rated Class IV to V, and includes such rapids as Rock Garden, Nemesis, Gray Grindstone, Hell's Kitchen, and Evangelist.

Current Road Information

Stanislaus National Forest
Groveland Ranger District
24545 Highway 120
Groveland, CA 95321
(209) 962-7825

Map References

BLM   Oakdale
USFS   Stanislaus National Forest
USGS   1:24,000   Duckwall Mtn.,
       Jawbone Ridge
       1:100,000 Oakdale
Maptech CD-ROM: High Sierra/Yosemite
Northern California Atlas & Gazetteer, p. 109
California Road & Recreation Atlas, p. 72

Route Directions

▼ 0.0   From Northern Sierra #1: Clavey Bridge Road, 2.7 miles west of the intersection with FR 31, zero trip meter and turn southwest onto 1N10 following the sign to Groveland. Jawbone USFS Station (closed) is at the intersection.

Lumsden Bridge crosses the Tuolumne River

NORTHERN SIERRA #2: LUMSDEN BRIDGE ROAD

5.0 ▲ Trail ends at intersection with Northern Sierra #1: Clavey Bridge Road. Jawbone USFS Station (closed) is at the intersection. Turn left for Tuolumne; turn right to exit to FR 31 and FR 17.
GPS: N37°53.97' W120°00.05'

▼ 0.3 SO Track on left.
4.7 ▲ SO Track on right.
▼ 0.5 SO Track on right.
4.5 ▲ SO Track on left.
▼ 1.4 SO Seasonal closure gate; then cattle guard; then cross over Corral Creek.
3.6 ▲ SO Cross over Corral Creek; then cattle guard; then seasonal closure gate.
GPS: N37°53.38' W120°01.03'

▼ 1.8 SO Cross over creek.
3.2 ▲ SO Cross over creek.
▼ 2.0 SO Start of shelf road.
3.0 ▲ SO End of shelf road.
▼ 2.2 SO Entering Tuolumne Wild and Scenic River Area. Camping is allowed in designated sites only.
2.8 ▲ SO Leaving Tuolumne Wild and Scenic River Area.
GPS: N37°52.87' W120.01.14'

▼ 2.9 SO Access to hiking trail along the Tuolumne River at pull-off on left by fishing regulation sign.

2.1 ▲ SO Access to hiking trail along the Tuolumne River at pull-off on right by fishing regulation sign.
▼ 4.8 SO Cross over Alder Creek.
0.2 ▲ SO Cross over Alder Creek.
GPS: N37°50.98' W120°01.71'

▼ 5.0 TL End of descent. Track straight ahead goes 0.2 miles into Lumsden Bridge USFS Campground. Zero trip meter. Turn left and cross over the Tuolumne River on Lumsden Bridge.
0.0 ▲ Continue to the northeast.
GPS: N37°50.92' W120°01.75'

▼ 0.0 Continue to the southeast.
6.5 ▲ TR Cross over the Tuolumne River on Lumsden Bridge; then track on left goes 0.2 miles into Lumsden Bridge USFS Campground. Zero trip meter.
▼ 0.8 SO Cross through Drew Creek.
5.7 ▲ SO Cross through Drew Creek.
▼ 1.3 SO Track on left into South Fork USFS Campground.
5.2 ▲ SO Track on right into South Fork USFS Campground.
GPS: N37°50.40' W120°02.70'

▼ 1.5 TR Cross over South Fork Tuolumne River on bridge; then T-intersection.
5.0 ▲ TL Track straight ahead. Turn left and

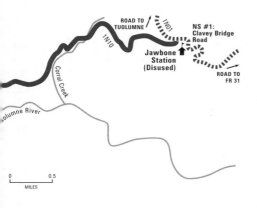

California 120 and Groveland Ranger Station; turn right for alternate route to Groveland.

0.0 ▲ From Groveland Ranger Station, proceed southwest on California 120 for 0.3 miles; then turn northwest onto small paved Ferretti Road. Proceed northwest for 1 mile; then zero trip meter and turn north onto graded dirt road, following the sign for Tuolumne River. Cross cattle guard and pass through seasonal closure gate. Track on left under power lines.

GPS: N37°49.71′ W120°07.02′

cross over South Fork Tuolumne River on bridge.

GPS: N37°50.28′ W120°02.83′

▼ 1.7	SO	Lumsden USFS Campground on right.
4.8 ▲	SO	Lumsden USFS Campground on left.
▼ 1.8	SO	Parking area, river information, and raft put-in on right.
4.7 ▲	SO	Parking area, river information, and raft put-in on left.

GPS: N37°50.20′ W120°03.14′

▼ 2.8	SO	Cross over creek. Small waterfall on left.
3.7 ▲	SO	Cross over creek. Small waterfall on right.
▼ 3.3	SO	Leaving Tuolumne Wild and Scenic River Area.
3.2 ▲	SO	Entering Tuolumne Wild and Scenic River Area. Camping in designated sites only.

GPS: N37°50.22′ W120°04.32′

▼ 4.2	SO	Cross over creek.
2.3 ▲	SO	Cross over creek.
▼ 5.1	SO	Closed track on right.
1.4 ▲	SO	Closed track on left.
▼ 6.4	SO	Track on right. End of shelf road.
0.1 ▲	BR	Track on left. Start of shelf road.
▼ 6.5		Track on right under power lines; then seasonal closure gate; then cattle guard. Trail ends at T-intersection with paved Ferretti Road. Turn left for

---

NORTHERN SIERRA #3

Bourland Trestle Trail

STARTING POINT FR 31 (3N01), 16.5 miles south of California 108 and Long Barn
FINISHING POINT Bourland Trestle
TOTAL MILEAGE 6.7 miles (one-way)
UNPAVED MILEAGE 6.7 miles
DRIVING TIME 1 hour (one-way)
ELEVATION RANGE 5,000–5,600 feet
USUALLY OPEN April to November
BEST TIME TO TRAVEL Dry weather
DIFFICULTY RATING 2
SCENIC RATING 8
REMOTENESS RATING +0

Special Attractions

■ Easy trail along the old West Side Lumber Company Railroad grade.
■ Remains of the Bourland Trestle—until recently the last intact narrow-gauge logging railroad trestle in the western United States.
■ Excellent mountain bike route.

History

In 1899, the West Side Flume and Lumber Company purchased a sawmill site in a small gold mining community called Summerville. Tuolumne, as it was later named, grew quickly as the company expanded to include 250 miles of temporary railroad

Bourland Trestle, built in 1922, was part of the West Side Lumber Company's railroad system

spurs and 45 logging camps. Ponderosas and sugar pines were the company's mainstay. A narrow-gauge railroad system (36 inches wide) was chosen over standard gauge (56.5 inches wide) to cope with the mountainous terrain. This system reduced overall costs and required less grading.

Remains of the Bourland Trestle are the last of many high trestles that connected nearly 70 miles of railroad developed by the West Side Lumber Company. Built in 1923, the six-tiered trestle stood 75 feet high and spanned more than 315 feet across Bourland Creek. A railroad tender was stationed at the Bourland Trestle to walk and inspect the high structure for smoldering fires started by sparks from the trains heading to the sawmill.

Enough logs went to the sawmill during warmer months to keep the mill operating throughout the winter. For the railroad, winter was a time of rebuilding and repairing locomotives and railcars. A series of Heisler and Shay locomotives were used on the logging railroads.

By the late 1940s, trucks were replacing trains on the old railroad grades. The Bourland Trestle remained in use until the 1950s. By the early 1960s, much of the railroad was falling into disuse because of labor and market demand issues. In 1967, the railroad tracks were removed and materials salvaged.

Bourland Creek, as with the trestle, was named after John L. Bourland, sheriff of Tuolumne County from 1865 to 1868.

Description

This short easy trail travels along graded dirt roads to the Bourland Trestle, following close to the original West Side Lumber Company Railroad grade. In places you can see the raised path of the grade.

Bourland Trestle Trail

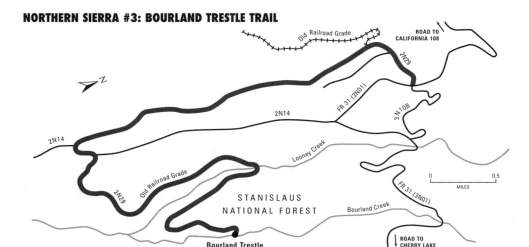

The first part of the trail follows a shelf road high above the Clavey River. The single-track shelf road has adequate passing places. The trail ends at the trestle itself, which spans Bourland Creek. Until recently the trestle was intact, but the middle section collapsed in the mid 1990s during heavy flooding of Bourland Creek. It is possible to walk down to the creek from the end of the vehicle trail along an old hiking trail. Do not attempt to walk onto the trestle; it is not stabilized and is considered unsafe.

Current Road Information

Stanislaus National Forest
Mi-Wok Ranger District
24695 Highway 108
Mi-Wuk Village, CA 95346
(209) 586-3234

Map References

BLM   San Andreas, Bridgeport
USFS   Stanislaus National Forest
USGS   1:24,000   Hull Creek, Cherry
          Lake North
          1:100,000 San Andreas, Bridgeport
Maptech CD-ROM: High Sierra/Yosemite
Northern California Atlas & Gazetteer,
          pp. 99, 100
California Road & Recreation Atlas,
          p. 72 (incomplete)

Route Directions

▼ 0.0		From paved FR 31 (3N01), 16.5 miles south of California 108 and Long Barn, and opposite 3N10B, zero trip meter and turn south on graded dirt road, marked 2N29.
3.4 ▲		Trail ends at T-intersection with paved FR 31. Turn left for Long Barn and California 108; turn right for Cherry Lake. **GPS: N38°03.94' W120°00.63'**

▼ 0.4	BR	Track on left.
3.0 ▲	SO	Track on right.
▼ 0.7	SO	Trail joins the railroad grade.
2.7 ▲	SO	Trail leaves the railroad grade. **GPS: N38°03.78' W120°01.07'**

▼ 1.4	SO	Start of shelf road.
2.0 ▲	SO	End of shelf road.
▼ 2.6	SO	End of shelf road.
0.8 ▲	SO	Start of shelf road.
▼ 2.7	SO	Cross through creek.
0.7 ▲	SO	Cross through creek.
▼ 3.1	SO	Seasonal closure gate; then track on right is 2N45.
0.3 ▲	SO	Track on left is 2N45; then seasonal closure gate.
▼ 3.2	TL	T-intersection with 2N14.
0.2 ▲	TR	2N14 continues straight ahead. Turn right onto 2N29. **GPS: N38°01.74' W120°01.11'**

▼ 3.4	TR	2N14 continues straight ahead and rejoins FR 31 in 2.6 miles. Turn right onto 2N29 and zero trip meter.
0.0 ▲		Continue to the southwest. **GPS: N38°01.86′ W120°00.97′**

▼ 0.0		Continue to the east on the old railroad grade.
▼ 1.9	SO	Cross over Looney Creek. **GPS: N38°02.83′ W120°00.40′**

▼ 2.7	SO	Seasonal closure gate.
▼ 3.3		Trail ends at Bourland Trestle. **GPS: N38°02.54′ W119°59.93′**

NORTHERN SIERRA #4

Dodge Ridge Trail

STARTING POINT Merrill Springs Road (FR 31) opposite Fahey Cabin, 5.3 miles east of California 108

FINISHING POINT Crabtree Road (4N26), 4 miles east of Pinecrest

TOTAL MILEAGE 11.9 miles

UNPAVED MILEAGE 9.9 miles

DRIVING TIME 2.5 hours

ELEVATION RANGE 5,400–7,000 feet

USUALLY OPEN May to November, exact dates vary

BEST TIME TO TRAVEL Dry weather

DIFFICULTY RATING 3

SCENIC RATING 8

REMOTENESS RATING +0

Special Attractions

■ Scenic drive along the U.S. Forest Service's marked auto tour.

■ Sweeping views from Dodge Ridge that will appeal to landscape photographers and artists.

History

Dodge Ridge Trail commences at an old wooden cabin used by the Fahey family in the late 1800s. The Faheys, along with a number of other families, ran dairy cows in the region as far north as Bell Meadow, east of the northern end of Dodge Ridge. The Fahey family sailed to America from Ireland in the hope of new opportunities. Michael and John Fahey crossed the Atlantic in 1849 and settled in New Orleans, where their two brothers and sisters soon joined them. By the early 1850s, the entire Fahey family had relocated to the vicinity of Sonora, California. Though most immigrants of that era sought fortunes in the goldfields, the Faheys decided to raise cattle. Their land and cattle concerns grew considerably in the years that followed. Their cabin at Wrights Creek was in a summer range area where they developed a reputation for producing high-quality butter. The Fahey's cabin and holdings remained in the family until 1938, when the forest service purchased them. The cabin has been the subject of a recent stabilization project.

The historic Sierra crossing made by the Duckwall party in 1852 passed close to the Aspen Meadow Pack Station at the north end of the trail. The difficult wagon route took the emigrants past Burst Rock, high above Relief Valley, then dropped some 2,000 feet to Aspen Meadow. From there the group descended Dodge Ridge to Strawberry Meadow, near today's Pinecrest Lake, and continued southwest close to the route of today's California 108. Wagon trains stopped using this dangerous trail in 1853.

Description

Dodge Ridge Trail, also known as the Sierra Grandstand Tour, is a marked auto tour described on a leaflet put out by the U.S. Forest Service. It takes you through pine forests to the open top of Dodge Ridge, where several viewpoints overlook the Dardanelles, Bald Mountain, and Browns Meadow.

The route described below follows the forest service tour in reverse, giving it a 3 difficulty rating because of a couple of loose, scrabbly climbs onto the ridge. In reverse, the drive rates a 2.

The trail leaves road 3N96 east of Long Barn at the wooden Fahey Cabin, which stands in a meadow opposite the start of the trail. Initially, the road follows a graded, gravel road that climbs toward Dodge Ridge. An alternate

Sparse vegetation on Dodge Ridge

route travels a smaller trail to Lightning Lookout, but this way can be slightly brushy. A short detour goes to Artists' Point and the famous view of the Dardanelles often captured by landscape artists and photographers. Additional viewpoints along the trail offer equally spectacular views of the steep volcanic cliffs that characterize the region.

The trail drops gradually from Dodge Ridge along progressively better maintained trails, finally joining small paved roads to finish at Aspen Meadow. The final viewpoint is just off the end of the trail. Large boulders called glacial erratics, dropped by retreating glaciers thousands of years ago, are visible from here.

If traveling the trail in reverse, it is well marked by Sierra Grandstand Tour markers, with each point of interest indicated by a numbered post.

Current Road Information
Stanislaus National Forest
Mi-Wok Ranger District
24695 Highway 108
Mi-Wuk Village, CA 95346
(209) 586-3234

Map References
BLM   San Andreas, Bridgeport
USFS   Stanislaus National Forest
USGS 1:24,000   Hull Creek, Pinecrest,
        Strawberry
        1:100,000 San Andreas, Bridgeport
Maptech CD-ROM: High Sierra/Yosemite
Northern California Atlas & Gazetteer,
    pp. 99, 100
California Road & Recreation Atlas,
    p. 72

Route Directions

▼ 0.0   From California 108 at Long Barn, 3.8 miles northeast of Mi-Wok Ranger Station, zero trip meter and turn east at the sign for Long Barn (note that this is the second entrance to Long Barn if traveling north from Mi-Wuk Village) and zero trip meter. After 0.1 miles, turn left onto Merrill Springs

Twisted conifer at the top of the ridge

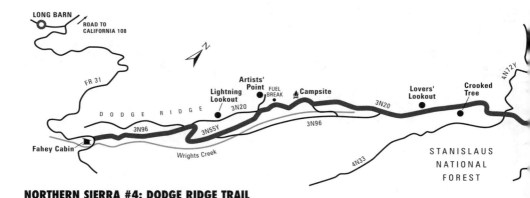

NORTHERN SIERRA #4: DODGE RIDGE TRAIL

Road (FR 31), following the sign for the North Fork of the Tuolumne River, and proceed 5.2 miles to the start of the trail. On a right-hand bend, zero trip meter and turn northeast on graded dirt road marked 3N96. Fahey Cabin, alongside Wrights Creek, is opposite the start of the trail.

3.3 ▲ Trail ends at T-intersection with paved Merrill Springs Road (FR 31). Turn right for Mi-Wuk Village. Fahey Cabin is opposite the end of the trail.
GPS: N38°04.73' W120°05.82'

▼ 0.9 SO Track on right is 3N28Y.
2.4 ▲ SO Track on left is 3N28Y.
▼ 1.5 SO Two tracks on left at turnout.
1.8 ▲ SO Two tracks on right at turnout.
GPS: N38°05.66' W120°04.77'

▼ 1.6 SO Track on left is 3N20, marked for 4WDs, ATVs, and motorbikes, which goes 0.6 miles to Lightning Lookout and rejoins the main trail 0.6 miles after that. This alternate route is 3-rated and somewhat brushy.
1.7 ▲ SO Alternate route 3N20 rejoins on right.
GPS: N38°05.73' W120°04.70'

▼ 2.0 SO Track on left and track on right.
1.3 ▲ SO Track on left and track on right.
▼ 2.4 BL 3N96 continues straight ahead. Bear left onto 3N55Y.
0.9 ▲ SO 3N96 joins from the left.
GPS: N38°05.78' W120°04.24'

▼ 3.0 SO Track on left is Trail #26 for 4WDs, ATVs, and motorbikes.
0.3 ▲ SO Track on right is Trail #26 for 4WDs, ATVs, and motorbikes.
▼ 3.3 TR 4-way intersection. Track on left is 3N20, which is the end of alternate route via Lightning Lookout. Track straight ahead is 3N42, which goes 0.2 miles to Artists' Point. Zero trip meter and turn right onto 3N20.
0.0 ▲ Continue to the southeast.
GPS: N38°06.53' W120°03.96'

▼ 0.0 Continue to the northeast.
4.2 ▲ TL 4-way intersection. Track on right is 3N42, which goes 0.2 miles to Artists' Point. Track straight ahead is 3N20, which goes 0.6 miles to Lightning Lookout and rejoins the main trail 0.6 miles after that. This alternate route is 3-rated and somewhat brushy. Zero trip meter and turn left onto 3N55Y.
▼ 0.3 SO Pass through fuel break (open area)—point 6 on Sierra Grandstand Tour.
3.9 ▲ SO Pass through fuel break (open area)—point 6 on Sierra Grandstand Tour.
▼ 0.7 SO Campsite and viewpoint on left.
3.5 ▲ SO Campsite and viewpoint on right.
▼ 0.8 TR Track on left is 3N49. Remain on 3N20.
3.4 ▲ TL Track straight ahead is 3N49. Remain on 3N20.
GPS: N38°07.05' W120°03.42'

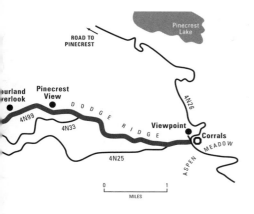

ROAD TO PINECREST

Pinecrest Lake

Bourland Overlook
Pinecrest View
4N99   4N33   DODGE RIDGE   Viewpoint   4N26
4N25   ASPEN MEADOW   Corrals

0   1
MILES

▼ 0.9   BL   Track on right is 3N53Y. Remain on 3N20.

3.3 ▲   SO   Track on left is 3N53Y. Remain on 3N20.

▼ 2.1   SO   Track on right is 3N96. Follow sign to Pinecrest.

2.1 ▲   SO   Track on left is 3N96. Follow sign to Fahey Cabin.

    GPS: N38°07.56′ W120°02.29′

▼ 2.8   SO   Lovers' Lookout on left—point 5 on Sierra Grandstand Tour.

1.4 ▲   SO   Lovers' Lookout on right—point 5 on Sierra Grandstand Tour.

    GPS: N38°07.95′ W120°01.74′

▼ 3.4   SO   Crooked Tree on right—point 4 on Sierra Grandstand Tour.

0.8 ▲   SO   Crooked Tree on left—point 4 on Sierra Grandstand Tour.

    GPS: N38°08.37′ W120°01.32′

▼ 4.2   SO   Track on left is 4N72Y and graded road on right is 4N33. Zero trip meter.

0.0 ▲   Continue to the southwest on 3N20.

    GPS: N38°08.64′ W120°00.61′

▼ 0.0   Continue to the east on 4N33.

4.4 ▲   SO   Track on right is 4N72Y and graded road on left is 4N33. Zero trip meter.

▼ 0.1   SO   Trail #24 on left for ATVs and motor-bikes only—rated blue.

4.3 ▲   SO   Trail #24 on right for ATVs and motor-bikes only—rated blue.

▼ 0.6   BL   Trail #12 on right for 4WDs, ATVs, and motorbikes—rated blue. 4N33 continues straight ahead. Bear left onto 4N99.

3.8 ▲   BR   Track on left is 4N33. Trail #12 straight ahead for 4WDs, ATVs, and motorbikes—rated blue. Bear right onto 4N33.

    GPS: N38°08.97′ W120°00.12′

▼ 1.3   SO   Bourland Overlook, which looks east to Bourland Mountain and Bell Mountain—point 3 on Sierra Grandstand Tour.

3.1 ▲   SO   Bourland Overlook, which looks east to Bourland Mountain and Bell Mountain—point 3 on Sierra Grandstand Tour.

    GPS: N38°09.37′ W119°59.83′

▼ 1.9   SO   View north of Pinecrest Lake and the effects of a 1997 wildfire—point 2 on Sierra Grandstand Tour.

2.5 ▲   SO   View north of Pinecrest Lake and the effects of a 1997 wildfire—point 2 on Sierra Grandstand Tour.

    GPS: N38°09.74′ W119°59.37′

▼ 2.4   TL   T-intersection with 4N33. Road becomes paved.

2.0 ▲   TR   4N33 continues straight ahead. Turn right onto 4N99. Road turns to graded dirt.

    GPS: N38°09.92′ W119°58.93′

▼ 2.5   SO   Cattle guard; then track on right; then track on left is 4N71.

1.9 ▲   SO   Track on right is 4N71; then track on left; then cattle guard.

▼ 2.7   SO   Track on left is 4733B.

1.7 ▲   SO   Track on right is 4733B.

▼ 4.1   TL   T-intersection with paved 4N25.

0.3 ▲   TR   4N25 continues straight ahead. Turn right onto 4N33.

    GPS: N38°10.41′ W119°57.39′

▼ 4.2   SO   Track on right to Kerrick Corrals Horse Camp.

0.2 ▲   SO   Track on left to Kerrick Corrals Horse Camp.

▼ 4.4   Trail ends at T-intersection with 4N26 opposite corrals. Turn left for Pinecrest; turn right for Gianelli Trailhead and Emigrant Wilderness. To reach Point 1 on the Sierra Grandstand Tour, turn left and head west past the sign marking the start of the Sierra Grandstand Scenic Drive. Proceed up the small dirt trail following the Sierra Grandstand Tour marker. The viewpoint is 0.1 miles up that trail.

0.0 ▲   From California 108, 2 miles southwest of the Summit Ranger Station at Strawberry, turn southeast on Crabtree Road (4N26) and proceed 6.3 miles to the start of trail. Trail commences on paved 4N26, 4 miles from Pinecrest. Zero trip meter opposite corrals and turn south on paved road 4N25, following the sign for Bell Meadow. There is a sign marking the start of the Sierra Grandstand Scenic Drive. To reach Point 1 of the tour, turn west up the small dirt trail, following the Sierra Grandstand Tour marker. The viewpoint is 0.1 miles up that trail.

GPS: N38°10.61′ W119°57.17′

Crandall Peak Trail

STARTING POINT California 108, 2 miles north of Strawberry

FINISHING POINT Parrots Ferry Road (CR E18), 1 mile southeast of California 4

TOTAL MILEAGE 36.6 miles, plus 6.9-mile spur to Sand Bar Flat

UNPAVED MILEAGE 28.8 miles, plus 6.9-mile spur

DRIVING TIME 5 hours

ELEVATION RANGE 1,000–6,000 feet

USUALLY OPEN April to November

BEST TIME TO TRAVEL Dry weather

DIFFICULTY RATING 3

SCENIC RATING 9

REMOTENESS RATING +1

Special Attractions

■ Access to the Middle Fork of the Stanislaus River at two points.

■ Long winding ridge top trail with many excellent views.

■ Access to the Crandall Peak OHV Area.

History

Laurence G. Crandall, for whom the peak and fire lookout were named, was a logging superintendent and camp boss at Camp Rath in the 1920s.

Crandall Peak Trail passes many examples of the development of California's natural resources, mainly timber and water. Strawberry Peak, at the eastern end of the trail, offers glimpses of Pinecrest Lake, a reservoir created to dam the South Fork of the Stanislaus River in 1916 by the predecessor of Pacific Gas & Electric (PG&E). Originally known as Strawberry Lake, it is part of a water storage system connecting the South and Middle Forks of the Stanislaus River. These waters combine to operate the Spring Gap Powerhouse on the south banks of the river's middle fork. The original Philadelphia Ditch was built in 1899 to provide water for mining operations near the western end of this trail. Modified since, the ditch diverts water to Spring Gap, which in turn drives the powerhouse. The Spring Gap Powerhouse, set 1,800 feet below the gap, was commissioned in 1921.

Schoettgen, pronounced Shotgun, Pass was a busy railroad junction on the Sugar Pine Railroad's network of tracks. The main railroad line operated out of Standard, just east of Sonora, and gradually made its way up the mountains to Long Barn, just southwest of Lyons Reservoir. From there it climbed to Schoettgen Junction at the northern end of the reservoir and began the long twisting route below Crandall Peak to Camp Strawberry. The busy railroad snaked past a logging camp called Crandall-in-the-Hole, carrying logs from the Strawberry region until 1929.

In 1927, a new railroad grade was constructed from Schoettgen Junction, up and over Schoettgen Pass, along what is today's 4N81. In 1929, a new logging camp was to be established below Spring Gap. The old buildings, including furniture, were loaded onto flatcars and moved nearly 50 miles from Camp Strawberry to Tunnell Creek Camp. Tunnell Creek Camp was named for a tunnel built in the 1850s as part of the Miners' Ditch Scheme to connect the South and

The Stanislaus River at the far reaches of New Melones Lake

Manzanitas edge the lower part of the ridge trail

Middle Forks of the Stanislaus River. Surely the small town on wheels was a sight to behold as the train slowly negotiated its way around Crandall Peak. Even the massive steel-banded wooden water tank from Bumblebee Siding, near the start of the trail, was relocated.

The main railroad grade continued to lengthen, proceeding northeast past the new camp. Many high, curved trestles were constructed as the line descended to cross the Middle Fork of the Stanislaus River at Beardsley Flat. From there the grade swung west through Sourdough Camp, on to Soap Creek Camp and Camp Grahl. Steam engine Shay #3, purchased from the Pickering Lumber Company, hauled massive quantities of logs up and over the 2.5-percent grade to Schoettgen Pass. Shay #3 is now on exhibit at the Sonora Fairgrounds.

In the 1950s, logging trains crossed Beardsley Dam along the grade that is today's FR 15. The rail lines past Soap Creek Camp were becoming redundant by the late 1950s, and by 1961 more efficient and versatile logging

trucks were introduced—the beginning of the end of a much-worked railroad system.

The last logging train crossed Beardsley Dam in 1963. The train consisted of open cars carrying employees bidding farewell to a major section of the Sugar Pine Railway. They had dinner at Soap Creek Camp to mark the closing of 32 miles of track. From then on, logging trucks were used to move felled trees to Schoettgen Pass, where they were loaded onto railcars.

Description
This long ridge top trail gets its difficulty rating of 3 from the section along Strawberry Ridge and the final descent to the Stanislaus River. Most of the trail is rated 2, and high-clearance 2WD vehicles can generally reach the middle sections by following one of the other graded dirt roads into the region.

The trail leaves California 108 north of Strawberry. Initially, it follows a well-used, formed trail to the radio towers on Strawberry Peak; past the peak, the trail is less used. It winds along Strawberry Ridge, through open woodlands carpeted with bear clover. The Stanislaus River Valley can be seen to the south, and Beardsley Lake and Whittakers Dardanelles can be seen to the north.

The trail joins a major graded road just east of the start of the spur to Sand Bar Flat. The 6.9-mile spur descends to a U.S. Forest Service campground beside the Stanislaus River. From the campground, you can take a dip in some great swimming holes or head out on 6 miles of hiking trails along the river. Note that the road shown as crossing the river from the campground is not open to the public. There is trailhead parking for the Crandall Peak OHV Area at the start of the spur, and a network of small trails, mostly suitable for motorbikes and ATVs only, crisscross the region.

A couple of miles past the spur, a rough, loose-surfaced trail suitable for high-clearance 4WDs goes 2 miles to the site of an old fire lookout on Crandall Peak, built by the CCC in 1934. Continuing along the ridge top, the main trail crosses over Schoettgen Pass and skirts the north side of Mount Knight. It gradually descends the long ridge through oak and manzanita forest. The descent to the bridge over the Stanislaus River can be rough. It becomes extremely greasy in wet weather and is not recommended at those times. A keen eye will spot some old mining equipment half-hidden in the undergrowth in a gully near the bottom of the descent. The trail joins a paved road at the Stanislaus River and follows it around Bald Mountain to finish on Parrots Ferry Road near Vallecito.

Current Road Information
Stanislaus National Forest
Mi-Wok Ranger District
24695 Highway 108
Mi-Wuk Village, CA 95346
(209) 586-3234

Map References
BLM   San Andreas
USFS Stanislaus National Forest
USGS 1:24,000   Strawberry, Crandall
      Peak, Stanislaus, Murphys,
      Columbia, Columbia SE
      1:100,000 San Andreas

Maptech CD-ROM: High Sierra/Yosemite
Northern California Atlas & Gazetteer,
  pp. 98, 99
California Road & Recreation Atlas,
  pp. 72, 71

Route Directions

▼ 0.0   From California 108, 2 miles north of Strawberry, zero trip meter and turn southwest on graded dirt road 4N39. Pass through seasonal closure gate.
5.5 ▲   Seasonal closure gate; then trail ends at T-intersection with California 108. Turn right for Strawberry; turn left for Sonora Pass.
           GPS: N38°12.37′ W120°01.06′

▼ 0.1   SO   Track on right.
5.4 ▲   SO   Track on left.
▼ 0.5   SO   Track on right.
5.0 ▲   SO   Track on left.
▼ 0.9   BL   Track on right goes 0.3 miles to the radio towers on top of Strawberry Peak.
4.6 ▲   SO   Track on left goes 0.3 miles to the radio towers on top of Strawberry Peak.
           GPS: N38°11.85′ W120°01.72′

▼ 1.4   SO   Cattle guard.
4.1 ▲   SO   Cattle guard.
▼ 4.9   SO   Track on left.
0.6 ▲   SO   Track on right.
           GPS: N38°10.29′ W120°05.40′

▼ 5.5   TL   T-intersection with 4N14. Road on right goes to Beardsley Lake. Zero trip meter.
0.0 ▲   Continue to the east.
           GPS: N38°10.13′ W120°06.06′

▼ 0.0   Continue to the southeast and cross cattle guard.
2.0 ▲   TR   Cattle guard; then turn right following sign for Strawberry Ridge Road. Road continues straight ahead to Beardsley Lake. Zero trip meter.
▼ 0.1   TL   Cross over small aqueduct; then turn left in front of work station following sign for Fraser Flat. This does not

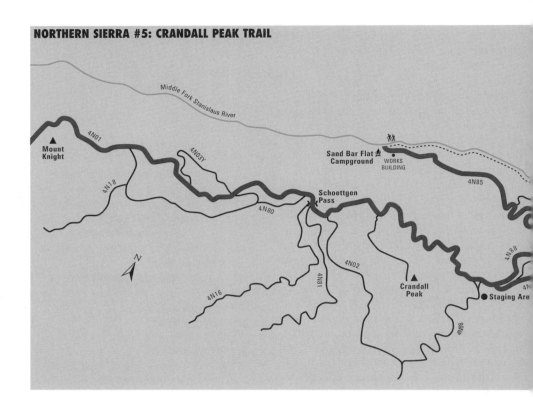

appear on the map—it has been re-routed past the work station

1.9 ▲ TR Turn right in front of work station onto 4N14 following sign to Strawberry and cross over aqueduct.
GPS: N38°10.09′ W120°06.07′

▼ 0.3 TR Turn sharp right onto graded road 4N01 following sign to Sand Bar Flat.

1.7 ▲ TL Turn sharp left onto 4N42 following sign for Spring Gap.
GPS: N38°10.05′ W120°05.89′

▼ 0.8 SO Two tracks on right.
1.2 ▲ SO Two tracks on left.
▼ 1.3 SO Track on right and track on left.
0.7 ▲ SO Track on right and track on left.
GPS: N38°09.90′ W120°06.78′

▼ 1.4 BR Track on left. Remain on 4N01.
0.6 ▲ SO Track on right. Remain on 4N01.
▼ 1.6 SO Track on right is 4N42.
0.4 ▲ SO Track on left is 4N42.
▼ 2.0 BR Track on left is 4N88, which goes to

Crandall Peak OHV Staging Area. Track on right is 4N88, which is the spur to Sand Bar Flat. Zero trip meter and bear right, remaining on 4N01 and following the sign to Mount Knight.

0.0 ▲ Continue to the northeast on 4N01.
GPS: N38°09.68′ W120°07.39′

Spur to Sand Bar Flat

▼ 0.0 From the intersection of 4N01 and 4N88, zero trip meter and proceed northeast on 4N88—the lower of the two roads heading northeast—following the sign to Sand Bar Flat.

▼ 2.1 SO Track on right is 4N86, which goes to a locked gate.
GPS: N38°10.51′ W120°06.45′

▼ 4.1 TL 4-way intersection. Turn left onto 4N85, following the sign for camping area; then turnout on left.
GPS: N38°10.73′ W120°07.26′

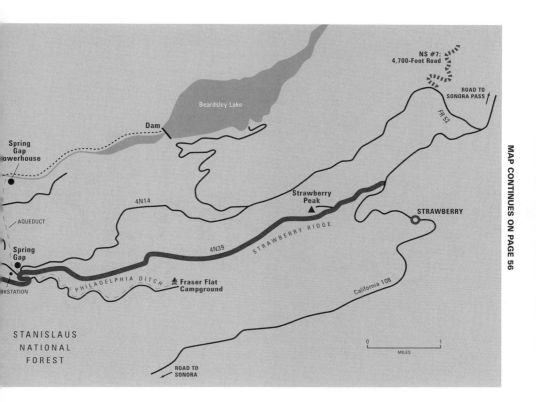

MAP CONTINUES ON PAGE 56

▼ 6.7   SO Works buildings on left.
▼ 6.9   Spur ends at the Sand Bar Flat USFS
             Campground and day-use area—fee
             required. Road over the river is closed
             to the public. Excellent swimming
             holes at the campground. Hiking trail
             continues along river for 6 miles.
             GPS: N38°11.09′ W120°09.24′

Continuation of Main Trail

▼ 0.0   Continue to the northwest on 4N01.
2.8 ▲   SO Track on right is 4N88, which goes to
             Crandall Peak OHV Staging Area. Track
             on left is 4N88, which is the spur to
             Sand Bar Flat. Zero trip meter and
             remain on 4N01—the upper of the two
             roads heading northeast.
             GPS: N38°09.68′ W120°07.39′

▼ 0.1   SO Track on left.
2.7 ▲   SO Track on right.
▼ 0.2   SO Track on left.
2.6 ▲   SO Track on right.
▼ 2.8   SO Track on left goes to the site of

Crandall Peak Fire Lookout. Zero trip
meter.
0.0 ▲   Continue to the southeast.
             GPS: N38°10.20′ W120°09.25′

▼ 0.0   Continue to the northwest.
8.2 ▲   SO Track on right goes to the site of
             Crandall Peak Fire Lookout. Zero trip
             meter.

▼ 0.1   SO Track on right.
8.1 ▲   SO Track on left.
▼ 0.8   BR Well-used track on left is 4N02.
             Remain on 4N01.
7.4 ▲   BL Well-used track on right is 4N02.
             Remain on 4N01.
             GPS: N38°10.02′ W120°09.99′

▼ 1.2   TR 4-way intersection at Schoettgen Pass.
             Track on left is 4N81 and track straight
             ahead is 4N16. Turn right, remaining
             on 4N01; then track on right.
7.0 ▲   TL Track on left; then 4-way intersection
             at Schoettgen Pass. Track on right is
             4N16 and track straight ahead is

NORTHERN SIERRA REGION   **55**

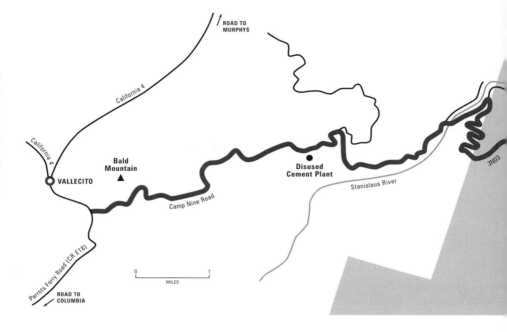

4N81. Turn left, remaining on 4N01.
GPS: N38°10.11′ W120°10.21′

▼ 1.3 BR Track on left is 4N80.
6.9 ▲ SO Track on right is 4N80.
▼ 1.5 SO Track on left.
6.7 ▲ SO Track on right.
▼ 2.6 SO Track on left and track on right.
5.6 ▲ SO Track on left and track on right.
▼ 3.3 SO Logging track on left.
4.9 ▲ SO Logging track on right.
▼ 3.4 SO Track on right is 4N03Y.
4.8 ▲ SO Track on left is 4N03Y.
▼ 4.8 SO Track on left is 4N18.
3.4 ▲ SO Track on right is 4N18.
     GPS: N38°10.16′ W120°13.30′
▼ 5.2 SO Seasonal closure gate.
3.0 ▲ SO Seasonal closure gate.
     GPS: N38°10.14′ W120°13.70′
▼ 5.3 SO Track on left.
2.9 ▲ SO Track on right.
▼ 5.4 SO Track on left.
2.8 ▲ SO Track on right.
▼ 5.5 SO Track on left.

2.7 ▲ SO Track on right.
▼ 6.7 SO Track on right and track on left through gate are private property.
1.5 ▲ SO Track on left and track on right through gate are private property.
     GPS: N38°09.78′ W120°14.67′
▼ 7.4 SO Track on left.
0.8 ▲ SO Track on right.
▼ 7.5 SO Track on left.
0.7 ▲ SO Track on right.
▼ 7.6 SO Track on right is 4N15Y.
0.6 ▲ SO Track on left is 4N15Y.
▼ 7.9 SO Track on right is 4N16Y.
0.3 ▲ SO Track on left is 4N16Y.
▼ 8.2 TR 4-way intersection. 4N01 continues straight ahead and small track on left. Zero trip meter and turn right onto 4N04.
0.0 ▲   Continue to the east.
     GPS: N38°09.61′ W120°15.64′

▼ 0.0   Continue to the north.
6.2 ▲ TL 4-way intersection. Small track straight ahead. Track on left and track

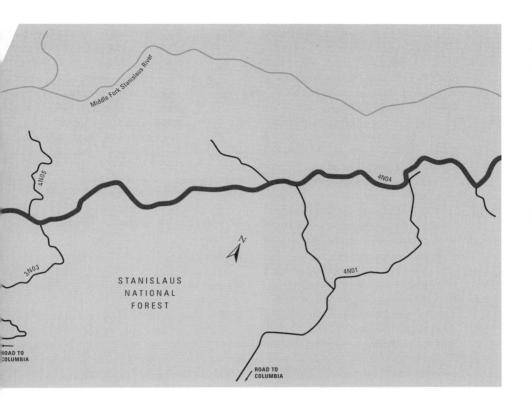

on right are both 4N01. Zero trip meter
and turn left onto 4N01.

▼ 0.3   SO   Track on left.
5.9 ▲   SO   Track on right.
▼ 0.9   SO   Track on left.
5.3 ▲   SO   Track on right.
▼ 1.5   BL   Two tracks on right.
4.7 ▲   BR   Two tracks on left.
         GPS: N38°09.42′ W120°17.03′

▼ 1.9   BR   Track on left.
4.3 ▲   BL   Track on right.
▼ 2.4   SO   Two tracks on right into private property.
3.8 ▲   SO   Two tracks on left into private property.
▼ 5.3   SO   Trail starts to descend from ridge.
0.9 ▲   SO   Top of ridge.
▼ 5.6   SO   Track on left.
0.6 ▲   SO   Track on right.
▼ 6.0   SO   Private property on right.
0.2 ▲   SO   Private property on left.
▼ 6.2   BR   Graded road on left is 3N03 to
            Columbia and Twain Harte. Zero trip
            meter and follow sign to Stanislaus
            River and Vallecito.

0.0 ▲   Continue to the northeast.
         GPS: N38°07.70′ W120°20.86′

▼ 0.0   Continue to the west.
4.1 ▲   BL   Graded road on right is 3N03 to
            Columbia and Twain Harte. Zero trip
            meter and bear left onto 4N04 follow-
            ing sign to Mount Knight.
▼ 0.2   SO   Track on right is 4N05. Remain on
            3N03.
3.9 ▲   SO   Track on left is 4N05. Remain on 3N03.
▼ 0.4   SO   Cattle guard.
3.7 ▲   SO   Cattle guard.
▼ 0.9   SO   Cattle guard.
3.2 ▲   SO   Cattle guard.
▼ 1.8   SO   Track on left.
2.3 ▲   SO   Track on right.
         GPS: N38°07.23′ W120°22.44′

▼ 1.9   SO   Start of shelf road.
2.2 ▲   SO   End of shelf road.
▼ 2.2   SO   View to the left of the Stanislaus River
            at the north end of New Melones Lake.
1.9 ▲   SO   View to the right of the Stanislaus

River at the north end of New Melones Lake.

▼ 3.3 SO Exiting Stanislaus National Forest at sign.
0.8 ▲ SO Entering Stanislaus National Forest at sign.
GPS: N38°07.58′ W120°22.76′

▼ 4.0 SO Mine workings on left with machinery in gully, and shaft on right.
0.1 ▲ SO Mine workings on right with machinery in gully, and shaft on left.
GPS: N38°07.91′ W120°22.49′

▼ 4.1 TL T-intersection with paved road along the Stanislaus River. Zero trip meter.
0.0 ▲ Continue to the east. Start of shelf road.
GPS: N38°07.96′ W120°22.57′

▼ 0.0 Continue to the south. End of shelf road.
7.8 ▲ TR Turn right onto 3N03 and start to climb away from the river. Road is now graded dirt. Zero trip meter.

▼ 0.6 SO Cross over Stanislaus River on bridge.
7.2 ▲ SO Exit bridge.
GPS: N38°07.50′ W120°22.95′

▼ 0.7 SO Exit bridge. Paved road on right. Trail now follows paved Camp Nine Road. Start of shelf road.
7.1 ▲ SO Paved road on left. End of shelf road. Cross over Stanislaus River on bridge.
GPS: N38°07.50′ W120°23.05′

▼ 2.5 SO Road veers away from river.
5.3 ▲ SO Road follows alongside the Stanislaus River.

▼ 3.1 SO Track on right.
4.7 ▲ SO Track on left.
GPS: N38°06.94′ W120°24.52′

▼ 3.9 SO End of shelf road. Disused cement plant on left.
3.9 ▲ SO Disused cement plant on right. Start of shelf road.

▼ 7.4 SO Paved road on right.
0.4 ▲ SO Paved road on left.
GPS: N38°05.17′ W120°27.28′

▼ 7.8 T-intersection with paved Parrots Ferry Road (CR E18). Turn right for Vallecito; turn left for Columbia.

0.0 ▲ Trail commences on Parrots Ferry Road (CR E18), 1 mile southeast of California 4 and Vallecito and 3.8 miles north of bridge over the Stanislaus River. Zero trip meter and turn east onto small paved Camp Nine Road following sign to Stanislaus Power House.
GPS: N38°05.05′ W120°27.59′

Pinecrest Peak Trail

STARTING POINT 4N12, 13.1 miles northeast of Strawberry
FINISHING POINT 4N12, 11.4 miles northeast of Strawberry
TOTAL MILEAGE 5.6 miles, plus 1.1-mile spur to Pinecrest Fire Lookout site
UNPAVED MILEAGE 5.6 miles, plus 1.1-mile spur
DRIVING TIME 2 hours
ELEVATION RANGE 7,900–8,700 feet
USUALLY OPEN May to November, exact dates vary
BEST TIME TO TRAVEL Dry weather
DIFFICULTY RATING 4
SCENIC RATING 10
REMOTENESS RATING +0

Special Attractions

- Moderate trail suitable for high-clearance 4WDs.
- Unparalleled views of the Dardanelles and the Emigrant Wilderness.
- Numerous backcountry campsites.
- Snowmobile trails in winter.

History

Pinecrest Peak Trail begins east of the old Bumblebee railroad siding, Cow Creek Camp, and Fiddlers Green. In the 1920s, the Sugar Pine Railroad ran through Strawberry to Bumblebee. This railroad spur was part of a massive network that grew to 70 miles of mainline railroad and more than 300 miles of spur lines. Large quantities of old growth trees were hauled out of Fiddlers Green to a sawmill at Standard, a few miles east of Sonora.

The toll wagon road over Sonora Pass, completed in 1868, was an important trade route from Sonora to Bodie and the Mono Lake region on the east side of the Sierra Nevada. A stage station catering to toll road traffic was established on Cow Creek, and in 1902, a forest service guard station was constructed at the same place at a cost of $65. Most of the lumber for the structure came from the Conlin Brothers sawmill at nearby Strawberry. In 1911, mule teams used the road to haul construction materials for the Relief Dam, high in the range at the present-day boundary of the Emigrant Wilderness.

An outbreak of hoof-and-mouth disease occurred in this region between 1923 and 1925. Cattle were rounded up, driven into an abandoned cutting along the old Sugar Pine Railroad, and slaughtered. The carcasses were heavily doused with quicklime and buried. During and after this outbreak, all railroad employees were under strict orders not to exit the railcars unnecessarily. Employees were sprayed with disinfectant on a regular basis in an effort to contain the disease. The main concern was that the railroad would spread the disease to the sawmill and thus release it to an even broader region.

Signs along Pinecrest Peak Trail

Description

This short trail starts and finishes on the loop road 4N12 and can be driven in either direction. In itself, 4N12 is a highly scenic, easy drive that gives access not only to Pinecrest Peak Trail, but also to Eagle Peak Trail, campgrounds at Herring Creek Reservoir, and hiking trails into the Emigrant Wilderness. In winter, the 12.8-mile loop of 4N12 is used by snowmobilers and cross-country skiers, though it is not groomed.

The forest service only allows 4WD vehicles on the Pinecrest Peak Trail, also known as Madhatters Rim Trail, because the loose surface is easily disturbed by the spinning tires of 2WD vehicles. Initially, the graded dirt road heads southeast to the Cooper Meadow Trailhead. Past the trailhead, parking, and horse camping area, the small, formed trail becomes 4WD only. It climbs steeply up the ridge, passing volcanic slopes covered with yellow mule's ears in late spring and summer. This hardy plant thrives in the region's volcanic soils. The trail surface is smooth, but loose. You will see spots where other vehicles have lost traction and spun wheels. From the top of the ridge, there are unparalleled views east over the Emigrant Wilderness and Eagle Peak and north to the Dardanelles.

The trail drops from the ridge along a sloping off-camber section, before joining a roughly graded road to the Waterhouse Lake Trailhead. Waterhouse Lake Trail is a steep, moderately strenuous hike that goes to Waterhouse Lake in the Emigrant Wilderness. From the trailhead, the vehicle trail follows a small loop to Pinecrest Peak and the site of an old fire lookout. The lookout site is the best place to take in the scenery, with views over Pinecrest Lake, Double Dome, Herring Creek, Hammill Canyon, Eagle Peak, and the Dardanelles. From Pinecrest Peak itself, there are views over the ski runs at Pinecrest and the Emigrant Wilderness.

Campers will enjoy this region. In addition to campgrounds at Herring Creek Reservoir and Herring Creek (not marked on the forest map), there are many backcountry sites along the trail, most with shade and excellent views. The campgrounds do not have tables, but they do have fire rings and pit toilets. Anglers can fish for eastern brook, German brown, and rainbow trout in Herring Creek and Herring Creek Reservoir.

A short hiking trail called Trail of the Gargoyles begins near the campground at Herring Creek Reservoir. The 1.5-mile trail passes a variety of geologic features and viewpoints. An interpretive leaflet for the trail is available at the trailhead, which can be found on a small, unmarked vehicle trail that heads west from the start of the loop section of 4N12.

Current Road Information
Stanislaus National Forest
Summit Ranger District
1 Pinecrest Lake Road
Pinecrest, CA 95364
(209) 965-3434

Map References
BLM   Bridgeport
USFS   Stanislaus National Forest

USGS   1:24,000   Pinecrest
       1:100,000   Bridgeport
Maptech CD-ROM: High Sierra/Yosemite
Northern California Atlas & Gazetteer, p. 100
California Road & Recreation Atlas, p. 72
       (incomplete)

Route Directions

▼ 0.0   From Strawberry, proceed 2.3 miles north on California 108; then turn northeast on paved Herring Creek Road. Continue along this road for 6.5 miles; then bear right on 4N12, following the sign to Pinecrest Peak. After 2.6 miles, pass the western end of the trail (5N31). Continue on 4N12 for another 1.7 miles to the start of the trail. Zero trip meter and turn south on graded dirt road 5N67, following the sign for Cooper Meadows Trailhead.

3.1 ▲   Trail ends back on 4N12. Turn left to exit back to Strawberry.

GPS: N38°15.04' W119°53.09'

The trail offers unparalleled views north toward the Dardenelles

NORTHERN SIERRA #6: PINECREST PEAK TRAIL

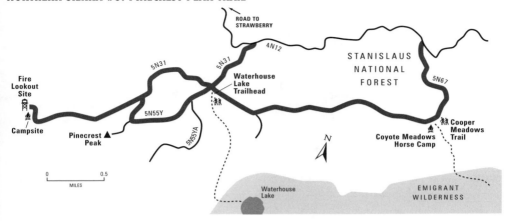

▼ 0.9   SO   Cooper Meadows Trailhead on left at Coyote Meadows Horse Camp.

2.2 ▲   SO   Cooper Meadows Trailhead on right at Coyote Meadows Horse Camp.
GPS: N38°14.45′ W119°52.71′

▼ 1.0   BL   Bear left out of camp and trailhead parking area. Trail drops in standard to become a narrow formed trail and starts to climb. 4WD-only past this point.

2.1 ▲   SO   Pass through trailhead parking and camp area. Trail is now a roughly graded dirt road.

▼ 1.7   SO   Top of climb. Walk to the north side of the trail for views over Eagle Peak and the Dardanelles.

1.4 ▲   SO   Walk to the north side of the trail for views over Eagle Peak and the Dardanelles. Start of descent.

▼ 2.2   SO   Trail starts to descend from ridge.
0.9 ▲   SO   Top of ridge.

▼ 2.7   TR   End of descent. Turn right at T-intersection.
0.4 ▲   TL   Turn left on 5N67 and start to climb. 4WD-only past this point.
GPS: N38°14.03′ W119°54.40′

▼ 3.1   SO   Waterhouse Lake Trailhead on left; then 4-way intersection. Graded road on left is 5N55Y. Track straight ahead and to the right is 5N31. Zero trip meter.

0.0 ▲   Continue to the east on 5N67.
GPS: N38°14.12′ W119°54.82′

▼ 0.0   Continue to the west on 5N31.

0.8 ▲   SO   4-way intersection. Graded road on right is 5N55Y and track on left is 5N31. Waterhouse Lake Trailhead on right. Zero trip meter.

▼ 0.8   BL   Track straight ahead is spur to Pinecrest Lookout site. Zero trip meter and bear left onto 5N55Y.

0.0 ▲   Continue to the north.
GPS: N38°13.87′ W119°55.41′

Spur to Pinecrest Lookout Site

▼ 0.0   Proceed to the southwest on 5N55Y.
▼ 0.9   SO   Viewpoint on left.
▼ 1.0   SO   Track on right.
▼ 1.1   Spur ends at viewpoint and campsite at Pinecrest Lookout site.
GPS: N38°13.49′ W119°56.44′

Continuation of Main Trail

▼ 0.0   Continue to the south.
1.1 ▲   SO   Track on left is spur to Pinecrest Lookout site. Zero trip meter and continue on 5N31.
GPS: N38°13.87′ W119°55.41′

▼ 0.3   TL   T-intersection. Track on right goes 0.2 miles to Pinecrest Peak.
0.8 ▲   TR   Track straight ahead goes 0.2 miles to Pinecrest Peak.
GPS: N38°13.64′ W119°55.44′

▼ 0.9   SO   Track on right is 5N55YA.

0.2 ▲   SO   Track on left is 5N55YA.

▼ 1.1   SO   4-way intersection at Waterhouse Lake Trailhead. Zero trip meter.

0.0 ▲   Continue to the south on graded road, 5N55Y.

     GPS: N38°14.12′ W119°54.82′

▼ 0.0   Continue to the north on 5N31.

0.6 ▲   SO   4-way intersection at Waterhouse Lake Trailhead. Track on left is 5N67 and track on right is 5N31. Zero trip meter.

▼ 0.6   Trail ends at T-intersection with 4N12. Turn left to exit to Strawberry.

0.0 ▲   From Strawberry, proceed north for 2.3 miles on California 108; then turn northeast on paved Herring Creek Road. Continue along this road for 6.5 miles; then bear right on 4N12, following the sign to Pinecrest Peak. Proceed 2.6 miles to the start of the trail. Zero trip meter and turn east on graded dirt road, signposted to Pinecrest Peak.

     GPS: N38°14.56′ W119°54.59′

NORTHERN SIERRA #7

4,700-Foot Road

STARTING POINT Beardsley Road (FR 52), 0.9 miles west of California 108

FINISHING POINT Gate before Donnell Lake

TOTAL MILEAGE 10 miles (one-way)

UNPAVED MILEAGE 10 miles

DRIVING TIME 1.25 hours (one-way)

ELEVATION RANGE 4,400–5,300 feet

USUALLY OPEN May to November, exact dates vary

BEST TIME TO TRAVEL May to November

DIFFICULTY RATING 2

SCENIC RATING 9

REMOTENESS RATING +0

Special Attractions

■ Waterfalls and wildflower viewing in spring.

■ Panoramic views over Dome Rock and the Middle Fork of the Stanislaus River.

NORTHERN SIERRA #7: 4,700 FOOT ROAD

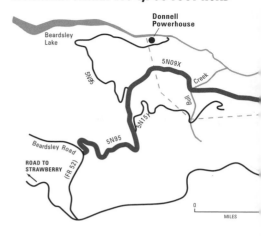

History

During the 1850s, the Middle Fork of the Stanislaus River near 4,700-Foot Road looked completely different. A wide, riverside flat sat below the massive granite outcrops where Donnell Lake now occupies the full width of the canyon. A sawmill, constructed by an enterprising merchant from the nearby town of Columbia, operated on the flat. The mill supplied lumber for buildings in the booming gold rush town of Columbia as well as for aqueducts throughout the region. Wooden aqueducts and earthen ditches carried the water needed for the ecologically destructive practice of hydraulic mining.

Donnell Lake Dam was constructed in the mid-1950s as part of an irrigation system known as the Tri-Dam project. In the late 1930s, the Oakdale and South San Joaquin Irrigation District made plans for an improved system that would hedge against drought. Work on the project did not get started until 1948, and it was finally completed in June 1957. The Tri-Dam project involved the construction and linkage of Beardsley and Donnell Lakes, associated powerhouses, penstocks, and tunnels. The Melones Dam, already completed by November 1926, was the third dam in the system. The Tri-Dam project was a major engineering feat for its time.

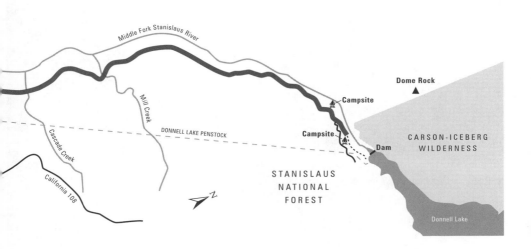

Description

4,700-Foot Road is so-named by locals and U.S. Forest Service workers because it closely follows the 4,700-foot contour line with little change in elevation.

The trail is generally easygoing for high-clearance 2WDs. It is rough and lumpy in places but with no difficult grades or maneuvers requiring four-wheel drive. The trail leaves paved Beardsley Road and follows graded dirt

4,700-Foot Road, carved into granite canyon walls during the construction of the Donnell Lake Dam

Donnell Lake, dedicated in 1957

5N95 for 2 miles before turning onto the trail that runs north to Donnell Lake. The Stanislaus National Forest map shows this road as 5N06, but on the ground it is clearly marked 5N09X. The wide shelf road travels high above the Middle Fork of the Stanislaus River for most of its length. Two vehicles can pass easily along most of the road, but the sheer drop may make some nervous.

Along the way, the trail passes several small cascades and waterfalls. These are particularly spectacular in spring, when running full of snowmelt. Wildflowers are abundant along the trail in April and early May.

Camping is limited because of the road's shelf aspect, but a good site can be found at the end of the trail. From the gate at the end of the trail, a half-mile, 20-minute hike takes you to the Donnell Lake Dam. There are no public recreation facilities at the reservoir. A short distance past the end of the vehicle trail is a good view north of Dome Rock, which towers above the dam.

Current Road Information
Stanislaus National Forest

Summit Ranger District
1 Pinecrest Lake Road
Pinecrest, CA 95364
(209) 965-3434

Map References
BLM   San Andreas, Bridgeport
USFS   Stanislaus National Forest
USGS   1:24,000   Strawberry, Liberty Hill,
Donnell Lake
1:100,000 San Andreas, Bridgeport
Maptech CD-ROM: High Sierra/Yosemite
Northern California Atlas & Gazetteer,
pp. 99, 100
California Road & Recreation Atlas, p. 72

Route Directions

▼ 0.0   From California 108, 3.6 miles north of Strawberry, turn northwest on Beardsley Road (FR 52) and proceed 0.9 miles to the start of the trail. Zero trip meter and turn northwest on graded dirt road, marked 5N95. Pass through seasonal closure gate.
GPS: N38°13.63′ W120°00.72′

▼ 1.2	SO	Cross over Cow Creek.
▼ 1.3	SO	Track on right is 5N15Y.
▼ 1.9	SO	Track on right.
▼ 2.0	BR	Graded road on left is 5N95. Bear right onto 5N09X and zero trip meter.

GPS: N38°14.38′ W120°01.38′

▼ 0.0		Continue to the north past track on left.
▼ 0.1	SO	Seasonal closure gate. Track is marked as suitable for ATVs and motorbikes as well as larger vehicles.
▼ 0.3	SO	Start of shelf road.
▼ 0.5	SO	Cross over Donnell Lake Penstock. Donnell Powerhouse is below the trail to the left; then track on left.
▼ 1.1	SO	Cross over Bull Creek.
▼ 2.1	SO	Track on left to tunnel works area.
▼ 2.9	SO	Three cascades on right are part of Cascade Creek.

GPS: N38°16.43′ W120°00.34′

| ▼ 3.9 | SO | Track on left. |
| ▼ 4.0 | SO | Cross over Mill Creek on bridge. |

GPS: N38°17.32′ W120°00.19′

| ▼ 5.3 | SO | Pass beside bare granite rock face. |

GPS: N38°18.33′ W120°00.01′

| ▼ 5.7 | SO | Waterfall on right. |
| ▼ 7.6 | SO | Campsite on left. |

GPS: N38°19.56′ W119°58.46′

| ▼ 7.9 | SO | Track on right. |
| ▼ 8.0 | | Trail ends at a campsite and gate before Donnell Lake. There is usually hiking access to the dam, which is 0.5 miles past the gate. |

GPS: N38°19.62′ W119°58.16′

NORTHERN SIERRA #8

Black Springs Route

STARTING POINT California 4, 3.5 miles north of Dorrington

FINISHING POINT 7N09, 0.1 miles west of Northern Sierra #9: Calaveras Dome Trail

TOTAL MILEAGE 18.4 miles
UNPAVED MILEAGE 18.4 miles
DRIVING TIME 2 hours
ELEVATION RANGE 5,300–7,400 feet
USUALLY OPEN May to November
BEST TIME TO TRAVEL Dry weather
DIFFICULTY RATING 4
SCENIC RATING 7
REMOTENESS RATING +0

Special Attractions

■ Access to a network of trails within the Black Springs OHV Area.
■ Views from Summit Level Ridge and Bailey Ridge.

History

Black Springs Route starts north of Dorrington, formerly called Cold Spring Ranch. A stage stop at this location served travelers on the Big Trees–Carson Valley Road. Prospec-

Some old U.S. Forest Service signs remain on Bailey Ridge

tors used this route to the southern mines of the Mother Lode as early as 1849. That same year, a Dr. Clark from Missouri was noted as being the first newcomer to see the nearby giant sequoia grove. In April 1851, Major John Ebbetts discovered an 8,731-foot pass over the Sierra Nevada (now called Ebbetts Pass) that had no snow on it in April. By 1855, a wagon road called Big Trees Route was established through Dorrington and over the Sierra Nevada via Ebbetts Pass. The route became a toll road in 1863 and fees were charged until 1910, two years after the first automobile crossed the Sierra Nevada via the Big Trees–Carson Valley Road.

Calaveras Big Trees State Park, established in 1931, lies just south of Dorrington. Research indicates that giant sequoias are related to a species that thrived in the region about 7 million years ago. Prior to the arrival of Euro-American settlers, the Northern Miwok lived on this rich land, making use of abundant resources in the lower foothills. Mule deer, rabbit, tule elk, and pronghorn inhabited the region. Seed-producing grasses, forbs, and various trees provided additional diversity to their diets.

Description

This is one of the U.S. Forest Service's listed OHV trails within the Black Springs OHV Area. The single-track trail, rated moderately difficult by the forest service, climbs onto the northern end of Summit Level Ridge. This first climb is the most difficult. Although the grade is only moderately steep, the loose, fist-size rubble on top of soft earth provides very little in the way of traction. A few tree roots and moguls add to the difficulty.

The trail gets easier on top of Summit Level Ridge. Although it is single vehicle width and edged with manzanitas, the trail gets sufficient use that only the widest vehicles will find it lightly brushy.

The trail travels among sugar pines and scattered oaks. After crossing paved 7N23, it begins to climb onto Bailey Ridge. This climb is easier than the earlier climb onto Summit Level Ridge; the surface here is loose, but it lacks the rubble of the first ascent. The predominant veg-

NORTHERN SIERRA #8: BLACK SPRINGS ROUTE

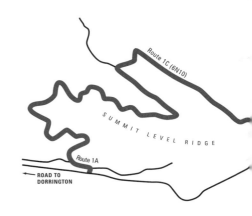

etation along this section of trail is white fir.

The trail descends along a loose, moguled surface to finish on well-graded 7N09, just west of Northern Sierra #9: Calaveras Dome Trail, and a short distance north of California 4.

The opening and closing dates for this trail are approximate; most of the time it closes naturally with snowfall.

Current Road Information

Stanislaus National Forest
Calaveras Ranger District
PO Box 500
Hathaway Pines, CA 95233
(209) 795-1381

Map References

BLM   San Andreas
USFS Stanislaus National Forest
USGS 1:24,000   Boards Crossing,
      Calaveras Dome, Dorrington
      1:100,000 San Andreas
Maptech CD-ROM: High Sierra/Yosemite
Northern California Atlas & Gazetteer, p. 99
California Road & Recreation Atlas, p. 71
      (incomplete)
Other: Calaveras Ranger District OHV
      Routes (U.S.F.S. leaflet)

Route Directions

▼ 0.0   From California 4, 3.5 miles north of
           Dorrington, zero trip meter and turn

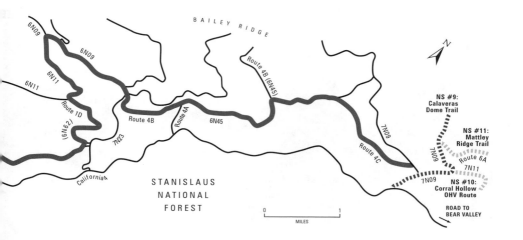

northwest on graded dirt road, marked 6N58. Immediately track on right and track on left.

5.5 ▲   Track on left and track on right. Trail ends at T-intersection with California 4. Turn left for Bear Valley; turn right for Dorrington.
GPS: N38°19.86' W120°14.16'

▼ 0.1   TL   Track on right. Trail is now marked Route 1A.
5.4 ▲   TR   Track on left.
▼ 0.3   SO   Track on left.
5.2 ▲   SO   Track on right.
▼ 1.5   SO   Campsite on left.
4.0 ▲   SO   Campsite on right.
▼ 2.0   SO   Track on left; then cattle guard.
3.5 ▲   SO   Cattle guard; then track on right.
GPS: N38°19.97' W120°15.48'

▼ 4.5   SO   Track on right.
1.0 ▲   SO   Track on left.
▼ 4.6   SO   Track on left.
0.9 ▲   SO   Track on right.
▼ 5.5   TR   Graded road continues ahead. Zero trip meter and turn right onto formed trail 6N10 (Route 1C) suitable for 4WDs, ATVs, and motorbikes.
0.0 ▲   Continue to the east.
GPS: N38°20.97' W120°15.02'

▼ 0.0   Continue to the north.
4.2 ▲   TL   T-intersection with graded road 6N58

(Route 1A). Zero trip meter.

▼ 3.6   SO   Track on right into private property. Trail now follows along small power lines.
0.6 ▲   SO   Trail leaves power lines. Track on left into private property.
▼ 4.1   TL   Track on right. Then turn left, following marker for the OHV route. Trail leaves power lines.
0.1 ▲   TR   T-intersection. Turn right onto Route IC, suitable for 4WDs, ATVs, and motorbikes, following along small power lines. Immediately track on left.
GPS: N38°22.62' W120°11.74'

▼ 4.2   TL   T-intersection with graded dirt road. Zero trip meter and turn left onto 6N62 (Route 1D), suitable for 4WDs, ATVs, and motorbikes.
0.0 ▲   Continue to the southeast.
GPS: N38°22.68' W120°11.74'

▼ 0.0   Continue to the west.
3.7 ▲   TR   Graded road continues straight ahead. Zero trip meter and turn right onto small formed trail marked Route 1C.
▼ 1.1   BL   Track on right.
2.6 ▲   SO   Track on left.
▼ 1.2   BR   Graded road 6N11 joins from left. Bear right onto 6N11.
2.5 ▲   BL   Graded road 6N11 leaves to the right. Bear left onto 6N62.
GPS: N38°22.91' W120°12.45'

Views northeast toward the Carson-Iceberg Wilderness

▼ 1.4   BR   Track on left goes into private property. Follow marker for Route 1D.

2.3 ▲   BL   Track on right goes into private property. Remain on Route 1D.

▼ 2.3   TR   T-intersection with 6N09.

1.4 ▲   TL   6N09 continues ahead. Turn left onto 6N11.

        GPS: N38°23.27′ W120°13.33′

▼ 2.5   BR   Graded road on left goes into private property. Remain on small formed trail.

1.2 ▲   BL   Graded road on right goes into private property. Remain on small formed trail.

        GPS: N38°23.32′ W120°13.14′

▼ 3.5   SO   Track on left. Remain on Route 1E.

0.2 ▲   SO   Track on right. Remain on Route 1E.

▼ 3.7   SO   4-way intersection with paved 7N23. Zero trip meter.

0.0 ▲   Continue to the northwest on 6N09 (Route 1E).

        GPS: N38°23.39′ W120°11.85′

▼ 0.0   Continue to the east on Route 4B.

2.5 ▲   SO   4-way intersection with paved 7N23. Zero trip meter.

▼ 1.0   SO   Route 4A on right goes to California 4.

Continue on 6N45, following sign to Hermit Springs.

1.5 ▲   SO   Route 4A on left goes to California 4. Continue on Route 4B, following sign to Buck Ranch.

        GPS: N38°23.76′ W120°11.17′

▼ 2.5   TR   Track on left is continuation of Route 4B (6N45), which runs along Bailey Ridge. Turn right onto Route 4C and pass through gate. Zero trip meter.

0.0 ▲   Continue to the southeast.

        GPS: N38°24.54′ W120°10.28′

▼ 0.0   Continue to the east.

2.5 ▲   TL   Gate; then turn left onto 6N45 (Route 4B). Track on right is also Route 4B, which runs along Bailey Ridge. Zero trip meter.

▼ 0.3   SO   Track on right.

2.3 ▲   SO   Track on left.

▼ 0.9   BR   Track on left is Route F for 4WDs, ATVs, and motorbikes. Remain on Route 4C.

1.6 ▲   BL   Track on right is Route F for 4WDs, ATVs, and motorbikes. Remain on Route 4C.

        GPS: N38°25.11′ W120°09.58′

▼ 1.3	BR	Track on left.
1.2 ▲	SO	Track on right.
▼ 2.5		Trail ends at T-intersection with graded dirt 7N09. Turn right for California 4 and Bear Valley.
0.0 ▲		Trail commences on graded dirt 7N09, 0.6 miles north of California 4. From the highway, 6.7 miles southwest of Bear Valley and 0.3 miles south of Cabbage Patch Station, proceed north on Northern Sierra #9: Calaveras Dome Trail (7N09). Bear left after 0.5 miles, following sign to Pumpkin Patch. After 0.1 miles, zero trip meter and turn south on formed dirt trail marked Route 4C, suitable for 4WDs, ATVs, and motorbikes—rated blue.

GPS: N38°25.14′ W120°08.14′

Calaveras Dome Trail

STARTING POINT California 4, 6.7 miles south-west of Bear Valley

FINISHING POINT FR 91 (8N05), southwest of Lower Bear River Reservoir

TOTAL MILEAGE 42 miles, plus 3.9-mile spur to Calaveras Dome and 4-mile spur to Salt Springs Reservoir

UNPAVED MILEAGE 40.4 miles, plus spurs

DRIVING TIME 5 hours

ELEVATION RANGE 3,100–7,600 feet

USUALLY OPEN April to November

BEST TIME TO TRAVEL Dry weather

DIFFICULTY RATING 2

SCENIC RATING 9

REMOTENESS RATING +0

Special Attractions

■ Long trail through a wide variety of forest scenery.

■ Angling, camping, and swimming on the North Fork of the Mokelumne River.

■ Excellent rock climbing opportunities on Calaveras Dome.

History

The Mokelumne Wilderness, situated within Eldorado, Stanislaus, and Toiyabe National Forests, was established in 1964 and expanded in 1984. The wilderness encompasses 104,461 acres of remote mountainous terrain and the headwaters of the Mokelumne River, which flows about 140 miles west to join the San Joaquin River northwest of Stockton. Mokelumne Peak (9,334 feet) can be seen northeast of Salt Springs Reservoir.

Mokelumne is Miwok, meaning "the people of Mok." The suffix -umne means "people," and is also used in the Cosumnes River to the north and Tuolumne River to the south.

Salt Springs Reservoir, with a capacity of 141,817 acre-feet of water, was constructed in 1931 as part of a hydroelectric power system named Project 137. The Tiger Creek Regulatory Canal can be seen below the trail on the northern side of the Mokelumne River. The canal, made up of flumes, tunnels, trestles, and penstocks, flows southwest to Tiger Creek Reservoir. It was built in 1931 to attain greater elevation drop for power generation at the powerhouse on Tiger Creek Reservoir.

The trail commences near Cabbage Patch Station on the old Big Trees–Carson Valley Road. After the toll road was taken over by the state in 1910 it was renamed California 24 and later California 4. Will and Chas Gann ran stock near Cabbage Patch during summer. They purchased land from Dave Felipini, the original patent holder of this land. Their name lingers on in the settlement Gann, just over a mile west along the old toll road.

Description

Both ends of this long easy trail are generally suitable for passenger vehicles, but in its entirety the trail requires a high-clearance vehicle. It should be driven in dry weather only because some sections become very greasy and difficult when wet.

The trail leaves California 4 and initially follows the graded dirt and gravel forest road 7N09, which takes you past the western end of Northern Sierra #10: Corral Hollow OHV

Calaveras Dome rises nearly 1,500 feet above the Mokelumne River

Route and both ends of Northern Sierra #11: Mattley Ridge Trail. It wraps around the small meadow at Hay Gulch, a good place to see wildflowers in late spring and early summer.

The first spur goes to the top of Calaveras Dome, one of the main features of this trail. From the spur's end, you can walk a short distance to the top of the dome for a view over Salt Springs Reservoir. The dome itself is better seen from the lower road along the North Fork of the Mokelumne River. An excellent campsite and picnic spot can be found near the end of this spur.

The main trail continues on 7N09, traveling through the forest to join paved Winton Road. Passenger vehicles can return to California 4 along the continuation of 7N09 or continue along paved Winton Road to West Point, on California 26.

High-clearance vehicles can follow the main route, turning off Winton Road to head northeast on 7N08. This single-track trail descends through thick forest along a shelf road. It crosses Blue Creek, a pleasant place to cool off in summer, en route to the North Fork of the Mokelumne River. Once the trail reaches the river, campers will find many sites to choose from. Most have shade and many provide river access. Anglers can fish for rainbow trout—the river is stocked annually by the California Department of Fish and Game. Although the national forest map shows a number of campgrounds along the river, they are primarily undeveloped and have no picnic tables or trash collection.

The main trail crosses the North Fork of the Mokelumne River at Moore Creek Campground and turns southwest. A spur from this point heads northeast on a paved road and takes you 4 miles to Salt Springs Reservoir. There are plenty of camping, fishing, swimming, and picnicking opportunities, as well as views of the premier climbing destinations of Calaveras Dome and Hammer Dome. The granite monolith of Calaveras Dome, south of the trail, is the better known of the two. Climbing access to the dome's base is via very small, unmarked hiking trails. The dome has long routes for sport climbers as well as a number of bouldering opportunities. The dome's many different routes offer a challenge to climbers of all skill levels. Climbing the entire 1,200-foot vertical face often requires a night on the face.

The spur finishes at a picnic area at the base of the Salt Springs Dam. No overnight camping is allowed at the dam. From here, a hiking trail into the Mokelumne Wilderness snakes up the mountain to the left of the dam. A permit is required for overnight stays in the wilderness. The Mokelumne River Canyon is a rugged area dominated by volcanic ridges and peaks. Salt Springs Reservoir, at the southern edge of the wilderness, is at an elevation of about 3,900 feet.

The main trail continues along the Mokelumne River past a few more campsites and gradually climbs above the river. An aqueduct follows below this part of the trail. The trail ends at the intersection with FR 91 (8N05). From here you can exit north to California 88 or continue west along the small paved road to Tiger Creek Reservoir.

Current Road Information

Stanislaus National Forest
Calaveras Ranger District
PO Box 500
Hathaway Pines, CA 95233
(209) 795-1381

Map References

BLM   San Andreas
USFS   Stanislaus National Forest;
       El Dorado National Forest
USGS   1:24,000   Calaveras Dome,
       Garnet Hill
       1:100,000 San Andreas
Maptech CD-ROM: High Sierra/Yosemite
Northern California Atlas & Gazetteer, p. 99
California Road & Recreation Atlas, p. 71

Route Directions

▼ 0.0   From California 4, 6.7 miles southwest
           of Bear Valley, zero trip meter and turn
           north on 7N09 at the marker. There is
           an information board immediately after
           the turn.
1.4 ▲   Trail ends at T-intersection with
           California 4. Turn left for Bear Valley;
           turn right for Dorrington.
           GPS: N38°24.79' W120°08.14'

▼ 0.1   SO Track on right.
1.3 ▲   SO Track on left.
▼ 0.5   SO Graded road on left is 7N09 and small
              track on right. Continue straight ahead on
              7N09 following the sign to Hay Gulch.
0.9 ▲   SO Graded road on right is 7N09 and small
              track on left. Continue straight ahead
              on 7N09.
▼ 0.9   SO Cattle guard; then track on right is North-
              ern Sierra #10: Corral Hollow OHV Route.
0.5 ▲   SO Track on left is Northern Sierra #10:
              Corral Hollow OHV Route; then cattle
              guard.
           GPS: N38°25.40' W120°07.66'

▼ 1.1   SO Track on left.
0.3 ▲   SO Track on right.
▼ 1.4   SO Track on right is Northern Sierra #11:
              Mattley Ridge Trail. Zero trip meter.
0.0 ▲   Continue to the south.
           GPS: N38°25.54' W120°08.14'

▼ 0.0   Continue to the north.
6.6 ▲   SO Track on left is Northern Sierra #11:
              Mattley Ridge Trail. Zero trip meter.
▼ 0.2   SO Track on right is 7N09H.
6.4 ▲   SO Track on left is 7N09H.

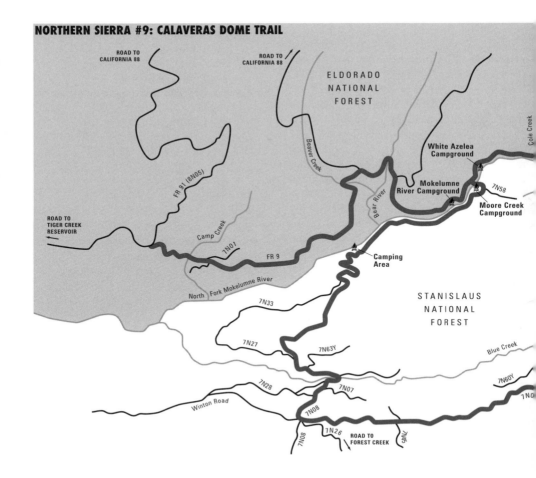

▼ 1.1   SO Track on left is 7N09G.
5.5 ▲   SO Track on right is 7N09G.
▼ 1.3   SO Track on left.
5.3 ▲   SO Track on right.
▼ 1.7   SO Track on right; then cross over Middle
         Gulch.
4.9 ▲   SO Cross over Middle Gulch; then track
         on left.
         GPS: N38°26.36' W120°08.26'

▼ 2.3   SO Track on right is 7N69 (Route 6C) for
         4WDs, ATVs, and motorbikes.
         Camping area on left.
4.3 ▲   SO Track on left is 7N69 (Route 6C) for
         4WDs, ATVs, and motorbikes.
         Camping area on right.
▼ 3.4   SO Cross over Hay Gulch; then pass
         around the end of a meadow.
3.2 ▲   SO Pass around the end of a meadow;

then cross over Hay Gulch.
▼ 3.7   SO Two tracks on right.
2.9 ▲   SO Two tracks on left.
▼ 3.9   SO Track on left to campsite.
2.7 ▲   SO Track on right to campsite.
▼ 5.3   SO Cross over Cottonwood Gulch; then
         track on right.
1.3 ▲   SO Track on left; then cross over
         Cottonwood Gulch.
         GPS: N38°27.47' W120°09.56'

▼ 5.6   SO Track on left.
1.0 ▲   SO Track on right.
▼ 6.2   SO Two tracks on left are 7N05.
0.4 ▲   SO Two tracks on right are 7N05.
▼ 6.6   SO 4-way intersection. Track on right and
         track on left are both 7N59. Northern
         Sierra #11: Mattley Ridge Trail is to
         the right. Zero trip meter.

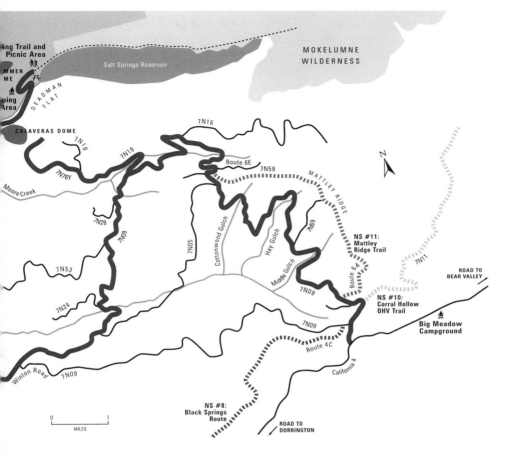

0.0 ▲		Continue to the southeast. **GPS: N38°27.94′ W120°10.10′**
▼ 0.0		Continue to the northeast.
4.1 ▲	SO	4-way intersection. Track on right and track on left are both 7N59. Northern Sierra #11: Mattley Ridge Trail is to the left. Zero trip meter.
▼ 0.2	BL	Track on right is Route 6E.
3.9 ▲	BR	Track on left is Route 6E.
▼ 0.6	SO	Track on left.
3.5 ▲	SO	Track on right.
▼ 1.0	SO	Cross over Moore Creek.
3.1 ▲	SO	Cross over Moore Creek.
▼ 1.9	BL	Graded road on right is 7N16 (Route 6H).
2.2 ▲	BR	Graded road on left is 7N16 (Route 6H). **GPS: N38°28.59′ W120°10.43′**
▼ 2.2	BL	Graded road on right.

1.9 ▲	BR	Graded road on left.
▼ 2.4	SO	Track on right.
1.7 ▲	SO	Track on left.
▼ 2.7	SO	Cross over Moore Creek.
1.4 ▲	SO	Cross over Moore Creek.
▼ 4.1	SO	Track on right is 7N19, spur to the top of Calaveras Dome. Zero trip meter.
0.0 ▲		Continue to the northeast. **GPS: N38°28.15′ W120°11.61′**

Spur to the top of Calaveras Dome

▼ 0.0		Continue to the north and pass through seasonal closure gate.
▼ 0.2	SO	Track on left.
▼ 0.5	SO	Cross over Moore Creek.
▼ 1.8	BL	Track on right is 7N19. Bear left onto 7N76Y. **GPS: N38°28.33′ W120°12.45′**

▼ 2.3 SO Track on right. Road turns from gravel to graded dirt.
▼ 2.8 SO Track on left ends after 0.2 miles.
GPS: N38°28.49′ W120°13.26′

▼ 3.2 SO Seasonal closure gate.
▼ 3.5 SO Track on left to campsite. This is the best access to the top of Calaveras Dome.
▼ 3.9 Trail is blocked by rockslide. Far below the trail to the north is Salt Springs Reservoir.
GPS: N38°29.00′ W120°13.02′

Continuation of Main Trail

▼ 0.0 Continue to the south.
6.2 ▲ SO Track on left is 7N19, spur to the top of Calaveras Dome. Zero trip meter.
GPS: N38°28.15′ W120°11.61′

▼ 0.4 SO Cross over creek.
5.8 ▲ SO Cross over creek.
▼ 0.5 BL Graded road on right is 7N28.

5.7 ▲ BR Graded road on left is 7N28.
▼ 1.5 SO Cattle guard; then track on right is 7N53.
4.7 ▲ SO Track on left is 7N53; then cattle guard.
GPS: N38°27.18′ W120°12.29′

▼ 2.1 SO Track on left; then track on right.
4.1 ▲ SO Track on left; then track on right.
▼ 3.1 SO Track on left.
3.1 ▲ SO Track on right.
▼ 3.3 BL Graded road on right is 7N24.
2.9 ▲ BR Graded road on left is 7N24.
▼ 3.5 SO Track on right to campsite; then cross over Blue Creek on bridge; then track on right.
2.7 ▲ SO Track on left; then cross over Blue Creek on bridge; then track on left to campsite.
GPS: N38°26.14′ W120°12.59′

▼ 3.8 SO Track on left.
2.4 ▲ SO Track on right.
▼ 3.9 SO Track on left.
2.3 ▲ SO Track on right.
▼ 4.2 SO Track on left.
2.0 ▲ SO Track on right.

Calaveras Dome Trail winds down from Mattley Ridge

▼ 4.5 SO Graded road 7N05 enters on left.
1.7 ▲ BL Graded road 7N05 continues to the right and joins California 4 in 14 miles. Follow the sign for Loop Road to Cabbage Patch Road.
        GPS: N38°25.83′ W120°12.87′

▼ 5.0 SO Track on left.
1.2 ▲ SO Track on right.
▼ 5.9 SO Track on right.
0.3 ▲ SO Track on left.
▼ 6.2 SO Paved Winton Road (7N09) joins from the left. Zero trip meter and continue straight ahead on paved Winton Road, marked 7N03, following sign to West Point. Pass through seasonal closure gate.
0.0 ▲   Continue to the north.
        GPS: N38°25.57′ W120°14.47′

▼ 0.0   Continue to the south.
5.6 ▲ SO Seasonal closure gate; then paved Winton Road swings right and becomes 7N09. Zero trip meter and continue straight ahead on graded dirt road, also 7N09, following the sign to Blue Creek.
▼ 0.7 SO Graded road on right is 7N60Y.
4.9 ▲ SO Graded road on left is 7N60Y.
▼ 3.5 SO Track on right is 7N49 (also called Spur 3).
2.1 ▲ SO Track on left is 7N49 (also called Spur 3).
▼ 3.7 SO Track on right.
1.9 ▲ SO Track on left.
▼ 3.8 SO Track on left is 7N45 (also called Spur 2).
1.8 ▲ SO Track on right is 7N45 (also called Spur 2).
▼ 5.6 TR Graded road on left is 7N26 to Forest Creek; then track on left and track on right are both 7N08. Zero trip meter and turn right onto formed trail 7N08.
0.0 ▲   Continue to the east.
        GPS: N38°25.84′ W120°20.11′

▼ 0.0   Continue to the north.
6.6 ▲ TL T-intersection with paved Winton Road. Zero trip meter and turn left. Track opposite is also 7N08; then graded road on right is 7N26 to Forest Creek.
▼ 0.4 SO Track on right.
6.2 ▲ SO Track on left.

▼ 0.5 SO Track on left.
6.1 ▲ SO Track on right.
▼ 0.7 BR Track on right; then bear right at fork.
5.9 ▲ BL Bear left past track on right; then track on left.
        GPS: N38°26.09′ W120°19.69′

▼ 0.9 SO Track on right is 7N07 and track on left.
5.7 ▲ SO Track on left is 7N07 and track on right.
▼ 1.2 BR Join graded road 7N28, which enters from the left. Cross over Blue Creek on bridge.
5.4 ▲ BL Cross over Blue Creek on bridge; then graded road 7N28 continues to the right.
▼ 1.3 TL Turn left immediately after bridge, remaining on 7N08. Track on right.
5.3 ▲ TR Graded road continues straight ahead. Turn right toward bridge.
        GPS: N38°26.36′ W120°19.18′

▼ 1.4 SO Track on left.
5.2 ▲ SO Track on right.
▼ 1.9 SO Track on right is 7N63Y.
4.7 ▲ SO Track on left is 7N63Y.
▼ 2.2 SO Track on left is 7N27.
4.4 ▲ SO Track on right is 7N27.
▼ 2.7 SO Track on left is 7N80 and track on right.
3.9 ▲ SO Track on right is 7N80 and track on left.
▼ 2.9 SO Track on right.
3.7 ▲ SO Track on left.
▼ 3.5 SO Track on left.
3.1 ▲ SO Track on right.
▼ 4.2 SO Track on right is 7N40.
2.4 ▲ SO Track on left is 7N40.
        GPS: N38°27.75′ W120°18.82′

▼ 4.4 SO Seasonal closure gate.
2.2 ▲ SO Seasonal closure gate.
▼ 4.5 BR Track on left is 7N33. Follow the sign for North Fork Mokelumne River and start to descend shelf road.
2.1 ▲ BL End of shelf road. Track on right is 7N33.
        GPS: N38°27.87′ W120°18.69′

▼ 5.4 SO Cross over creek.
1.2 ▲ SO Cross over creek.
▼ 6.1 SO Cross over creek.
0.5 ▲ SO Cross over creek.
▼ 6.6 SO Unmarked track on left goes 0.1 miles

		to camping area alongside North Fork Mokelumne River. End of shelf road. Zero trip meter.
0.0 ▲		Continue to the south.
		GPS: N38°28.35' W120°18.11'

▼ 0.0		Continue to the northeast. Many campsites and tracks on left to campsites for next 0.6 miles.
2.7 ▲	SO	Unmarked track on right goes 0.1 miles to camping area alongside North Fork Mokelumne River. Start of shelf road. Zero trip meter.
▼ 1.2	SO	Track on left to camping area.
1.5 ▲	SO	Track on right to camping area.
▼ 2.1	SO	Start of Moore Creek Campground on left and right.
0.6 ▲	SO	Exit Moore Creek Campground.
▼ 2.3	SO	Track on left is 7N23; then cross over creek on concrete ford.
0.4 ▲	SO	Cross over creek on concrete ford; then track on right is 7N23.
		GPS: N38°28.81' W120°15.88'

▼ 2.5	BL	Track on right is 7N58.
0.2 ▲	BR	Track on left is 7N58.
▼ 2.7	TL	Cross over Mokelumne River on bridge; then T-intersection with paved road. Road on right is the spur to Calaveras Dome and Salt Springs Reservoir. Zero trip meter and exit Moore Creek Campground.
0.0 ▲		Continue to the southeast on dirt road.
		GPS: N38°28.95' W120°15.87'

Spur to Calaveras Dome and Salt Springs Reservoir

▼ 0.0		Proceed to the northeast on paved road. Many tracks on right and left to camping areas.
▼ 0.3	SO	White Azalea USFS Campground on right.
▼ 1.7	SO	Cross over Cole Creek on bridge.
▼ 1.9	SO	Cross over North Fork Mokelumne River on bridge. Faint hiking trails between here and the next bridge give climbing access to Calaveras Dome and Hidden Wall.
▼ 2.1	SO	Regulatory canal enters tunnel on far side of river and sometimes spills over at this point.
▼ 2.4	SO	Faint hiking trail on right gives climbing access to Calaveras Dome. Small cairn below pylon marks the spot.
		GPS: N38°29.33' W120°13.57'

▼ 2.8	TL	Turn left and cross North Fork Mokelumne River on bridge. Deadman Flat (private property) is straight ahead.
▼ 3.0	SO	Hiking trail on left gives climbing access to Hammer Dome; then cross over aqueduct. Power station on right.
		GPS: N38°29.75' W120°13.15'

▼ 3.4	SO	Track on left under power lines.
▼ 3.6	SO	Hiking trail on left gives climbing access to Hammer Dome.
		GPS: N38°29.76' W120°13.32'

▼ 3.7	SO	Camping area on left.
▼ 4.0		Spur ends at Salt Springs Reservoir dam. Salt Springs Trail starts here and provides hiking access into the Mokelumne Wilderness. There is a small picnic area at the dam.
		GPS: N38°30.01' W120°12.94'

Continuation of Main Trail

▼ 0.0		Continue to the southwest.
2.8 ▲	TR	Paved road straight ahead is the spur to Calaveras Dome and Salt Springs Reservoir. Zero trip meter and turn right and cross over Mokelumne River on bridge and enter Moore Creek Campground.
		GPS: N38°28.95' W120°15.87'

▼ 0.5	SO	Mokelumne River USFS Campground on left.
2.3 ▲	SO	Mokelumne River USFS Campground on right.
		GPS: N38°28.73' W120°16.21'

▼ 1.6	SO	Cross over aqueduct.
1.2 ▲	SO	Cross over aqueduct.
▼ 1.8	SO	Track on right and track on left.
1.0 ▲	SO	Track on left and track on right.
		GPS: N38°28.95' W120°17.46'

Tiger Creek Regulatory Canal runs below the trail along FR 9

▼ 2.3	SO	Paved road on right goes 10 miles to Bear River Reservoir. Follow the sign to California 88 (9 miles).
0.5 ▲	SO	Paved road on left goes 10 miles to Bear River Reservoir. Follow the sign to Salt Springs Reservoir.

GPS: N38°29.38' W120°17.34'

▼ 2.5	SO	Cross over Bear River on bridge; then track on right.
0.3 ▲	SO	Track on left; then cross over Bear River on bridge.
▼ 2.8	TL	Paved road ahead goes 8 miles to California 88. Zero trip meter and turn left onto gravel FR 9, following the sign to Tiger Creek Reservoir. Start of wide shelf road.
0.0 ▲		Continue to the northeast.

GPS: N38°29.43' W120°17.51'

▼ 0.0		Continue to the south and pass through seasonal closure gate.
6.0 ▲	TR	Seasonal closure gate; then T-intersection with paved FR 92 (8N25). Zero trip meter and turn right following the sign to Salt Springs Reservoir. End of shelf road.
▼ 0.9	SO	Cross over Beaver Creek.
5.1 ▲	SO	Cross over Beaver Creek.
▼ 1.6	SO	Track on left and track on right.
5.4 ▲	SO	Track on left and track on right.
▼ 3.1	SO	Track on left; then track on right.
2.9 ▲	SO	Track on left; then track on right.

GPS: N38°28.33' W120°19.62'

▼ 3.7	SO	Track on right.
2.3 ▲	SO	Track on left.
▼ 4.7	SO	Gravel road on left. End of shelf road.
1.3 ▲	SO	Start of shelf road. Gravel road on right.
▼ 4.9	SO	Track on right is 7N01.
1.1 ▲	SO	Track on left is 7N01.

GPS: N38°28.61' W120°21.32'

▼ 5.1	SO	Cross over Camp Creek.
0.9 ▲	SO	Cross over Camp Creek.
▼ 6.0		Trail ends at intersection with paved FR 91 (8N05). Turn right to exit to California 88 and Cooks Station; continue straight ahead to Tiger Creek Reservoir.

0.0 ▲		Trail commences at the intersection of FR 91 (8N05) and FR 9, 11 miles south of California 88. Zero trip meter and turn northeast on graded dirt FR 9, following the sign to Salt Springs Reservoir. Trail begins within State Game Refuge—no firearms allowed.

GPS: N38°28.97' W120°22.15'

NORTHERN SIERRA #10

Corral Hollow OHV Route

STARTING POINT California 4, 0.6 miles southwest of Bear Valley

FINISHING POINT Northern Sierra #9: Calaveras Dome Trail (7N09), 0.9 miles north of California 4

TOTAL MILEAGE 12.5 miles

UNPAVED MILEAGE 12.5 miles

DRIVING TIME 2 hours

ELEVATION RANGE 6,800–8,100 feet

USUALLY OPEN May to November

BEST TIME TO TRAVEL Dry weather

DIFFICULTY RATING 5

SCENIC RATING 10

REMOTENESS RATING +0

Special Attractions

■ Wildflower viewing in spring.

■ Historic Bear Trap Cabin.

■ Extremely scenic ridge top trail with many beautiful views.

■ Part of the trail forms a popular mountain bike trail called Bear Trap Basin Loop.

History

Corral Hollow OHV Route commences near Bloods Point, south of Bloods Ridge. These features were named for Harvey S. Blood, operator of a toll station and hotel at Bear Valley Meadow. The toll road, known as the Big Trees–Carson Valley Road, operated from 1863 to 1910. Mount Reba, to the north of the trail, was named after Harvey's daughter.

Before the toll road was put through, emigrants and prospectors used a basic pack trail

Bear Trap Cabin

to cross the Sierra Nevada at Ebbetts Pass, northeast of this trail. Major John Ebbetts led a group of miners over this newly found pass in 1850. Traffic increased greatly in 1859 with the discovery of silver at Nevada's Comstock Lode. Harvey Blood and Joethean Curtis were instrumental in getting the Big Trees–Carson Valley Turnpike Company to complete a wagon road over the pass.

Camp Tamarack, just south of the start of the trail, was originally called Onion Valley because of the abundance of onions in this summer pasturage. From the late 1860s to early '70s, C. Brown operated a sawmill at this location. A man known as Turkey Johnson later ran swine, chickens, sheep, and turkeys in the area. In the early 1920s, W. H. Hutchins constructed the first store, saloon, and dance hall here and named his resort Camp Tamarack. These buildings were relocated when California 4 was widened.

Thompson Meadow, just before the end of the trail, is a reminder of the legendary character John "Snowshoe" Thompson, who passed through the region regularly from 1856 to 1876. Thompson delivered mail along a 90-mile route across the snow-covered Sierra Nevada. Thompson, born Jon Torsteinsin-Rue, hailed from Norway. At 24 years of age, he answered a call from Uncle Sam to deliver mail through the near impassable terrain between Placerville and Carson Valley, on the east side of the Sierra. Thompson hand-carved his own crude 25-pound oak skis, or snowshoes as he called them, and commenced bimonthly deliveries. All prior attempts by mail carriers using snowshoes had failed. The round-trip solo journey took Thompson five days to complete. He rubbed charcoal on his face to prevent sunburn and snow-blindness. He did not carry a rifle or blankets because his mail sack weighed anywhere from 60 to 120 pounds. Snowshoe, as he was affectionately known, passed away in 1876. Many attribute him as being the father of skiing in the West.

Southern face of Mokelumne Peak

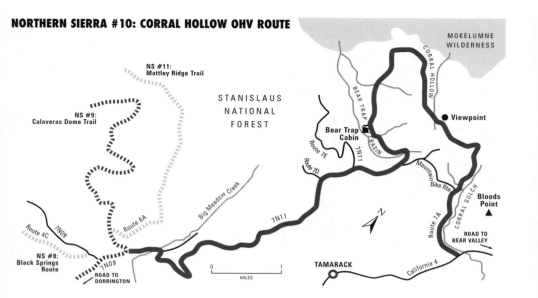

Description

Corral Hollow is a beautiful, moderately rated 4WD trail that passes a variety of scenery, from forest gullies to open ridge tops. Rated black, meaning most difficult, by the National Forest Service, only the eastern 4 miles rates a 5 for difficulty; the rest rates a 3.

The trail leaves California 4 on the Alpine-Calaveras County line, southwest of Bear Valley. The turn is not well signed on the highway; a small Jeep symbol is all that marks the turn. Once off the highway you will see an information board. Initially, the trail is lumpy as it heads toward Corral Hollow. Careful wheel placement will allow most vehicles to make it through unscathed. The trail as a whole is best suited for compact and subcompact vehicles because of a few tight turns through trees. Full-size vehicles should make it through with careful driving and maybe a bit of backing up to complete turns.

As the trail leaves Corral Hollow, it starts to climb up to a ridge. Like many in the region, this climb has a dry, loose surface that means poor traction for vehicles. Some sections are moguled, and a few short off-camber sections will tilt vehicles to the side. The trail passes a few small meadows, which in spring and early summer are ablaze with wildflowers, predominantly yellow mule's ears. As you reach the top of the ridge, there are views to the north over Grouse Valley and Mokelumne Peak. Mount Reba Ski Area borders this point.

The trail follows along the ridge for few miles, with great views on either side, before descending gradually toward Bear Trap Basin and the old two-story Bear Trap Cabin. Owned by the forest service, the cabin is maintained as an emergency refuge and is generally stocked with dry food and firewood in winter. It can be used at other times under a special use permit from the Calaveras Ranger District. The cabin is sparsely furnished and has a stove for heat. If you visit the cabin, please leave it in better condition than you found it; contributions of non-perishable foodstuffs and firewood are always welcome. There is a visitor book inside the cabin.

Past the cabin the trail becomes easier, crossing small meadows and passing a series of spurs before crossing Big Meadow Creek and coming to an end on 7N09, a short distance north of California 4.

A popular moderately difficult mountain bike route called Bear Trap Basin Loop follows this trail for part of the way, diverging near the end to return to the parking area on California 4.

Corral Hollow OHV Route

Current Road Information

Stanislaus National Forest
Calaveras Ranger District
PO Box 500
Hathaway Pines, CA 95233
(209) 795-1381

Map References

BLM   San Andreas
USFS Stanislaus National Forest
USGS 1:24,000   Tamarack, Calaveras Dome
          1:100,000 San Andreas
Maptech CD-ROM: High Sierra/Yosemite
Northern California Atlas & Gazetteer, p. 99
California Road & Recreation Atlas, p. 72
          (incomplete)
Other: Calaveras Ranger District OHV
          Routes (U.S.F.S. leaflet)

Route Directions

▼ 0.0   From California 4 on the Alpine-
             Calaveras County line, 0.6 miles south-
             west of Bear Valley, zero trip meter
             and turn west on small formed trail.
             There is a jeep marker on the highway

and a Corral Hollow information board
visible once you turn off the highway.
The route is marked Route 7A, suitable
for 4WDs, ATVs, motorbikes, and
mountain bikes.

6.1 ▲   Trail ends at T-intersection with
             California 4. Turn left for Bear Valley;
             turn right for Dorrington.
             GPS: N38°27.42′ W120°03.11′

▼ 1.1   SO Cross through creek.
5.0 ▲   SO Cross through creek.
             GPS: N38°27.92′ W120°03.65′

▼ 1.4   SO Cross through creek. Trail starts to climb.
4.7 ▲   SO End of descent. Cross through creek.
▼ 2.3   BL Turnout on right.
3.8 ▲   BR Turnout on left.
             GPS: N38°28.77′ W120°03.78′

▼ 2.8   SO Pass through wire gate.
3.3 ▲   SO Pass through wire gate.
             GPS: N38°28.66′ W120°04.25′

▼ 3.0   SO Turnout and viewpoint on right.
3.1 ▲   SO Turnout and viewpoint on left.

▼ 3.3   SO Cross through creek.
2.8 ▲   SO Cross through creek.
        GPS: N38°28.82' W120°04.66'

▼ 5.0   SO Cross through creek.
1.1 ▲   SO Cross through creek.
▼ 5.4   SO Cross through creek.
0.7 ▲   SO Cross through creek.
        GPS: N38°28.82' W120°05.64'

▼ 6.1   SO Cross through creek; then track on right goes short distance to Bear Trap Cabin. Zero trip meter.
0.0 ▲   Continue to the northeast and cross through creek.
        GPS: N38°28.30' W120°05.43'

▼ 0.0   Continue to the southeast.
6.4 ▲   SO Track on left goes short distance to Bear Trap Cabin. Zero trip meter.
▼ 0.2   SO Cross through creek.
6.2 ▲   SO Cross through creek.
▼ 0.8   SO Cross through creek.
5.6 ▲   SO Cross through creek.
▼ 1.1   SO Track on left.
5.3 ▲   SO Track on right.
▼ 1.7   SO Track on right.
4.7 ▲   SO Track on left.
▼ 1.8   SO Track on right is 7N11 (Route 7E). Continue straight ahead and join 7N11.
4.6 ▲   BR Track on left is 7N11 (Route 7E). Zero trip meter and bear right onto 7N11A.
        GPS: N38°27.67' W120°05.30'

▼ 2.2   SO Track on right is Route 7D.
4.2 ▲   SO Track on left is Route 7D.
        GPS: N38°27.39' W120°05.61'

▼ 4.0   SO Track on right.
2.4 ▲   SO Track on left.
        GPS: N38°26.11' W120°06.25'

▼ 4.4   SO Track on right.
2.0 ▲   SO Track on left.
▼ 5.1   SO Turnout on left.
1.3 ▲   SO Turnout on right.
▼ 5.7   SO Cattle guard.
0.7 ▲   SO Cattle guard.
▼ 5.8   BL Track on right goes to private property.
0.6 ▲   BR Track on left goes to private property.

        GPS: N38°25.63' W120°07.22'

▼ 5.9   SO Cross over Big Meadow Creek on bridge.
0.5 ▲   SO Cross over Big Meadow Creek on bridge.
▼ 6.3   SO Track on left is Route 7B for ATVs and motorbikes.
0.1 ▲   SO Track on right is Route 7B for ATVs and motorbikes.
▼ 6.4   SO Trail ends at T-intersection with graded Northern Sierra #9: Calaveras Dome Trail (7N09). Turn left to exit to California 4; turn right to join Northern Sierra #11: Mattley Ridge Trail.
0.0 ▲   From California 4, 6.7 miles southwest of Bear Valley, zero trip meter and turn north on graded Northern Sierra #9: Calaveras Dome Trail (7N09) at the marker. Proceed 0.9 miles north; then zero trip meter and turn southeast on formed trail marked 7N11. There is an information board at the intersection.
        GPS: N38°25.40' W120°07.66'

           NORTHERN SIERRA #11

Mattley Ridge Trail

STARTING POINT Northern Sierra #9: Calaveras Dome Trail (7N09), 1.4 miles north of California 4

FINISHING POINT Northern Sierra #9: Calaveras Dome Trail (7N09), 8 miles north of California 4

TOTAL MILEAGE 5 miles

UNPAVED MILEAGE 5 miles

DRIVING TIME 1 hour

ELEVATION RANGE 6,800–7,800 feet

USUALLY OPEN April to November

BEST TIME TO TRAVEL Dry weather

DIFFICULTY RATING 4

SCENIC RATING 8

REMOTENESS RATING +0

Special Attractions

■ Ridge top trail with views of Mokelumne Peak.

■ Moderate trail suitable for most high-clearance 4WDs.

History

The Mokelumne Coast to Crest Trail (MC-CT) is a non-motorized, multi-use trail from the Pacific Ocean near San Francisco to the crest of the Sierra Nevada. Efforts to develop the trail commenced in 1990 and look promising to date. The ambitious trail will finish at Ebbetts Pass, an historic point on the old Big Trees–Carson Valley Toll Road. In 1993, Stanislaus National Forest completed an environmental analysis of constructing a section of the MCCT from Tiger Creek Reservoir to Mattley Creek and the Blue Hole Trailhead. In 2000, the forest service allocated $750,000 for the 15-mile section between Moore Creek Campground, downstream from Calaveras Dome, and Mattley Creek.

Mattley Creek begins below Flag Pole Point, east of the trail, and falls sharply more than 3.5 miles to join the North Fork of the Mokelumne River at Blue Hole. A pack trail follows close to the creek, zigzagging to the floor of the canyon—a drop of 3,600 feet.

Prospectors worked the North Fork of the Mokelumne River after the massive 1848 discovery of gold downstream at Mokelumne Hill. The Big Trees–Carson Valley Toll Road, near the start of the trail, was formerly a pack trail used by emigrants to the California goldfields. Prospectors and emigrants might turn in their shallow graves if they saw the funds available to develop recreational trails in the twenty-first century.

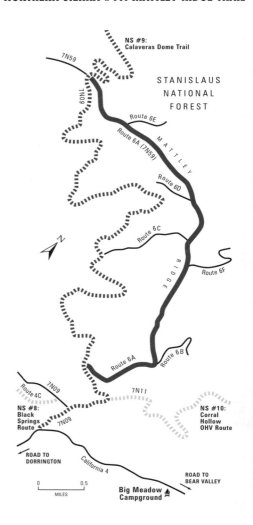

Description

This short, scenic trail leaves graded road 7N09 to climb along Mattley Ridge, passing open meadows carpeted with yellow mule's ears and interspersed with logged areas, before descending to rejoin 7N09. The initial climb up the ridge is loose, with a gently moguled surface that can make traction difficult.

The trail undulates through stands of white firs on top of the ridge, passing recently logged-over areas. The very loose surface, particularly in the logged areas, can make getting adequate traction difficult, even on foot. This part of the trail

can become difficult to impossible in wet weather and is best avoided then.

Excellent views to the north over Mokelumne Peak and the Mokelumne Wilderness can be glimpsed from the ridge top.

Current Road Information

Stanislaus National Forest
Calaveras Ranger District
PO Box 500
Hathaway Pines, CA 95233
(209) 795-1381

Luminous lichen on fir trees

Mule's ears along the trail as it climbs Mattley Ridge

Map References

BLM   San Andreas
USFS   Stanislaus National Forest
USGS   1:24,000   Calaveras Dome, Tamarack
         1:100,000 San Andreas
Maptech CD-ROM: High Sierra/Yosemite
Northern California Atlas & Gazetteer, p. 99
California Road & Recreation Atlas, p. 72
         (incomplete)
Other: Calaveras Ranger District OHV
         Routes (U.S.F.S. leaflet)

Route Directions

▼ 0.0   Trail commences on Northern Sierra
           #9: Calaveras Dome Trail (7N09), 1.4
           miles north of California 4. Zero trip
           meter and turn northeast on Route 6A
           and 6B.
5.0 ▲   Trail ends at T-intersection with
           Northern Sierra #9: Calaveras Dome

Trail (7N09). Turn left for California 4
and Bear Valley; turn right to follow
Calaveras Dome Trail.
GPS: N38°25.54′ W120°08.14′

▼ 0.1   SO Route 7B on right connects to
              Northern Sierra #10: Corral Hollow
              OHV Route for ATVs and motorbikes.
4.9 ▲   SO Route 7B on left connects to Northern
              Sierra #10: Corral Hollow OHV Route
              for ATVs and motorbikes.

▼ 0.9   TL Route 6B continues straight ahead. Turn
              left on formed trail Route 6A, which
              climbs up the side of a hill. Trail is
              unmarked except for a yellow OHV sign.
4.1 ▲   TR T-intersection with the larger Route 6B.
              GPS: N38°25.94′ W120°07.44′

▼ 2.1   BL Track on right is Route 6F.
2.9 ▲   BR Track on left is Route 6F.
              GPS: N38°26.92′ W120°07.80′

▼ 2.2	SO	Start to cross meadow.
2.8 ▲	SO	Exit meadow.
▼ 2.4	TR	Exit meadow. Track on left is Route 6C. Turn right, remaining on Route 6A, and follow the sign to Mattley Ridge.
2.6 ▲	TL	Track on right is Route 6C. Turn left, remaining on Route 6A, and start to cross meadow.

GPS: N38°27.13' W120°07.97'

▼ 2.8	SO	Track on right.
2.2 ▲	SO	Track on left.
▼ 2.9	BR	Track straight ahead is Route 6D. Bear right onto Route 6A.
2.1 ▲	SO	Track on right is Route 6D. Remain on Route 6A.

GPS: N38°27.46' W120°08.19'

▼ 3.1	SO	Track on right is Route 6G.
1.9 ▲	SO	Track on left is Route 6G.

GPS: N38°27.58' W120°08.33'

▼ 3.2	SO	Track on right.
1.8 ▲	BR	Track on left.
▼ 3.6	SO	Track on left.
1.4 ▲	SO	Track on right.
▼ 3.7	BL	Track on right.
1.3 ▲	SO	Track on left.
▼ 4.2	SO	Track on right is Route 6E.
0.8 ▲	SO	Track on left is Route 6E.

GPS: N38°27.75' W120°09.44'

▼ 4.5	SO	Small track on left.
0.5 ▲	SO	Small track on right.
▼ 5.0		Trail ends at 4-way intersection with graded dirt Northern Sierra #9: Calaveras Dome Trail (7N09). Turn left to return to California 4; turn right to travel Calaveras Dome Trail.
0.0 ▲		Trail commences at 4-way intersection on Northern Sierra #9: Calaveras Dome Trail (7N09), 8 miles northwest of California 4. Zero trip meter and turn southeast on small dirt road marked 7N59. The turn is on a sharp right-hand bend when approaching from the south. Track opposite the start is also 7N59.

GPS: N38°27.94' W120°10.10'

Red and Blue Lakes Trail

STARTING POINT California 88, at the eastern end of Red Lake

FINISHING POINT Blue Lakes Road, 9.5 miles south of California 88

TOTAL MILEAGE 10 miles, plus 2.4-mile spur to Meadow Lake

UNPAVED MILEAGE 9.3 miles, plus 2.3 miles of the spur

DRIVING TIME 2 hours

ELEVATION RANGE 7,700–8,900 feet

USUALLY OPEN June to November

BEST TIME TO TRAVEL June to November

DIFFICULTY RATING 3

SCENIC RATING 9

REMOTENESS RATING +0

Special Attractions

- Fishing and camping at the many lakes along the trail.
- Spectacular open scenery above tree line.
- Basque carvings and the Alpine Sportsman Cabin.

History

Red and Blue Lakes Trail begins along an early emigrant trail over Carson Pass, which is above the western end of Red Lake. Kit Carson discovered the pass that retains his name. The renowned scout led Captain John C. Frémont and his group of explorers over the pass when traversing the Sierra Nevada in late June 1844. Emigrants had a choice of using this pass, or more northerly passes, one of which was named Donner Pass, after the unfortunate experiences of the Donner-Reed Party of 1846.

Upper and Lower Blue Lakes, Twin Lake, and Meadow Lake are all part of the Upper Mokelumne River Hydroelectric Project. The Alpine Sportsman Cabin was a grocery store built in 1938. The store, originally half its present size, catered to the many cabins scattered in this vicinity. Construction crews lived in the cabins while building dams for the hydroelectric project in the 1930s and '

Old stables at Lower Blue Lake

'40s, and their needs kept the outpost busy. At other times campers and hunters were the store's main customers. The old log building below Lower Blue Lake Dam was an active stable in its heyday. The structure has been stabilized over the years and further restoration efforts are currently underway.

Micky Green was the original storekeeper at the Alpine Sportsman Cabin. Her husband, Norm, was a caretaker for the surrounding dams. Sadly, Micky passed away at an early age, leaving Norm to care for their two children. Schooling was an obvious problem for a single parent in this remote region, so Norm sent the children off to boarding school. He remained at the old camp throughout the winter with his faithful dog. To stock up on supplies, Norm had to snowshoe approximately 15 miles into Markleeville, located east of the trail on present-day California 89. The journey had an elevation loss of 2,500 feet from his cabin. In the late 1940s, Norm's dog arrived in Markleeville without his master. Fearing the worst, a search party headed out and found Norm dead of a heart attack in his mountain cabin. The children were left orphans.

Current owners of the old Alpine Sportsman Cabin have managed to keep the heritage of the region alive. Efforts to pave the road to this little-changed region have resulted in the separation of the old store from its outhouse, an historic building in its own right.

A number of noteworthy Basque shepherd carvings can be found in the area, reminders of the many sheepherders who tended stock in the high subalpine country. Sheepherding across the Sierra Nevada dates back to the late 1840s when Basques, like other emigrants, came to California to seek fortunes. Many became shepherds, a traditional occupation in their region of the Pyrenees. Tending sheep is a lonely profession, and carving tales and images on aspen trees was a form of storytelling that passed the time. Shepherds marked their favorite meadows and watering holes in this way. Some carvings give shepherds' names, where they came from, and the relevant date. Some are human images like one of the carvings near the Alpine Sportsman Cabin, which depicts a woman, seemingly representative of a prostitute. It was also a marker for her cabin in the meadow opposite.

These old, culturally rich inscriptions may be hard to decipher because they are written in Euskara, a native Basque language thought to be the earliest European language. As aspen trees die off, the carvings go too. Families of these Basque shepherds populated many towns and settlements in the Sierra Nevada, and their rich traditions remain in present-day Basque restaurants throughout the West.

Description

Red and Blue Lakes Trail is a pleasant, quiet road that accesses the Blue Lakes. The trail starts a short distance east of Carson Pass at Red Lake, a popular place to fish for rainbow trout. The Old Carson Pass Road, which runs along the south side of Red Lake to Carson Pass, is closed to motor vehicles, but it is popular with mountain bikers and hikers.

From Red Lake, the roughly graded dirt road climbs through stands of aspens onto an open ridge. The road is rough enough, with a loose uneven surface, to make 4WD preferable. From the ridge top there are views west to the humped peaks of Elephants Back (9,603 feet) and Round Top (10,381 feet) and north over the Carson Range. Photographers and landscape painters will especially enjoy the view. The trail continues along a narrow shelf road for some distance with the Pacific Crest National Scenic Trail running

Red and Blue Lakes Trail passes through a sparsely vegetated landscape

close to it. A side trail goes to campsites at Lost Lakes Dam and provides a good view of The Nipple, a prominent rock outcrop to the east.

From Lost Lakes, the trail descends to join a graded road at Upper Blue Lake. Four developed campgrounds owned and operated by the Pacific Gas & Electric Company are situated along the shores of Upper and Lower Blue Lakes. The campgrounds are normally open from May 1 to September 30; camping is limited to developed campgrounds on PG&E–owned land.

The Alpine Sportsman Cabin sits at the southern end of Lower Blue Lake. This historic cabin is privately owned and still uses its original outhouse, set back from the road a short distance away. The spur to Twin Lake and Meadow Lake leads off from the intersection in front of the cabin and heads past the stone-block dam of Lower Blue Lake. The old timber and shingle building you see here was a stable.

Anglers will enjoy the choice of lakes along the trail. Upper Blue Lake has excellent trout fishing. A particularly good spot is near the dam. Lost Lakes appear to have leaner pickings. All of the lakes along this trail are good for boating and boat-based fishing. Red Lake and Lower Blue Lake both have boat launches. Pacific Gas & Electric land along this spur is for day use only; no camping is allowed.

In addition to the developed campgrounds, campers will find many lovely backcountry sites along the trail. A large informal camping area can be found near the start, and other sites can be found tucked in the trees at Lost Lakes.

In winter, snowmobiles and cross-country skiers can reach the frozen lakes along ungroomed trails. The lakes have unstable ice and snow in winter and you should not attempt to venture onto them.

The section of graded road from the Alpine Sportsman Cabin north to the existing paved road is tentatively scheduled to be paved in 2002. Should this happen, the aligned road will no longer pass close to the Basque carving. Use the GPS coordinates to locate the tree and avoid rubbing or marking it in any way. The tree is marked by a plaque and the carving is about waist high.

Mountain bikers use this trail, and it is rated moderate for them, with some long climbs and a few difficult, technical sections.

Current Road Information

Eldorado National Forest
Amador Ranger District
26820 Silver Drive
Pioneer, CA 95666
(209) 295-4251

Map References

BLM   Smith Valley
USFS   Eldorado National Forest; Toiyabe
National Forest: Carson Ranger District
USGS 1:24,000   Carson Pass, Pacific
         Valley
         1:100,000 Smith Valley
Maptech CD-ROM: High Sierra/Tahoe
Northern California Atlas & Gazetteer, p. 90
California Road & Recreation Atlas, p. 67
Other: Fine Edge Productions—South Lake
         Tahoe Basin Recreation Topo Map

Route Directions

▼ 0.0   From California 88 at the eastern end
           of Red Lake, 6.5 miles west of the
           intersection with California 89 and 7.5
           miles east of Kirkwood, zero trip meter
           and turn southeast on Forestdale
           Divide Road at the sign for Red Lake.
           Immediately paved road on right to
           Red Lake. Trail initially passes through
           private property.
5.4 ▲   Paved road on left to Red Lake; then
           trail ends on paved California 88. Turn
           left for Kirkwood; turn right for Lake
           Tahoe.
           GPS: N38°41.95' W119°57.91'

▼ 0.1   SO Cattle guard.
5.3 ▲   SO Cattle guard.
▼ 0.9   SO Track on right.
4.5 ▲   SO Track on left.
▼ 1.1   SO Track on left.
4.3 ▲   SO Track on right.

▼ 1.4   SO   Track on left is 013A for 4WDs, and motorbikes.

4.0 ▲   SO   Track on right is 013A for 4WDs, ATVs, and motorbikes.
GPS: N38°40.82′ W119°57.61′

▼ 1.5   SO   Cross over Forestdale Creek on bridge; then track on right through large camping area.

3.9 ▲   SO   Track on left through large camping area; then cross over Forestdale Creek on bridge.

▼ 1.6   SO   Track on left is FR 146.

3.8 ▲   SO   Track on right is FR 146.

▼ 2.0   SO   Track on left.

3.4 ▲   SO   Track on right.

▼ 3.0   SO   Track on right goes 0.1 miles to the start of the Summit City-Carson Trail (18E13).

2.4 ▲   SO   Track on left goes 0.1 miles to the start of the Summit City-Carson Trail (18E13).
GPS: N38°39.69′ W119°57.96′

▼ 3.3   SO   Pacific Crest Trail crosses.

2.1 ▲   SO   Pacific Crest Trail crosses.
GPS: N38°39.64′ W119°57.70′

▼ 4.6   BR   Track on left is FR 018, which runs 0.3 miles around the side of Lost Lakes to the dam. Follow sign to Hope Valley. Pacific Crest Trail runs near this intersection.

0.8 ▲   BL   Track on right is FR 018, which runs 0.3 miles around the side of Lost Lakes to the dam. Follow sign to Red Lake. Pacific Crest Trail runs near this intersection.
GPS: N38°38.87′ W119°57.09′

Canadian geese on Lower Blue Lake

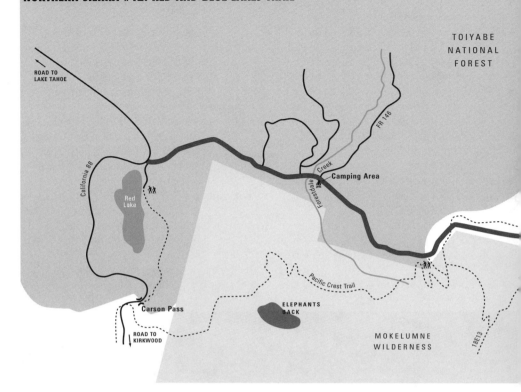

▼ 5.4   TL   T-intersection at the north end of Upper Blue Lake. Track on right goes to Upper Blue Lake Campground. Zero trip meter. Evergreen Trailhead (18E21) on the right enters the Mokelumne Wilderness.

0.0 ▲   Continue to the northwest away from Upper Blue Lake.
GPS: N38°38.46' W119°57.22'

▼ 0.0   Continue to the east and along the shore of Upper Blue Lake.

2.8 ▲   TR   Road continues straight ahead into Upper Blue Lake Campground. Evergreen Trailhead (18E21) on left enters the Mokelumne Wilderness. Zero trip meter and turn right onto roughly graded dirt road, marked suitable for 4WDs, ATVs, and motorbikes.

▼ 1.0   SO   Trail becomes paved as it passes through Upper Blue Lake Damsite Campground. Roads on right and left to campsites.

1.8 ▲   SO   Trail returns to graded dirt after the campground.

▼ 1.1   SO   Exit campground.

1.7 ▲   SO   Road passes through Upper Blue Lake Damsite Campground. Roads on right and left to campsites.
GPS: N38°37.80' W119°56.27'

▼ 1.2   SO   Grouse Lake Trail (18E08) on right for hikers only.

1.6 ▲   SO   Grouse Lake Trail (18E08) on left for hikers only.

▼ 1.4   SO   Pass through Middle Creek Campground. Road turns back to graded dirt.

1.4 ▲   SO   Road turns to paved and passes through Middle Creek Campground. Start to follow along the shore of Upper Blue Lake.

▼ 2.0   SO   Trail passes the east side Lower Blue Lake.

0.8 ▲   SO   Trail leaves Lower Blue Lake.

▼ 2.5   SO   Road becomes paved as it enters

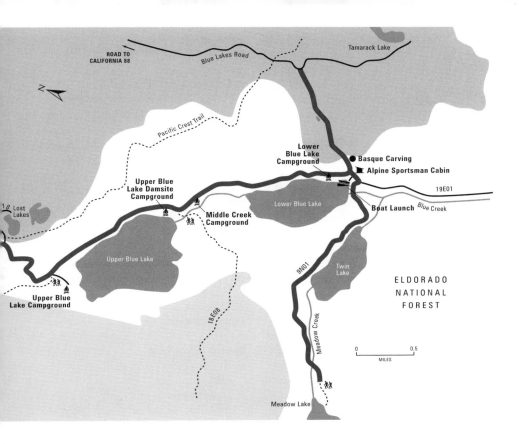

Lower Blue Lake Campground. Roads on left and right to campsites.

0.3 ▲   SO   Road returns to graded dirt as it leaves Lower Blue Lake Campground.

▼ 2.8   BL   Exit campground. Paved road on right is the spur to Twin Lake and Meadow Lake. Zero trip meter and bear left away from Lower Blue Lake. Alpine Sportsman Cabin is at the intersection—private property.

0.0 ▲   Continue to the northwest. Road becomes paved.

GPS: N38°36.58′ W119°55.39′

Spur to Twin Lake and Meadow Lake

▼ 0.0   From the entrance to Lower Blue Lake Campground, proceed southwest on 9N01 and zero trip meter. Immediately road on left to campground supervisor and road on right to Lower Blue Lake Boat Launch. Follow sign to Meadow Lake.

▼ 0.1   BR   Road turns to dirt; then track on left is Deer Valley Trail (19E01) for 4WDs, ATVs, and motorbikes. Follow sign to Meadow Lake.

▼ 0.2   SO   Old cabin on left.

▼ 0.3   SO   Cross over Blue Creek below dam; then track on right to dam.

▼ 0.5   SO   Track on left.

▼ 0.8   SO   Track on left to Twin Lake.

GPS: N38°36.44′ W119°56.02′

▼ 1.9   SO   Track on right.

▼ 2.2   SO   Cross over Meadow Creek.

▼ 2.4   Trail ends at a viewpoint over Meadow Lake. It is a 0.3-mile's hike to the lake.

GPS: N38°36.28′ W119°57.46′

Continuation of Main Trail

▼ 0.0   Continue to the northeast. Road returns to graded dirt.

1.8 ▲   BR   Enter Lower Blue Lake Campground.

Paved road on left is the spur to Twin Lake and Meadow Lake. Zero trip meter and bear right, following the sign for campgrounds and start to pass along the eastern shore of Lower Blue Lake. Alpine Sportsman Cabin is at the intersection—private property.
GPS: N38°36.58' W119°55.39'

▼ 0.2 SO Basque carving on pine tree on right. The carving is about 3 feet up from the bottom with a wildlife tree marker directly above it. A second carving can be found slightly to the northeast on the opposite side of the road. The prostitute's cabin used to stand in the meadow opposite.

1.6 ▲ SO Basque carving on pine tree on left. The carving is about 3 feet up from the bottom with a wildlife tree marker directly above it. A second carving can be found slightly to the northeast on the opposite side of the road. The prostitute's cabin used to stand in the meadow opposite.
GPS: N38°36.68' W119°55.23'

▼ 0.3 SO Entering Toiyabe National Forest.
1.5 ▲ SO Entering Eldorado National Forest.
▼ 0.7 SO Small lake on left.
1.1 ▲ SO Small lake on right.
GPS: N38°36.92' W119°54.91'

▼ 1.8 SO Trail ends at intersection with Blue Lakes Road. Turn right for Tamarack Lake and Wet Meadows Trailhead; continue straight ahead on graded Blue Lakes Road, which becomes paved and joins California 88.

0.0 ▲ Trail commences on Blue Lakes Road. The turn from California 88 is 2.4 miles west of the intersection of California 88 and California 89. Turn south, following the sign to Blue Lakes Road and proceed 9.5 miles to the start of the trail. At the intersection with Tamarack Lake Road, zero trip meter and continue southwest, following sign to Lower Blue Lake.
GPS: N38°37.17' W119°54.61'

Baltic Ridge Trail

STARTING POINT Mormon Emigrant Trail (FR 5), 2.7 miles west of California 88
FINISHING POINT Intersection of Cosumnes Mine Road and Bonetti Road, 6 miles south of CR 5
TOTAL MILEAGE 15.6 miles
UNPAVED MILEAGE 15.5 miles
DRIVING TIME 2 hours
ELEVATION RANGE 4,600–7,400 feet
USUALLY OPEN June to October
BEST TIME TO TRAVEL June to October
DIFFICULTY RATING 3 (forward direction); 4 (reverse direction)
SCENIC RATING 7
REMOTENESS RATING +1

Special Attractions
■ Trail follows part of the historic Mormon Emigrant Trail.
■ Trail travels along a ridge top with views over Iron Mountain Ridge and Eldorado National Forest.

History
Baltic Ridge got its name from a mine of the same name on the western end of the ridge. Baltic Mine was a lode gold operation established in 1896 on the north face of Baltic Peak. To extract the ore, an adit was dug more than 500 feet into the mountainside with a 130-foot inclined shaft. A 10-stamp mill was constructed at the mine to process the ore. By 1907, operations were complete and all was quiet again at the mine site.

The trail starts at the junction of the Mormon Emigrant Trail and an early side trail that ran down Baltic Ridge. Kit Carson and John C. Frémont's expedition crossed the Sierra Nevada in the winter of 1844 en route to Sutter's Fort in the Sacramento Valley. Carson discovered a pass some 20-odd miles east of Baltic Ridge Trail. He carved his name on a tree at the pass that would come to bear his name and returned to camp. The Carson Trail, as it became known, followed close to today's Iron

Mountain Road. From California 88, it traveled the length of Iron Mountain Ridge to Sly Park and Pleasant Valley.

Baltic Ridge Trail follows part of Grizzly Flat Road, a side trail developed by emigrants in 1848. The trail ran down Baltic Ridge roughly as far as North-South Road, bore south to cross the North Fork of the Cosumnes River, and continued toward Grizzly Flat.

Description

Baltic Ridge Trail follows a series of lightly-used forest roads within Eldorado National Forest, traveling through a mixture of revegetated forest and more recently logged areas. There are views north over the South Fork of the American River.

The trail is rated a 3 for difficulty in the forward direction, but in reverse it is rated a 4. The difference comes from one short section of shallow, loose rock steps that is harder to climb than descend. Approximately 0.4 miles of the trail around this section is lightly brushy.

The trail is sporadically marked and can be a little hard to follow through areas that have seen recent logging activity. Newly constructed logging tracks often appear better used than the main trail and can make for confusing navigation. The final section of the trail travels through open forest and descends the northwestern end of Baltic Ridge to finish on small paved forest roads just south of Pollock Pines.

Current Road Information

Eldorado National Forest
Placerville Ranger District
4260 Eight Mile Road
Camino, CA 95709
(530) 644-2324

Baltic Ridge Trail overlooks Camp Creek Valley

Map References

BLM   Placerville
USFS Eldorado National Forest
USGS 1:24,000 Tragedy Spring, Leek
      Spring Hill, Stump Spring
      1:100,000 Placerville
Maptech CD-ROM: High Sierra/Tahoe
Northern California Atlas & Gazetteer,
      pp. 89, 88
California Road & Recreation Atlas,
      p. 66 (incomplete)

NORTHERN SIERRA #13: BALTIC RIDGE TRAIL

Route Directions

▼ 0.0   From California 88, 7 miles northeast
           of the turn to Lower Bear River
           Reservoir and 0.7 miles southwest of
           Shot Rock Vista Point, turn northwest
           on paved road signposted for the
           Mormon Emigrant Trail (FR 5) and pass
           the closed Iron Mountain Ski Resort.
           Proceed 2.7 miles to the start of the
           trail and turn southwest on graded dirt
           road, marked 9N20. Zero trip meter.
           The turn is immediately south of a cat-
           tle guard. Immediately track on right.
3.4 ▲   Track on left; then trail finishes at T-
           intersection with the Mormon Emigrant
           Trail (FR 5). Turn left for Pollock Pines
           and US 50; turn right for California 88
           and Lower Bear River Reservoir.
           GPS: N38°38.46′ W120°14.87′

▼ 1.4   SO Track on right; then cattle guard.
2.0 ▲   SO Cattle guard; then track on left.
▼ 1.7   BR Unmarked track on left.
1.7 ▲   SO Unmarked track on right.
           GPS: N38°38.55′ W120°16.24′

▼ 2.0   SO Track on right.
1.4 ▲   SO Track on left.
▼ 2.3   SO Track on left.
1.1 ▲   SO Track on right.
▼ 2.5   SO Track on left is 9N20D.
0.9 ▲   SO Track on right is 9N20D.
▼ 2.6   TL T-intersection with graded dirt Meiss
           Road. To the right returns to the
           Mormon Emigrant Trail. Turn left, fol-
           lowing sign for Capps Crossing.
0.8 ▲   TR Meiss Road continues ahead to the

           Mormon Emigrant Trail. Turn right onto
           formed dirt trail, following small sign to
           California 88.
           GPS: N38°38.92′ W120°17.00′

▼ 3.3   SO Track on left.
0.1 ▲   SO Track on right.
▼ 3.4   BR Bear right onto unmarked, formed
           Baltic Ridge Road. Zero trip meter.
0.0 ▲   Continue to the southeast.
           GPS: N38°39.03′ W120°17.82′

▼ 0.0   Continue to the north.
5.7 ▲   BL Bear left onto unmarked, small, graded
           Meiss Road. Zero trip meter.
▼ 1.6   BR Track on left. Bear right at marker for
           9N20.
4.1 ▲   BL Track on right. Bear left at marker for
           9N20.
           GPS: N38°39.78′ W120°19.14′

▼ 5.0   BL Track on right. Trail forks and rejoins
           almost immediately.
0.7 ▲   BR Track on left. Trail forks and rejoins
           almost immediately.
           GPS: N38°40.12′ W120°22.52′

▼ 5.7   TR Unmarked T-intersection with 10N46.
           Zero trip meter.
0.0 ▲   Continue to the east.
           GPS: N38°40.07′ W120°23.25′

▼ 0.0   Continue to the north on wider trail.
3.6 ▲   TL Wider trail 10N46 continues ahead.
           Zero trip meter and turn left onto small,
           formed trail marked 9N20.
▼ 0.6   TL Turn sharp left onto small, formed trail,
           marked 9N20, that descends the hill.

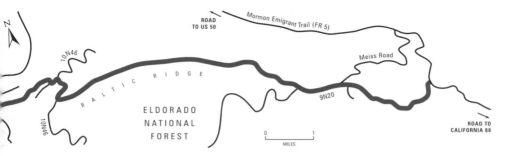

3.0 ▲ TR Turn sharp right onto wider unmarked trail.
       GPS: N38°40.45' W120°23.07'

▼ 0.8 BR Track on left. Remain on 9N20.
2.8 ▲ SO Track on right. Continue up the hill.
▼ 2.4 BR Track on left. Remain on 9N20.
1.2 ▲ BL Track on right. Remain on 9N20.
       GPS: N38°40.17' W120°24.89'

▼ 2.75 TL T-intersection.
0.85 ▲ TR Track continues straight ahead.
       GPS: N38°40.39' W120°25.17'

▼ 2.8 BR Track on left. Follow marker for 9N20.
0.8 ▲ SO Track on right.
▼ 3.6 SO Cross over paved road, remaining on small trail, and zero trip meter. Trail is marked Baltic Ridge Road on paved road.
0.0 ▲   Continue to the southeast.
       GPS: N38°40.40' W120°26.11'

▼ 0.0   Continue to the northwest.
2.9 ▲ SO Cross over paved road, remaining on small trail, and zero trip meter. Trail is marked Baltic Ridge Road on paved road.
▼ 2.4 SO Track on left.
0.5 ▲ SO Track on right.
       GPS: N38°41.43' W120°28.41'

▼ 2.8 TR T-intersection with small paved Bonetti Road.
0.1 ▲ TL Bonetti Road continues ahead. Turn left on small, unmarked trail 10N61.
       GPS: N38°41.55' W120°28.80'

▼ 2.9   Trail ends at T-intersection with paved Cosumnes Mine Road (FR 51). Turn left to exit to US 50.
0.0 ▲   Trail begins on paved Cosumnes Mine Road (FR 51), 6 miles south of CR 5. Zero trip meter at the intersection of FR 51 and Bonetti Road and turn southeast on Bonetti Road, following sign to Capps Crossing.
       GPS: N38°41.57' W120°28.84'

Western end of Baltic Ridge

Slate Mountain Trail

STARTING POINT Mosquito Road (CR 60), 9.5 miles northeast of US 50 and Placerville

FINISHING POINT CR 63 (FR 1), 6.4 miles east of Georgetown

TOTAL MILEAGE 18.5 miles, plus 2.8-mile spur to Slate Mountain Fire Lookout

UNPAVED MILEAGE 14.3 miles, plus 2.8-mile spur

DRIVING TIME 2 hours

ELEVATION RANGE 2,600–3,700 feet

USUALLY OPEN May to November

BEST TIME TO TRAVEL Dry weather

DIFFICULTY RATING 2

SCENIC RATING 8

REMOTENESS RATING +0

Special Attractions

■ Slate Mountain Fire Lookout.
■ Access to a network of 4WD, ATV, and motorbike trails.
■ Cool shady, forest drive in Eldorado National Forest.

History

Slate Mountain Road commences just east of Mosquito Camp, originally a Civilian Conservation Corps camp that housed CCC workers while they completed projects in the region. The CCC boys, as they were called, received about $30 a month. Expenses were minimal: a lunch truck accompanied road crews, and the meals at the camp, which everyone helped prepare, cost about 13 cents. Movies were shown regularly at a cost of about 10 cents. Time off meant an opportunity to visit Motor City, south of the South Fork of the American River. Bed bugs were a major problem at the old camp and though regularly fumigated, the name "Camp Mosquito" seemed appropriate.

As early as 1849, gold miners were well rewarded around Mosquito and Little Mosquito Creeks. By 1854, the Mosquito Water Company had built a ditch to supply the growing number of miners, merchants, and fruit growers. The ditch drew water from Slab Creek, east of this trail near Cable Point on the old logging railroad.

Description

Slate Mountain Road begins north of Placerville near Finnon Reservoir. The graded dirt road is not suitable for passenger vehicles because of several rough, uneven sections interspersed with the smoother sections. To reach the start of the trail from Placerville, head northeast on Mosquito Road, ignoring turns to Finnon Reservoir. Once at the start of the trail, navigation is easy. Side roads and trails become quite numerous in the Rock Creek OHV Area, but the main trail is well marked. A spur from the main trail leads to the fire lookout on Slate Mountain; the reason for mountain's name becomes obvious along the spur because the shelf road cuts through layers of slate on its way to the top of the mountain. This route to the lookout is less used and slightly brushy. The tower is manned as needed during fire season, and the fire spotter travels to the tower from the other side, on CR 60. The gate to the lookout may be locked, but it is less than 0.1 miles to the tower.

The Slate Mountains, including Darling Ridge, is the winter habitat of the Pacific deer herd. Winter is the most stressful part of their year, with limited food, cold temperatures, and a concentration of their population. Adult does are typically in the later stages of pregnancy in April, with their bodies already weakened from winter hardships. The OHV area is closed from November 10 to May 1 to protect the herd.

Many trails lead off from Slate Mountain Road, and there is a network of trails in the Rock Creek OHV Area, mainly for motorbikes and ATVs although some trails are suitable for 4WDs.

Current Road Information

Eldorado National Forest
Georgetown Ranger District
7600 Wentworth Springs Road
Georgetown, CA 95634
(530) 333-4312

Map References

BLM   Placerville
USFS Eldorado National Forest
USGS 1:24,000 Slate Mtn., Tunnel Hill
         1:100,000 Placerville
Maptech CD-ROM: High Sierra/Tahoe
Northern California Atlas & Gazetteer, p. 88
California Road & Recreation Atlas, p. 66

Route Directions

▼ 0.0   From Mosquito Road (CR 60), 9.5 miles
           northeast of US 50 and Placerville, zero
           trip meter and turn northwest on small
           paved road marked 12N70 (shown on
           forest map as FR 12).

4.8 ▲   Trail ends at T-intersection with paved
           Mosquito Road (CR 60). Turn right for
           Placerville and US 50, remaining on
           Mosquito Road and ignoring turns to
           Finnon Reservoir.
           GPS: N38°48.24' W120°43.16'

▼ 0.2   SO Track on left; then cross over creek;
                then second track on left.
4.6 ▲ SO Track on right; then cross over creek;
                then second track on right.
▼ 0.3   SO Cattle guard. Entering Eldorado
                National Forest; then track on right is
                Crosier Run Loop 7 (11N81) for ATVs,
                motorbikes, hikers, horses, and moun-
                tain bikes—rated blue. This is closed
                to OHV travel November 10 to May 1.
4.5 ▲ SO Track on left is the return of Crosier
                Run Loop 7 (11N81).
               GPS: N38°48.46' W120°43.21'

▼ 1.1   SO Track on left.
3.7 ▲ SO Track on right.
▼ 1.2   SO Track on left.
3.6 ▲ SO Track on right.
▼ 1.7   SO Track on right is the return of Crosier
                Run Loop 7 (11N81).
3.1 ▲ SO Track on left is Crosier Run Loop 7
                (11N81) for ATVs, motorbikes, hikers,
                horses, and mountain bikes—rated

View from the Slate Mountain Fire Lookout

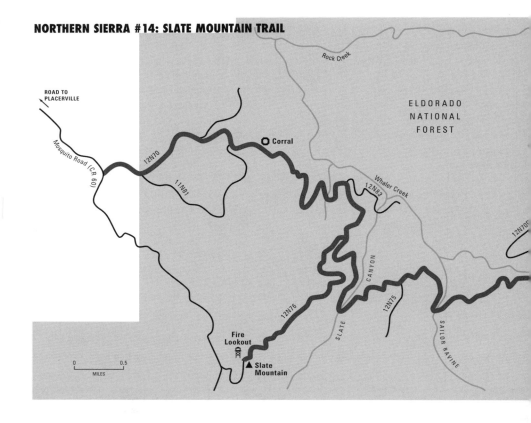

blue. This is closed to OHV travel
November 10 to May 1.

▼ 1.9   SO   Track on right.

2.9 ▲   SO   Track on left.

▼ 2.1   SO   Corral on left and track on right. Road
turns to graded dirt and is marked L7.

2.7 ▲   SO   Corral on right and track on left. Road
is now paved.
GPS: N38°49.59' W120°43.53'

▼ 3.8   SO   Cross over creek.

1.0 ▲   SO   Cross over creek.

▼ 4.0   BR   Track on right; then track on left is Trail
L6 (12N83). Bear right on Trail L6 and
L7, following sign to Georgetown.

0.8 ▲   SO   Track on right is Trail L6 (12N83). Follow
sign to Mosquito; then track on left.
GPS: N38°50.30' W120°43.04'

▼ 4.8   BL   Track on right is 12N76, the spur to
Slate Mountain Fire Lookout. Zero trip
meter and bear left, following Trail L6.

0.0 ▲   Continue to the southwest.
GPS: N38°50.37' W120°42.50'

Spur to Slate Mountain Fire Lookout

▼ 0.0   Proceed northeast on the upper road,
marked Trail L7 (12N76) and zero trip
meter. Trail starts to climb shelf road.

▼ 1.8   SO   Small trail for motorbikes crosses road.

▼ 2.3   SO   Small track on left is Trail 23-16 for
motorbikes only—rated blue.
GPS: N38°49.68' W120°41.24'

▼ 2.6   SO   Track on right on saddle.
GPS: N38°49.48' W120°41.14'

▼ 2.8   Track on right goes through gate. Slate
Mountain Fire Lookout and radio towers
are 0.1 miles past the gate. Trail L7 continues straight ahead and joins CR 60.
GPS: N38°49.44' W120°41.00'

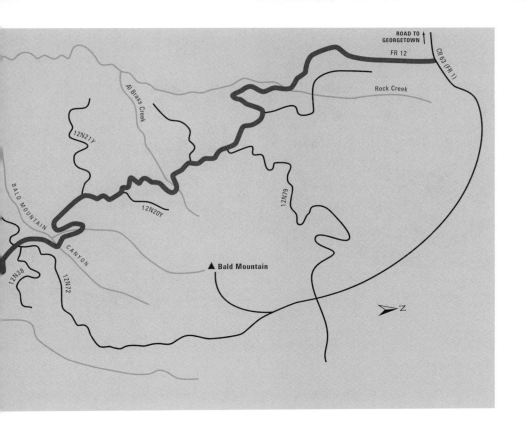

Continuation of Main Trail

▼ 0.0
5.9 ▲   SO   Continue to the north on the lower road.

5.9 ▲   SO   Track on sharp left is 12N76, the spur to Slate Mountain Fire Lookout. Zero trip meter and continue on Trail L7.
GPS: N38°50.37' W120°42.50'

▼ 1.4   SO   Cross over creek in Slate Canyon.
4.5 ▲   SO   Cross over creek in Slate Canyon.

▼ 2.4   SO   Track on right is 12N75 for 4WDs, ATVs, and motorbikes; then two small tracks on left.
3.5 ▲   SO   Two small tracks on right; then track on left is 12N75 for 4WDs, ATVs, and motorbikes.
GPS: N38°50.79' W120°41.93'

▼ 3.4   SO   Cross over Sailor Ravine; then track on right is 12N74 for 4WDs, ATVs, and motorbikes.
2.5 ▲   SO   Track on left is 12N74 for 4WDs, ATVs, and motorbikes; then cross over Sailor Ravine.

GPS: N38°51.09' W120°41.55'

▼ 4.1   SO   Track on left; then track on right is 12N69.
1.8 ▲   BR   Track on left is 12N69. Bear right, remaining on the main trail; then track on right.

▼ 4.5   SO   Road becomes paved.
1.4 ▲   SO   Road turns to graded dirt.

▼ 5.1   SO   Cross over Whaler Creek; then track on right is 12N70H.
0.8 ▲   SO   Track on left is 12N70H; then cross over Whaler Creek.
GPS: N38°52.15' W120°41.79'

▼ 5.7   SO   Track on left is Trail L5 (12N70D).
0.2 ▲   SO   Track on right is Trail L5 (12N70D).

▼ 5.9   SO   Small track on left joins Ballarat Trail in 1 mile; then track on left is Ballarat Loop 5 (12N82) for 4WDs, ATVs, motorbikes, hikers, horses, and mountain bikes—rated blue. Paved road on

Slate Mountain Fire Lookout

right is 12N72 to Bald Mountain Lookout and Quintette. Immediately off that road is 12N38 for 4WDs, ATVs, and motorbikes. Zero trip meter and follow the sign to Georgetown.

0.0 ▲   Continue to the east. Road is now paved.
    GPS: N38°52.51' W120°42.44'

▼ 0.0   Continue to the west. Road turns to gravel.

4.1 ▲ SO Track on right is Ballarat Loop 5 (12N82) for 4WDs, ATVs, motorbikes, hikers, horses, and mountain bikes— rated blue; then small track on right joins Ballarat Trail in 1 mile. Paved road on left is 12N72 to Bald Mountain Lookout and Quintette. Immediately off that road is 12N38 for 4WDs, ATVs, and motorbikes. Zero trip meter and follow the sign to Mosquito.

▼ 0.5 SO Cross over creek in Bald Mountain Canyon.

3.6 ▲ SO Cross over creek in Bald Mountain Canyon.

▼ 0.8 SO Track on right; then cross over creek in Bald Mountain Canyon.

3.3 ▲ SO Cross over creek in Bald Mountain Canyon; then track on left.

▼ 1.5 SO Small track on right is 9-12 for motorbikes only—rated blue.

2.6 ▲ SO Small track on left is 9-12 for motorbikes only—rated blue.

▼ 1.6 BR Two tracks on left. First is small trail 9-28 for motorbikes only—rated blue; then second track through seasonal closure gate is Trail L4 (12N21Y).

2.5 ▲ BL Two tracks on right. First track through seasonal closure gate is Trail L4 (12N21Y); then second track is small trail 9-28 for motorbikes only— rated blue.
    GPS: N38°53.09' W120°43.03'

▼ 2.2 SO Track on right is Trail 9-12Y (12N20Y) for motorbikes only—rated blue. Track on left is 9-13 for motorbikes only— rated blue.

1.9 ▲ SO Track on left is Trail 9-12Y (12N20Y) for motorbikes only—rated blue. Track on right is 9-13 for motorbikes only— rated blue.

▼ 2.4 SO Small trail on left and right.

TRIGGER OF THE CALIFORNIA GOLD RUSH

Born October 8, 1810, James Wilson Marshall was raised in Lambertville, New Jersey, where his childhood home stands today. His father died in 1834 and much responsibility fell on the young man's shoulders. Marshall bolted for the West when he was jilted. He wandered to western Missouri, where land had recently been opened to homesteading. By 1837, he had built a cabin, started to farm, and fell in love again; however, the girl married another man. Marshall picked up and moved to Oregon in 1844. Dissatisfied with the weather, Marshall joined an emigrant party and reached the Sacramento Valley in 1845.

James Wilson Marshall

A skilled millwright and woodworker, he sought employment with John A. Sutter at Sutter's Fort. Marshall soon established his own ranch nearby.

When American settlers revolted against Mexican rule in 1846, Marshall volunteered to march with Captain John C. Frémont. He served as chief military carpenter before his discharge early in 1847. Upon returning to his ranch, he found it plundered. Again he looked to Sutter for work. Sutter sent Marshall to build a sawmill on the banks of the South Fork of the American River, in the Cullomah Valley, about 45 miles northeast of the settlement.

On January 24, 1848, James Marshall was tweaking the flow in the mill's tailrace when he saw pieces of a shiny metal glistening in the sunlight. Seizing a small nugget, he placed it on the ground and began pounding it with a rock. Instead of shattering like fool's gold (pyrite), the nugget thinned under the beating. Convinced he had found gold, Marshall rushed to tell his colleagues. Four days later he traveled back to the fort to consult with Sutter. The pair conducted a series of tests until they felt convinced that the metal was gold.

Sutter urged Marshall to keep the discovery a secret until work on the mill was complete. However, by mid-March when the mill began sawing logs, rumors had already spread and another strike had been made at Mormon Island. When Samuel Brannan announced the discovery, first shouting it on the streets of San Francisco and then in his newspaper, prospectors rushed to the valley.

Soon the mill's vicinity became the bustling town of Coloma. Marshall kept sawing logs and only dabbled in gold mining. When he tried to extract a percentage from other miners, he was nearly driven from town. By 1850, the mill's operation was crippled by lawsuits; litigation would eat away Marshall's wealth, eventually forcing him to sell the last of his real estate.

The rest of Marshall's life was spent in the shadow of the gold discovery. He tried his hand as a vintner at Coloma; his grapes even won prizes at the state fair. Bad luck dogged him: In 1862, his cabin burned down, destroying valuable papers and perhaps a historically priceless diary. He became a little too keen on drink and quit the wine business. In 1872, the state legislature granted him a small pension, but it was not extended when it was discovered that the money was spent mostly on booze. Nevertheless, the allowance did enable Marshall to establish a small blacksmith shop in Kelsey, a town not far from Coloma. The man who started the world's greatest gold rush was squeaking out a living in this little shop when he died peacefully on August 10, 1885. A charitable group, The Native Sons of the Golden West, built a statue of Marshall on a hill overlooking his original discovery. The Marshall Gold Discovery State Historic Park in Coloma preserves the site and honors him as well.

1.7 ▲	SO	Small trail on left and right.
▼ 3.1	SO	Cross over Al Brass Creek.
1.0 ▲	SO	Cross over Al Brass Creek.

GPS: N38°53.86′ W120°43.11′

▼ 3.5	BR	Trail L4 on left and second small trail on left for motorbikes.
0.6 ▲	BL	Small trail on right and Trail L4 on right for motorbikes.
▼ 3.7	SO	Track on right is Trail 9-1 (12N18Y) for ATVs and motorbikes only—rated blue.
0.4 ▲	SO	Track on left is Trail 9-1 (12N18Y) for ATVs and motorbikes only—rated blue.

GPS: N38°54.14′ W120°43.44′

▼ 3.8	SO	Cross over creek.
0.3 ▲	SO	Cross over creek.
▼ 4.1	BL	Track on right is 12N79, signposted to Quintette. Zero trip meter.
0.0 ▲		Continue to the south.

GPS: N38°54.33′ W120°43.51′

▼ 0.0		Continue to the northwest.
3.7 ▲	BR	Track on left is 12N79, signposted to Quintette. Zero trip meter.
▼ 0.1	SO	Track on left is Trail 4 (also 9-15)—rated green. Track on right is Trail 9-16 for ATVs and motorbikes—rated green.
3.6 ▲	SO	Track on right is Trail 4 (also 9-15)—rated green. Track on left is Trail 9-16 for ATVs and motorbikes—rated green.
▼ 0.3	SO	Track on left is Trail 9-15 for motorbikes—rated green; then second track on left is Trail 9-15 for motorbikes—rated black; then third track on left is 12N701 for ATVs and motorbikes. Track on right is 9-18-19 for motorbikes—rated blue.
3.4 ▲	SO	Track on left is 9-18-19 for motorbikes—rated blue. Track on right is 12N701 for ATVs and motorbikes; then second track on right is Trail 9-15 for motorbikes—rated black; then third track on right is Trail 9-15 for motorbikes—rated green.
▼ 0.7	SO	Track on right through fence line is 9-18-19 for motorbikes—rated blue.
3.0 ▲	SO	Track on left through fence line is 9-18-19 for motorbikes—rated blue.
▼ 1.8	SO	Cross over Rock Creek; then trail on left is Trail 9-21 for motorbikes and horses—rated blue.
1.9 ▲	SO	Trail on right is Trail 9-21 for motorbikes and horses—rated blue; then cross over Rock Creek.

GPS: N38°54.85′ W120°44.26′

▼ 2.0	SO	Cross over Rock Creek; then track on right is 9-16 for motorbikes and horses—rated blue. Street-legal vehicles only past this point.
1.7 ▲	SO	Track on left is 9-16 for motorbikes and horses—rated blue; then cross over Rock Creek. Green-sticker vehicles permitted past this point.
▼ 3.0	SO	Track on left is 12N70T and track on right. Exiting Eldorado National Forest on paved road. Remain on paved road, ignoring private roads and driveways to the left and right for the next 0.7 miles.
0.7 ▲	SO	Entering Eldorado National Forest on paved road. Track on right is 12N70T and track on left.
▼ 3.7		Trail ends at T-intersection with paved CR 63 (FR 1). Turn left for Georgetown; turn right for Quintette.
0.0 ▲		Trail commences at the intersection of paved CR 63 (FR 1) and FR 12, 6.4 miles east of Georgetown and 0.1 miles southwest of county mile marker 6.5. Zero trip meter and turn south on paved Rock Creek Road at the sign for FR 12 and marker 4 on the Georgetown District History Tour.

GPS: N38°56.18′ W120°44.55′

Pony Express Trail

STARTING POINT Ice House Road (FR 3), 3.5 miles north of US 50 and Riverton.

FINISHING POINT US 50, 0.3 miles west of Silver Fork

TOTAL MILEAGE 7.8 miles

UNPAVED MILEAGE 7.8 miles

DRIVING TIME 1 hour

ELEVATION RANGE 4,000–4,800 feet

USUALLY OPEN April to November
BEST TIME TO TRAVEL Dry weather
DIFFICULTY RATING 2
SCENIC RATING 8
REMOTENESS RATING +0

Special Attractions

■ Short, easygoing trail that travels high above the South Fork of the American River.
■ Pleasant detour to a trip along US 50.
■ Trail travels part of the historic Pony Express route.

History

Traveling sections of the Pony Express Trail is a less hurried experience for today's traveler when compared with the speed of fearless Pony Express riders delivering mail. The Pony Express was an ambitious effort to develop communication between the East and West, an achievement that helped open up the West. The Pony Express operated between April 1860 and November 1861, and it successfully achieved its objective to deliver mail between St. Joseph, Missouri, and San Francisco. St. Joseph was linked to the telegraph system and could therefore easily communicate with Washington, D.C. Before the Pony Express, it could take as long as a month for mail to reach California by ship from New York.

What now seems like tame country along the American River was a wild mountain canyon in 1860. Riverton, just east of the start of this trail, was called Moore's Station in the mid nineteenth century. John M. Moore, a former member of the San Francis-

Eastern end of the Pony Express Trail

co Vigilance Committee, built and operated an outpost along a toll road here. The Pioneer Stage Company had a stage stop here in the 1850s and 1860s. Coming from the west, this was the first place to change weary horses after Sportsman Hall, or the Twelve-Mile House as it was known, in Pollock Pines. Moore's Station was also a remount station for Pony Express riders, their first stop after the Sportsman Hall as well.

In 1864, Wells Fargo expanded service to transport thousands of Comstock-bound Californians over the Sierra Nevada to Virginia City, Nevada. In doing so, the company bought out the Pioneer Stage Company and took over this vital stagecoach and freight route.

Another remount station for Pony Express riders was at Kyburz, at the eastern end of the trail. Webster's Station, as it was known, was located at Webster's Sugar Loaf House, so named because it was set at the base of a natural sugarloaf shaped mountain. The route of the Pony Express is now a National Historic Trail.

In the late 1850s, stage stations saw additional traffic from the construction of water ditches in the region. The very even grade of the Eldorado Water Ditch can still be seen on the far side of the deep canyon. The intake for this old ditch is on the South Fork of the American River, just below the eastern end of this trail where it rejoins US 50. Water was channeled through ditches, tunnels, flumes, and the Pollock Pines Forebay before dropping 1,900 feet through a penstock to drive the Pelton waterwheels of the El Dorado Powerhouse, northeast of Pollock Pines. In 1997, heavy rains caused a major landslide on the far side of the canyon, taking out a section of the Eldorado Water Ditch. A decision was made to abandon this section of the grade; a 1.8-mile-long tunnel now connects the ditch between Mill and Bull Creeks.

Description
This short trail makes for a pleasant detour from US 50 or is a lovely destination in its own right. Paved Ice House Road is well marked from US 50 at Riverton and swiftly

climbs onto Peavine Ridge. A forest service information booth is passed after 2.8 miles, and the trail commences 0.7 miles after that. The graded road heads southeast from a turnout and travels slightly downhill, wrapping around the hillsides.

Initially the hills are open. The area was burned in the Cleveland Wildfire of 1992 and is still recovering. The trail provides excellent views over the South Fork of the American River, 1,200 feet below, as well as the small settlement of White Hall.

Little remains at the Weber Mill site; the most visible remnant is a loading ramp. The trail enters the forest before descending to finish on US 50. Shortly before finishing, it crosses the original route of the Pony Express Trail, which is now a hiking trail.

Pony Express Trail is marked "XP"

Current Road Information
Eldorado National Forest
Pacific Ranger District
7887 Highway 50
Pollock Pines, CA 95726
(530) 644-2349

Map References
BLM   Placerville
USFS   Eldorado National Forest
USGS   1:24,000   Riverton, Kyburz
      1:100,000   Placerville
Maptech CD-ROM: High Sierra/Tahoe
Northern California Atlas & Gazetteer, p. 89
California Road & Recreation Atlas, p. 66
      (incomplete)

Route Directions

▼ 0.0   Trail commences on Ice House Road,
            3.5 miles north of US 50 and Riverton.
            Ice House Road intersects with US 50,
            2.5 miles west of White Hall. Zero trip
            meter 0.7 miles north of Cleveland
            Corral USFS Information Center and
            turn southeast down graded dirt road
            signposted Weber Mill Road (11N38).
            Pass through seasonal closure gate.
            Start of shelf road.

4.6 ▲   Seasonal closure gate; then trail ends
            at T-intersection with paved Ice House
            Road. Turn left for US 50 and Pollock
            Pines; turn right for Ice House
            Reservoir.
            GPS: N38°47.11' W120°25.14'

▼ 0.4 SO Turnout on right.
4.2 ▲ SO Turnout on left.
▼ 1.7 SO Cross over creek.
2.9 ▲ SO Cross over creek.
▼ 1.8 BL Track on right through seasonal
            closure gate.
2.8 ▲ SO Track on left through seasonal
            closure gate.
            GPS: N38°47.05' W120°23.68'

▼ 2.0 SO Track on right through seasonal closure
            gate is 11N.
2.6 ▲ SO Track on left through seasonal closure
            gate is 11N.

NORTHERN SIERRA #15: PONY EXPRESS TRAIL

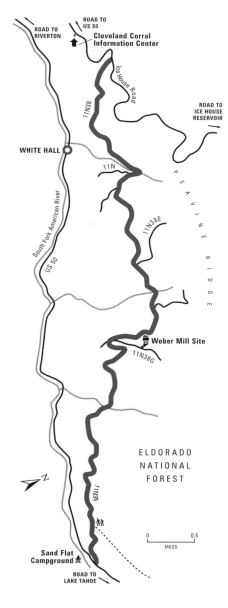

▼ 2.6 SO Track on right.
2.0 ▲ SO Track on left.
▼ 3.1 SO Track on left is 11N38E.
1.5 s SO Track on right is 11N38E.
            GPS: N38°46.90' W120°22.59'

▼ 3.3 SO Cross over creek.
1.3 ▲ SO Cross over creek.

▼ 3.6	SO	Cross over creek.
1.0 ▲	SO	Cross over creek.

GPS: N38°47.07' W120°22.19'

▼ 3.8	SO	Track on left.
0.8 ▲	SO	Track on right.
▼ 4.2	SO	Track on right goes to loading ramp.
0.4 ▲	SO	Track on left goes to loading ramp.
▼ 4.3	SO	Track on right is 11N38F.
0.3 ▲	SO	Track on left is 11N38F.

GPS: N38°46.74' W120°21.71'

▼ 4.6	SO	Track on left is 11N38G and unmarked track on right goes 0.1 miles to viewpoint. Zero trip meter.
0.0 ▲		Continue to the northwest.

GPS: N38°46.50' W120°21.71'

▼ 0.0		Continue to the northeast.
3.2 ▲	SO	Track on right is 11N38G and unmarked track on left goes 0.1 miles to viewpoint. Zero trip meter.
▼ 0.5	SO	Track on right.
2.7 ▲	SO	Track on left.
▼ 0.6	SO	Track on left is 11N38K.
2.6 ▲	SO	Track on right is 11N38K.
▼ 1.0	SO	Cross over creek.
2.2 ▲	SO	Cross over creek.
▼ 1.4	SO	Track on right.
1.8 ▲	SO	Track on left.
▼ 2.7	SO	Pony Express Hiking Trail on left, marked XP.
0.5 ▲	SO	Pony Express Hiking Trail on right, marked XP.

GPS: N38°45.98' W120°19.62'

▼ 2.9	SO	Seasonal closure gate.
0.3 ▲	SO	Seasonal closure gate.
▼ 3.2		Pass private property; then trail ends at intersection with US 50. Turn left for Lake Tahoe; turn right for Placerville.
0.0 ▲		Trail commences on US 50, 0.2 miles east of Sand Flat USFS Campground and 0.3 miles west of Silver Fork. Zero trip meter and turn north on small formed trail marked 31 Milestone Tract (11N38) and zero trip meter. Pass through private property.

GPS: N38°45.96' W120°19.13'

Angora Lakes Road

STARTING POINT Unmarked paved road, 0.4 miles east of Fallen Leaf Road and Fallen Leaf Lake

FINISHING POINT Parking area, 0.7 miles north of Angora Lakes

TOTAL MILEAGE 2.8 miles

UNPAVED MILEAGE 1.3 miles

DRIVING TIME 30 minutes

ELEVATION RANGE 6,700–7,200 feet

USUALLY OPEN May to September

BEST TIME TO TRAVEL May to September

DIFFICULTY RATING 1

SCENIC RATING 10

REMOTENESS RATING +0

Special Attractions

■ The historic complex of Angora Fire Lookout.

■ Views of Fallen Leaf Lake and Lake Tahoe.

■ Fishing, kayaking, and hiking at the scenic Angora Lakes.

■ Fallen Leaf Lake and Tallac Historic Site near the start of the trail.

History

The narrow, ridge-top trail toward Angora Lakes and Peak offers excellent views over Fallen Leaf Lake and its lakeshore community, some 900 feet below yet only a third of a mile away as the crow flies. The panoramic views from the ridge made this a suitable spot to build a much needed fire lookout. The three small buildings along this trail provide a record of fire lookouts in the early half of the twentieth century.

The first lookout, which is still standing, was built in 1925. The Civilian Conservation Corps constructed the next lookout alongside the original 10 years later. The third structure is simply a garage. All three buildings are eligible for inclusion on the National Register of Historic Places.

The far-reaching views of Lake Tahoe can't help but make today's visitors wonder

Mount Tallac rises above Fallen Leaf Lake

how idyllic and bountiful this mountain-ringed blue lake was for early inhabitants. Sadly, not many of these Washo people survived the influx of Euro-American settlers. The landscape the Washo knew was born out of turbulent geological times reaching back 10 million years (see Lake Tahoe, page 128). Waters once filled this massive basin to a depth several hundred feet deeper than we see today.

The Washo are possibly the oldest culture among the Sierran or Great Basin tribal groups. Their storytelling, a good indication of their background, goes no further than the region in which they lived. Their language has a somewhat distinct aspect, noticeably different from surrounding cultures. Like all native peoples, they lost out with the influx of newcomers to this magnificent region. Diseases, coupled with aggressive settlers brought about their demise. They knew Lake Tahoe as *dá'wa*, meaning "lake," which newcomers took on as Lake Tahoe. Dá'wa was a summer retreat for the Washo. They camped at the lakeshore, enjoying summer temperatures much more pleasant than the heat of Carson Valley, almost 2,000 feet lower. The remaining Washo still hope that one day they will once again hold the rights to their forefathers' land.

Description

This short, easy trail is a popular trip for visitors staying near South Lake Tahoe. The graded dirt and paved road, known as Angora Ridge Road, is suitable for passenger vehicles and passes a variety of spectacular scenery. It begins near Fallen Leaf Lake and travels gradually onto Angora Ridge. The whole trail is a moderate ride for mountain bikers, who can continue along the trail to the lakes and resort.

The old Angora Fire Lookout sits on top of the ridge. The site is currently undergoing restoration. Spectacular views from the lookout include Fallen Leaf Lake, Lake Tahoe, Mount Tallac, and farther south toward Angora Peak.

The vehicle trail ends at a parking area after 2.8 miles. From here, it is a short, extremely rewarding 0.7-mile hike to Angora Lakes along the vehicle trail that serves an old resort. A full view of the first lake is reached 0.4 miles from the parking area, a view of the second at 0.7 miles.

The Angora Lakes Resort, operating since 1917, offers light refreshments and accommodations in shingle-roofed cabins. There can be a waiting list for the cabins of more than a year at times. The clear Angora Lakes are suitable for swimming and snorkeling and there is a small beach. Boat rentals are available at the lodge, which is normally open from June to September. Dogs must be kept on a leash on the entire trail and are not allowed in the lakes.

The trail borders the Desolation Wilderness, 63,960 acres of subalpine forest and alpine tundra and glacially formed lakes. Permits are required year-round for both day and overnight use in the wilderness. Reservations are recommended.

In winter, the area around the northern end of Fallen Leaf Lake is marked for cross-country skiing. Advanced skiers can continue up Angora Lakes Road to the lookout and lakes. The road is also open to snowmobiles and snowshoers in winter. It is closed to motor vehicles until the surface dries.

Current Road Information

Lake Tahoe Basin Management Unit
35 College Drive
South Lake Tahoe, CA 96150
(530) 543-2600

Map References

BLM   Placerville
USFS   Toiyabe National Forest: Carson
       Ranger District; Eldorado National
       Forest
USGS   1:24,000   Emerald Bay, Echo Lake
       1:100,000 Placerville
Maptech CD-ROM: High Sierra/Tahoe
Northern California Atlas & Gazetteer, p. 89
California Road & Recreation Atlas, p. 67
Trails Illustrated, Lake Tahoe, Marin
       County and Pt. Reyes National
       Seashore Bike Map (505)
Other: Fine Edge Productions—South

Kayak on the lake at the foot of Angora Peak

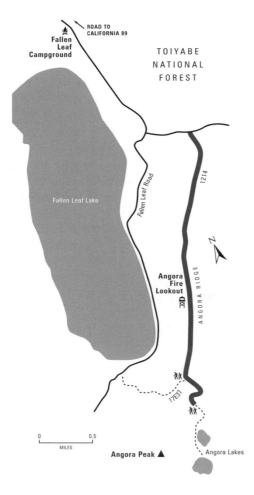

Lake Tahoe Basin Recreation Topo
Map; Tom Harrison Maps—Lake
Tahoe Recreation Map, A Guide to
the Desolation Wilderness

Route Directions

▼ 0.0   From California 89, opposite the Tallac
Historic Site and west of South Lake
Tahoe, turn south on Fallen Leaf Road
and proceed 2 miles. Turn left onto
unmarked paved road and head 0.4
miles east to the start of the trail. Zero
trip meter and turn south on graded
dirt road marked 1214 (marked on

Eldorado National Forest map as
12N14) and pass through closure gate.
GPS: N38°54.21′ W120°02.22′

▼ 0.6   SO Road becomes paved as it climbs
the ridge.
▼ 1.1   SO Road turns to graded dirt.
▼ 1.3   SO Road becomes paved.
▼ 1.4   SO Non-motorized vehicle track on right.
GPS: N38°53.25′ W120°03.07′

▼ 1.8   SO Angora Fire Lookout buildings on right.
GPS: N38°52.93′ W120°03.23′

▼ 2.3   SO Road turns to graded dirt.
▼ 2.4   SO Hiking trail on right is 17E37.
GPS: N38°52.48′ W120°03.67′

▼ 2.8   Trail ends at parking area for Angora
Lakes. Park and hike south along the old
vehicle trail for 0.7 miles to Angora Lakes.
GPS: N38°52.26′ W120°03.71′

McKinney Creek Trail

STARTING POINT California 89 in Tahoma
FINISHING POINT FR 03 at Barker Pass
TOTAL MILEAGE 11.5 miles
UNPAVED MILEAGE 9.1 miles
DRIVING TIME 3 hours
ELEVATION RANGE 6,200–7,700 feet
USUALLY OPEN July to November
BEST TIME TO TRAVEL Dry weather only
DIFFICULTY RATING 4
SCENIC RATING 8
REMOTENESS RATING +0

Special Attractions

■ Trail travels a short, easy section of the
notorious Rubicon Trail.
■ Access to the Pacific Crest National Scenic
Trail, Tahoe Rim Trail, and Ellis Peak Trail
for hikers.
■ Can be combined with Northern Sierra
#18: Blackwood Canyon Trail to make a
loop back to California 89.

History

A wagon road called Burton Pass Road evolved from a fur trappers' and prospectors' route, bringing trade, livestock, and mining traffic through this picturesque region. Various creeks and springs near the Rubicon River, just inside El Dorado County, enhanced travel for Native Americans and settlers alike.

The eastern end of the trail follows McKinney Creek, named after John Washington McKinney, who arrived in this region in 1861 and established a hay pasture. Within two years, the cabin retreat on the shores of Lake Tahoe had already become popular with miners, hunters, and passing travelers. With time and popularity, McKinney's resort grew to include a saloon and pier, with fishing as the main attraction. John Muir was one of many who frequented McKinney's resort, relishing the majestic forests around the spectacular lake.

By the late 1860s, John and George Hunsucker, miners from the Kelsey region, had arrived on the scene and began improving the land around Rubicon Springs. They ran stock and bottled spring water for distribution to local mining communities. The quality of the water drew many travelers to its source. One such person, Mrs. S. P. Clark, bought land around the springs and turned it into a successful resort, which, by the late 1880s, was complete with a two-story hotel. Her fine furnishings, silverware, and high-quality food attracted many visitors, who traveled to the resort via the rough Burton Pass Road, which by that time had gained recognition as a public thoroughfare.

Sadly, the Rubicon Springs Hotel and outbuildings received a thorough lashing from the flash floods of 1908. The resort continued to operate, changing ownership and gaining and losing popularity with time. In the 1920s, the resort was having a tough time making ends meet. It was finally sold off to the Sierra Power Company in 1930. The hotel lasted until 1953, when the weight of win-

Cothrin Cove sits below the trail to Barker Pass

ter snows destroyed what had been referred to as The Fountain of Youth Resort.

The lakeshore town of Tahoma, at the trail's start, was named after a hotel built by Joseph Bishop of San Francisco in 1916. Bishop seemingly played upon the combination of the words Tahoe and home, coming up with Tahoma. His well-appointed lakeside hotel enjoyed enormous popularity during the 1920s, boasting a swimming pool that stretched into the lake, a dance hall, and a dining room.

Description
McKinney Creek Trail follows a short section of the infamous Rubicon Trail (see page 118), a hardcore jeep trail for modified vehicles, before heading north to Barker Pass.

The trail leaves from the edge of Tahoma along a small paved road, following signs to the Rubicon OHV Trailhead. Past the trailhead, it becomes a rough dirt trail that has been stabilized with loose crushed rock to help minimize damage to the meadows and marshes. Please do not travel this trail in wet weather. Avoiding the trail when wet will minimize damage and help keep this historic route open.

Along McKinney Creek, the trail is loose in places with a few embedded rocks. The Sierra Nevada Fault, a major California fault line, crosses the trail near Lake Tahoe.

The trail passes several lakes: The first two, McKinney Lake and Lily Lake, are covered with water lilies; the third, Miller Lake, is open water. The lakes were formed when eastbound glaciers dropped moraine, forming natural dams. A few campsites can be found near the lakes.

The trail forks after 5.8 miles. The Rubicon Trail continues to the left on its long journey to Georgetown. A short distance past the intersection, the Rubicon starts to show its colors and becomes 7-rated as it crawls over large boulders. The Rubicon Trail in its entirety is not suitable for stock vehicles. The main trail turns right at this intersection and follows a roughly graded road, climbing toward Barker Pass. The trail passes Bear Lake, which is set below the trail, and the rock bowl of Cothrin Cove. The final part of the route leaves the graded road and winds along the uneven Barker Meadow OHV Trail, passing beside Barker Meadow.

The trail comes to an end at a Pacific Crest National Scenic Trailhead at Barker Pass. The more difficult Northern Sierra #18: Blackwood Canyon Trail leaves from Barker Pass and can be combined with McKinney Creek Trail to make a loop back to California 89. For a more direct way back to the highway, turn right on Barker Pass Road (FR 03), which quickly becomes paved and drops swiftly to join California 89.

At Barker Pass, a segment of the Tahoe Rim Trail and the Pacific Crest National Scenic Trail run concurrently. The TRT is a 150-mile loop around the Tahoe Basin open to hikers and equestrians and in some places to mountain bikers. In addition, the Ellis Peak Trail, a short moderate trail that climbs several switchbacks to Ellis Peak, leaves from the south side of the road, opposite the Pacific Crest National Scenic Trailhead.

In winter, most of this route is a cross-country ski trail. Snowmobilers also use some parts of it. A county ordinance closes the trail the last weekend in July and the first weekend in August each year for the annual Jeepers Jamboree. This organized trail run attracts hundreds of four-wheelers from all over the country.

Current Road Information
Lake Tahoe Basin Management Unit
35 College Drive
South Lake Tahoe, CA 96150
(530) 543-2600

Tahoe National Forest
Truckee Ranger District
9646 Donner Pass Road
Truckee, CA 96161
(530) 587-3558

Map References
BLM   Truckee
USFS   Eldorado National Forest; Tahoe
       National Forest
USGS   1:24,000   Homewood, Wentworth
       Springs

Lily Lake

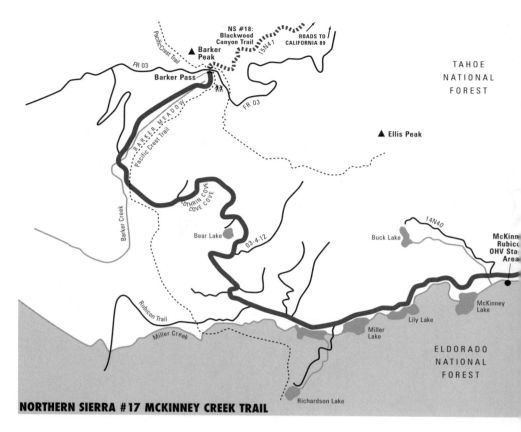

NORTHERN SIERRA #17 MCKINNEY CREEK TRAIL

1:100,000 Truckee
Maptech CD-ROM: High Sierra/Tahoe
Northern California Atlas & Gazetteer, p. 81
California Road & Recreation Atlas, p. 66
    (incomplete)
Trails Illustrated, Lake Tahoe, Marin
    County and Pt. Reyes National
    Seashore Bike Map (505)
Other: Fine Edge Productions—North
    Lake Tahoe Basin Recreation Topo
    Map; Fine Edge Productions—
    South Lake Tahoe Basin Recreation
    Topo Map (incomplete); Tom
    Harrison Maps—Lake Tahoe
    Recreation Map, A Guide to the
    Desolation Wilderness (incomplete)

Route Directions

▼ 0.0   From California 89, on the western
         shore of Lake Tahoe in Tahoma, zero
         trip meter and turn south on paved

McKinney-Rubicon Springs Road,
following sign for OHV Access.

2.4 ▲   Trail ends at T-intersection with California
         89 in Tahoma. Turn right for South Lake
         Tahoe; turn left for Tahoe City.
         GPS: N39°04.23′ W120°08.36′

▼ 0.3   TL   Turn left onto paved road following
              sign for Miller Lake Access and the
              Rubicon Trail.

2.1 ▲   TR   Turn right onto paved McKinney-
              Rubicon Springs Road, following the
              sign for California 89.

▼ 0.5   TR   T-intersection. Turn right onto
              McKinney Road, following the sign for
              Miller Lake. Road becomes Springs
              Court.

1.9 ▲   TL   Road becomes McKinney Road; then
              turn left onto Bellevue Avenue.

▼ 0.7   BL   Road on right. Bear left onto
              McKinney- Rubicon Road, following
              sign for the Rubicon Trail.

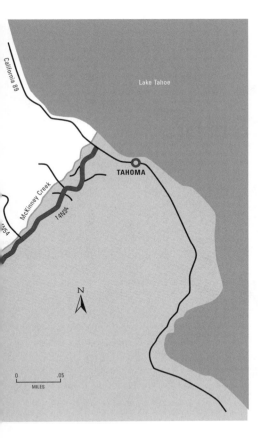

▼ 0.2   SO   Track on right is 14N40, which goes to Buck Lake.

3.2 ▲   SO   Track on left is 14N40, which goes to Buck Lake.

GPS: N39°02.74′ W120°10.30′

▼ 0.4   SO   Cross through wash.

3.0 ▲   SO   Cross through wash.

▼ 0.6   SO   McKinney Lake below road on the left.

2.8 ▲   SO   McKinney Lake below road on the right.

GPS: N39°02.60′ W120°10.62′

▼ 0.8   SO   Track on right.

2.6 ▲   SO   Track on left.

▼ 1.5   SO   Lily Lake on left.

1.9 ▲   SO   Lily Lake on right.

GPS: N39°02.40′ W120°11.29′

▼ 2.0   SO   Two tracks on left to campsites along Miller Lake.

1.4 ▲   SO   Two tracks on right to campsites along Miller Lake.

▼ 2.1   SO   Miller Lake on left.

1.3 ▲   SO   Miller Lake on right.

GPS: N39°02.22′ W120°11.94′

▼ 2.4   SO   Track on left to Richardson Lake.

1.0 ▲   SO   Track on right to Richardson Lake.

▼ 2.6   SO   Lake on left.

0.8 ▲   SO   Lake on right.

▼ 2.9   SO   Track on right; then cross through creek; then second track on right is OHV route for 4WDs, ATVs, and motorbikes.

0.5 ▲   SO   Track on left is OHV route for 4WDs, ATVs, and motorbikes; then cross through creek; then second track on left.

GPS: N39°02.18′ W120°12.82′

▼ 3.0   SO   Cross over two concrete fords.

0.4 ▲   SO   Cross over two concrete fords.

▼ 3.4   BR   Rubicon Trail continues to the left. Follow sign for Barker Pass. Zero trip meter.

0.0 ▲   Continue to the east.

GPS: N39°02.24′ W120°13.29′

▼ 0.0   Continue to the west and pass through seasonal closure gate.

1.7 ▲   BR   Road on left. Bear right onto Springs Court, following the sign for California 89.

▼ 0.8   SO   4-way intersection. Follow signs to the McKinney-Rubicon Staging Area.

1.6 ▲   SO   4-way intersection.

GPS: N39°03.74′ W120°08.75′

▼ 1.1   SO   Parking area on right.

1.3 ▲   SO   Parking area on left.

▼ 1.5   SO   Track on right is 14N54.

0.9 ▲   SO   Track on left is 14N54.

▼ 2.3   SO   Cross over McKinney Creek.

0.1 ▲   SO   Cross over McKinney Creek.

▼ 2.4   SO   McKinney-Rubicon OHV Staging Area. Road is now a rough formed trail. Zero trip meter.

0.0 ▲   Continue to the northeast.

GPS: N39°02.76′ W120°10.03′

▼ 0.0   Continue to the southwest.

3.4 ▲   SO   McKinney-Rubicon OHV Staging Area. Road is now paved. Zero trip meter.

RUBICON TRAIL

The Maidu Indians of the northern Sierra followed the Rubicon River Valley into the Sierra Nevada to Lake Tahoe to trade with the Washo tribe of western Nevada. George Ehrenhaft established a camp at what became Georgetown, just south of the river, in 1849; George Phipps, a sailor, arrived at about the same time, and it is not clear which George the site is named for. Georgetown is 10 miles northeast of Coloma, where James Marshall first discovered gold in 1848. Georgetown is the western start of the Rubicon Trail, which travels east to Lake Tahoe.

In 1864, a black trapper and trader built a cabin on the Rubicon, a site called Uncle Tom's Cabin, which is now a favorite stop of trail riders and hunters. Miners John and George Hunsucker built a cabin at Rubicon Springs in 1867 and began bottling spring water in 1880 to sell to visitors. The Rubicon Soda Springs Resort opened on the site of the brothers' cabin and catered to health-seeking vacationers. Its two-story hotel collapsed during the winter of 1953. The site is now the largest campground along the trail and a place for jeepers to swap trail stories.

Ranchers moved livestock along the trail to graze in mountain pastures from the 1880s to the 1940s. The El Dorado County Board of Supervisors ensured unlimited access to the trail by declaring it a public highway in 1887.

The first automobiles took to the trail in the 1920s, using ropes and planks to negotiate the hairiest obstacles. Tales of derelict and destroyed cars littering the trail served to warn drivers of its hazards. In 1952, Georgetown residents organized the first Jeepers Jamboree, and on August 29, 1953, 55 vehicles traversed the trail in two days. The annual event is still held the last weekend in July. Four-wheel drive manufacturers test their newest designs on the trail, considering it the ultimate test for prototypes. They swath their vehicles in canvas to hide cutting-edge designs. A successful negotiation of the Rubicon Trail means the 4WD is suitable to drive anywhere.

The Rubicon River was likely named for the river in northern Italy crossed by Caesar in 49 B.C. on his way to overthrow Pompey and gain control of Italy. Crossing the Rubicon means reaching the point of no return, an appropriate phrase for this extreme 4WD trail, which should only be attempted in its entirety by experienced four-wheel drivers with vehicles modified for extreme backcountry conditions.

4.0 ▲   SO   Seasonal closure gate; then track on right is the Rubicon Trail. Zero trip meter and join the Rubicon Trail, following sign for California 89 and Tahoe City.

▼ 0.3   SO   Track on left.

3.7 ▲   SO   Track on right.

▼ 0.4   BL   Track on right.

3.6 ▲   BR   Track on left.

▼ 1.2   BL   Track on right is 03-4-12 for 4WDs, ATVs, and motorbikes.

2.8 ▲   BR   Track on left is 03-4-12 for 4WDs, ATVs, and motorbikes.
GPS: N39°02.75' W120°13.56'

▼ 1.4   SO   Bear Lake below trail on the left.

2.6 ▲   SO   Bear Lake below trail on the right.
GPS: N39°02.87' W120°13.51'

▼ 1.8   SO   Track on left to Bear Lake and track on right.

2.2 ▲   SO   Track on right to Bear Lake and track on left.

▼ 3.1   SO   Track on right.

0.9 ▲   SO   Track on left.

▼ 3.6   SO   Track on left is OHV route.

0.4 ▲   SO   Track on right is OHV route.

▼ 4.0   TR   Cross over Barker Creek; then track on left. Turn right onto small trail marked as an OHV Route and zero trip meter. This is the Barker Meadow OHV Trail.

The trail is most commonly traveled from west to east starting at Georgetown, on California 193, 20 miles east of Auburn. The pavement ends at mile 24 and Uncle Tom's Cabin is passed just after mile 30. Beyond mile 38, the trail intersects paved Ice House Road, which joins US 50 at Riverton. A little more than 40 miles from Georgetown, the trail follows Loon Lake's shoreline to its staging area where the terrain gets rough for the first time.

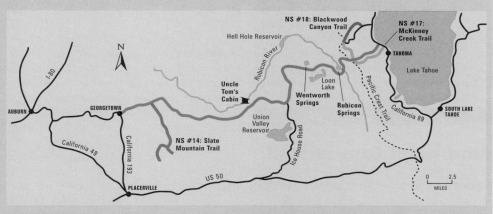

Rubicon Trail in red

The trail crosses Ice House Road again at the turnoff to Wentworth Springs. Because of the challenges of the road ahead, the next portion of the trail, from Wentworth Springs to Rubicon Springs, is named Devil's Playground. Just before the trail reaches Rubicon Springs, about 60 miles from Georgetown, it crosses the Rubicon River Bridge. The original log bridge was built in 1860, and it has been replaced by a steel structure and refurbished several times since. From Rubicon Springs the trail follows the river north. About 20 miles from trail's end at Lake Tahoe, the body of an old LaSalle marks Cadillac Hill, the beginning of the final extreme section. From Observation Point, where there is a noteworthy view of the Rubicon River Gorge and trail back toward Georgetown, the trail evens out. At Barker Pass, the route's highest elevation at 7,115 feet, the Pacific Crest Trail intersects the Rubicon Trail. The Rubicon ends just over 5 miles beyond this point.

0.0 ▲		Continue to the east and cross over Barker Creek.
		GPS: N39°03.55′ W120°15.07′

▼ 0.0		Continue to the north.
1.7 ▲	TL	4-way intersection with roughly graded road. Track straight ahead. Zero trip meter.
▼ 0.7	SO	Cross through wash; then cross through creek; then track on right.
1.0 ▲	SO	Track on left; then cross through creek; then cross through wash.
▼ 0.9	SO	Track on left; then cross through wash.
0.8 ▲	SO	Cross through wash; then track on right.
▼ 1.1	SO	Cross through wash.
0.6 ▲	SO	Cross through wash.
▼ 1.4	SO	Cross through wash.
0.3 ▲	SO	Cross through wash.
▼ 1.5	SO	Track on right is a dead end.
0.2 ▲	BR	Track on left is dead end. Bear right onto Barker Meadow OHV Trail.
▼ 1.7		Trail ends at 4-way intersection with graded Barker Pass Road (FR 03) at Barker Pass, opposite the Pacific Crest National Scenic Trailhead and the start of Northern Sierra #18: Blackwood Canyon Trail. Trailhead parking and picnic area at intersection. Turn right to exit to California 89. Continue straight ahead to exit to California 89 via the more difficult Blackwood Canyon Trail.

0.0 ▲   Trail commences on graded Barker Pass Road (FR 03) at Barker Pass, 7.2 miles southwest of California 89. The Pacific Crest National Scenic Trailhead and the start of Northern Sierra #18: Blackwood Canyon Trail is opposite. Trailhead parking and picnic area at intersection. Zero trip meter and turn southeast on small formed trail, which is the start of the Barker Meadow OHV Trail.

GPS: N39°04.60' W120°14.07'

Blackwood Canyon Trail

STARTING POINT Barker Pass Road (FR 03), 2.2 miles west of California 89 and Idlewild

FINISHING POINT Barker Pass Road (FR 03), opposite Northern Sierra #17: McKinney Creek Trail

TOTAL MILEAGE 3.6 miles

UNPAVED MILEAGE 3.6 miles

DRIVING TIME 45 minutes

ELEVATION RANGE 6,400–7,700 feet

USUALLY OPEN July to October

BEST TIME TO TRAVEL Dry weather

DIFFICULTY RATING 5

SCENIC RATING 8

REMOTENESS RATING +0

Special Attractions

■ Views of Blackwood Canyon and Lake Tahoe.

■ Moderately challenging trail for compact and subcompact, high-clearance 4WDs.

■ Can be combined with Northern Sierra #17: McKinney Creek Trail to make a loop back to California 89.

History

Blackwood Canyon Trail reaches its highest point (7,610 feet) when it crests Barker Pass, just below a peak of the same name. In the nineteenth century, William A. Barker ran stock in the meadows south of the pass.

Looking back from the pass, the trail zigzags down a steep ridge to run alongside Blackwood Creek, 1,300 feet below. The creek is named for Hampton C. Blackwood, who settled here in 1866. Another early arrival to the Lake Tahoe region, Jock Ellis left his name attached to Ellis Peak, the tall mountain to the east. Ellis owned a dairy and later a sheep ranch nearby in the late nineteenth century.

Description

This short trail begins along Blackwood Creek and climbs up the ridge to Barker Pass. The route parallels paved Barker Pass Road, but the paved road is not visible from the trail. Compact and subcompact, high-clearance 4WDs are best suited for this trail; extra wide or full size vehicles may not make the squeeze between two trees encountered 2.6 miles from the start of the trail.

The trail gets its difficulty rating from the long, moderately steep, loose climb up a single-vehicle width trail. A few embedded rocks must be negotiated along the trail. The hardest pinch is the final 50 yards before the top of the climb. However, a stock, high-clearance 4WD in low range should be able to negotiate the rocks with careful wheel placement.

Good views over Blackwood Canyon and a glimpse of Lake Tahoe make this a very scenic drive. The trail finishes at the Pacific Crest National Scenic Trailhead on Barker Pass. Northern Sierra #17: McKinney Creek Trail heads south from Barker Pass; the two trails can be combined for a longer loop back to California 89.

In winter, Blackwood Canyon Trail is used by cross-country skiers and snowmobilers. Avalanches are possible after snowstorms, and the trail is not marked for winter use.

Current Road Information

Lake Tahoe Basin Management Unit
35 College Drive
South Lake Tahoe, CA 96150
(530) 543-2600

Map References

BLM Truckee

USFS Eldorado National Forest; Tahoe National Forest

Distant view of Lake Tahoe

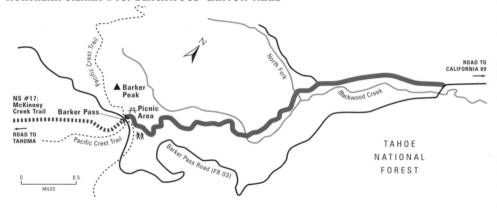

USGS 1:24,000   Homewood
       1:100,000 Truckee
Maptech CD-ROM: High Sierra/Tahoe
Northern California Atlas & Gazetteer, p. 81
California Road & Recreation Atlas, p. 66
       (incomplete)
Trails Illustrated, Lake Tahoe, Marin

County and Pt. Reyes National
Seashore Bike Map (505)
Other: Fine Edge Productions—North
Lake Tahoe Basin Recreation Topo
Map; Tom Harrison Maps—Lake
Tahoe Recreation Map

Blackwood Canyon Trail at Barker Pass

Route Directions

▼ 0.0　From Barker Pass Road (FR 03), immediately before it crosses over Blackwood Creek, 2.2 miles west of California 89 and Idlewild, zero trip meter and turn southwest on formed dirt trail, signposted to the OHV picnic and staging area.

3.6 ▲　Trail ends back on paved Barker Pass Road (FR 03). Turn left to return to California 89 and Lake Tahoe.
　　　GPS: N39°06.40′ W120°11.74′

▼ 0.4　SO Pass through OHV staging area. Track on right is 15N38A.

3.2 ▲　SO Track on left is 15N38A. Pass through OHV staging area.

▼ 0.5　SO Seasonal closure gate.

3.1 ▲　SO Seasonal closure gate.

▼ 0.8　SO Cross through wash.

2.8 ▲　SO Cross through wash.

▼ 1.1　BL Track on right.

2.5 ▲　BR Track on left.
　　　GPS: N39°05.78′ W120°12.74′

▼ 1.2　SO Cross through wash.

2.4 ▲　SO Cross through wash.

▼ 1.3　SO Cross over North Fork Blackwood Creek.

2.3 ▲　SO Cross over North Fork Blackwood Creek.

▼ 1.4　SO Cross over creek.

2.2 ▲　SO Cross over creek.

▼ 2.0　SO Cross through creek. Trail starts to climb.

1.6 ▲　SO End of descent. Cross through creek.
　　　GPS: N39°05.09′ W120°12.97′

▼ 2.6　SO Squeeze between two trees.

1.0 ▲　SO Squeeze between two trees.

▼ 3.4　SO Seasonal closure gate; then track on left. Trail is now graded dirt. End of climb.

0.2 ▲　SO Trail is now a formed trail. Track on right; then seasonal closure gate. Trail starts to descend.

▼ 3.6　SO Barker Pass. Picnic area on right and trailhead parking for the Pacific Crest and Tahoe Rim Trails. Trail ends at Barker Pass Road (FR 03). Turn left to return to California 89. Straight ahead is the start of Northern Sierra #17: McKinney Creek Trail.

0.0 ▲　Trail commences on Barker Pass Road (FR 03) at Barker Pass, 7.2 miles southwest of California 89 and Idlewild. Zero trip meter at the sign for Barker Pass and turn north on graded dirt road. Track opposite is the start of Northern Sierra #17: McKinney Creek Trail.
　　　GPS: N39°04.60′ W120°14.07′

NORTHERN SIERRA #19

Mount Watson Trail

STARTING POINT California 89 in Tahoe City, 0.2 miles southwest of the intersection with California 28

FINISHING POINT California 267, 0.4 miles south of Truckee

TOTAL MILEAGE 20.8 miles, plus 1.5-mile spur to Mount Watson and 0.9-mile spur to Watson Lake

UNPAVED MILEAGE 13.7 miles, plus spurs

DRIVING TIME 1.5 hours

ELEVATION RANGE 5,900–8,200 feet

USUALLY OPEN July to October

BEST TIME TO TRAVEL Dry weather

DIFFICULTY RATING 3

SCENIC RATING 8

REMOTENESS RATING +0

Special Attractions

■ Watson Lake.

■ Scenic route between Lake Tahoe and Truckee.

■ The trail is popular with mountain bikers and intersects with many hiking trails.

History

Mount Watson Trail begins in Tahoe City at the headwaters of the Truckee River, the only outlet from Lake Tahoe. California 89 crosses the Truckee River at this point on the Virginia Street Bridge, a landmark of some renown. In 1906, the dissatisfied spouse of a leading national businessman came to Reno, Nevada, to annul her marriage. The high-profile divorce made Reno the place to get separated with panache. The final statement for such a dissolution was to travel up to Tahoe City and cast the now defunct wedding ring off the side of Virginia Street Bridge. This ring-throwing ceremony was immortalized by Marilyn Monroe in her last movie, *The Misfits.*

Mount Pluto Ski Area, 200 feet higher than the 8,424-foot Mount Watson, is immediately north of Mount Watson along this trail. The name, first mentioned in 1874, is taken from the Roman god of the underworld because of the volcanic nature of the mountain.

Description

This route, also known as the Fiberboard Freeway, mainly follows a series of developed logging roads. Most of the trail is rated a 2 for difficulty; the 3 rating comes from the section leading out of Tahoe City. This small, formed trail can be loose and steep enough to require four-wheel-drive; this section is seasonally closed to motor vehicles to protect the trail surface.

The trail winds through Tahoe National Forest, passing a mix of aspens and conifers and offering many opportunities for hiking or camping along the way. A short spur leads to a small clearing at the top of Mount Watson, which provides fantastic views of Lake Tahoe. A second short spur leads to Watson Lake, which is a good place to camp or picnic. The banks of the lake are fringed with wildflowers in spring. It is normally quiet and sees little of the crowds that visit Lake Tahoe. The Western States Trail, part of the American Discovery Trail, and the Tevis Cup Trail both follow part of the Mount Watson route along the ridge.

Past the spur to Watson Lake, the trail follows better graded roads below Sawtooth Ridge, descending gradually toward Truckee. To the west is Squaw Valley, one of the region's popular ski areas. The trail passes through subdivisions on the edge of Truckee, before ending on California 267, 0.4 miles east of the center of Truckee.

The trail is popular with mountain bikers, for whom it is a moderate ride with some long climbs. Other mountain bike trails intersect the main route. In winter, snowmobilers enjoy this region.

Current Road Information

Lake Tahoe Basin Management Unit
35 College Drive
South Lake Tahoe, CA 96150
(530) 543-2600

Tahoe National Forest
Truckee Ranger District
9646 Donner Pass Road
Truckee, CA 96161
(530) 587-3558

Map References

BLM   Truckee
USFS   Eldorado National Forest; Tahoe
       National Forest
USGS   1:24,000   Tahoe City, Truckee
       1:100,000 Truckee
Maptech CD-ROM: High Sierra/Tahoe
Northern California Atlas & Gazetteer, p. 81
California Road & Recreation Atlas, p. 66
Trails Illustrated, Lake Tahoe, Marin
       County and Pt. Reyes National
       Seashore Bike Map (505)
Other: Fine Edge Productions—North
       Lake Tahoe Basin Recreation Topo
       Map; Tom Harrison Maps—Lake
       Tahoe Recreation Map (incomplete)

Route Directions

▼ 0.0   From California 89 in Tahoe City, 0.2
           miles southwest of the intersection
           with California 28, zero trip meter and
           turn northwest on paved Fairway
           Drive. Proceed 0.1 miles to the start of
           the trail. Zero trip meter and turn west
           on formed dirt trail. Pass through sea-
           sonal closure gate.
4.2 ▲   Seasonal closure gate; then trail ends
           on paved Fairway Drive. Turn right and
           proceed 0.1 miles to reach California
           89 in Tahoe City.
           GPS: N39°09.97′ W120°08.78′

▼ 0.1   BL Track on right is for 4WDs, ATVs, and
           motorbikes.
4.1 ▲   SO Track on left is for 4WDs, ATVs, and
           motorbikes.

▼ 0.3   SO Track on right.

3.9 ▲	SO	Track on left.
▼ 1.0	SO	Seasonal closure gate.
3.2 ▲	SO	Seasonal closure gate.
		GPS: N39°10.18′ W120°09.70′

▼ 3.6	SO	Tahoe Rim Trail for hikers crosses.
0.6 ▲	SO	Tahoe Rim Trail for hikers crosses.
		GPS: N39°11.10′ W120°09.98′

▼ 4.2	TL	Seasonal closure gate; then road becomes paved. Road on right is 16N71 for high-clearance vehicles. Zero trip meter.
0.0 ▲		Continue to the west.
		GPS: N39°11.27′ W120°09.59′

▼ 0.0		Continue to the north.
3.9 ▲	TR	Road straight ahead is 16N71. Zero trip meter and turn right onto 16N73 and pass through seasonal closure gate. Road turns to graded dirt.
▼ 1.1	SO	Track on left is 16N53.
2.8 ▲	SO	Track on right is 16N53.

▼ 2.6	SO	Track on left is 16N73G.
1.3 ▲	SO	Track on right is 16N73G.
▼ 3.4	SO	Track on right is 16N73F.
0.5 ▲	SO	Track on left is 16N73F.
▼ 3.6	SO	Track on left.
0.3 ▲	SO	Track on right.
		GPS: N39°13.15′ W120°09.67′

▼ 3.9	SO	Track on right is 16N73E, spur to Mount Watson. Zero trip meter.
0.0 ▲		Continue to the southwest.
		GPS: N39°13.34′ W120°09.33′

Spur to Mount Watson

▼ 0.0		Proceed southeast on formed trail.
▼ 0.3	SO	Track on right.
▼ 0.4	SO	Start of shelf road.
▼ 1.2	SO	End of shelf road.
▼ 1.4	SO	Track on right.
▼ 1.5		Spur ends below Mount Watson with a view east of Lake Tahoe. A hiking trail continues to the northeast.

Watson Lake

GPS: N39°13.16' W120°08.25'

Continuation of Main Trail

▼ 0.0   Continue to the northeast.
0.6 ▲   BR Track on left is 16N73E, spur to Mount
             Watson. Zero trip meter.
             GPS: N39°13.34' W120°09.33'

▼ 0.6   BL Bear left onto FR 06. Road turns to
             graded dirt. Zero trip meter. Paved road
             ahead is the spur to Watson Lake.
0.0 ▲   Continue to the southwest. Road
             becomes paved.
             GPS: N39°13.51' W120°08.85'

Spur to Watson Lake

▼ 0.0   Proceed to the north.
▼ 0.3   TR Turn right onto small paved road 16N50.
             GPS: N39°13.65' W120°08.67'

▼ 0.9   Road ends at Watson Lake. A spur of
        the Tahoe Rim Trail comes in from the
        southwest at this point. In winter, a
        snowmobile route continues farther.
        GPS: N39°13.45' W120°08.21'

Continuation of Main Trail

▼ 0.0   Continue to the northwest and pass
        through closure gate.
3.8 ▲   SO Closure gate; then paved road on left is
             the spur to Watson Lake. Zero trip meter.
             GPS: N39°13.51' W120°08.85'

▼ 0.7   SO Track on right is Spocket Mountain
             Bike Trail.
3.1 ▲   SO Track on left is Spocket Mountain
             Bike Trail.
▼ 1.1   BL Track on right is 06-26.
2.7 ▲   BR Track on left is 06-26.
▼ 1.8   BR Track on left is closed.
2.0 ▲   BL Track on right is closed.
▼ 2.5   SO Track on left is 06-22.
1.3 ▲   BL Track on right is 06-22.
        GPS: N39°13.85' W120°09.51'

▼ 3.8   BR Track on left is 06-18. Zero trip meter.
0.0 ▲   Continue to the southeast on FR 06.

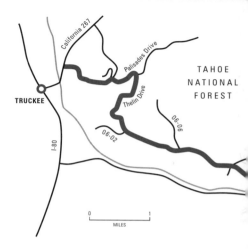

GPS: N39°14.39' W120°10.75'

▼ 0.0   Continue to the northwest on FR 06.
6.0 ▲   BL Track on right is 06-18. Zero trip meter.
▼ 0.3   SO Track on left.
5.7 ▲   SO Track on right.
▼ 0.4   SO Track on right.
5.6 ▲   SO Track on left.
▼ 0.8   SO Track on right; then track on left.
5.2 ▲   SO Track on right; then track on left.
▼ 1.1   SO Track on left and track on right.
4.9 ▲   SO Track on left and track on right.
▼ 1.4   SO Track on right.
4.6 ▲   SO Track on left.
▼ 1.6   SO Track on left.
4.4 ▲   SO Track on right.
▼ 1.9   SO Track on left.
4.1 ▲   SO Track on right.
▼ 2.6   SO Track on right.
3.4 ▲   SO Track on left.
        GPS: N39°16.16' W120°11.83'

▼ 2.8   SO Track on left; then second track on left.
3.2 ▲   SO Track on right; then second track
             on right.
▼ 2.9   SO Track on right.
3.1 ▲   SO Track on left.
▼ 3.4   SO Track on right.
2.6 ▲   SO Track on left.
▼ 3.7   SO 4-way intersection. Track on left and
             graded road on right.

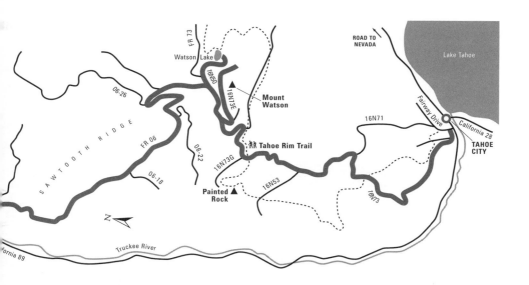

▼ 2.3 ▲	SO	4-way intersection. Track on right and graded road on left.		▼ 4.6	SO	Track on right is 06-06.
				1.4 ▲	SO	Track on left is 06-06.
		GPS: N39°16.97′ W120°11.86′				**GPS: N39°17.74′ W120°11.76′**

▼ 4.4	SO	Track on right.		▼ 5.6	SO	Track on left is 06-02.
1.6 ▲	SO	Track on left.		0.4 ▲	SO	Track on right is 06-02.

The spur climbs Mount Watson

LAKE TAHOE

The Lake Tahoe Basin began to form five to ten million years ago as a result of pull-apart faulting, which was so severe that it caused the earth's crust to break into massive blocks to the east and west of today's Tahoe Basin. The Sierra Nevada block to the west was uplifted and today includes Freel Peak at 10,891 feet and Monument Peak at 10,067 feet, on the basin's rim. The blocks uplifted to the east formed the Carson Range in Nevada. The blocks

Lake Tahoe in the distance

between the two ranges dropped to create a deep valley. Over time, rain, snowmelt, and run-off filled the valley's south end.

An estimated two million years ago, andesite lava flows from several volcanoes including Mount Pluto, north of the lake, cooled and dammed the northeastern end of the valley. Water collected in the enclosed basin. As the water level rose, it overflowed the lava dam and cut an outlet that became known as the Truckee River, which flows north and northeast to Pyramid Lake in Nevada. During the Ice Age, the vast snowpacks on the Sierra Nevada peaks froze to form glaciers that flowed down the mountain slopes. Glaciers also dammed the lake, raising its water level 800 feet above today's level. The terraces of sediments at the basin rim are evidence of the lake's higher levels.

Glaciers melted leaving piles of debris, or terminal moraines, that formed Emerald Bay,

Cascade Lake, and Fallen Leaf Lake. The water level waned after the glaciers melted, and a long drought caused shores to recede below their present level. Scientists have discovered tree trunks as much as 40 feet below today's surface, and studies revealed the trees were about a century old when they were drowned.

The lake's eastern shore is composed almost entirely of granite from the Sierra Nevada. Some volcanic rock can be found at Glenbrook Bay and Cave Rock. Between Crystal Bay and Tahoe City, the rock is volcanic, part of the lava flow that originally dammed the lake. Sediment covers the north shores, smoothing the landscape. The peaks of Carson Range to the east of the lake are smooth granite because the mountains, in the rain shadow of the towering Sierra Nevada, did not accumulate enough snow to create glaciers.

Lake Tahoe's deepest point is 1,645 feet near Crystal Bay. Its average depth is 989 feet, and it is the third deepest in North America, behind Oregon's Crater Lake (1,930 feet) and Canada's Great Slave Lake (2,010 feet), and tenth deepest in the world. Measuring roughly 22 miles long and 12 miles wide, Lake Tahoe holds 39 trillion gallons of water within its 71 miles of shoreline. Spread out, that volume would cover a flat area the size of California with 14 inches or supply each resident of the United States with 50 gallons daily for 5 years. The amount of water that evaporates from its 191-square-mile surface in 24 hours is enough to supply Los Angeles for one day. At 6,225 feet above sea level, it is the highest lake of its size in the United States. Thirty inches of average annual precipitation supplies Lake Tahoe, and 63 streams filtered by the granite-filled soil provide 300,000 acre-feet of water each year. Snowmelt keeps the lake cool, and it does not freeze because of its significant circulation. The surface temperature drops to 40 degrees during the winter and reaches nearly 70 degrees in the summer. Below 700 feet the temperature is constant at 39 degrees.

Although Lake Tahoe is clear to depths of up to 75 feet, the survival of its pristine waters is threatened. New development near the lake has increased the amount of sediment entering the water. These sediments carry nutrients into the lake that stimulate algae growth, which threaten to cloud its waters. Likewise, treated sewage water released into the lake stimulates algae grow. As a result, the waste from towns and businesses around the lake is treated and diverted from flowing directly into the lake. Lake Tahoe is also particularly susceptible to pollution because of its large volume and limited drainage. This means the lake can harbor pollutants for centuries before they circulate out. A dam in Tahoe City, at the outlet of the Truckee River, regulates its water level.

Seasonal temperature swings within the Tahoe Basin in the subalpine life zone have created flora and fauna unique to the region. For example, Clarkias, a member of the sunflower family, and buckwheat grow nowhere else on earth. Ponderosa, lodgepole, sugar pine, and Sierra juniper are a few of the tree species here. Wildlife includes black bears, pine martens, mule deer, and marmots. And likely birds to be seen are Calliope and broad-tailed humming birds, pygmy nuthatches, and western tanagers. The kokanee salmon is an interesting Lake Tahoe resident. Unlike most salmon, which migrate to the ocean to spawn, this fish lives its entire life within the lake, spawning nearby in its shallow tributaries.

▼ 5.7	SO	Track on left. Road becomes paved.
0.3 ▲	SO	Road turns to graded dirt. Track on right.
▼ 6.0	TR	Seasonal closure gate; then turn right onto paved Thelin Drive. Zero trip meter.
0.0 ▲		Continue to the southwest and pass through seasonal closure gate.
		GPS: N39°18.81′ W120°11.28′

▼ 0.0		Continue to the southeast on Thelin Drive.
2.3 ▲	TL	Turn left onto paved FR 06 and zero trip meter.
▼ 0.9	TL	T-intersection with Palisades Drive.
1.4 ▲	TR	Turn right onto Thelin Drive.
		GPS: N39°18.56′ W120°10.44′

▼ 1.3	TL	4-way intersection. Turn left onto Ponderosa Drive.
1.0 ▲	TR	4-way intersection. Turn right onto Palisades Drive.
		GPS: N39°18.87′ W120°10.61′

▼ 1.9	TR	Turn right onto Palisades Drive.
0.4 ▲	TL	Turn left onto Ponderosa Drive.
▼ 2.3		Trail ends on California 267. Turn left for the center of Truckee and I-80.
0.0 ▲		Trail starts on California 267, 0.4 miles south of the center of Truckee. Zero trip meter and turn south on Palisades Drive.
		GPS: N39°19.58′ W120°10.58′

NORTHERN SIERRA #20

Soda Springs Road

STARTING POINT Donner Pass Road, 0.8 miles south of I-80

FINISHING POINT FR 96 at the northeastern end of French Meadows Reservoir

TOTAL MILEAGE 26.4 miles, plus 2.1-mile spur to Snow Mountain Overlook and 1.8-mile spur to Talbot Campground

UNPAVED MILEAGE 24.3 miles, plus spurs

DRIVING TIME 4 hours

ELEVATION RANGE 5,400–7,300 feet

USUALLY OPEN May to October

BEST TIME TO TRAVEL May to October

DIFFICULTY RATING 2 from Soda Springs to The Cedars; 3 from The Cedars to French Meadows Reservoir

SCENIC RATING 9

REMOTENESS RATING +0

Special Attractions

■ Remains of the Lost Emigrant Mine.
■ Boating, angling, and camping at French Meadows Reservoir.
■ Spectacular views of the Royal Gorge from several points along the trail.

History

Soda Springs, for which this trail is named, are located on the upper reaches of the North Fork of the American River, east of The Cedars community. Sacramento businessmen Mark Hopkins and Leland Stanford established the summer resort in the early 1870s, calling it Hopkins Springs. Hopkins and Stanford were businessmen from Sacramento who, with Charles Crocker and Collis P. Huntington, made up the Big Four, financiers behind the construction of the Central Pacific Railroad in the 1860s.

Early visitors to the springs traveled by train to what was then called Tinker's Station. From there it was a bumpy stage ride down Onion Creek to the resort. J. A. Tinker operated the freight service between Soda Springs and the various mines on Foresthill Divide. His name is also attached to a prominent landmark of Tinker Knob, set high above the old springs to the east of the trail.

The southern section of Soda Springs Road follows an early emigrant trail that developed from west to east. It roughly went up the Foresthill Divide through Robertson Flat, past the Lost Emigrant Mine to Soda Springs, before crossing sharply over the Sierra Crest to Squaw Valley.

In the 1860s, mining at the upper end of French Meadows was far from fruitful. The name Picayune Valley reflects the paltry sum extracted from the location. A picayune is a Spanish coin worth half a real, a rather small amount.

Serena Creek cuts a deep gorge as it drops sharply to join the North Fork of the American River

Description

The trail starts in the settlement of Soda Springs and initially travels along a paved road to Serene Lakes (shown as Ice Lakes on some maps), where it turns to graded dirt. It passes some of the groomed cross-country ski trails maintained by the Royal Gorge Cross Country Ski Resort in winter. The start of the trail is also near Donner Summit, a popular rock climbing area with approximately 400 routes of every skill level, including bouldering opportunities, sport routes, and multi-pitch crack climbing. Difficulties range from easy scrambles to expert routes rated as high as 5.13b.

The route briefly follows Serena Creek, which drops into a deep rocky gorge that feeds the North Fork of the American River. There are good views of the open forest, scattered firs, and rocky outcrops at the gorge.

The route passes through a lot of private property. Right of way is restricted to the county road and stopping is not encouraged, especially around The Cedars. Please respect the rights of the property owners as you pass through this vicinity and make sure you are within public lands before camping or diverging from the main trail.

After crossing the North Fork of the American River, a lumber company owns the forest, and access to side trails may be restricted at times. A worthwhile side trip is the 3-rated loop to a stunning viewpoint over Snow Peak and the North Fork of the American River through Royal Gorge.

The trail passes the southern end of the Palisade Creek Trail, which is for hikers only; equestrians are not permitted. The hiking route north from here to the North Fork of the American River is not maintained by the forest service. The northern portion of the Palisade Creek Trail is rated extremely difficult with many steep climbs. Another major hiking trail that intersects this route is the Tevis Cup Trail, which leads into the Granite Chief Wilderness.

Tinker Knob rises high above Soda Springs

A second worthwhile detour is a short side trail that leads to the Lost Emigrant Mine. The turn is unmarked and easy to miss. This rough 4-rated spur leads 0.4 miles down a loose, moguled hill to remains of the mine. Two old cabins, one predominately timber and the other predominantly tin, are all that remain.

The main trail, which becomes rougher than the northern section, turns off Soda Springs Road and descends to enter a state wildlife refuge. No hunting or firearms are allowed in the refuge. If you wish to transport firearms or bows through the refuge they must be unloaded, unstrung, and either dismantled or carried in a case. No camping is allowed except in designated areas.

The trail ends at the northeastern end of French Meadows Reservoir. There are three campgrounds around the lake, plus a walk-in site about a mile down the hiking trail around the north side of the lake. Because of the refuge, bears abound in the region so campers should take the necessary precautions.

The trail from the intersection of Soda Springs Road and Foresthill Road to French Meadows Reservoir is a marked snowmobile route in winter that continues to the dam at the western end of the lake, a total distance of 7.8 miles. The snowmobile trail is part of the Mosquito Ridge Trail. It intersects with the groomed Soda Springs Trail and continues toward Duncan Peak and Robinson Flat.

Current Road Information

Tahoe National Forest
Truckee Ranger District
10646 Donner Pass Road
Truckee, CA 96161
(530) 587-3558

Tahoe National Forest
Foresthill Ranger District
22830 Foresthill Road
Foresthill, CA 95631
(530) 367-2224

Map References

BLM   Truckee

USFS   Tahoe National Forest
USGS   1:24,000   Soda Springs, Norden, Granite Chief, Royal Gorge
1:100,000 Truckee
Maptech CD-ROM: High Sierra/Tahoe
Northern California Atlas & Gazetteer, p. 81
California Road & Recreation Atlas, p. 66

Route Directions

▼ 0.0   From the Soda Springs exit on I-80, zero trip meter on the south side of the freeway and proceed 0.8 miles east on Donner Pass Road. Zero trip meter and turn south on paved Soda Springs Road, following the signpost to Serene Lakes. Cross over railroad. Remain on paved road, ignoring turns to right and left for the next 2.1 miles.
6.3 ▲   Cross over railroad; then trail ends at Donner Pass Road in Soda Springs. Turn left for I-80; turn right for Norden.
          GPS: N39°19.41' W120°22.70'

▼ 0.1 SO Soda Springs Alpine Resort on right.
6.2 ▲ SO Soda Springs Alpine Resort on left.
▼ 0.8 SO Royal Gorge Cross Country Ski Resort on right. Trails are privately owned and part of the resort.
5.5 ▲ SO Royal Gorge Cross Country Ski Resort on left.
▼ 2.1 SO Road turns to graded dirt. Serene Road and Serene Lakes on right.
4.2 ▲ SO Road becomes paved. Serene Road and Serene Lakes on left.
          GPS: N39°17.67' W120°22.90'

▼ 2.4 SO Three Nordic ski trails on right and one on the left.
3.9 ▲ SO Three Nordic ski trails on left and one on the right.
▼ 2.5 SO Leaving Royal Gorge Nordic ski track system.
3.8 ▲ SO Entering Royal Gorge Nordic ski track system. Trails are privately owned and part of the resort.
▼ 3.3 SO Two tracks on left. Views on right into the deep gorge of Serena Creek.
3.0 ▲ SO Two tracks on right. Views on left into the deep gorge of Serena Creek.

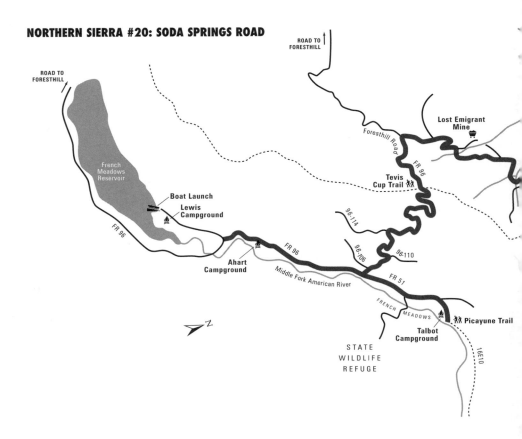

▼ 4.2	SO	Track on right.
2.1 ▲	SO	Track on left.
▼ 5.9	SO	Cross over creek.
0.4 ▲	SO	Cross over creek.
▼ 6.1	SO	Well-used track on right.
0.2 ▲	SO	Well-used track on left.
▼ 6.3	SO	Track on left to Onion Creek Snow Survey Cabin and Onion Creek Experimental Forest; then track on right; then cross over Onion Creek on bridge. Zero trip meter at bridge.
0.0 ▲		Continue to the north. Track on left; then track on right to Onion Creek Snow Survey Cabin and Onion Creek Experimental Forest.
		GPS: N39°16.54' W120°21.70'

▼ 0.0		Continue to the south.
3.0 ▲	SO	Cross over Onion Creek on bridge and zero trip meter.
▼ 0.2	SO	Track on left.
2.8 ▲	SO	Track on right.

▼ 0.8	SO	Cross over creek.
2.2 ▲	SO	Cross over creek.
▼ 1.6	SO	Track on left under The Cedars archway.
1.4 ▲	SO	Track on right under The Cedars archway.
		GPS: N39°15.31' W120°21.17'

▼ 1.8	SO	Cross through Cedar Creek.
1.2 ▲	SO	Cross through Cedar Creek.
▼ 2.2	BR	Private road on left.
0.8 ▲	BL	Private road on right.
▼ 2.3	SO	Cross over North Fork American River on bridge. Soda Springs are upstream along the river.
0.7 ▲	SO	Cross over North Fork American River on bridge. Soda Springs are upstream along the river.
		GPS: N39°14.85' W120°21.08'

▼ 2.5	SO	Cross through wash.
0.5 ▲	SO	Cross through wash.
▼ 3.0	SO	Track on left is Tevis Cup Trail. Zero trip meter and follow the sign to French

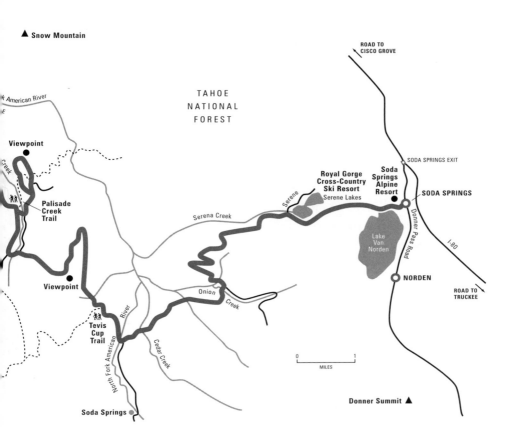

▲ Snow Mountain

ROAD TO CISCO GROVE

TAHOE NATIONAL FOREST

SODA SPRINGS EXIT

Viewpoint

Royal Gorge Cross-Country Ski Resort

Soda Springs Alpine Resort

SODA SPRINGS

Palisade Creek Trail

Serena Creek

Serene Lakes

Lake Van Norden

NORDEN

Viewpoint

Onion Creek

Donner Pass Road

I-80

ROAD TO TRUCKEE

Tevis Cup Trail

North Fork American River

Cedar Creek

MILES

Donner Summit ▲

Soda Springs

Meadows Reservoir.

0.0 ▲   Continue to the northeast.

GPS: N39°14.66′ W120°21.77′

▼ 0.0   Continue to the south.

4.3 ▲ SO Track on right is Tevis Cup Trail. Zero trip meter.

▼ 0.2 SO Track on left.

4.1 ▲ SO Track on right.

▼ 0.3 SO Track on right.

4.0 ▲ SO Track on left.

▼ 0.4 SO Cross over creek.

3.9 ▲ SO Cross over creek.

▼ 0.5 SO Track on left.

3.8 ▲ SO Track on right.

▼ 1.5 BL Track on right; then second track on right.

2.8 ▲ BR Track on left; then second track on left.

GPS: N39°14.58′ W120°23.35′

▼ 2.1 SO Track on right.

2.2 ▲ SO Track on left.

▼ 2.4 SO Viewpoint on left overlooks North Fork American River, Soda Springs, and behind them Mount Lincoln, Anderson Peak, Tinker Knob, Silver Peak, Granite Chief, and Needle Peak.

1.9 ▲ SO Viewpoint on right overlooks North Fork American River, Soda Springs, and behind them Mount Lincoln, Anderson Peak, Tinker Knob, Silver Peak, Granite Chief, and Needle Peak.

GPS: N39°14.23′ W120°22.60′

▼ 2.6 SO Track on left and track on right.

1.7 ▲ SO Track on left and track on right.

▼ 2.8 SO Track on right.

1.5 ▲ SO Track on left.

▼ 3.4 SO Track on left; then cross over Wabena Creek; then second track on left.

0.9 ▲ SO Track on right; then cross over Wabena Creek; then second track on right.

GPS: N39°13.51′ W120°23.14′

▼ 3.8 SO Track on left.
0.5 ▲ SO Track on right.
▼ 4.3 SO Track on right is the spur to Snow Mountain Overlook; then track on right is Palisade Creek Trail. Entering Tahoe National Forest. Zero trip meter at Palisade Creek Trail sign.
0.0 ▲ Continue to the east. Immediately track on left is the spur to Snow Mountain Overlook.
GPS: N39°13.71' W120°23.99'

Spur to Snow Mountain Overlook

▼ 0.0 At the track a short distance east of the Palisade Creek Trail sign, zero trip meter and turn north on unmarked formed trail and cross through Wabena Creek; then track on left.
▼ 0.1 TL Track on right.
▼ 0.25 SO 4-way intersection.
GPS: N39°13.80' W120°23.94'

▼ 0.55 BR Track on left is end of loop. Bear right and start loop.
GPS: N39°13.98' W120°24.22'

▼ 0.8 TL Track on right goes 0.5 miles to clearing and viewpoint. Palisade Creek Trail crosses.
GPS: N39°14.00' W120°24.51'

▼ 1.4 SO Viewpoint. To the west is Royal Gorge and Snow Mountain.
GPS: N39°13.87' W120°25.03'

▼ 2.1 End of loop. Turn right to exit.
GPS: N39°13.98' W120°24.22'

Continuation of Main Trail

▼ 0.0 Continue to the southwest
3.3 ▲ SO Track on left is Palisade Creek Trail. Leaving Tahoe National Forest. Zero trip meter at Palisade Creek Trail sign.
GPS: N39°13.71' W120°23.99'
▼ 0.7 SO Viewpoint on right of Snow Mountain and Royal Gorge.
2.6 ▲ SO Viewpoint on left of Snow Mountain and Royal Gorge.

GPS: N39°13.46' W120°24.56'

▼ 1.3 SO Track on left.
2.0 ▲ SO Track on right.
▼ 1.6 SO Cross through creek.
1.7 ▲ SO Cross through creek.
▼ 1.8 SO Cross through creek.
1.5 ▲ SO Cross through creek.
▼ 2.4 SO Track on right.
0.9 ▲ SO Track on left.
GPS: N39°12.57' W120°25.22'

▼ 3.1 SO Track on left.
0.2 ▲ SO Track on right.
▼ 3.2 SO Track on left.
0.1 ▲ SO Track on right.
▼ 3.3 SO Cross over creek; then track on right and track on left. Intersection is unmarked. Zero trip meter. Track on right goes 0.4 miles to the Lost Emigrant Mine. It crosses the clearing, descends the hill to the mine, and continues up to the diggings.
0.0 ▲ Continue to the east and cross over creek.
GPS: N39°11.93' W120°25.48'

▼ 0.0 Continue to the west.
1.6 ▲ SO Track on right and track on left. Intersection is unmarked. Zero trip meter. Track on left goes 0.4 miles to the Lost Emigrant Mine. It crosses the clearing, descends the hill to the mine, and continues up to the diggings.
▼ 1.0 SO Track on left and track on right.
0.6 ▲ SO Track on left and track on right.
GPS: N39°11.64' W120°25.82'

▼ 1.6 TL T-intersection with graded Foresthill Road. To the right goes to Foresthill, to the left goes to French Meadows. Zero trip meter and follow the sign to French Meadows.
0.0 ▲ Continue to the northwest.
GPS: N39°11.21' W120°26.02'

▼ 0.0 Continue to the northeast on FR 96.
5.4 ▲ TR End of FR 96. Foresthill Road continues straight ahead to Foresthill. Zero trip meter and turn right onto graded Soda Springs Road, following the sign to

Soda Springs.

▼ 1.1   SO   Entering state wildlife refuge. Camping and campfires in designated sites only. Tevis Cup Trail crosses on left and right.

4.3 ▲   SO   Tevis Cup Trail crosses on left and right. Leaving state wildlife refuge.

▼ 3.1   SO   Cross over creek.

2.3 ▲   SO   Cross over creek.

▼ 3.6   SO   Cross over creek.

1.8 ▲   SO   Cross over creek.

▼ 4.0   SO   Track on right is 96-114.

1.4 ▲   SO   Track on left is 96-114.
         GPS: N39°10.70′ W120°24.23′

▼ 4.8   BR   Track on left is 96-110.

0.6 ▲   BL   Track on right is 96-110.

▼ 5.1   SO   Cross over creek.

0.3 ▲   SO   Cross over creek.

▼ 5.2   SO   Cross over creek.

0.2 ▲   SO   Cross over creek.

▼ 5.3   SO   Track on right is 96-106.

0.1 ▲   SO   Track on left is 96-106.

▼ 5.4   TR   T-intersection. Graded road on left is FR 51, spur to Talbot USFS Campground. Zero trip meter and turn right following the sign to French Meadows Recreation Area.

0.0 ▲   Continue to the northwest.
         GPS: N39°10.18′ W120°23.47′

Spur to Talbot Campground

▼ 0.0   Proceed north on FR 51, following sign to Talbot Campground.

▼ 0.1   SO   Track on right.

▼ 0.2   SO   Track on left.

▼ 0.7   SO   Track on left.

▼ 0.8   SO   Track on right.

▼ 1.4   BR   Gravel road on left. Follow sign to Granite Chief Wilderness and Talbot Campground.
         GPS: N39°11.23′ W120°22.76′

▼ 1.7   SO   Picayune Hiking Trailhead and parking area on left. Trail heads into the Granite Chief Wilderness.
         GPS: N39°11.37′ W120°22.42′

▼ 1.8   Spur ends at Talbot Campground. Trail

16E10, part of the Western States Trail, for hikers and horses, on left leads to Picayune Valley and the Granite Chief Wilderness.
         GPS: N39°11.32′ W120°22.33′

Continuation of Main Trail

▼ 0.0   Continue to the south on FR 96.

2.5 ▲   TL   Graded road FR 51 straight ahead is the spur to Talbot USFS Campground. Zero trip meter and turn left on FR 96, following the sign to Soda Springs.
         GPS: N39°10.18′ W120°23.47′

▼ 1.1   SO   Two tracks on left.

1.4 ▲   SO   Two tracks on right.

▼ 1.3   SO   Track on right is 96-96.

1.2 ▲   SO   Track on left is 96-96.

▼ 1.5   SO   Cross over creek.

1.0 ▲   SO   Cross over creek.

▼ 1.8   SO   Track on left is 96-91 into Ahart USFS Campground. Track continues past campground.

0.7 ▲   SO   Track on right is 96-91 into Ahart USFS Campground. Track continues past campground.
         GPS: N39°08.76′ W120°24.44′

▼ 2.0   SO   Track on right is 96-90.

0.5 ▲   SO   Track on left is 96-90.

▼ 2.1   SO   Cross over creek.

0.4 ▲   SO   Cross over creek.

▼ 2.5   Trail ends at the start of the paved road at the northeastern end of French Meadows Reservoir. Road on right goes 1.4 miles to Lewis Campground and boat ramp. Continue straight ahead on FR 96 following the sign to Foresthill, 38 miles, or retrace your steps to Soda Springs.

0.0 ▲   Trail commences on FR 96 at the northeastern end of French Meadows Reservoir, 38 miles east of Foresthill. Zero trip meter at the end of the paved road at the intersection with the road to Lewis Campground and boat ramp. Turn northwest on graded gravel FR 96.
         GPS: N39°08.26′ W120°24.62′

Henness Pass Road

STARTING POINT I-80 in Verdi, NV
FINISHING POINT California 49 in Camptonville
TOTAL MILEAGE 76 miles, plus 1-mile spur to Little Truckee River Bridge
UNPAVED MILEAGE 67.3 miles
DRIVING TIME 1 day minimum, 2 days preferable
ELEVATION RANGE 2,700–7,000 feet
USUALLY OPEN May to November
BEST TIME TO TRAVEL May to November
DIFFICULTY RATING 2
SCENIC RATING 10
REMOTENESS RATING +0

Special Attractions

■ Long, easy road for high-clearance vehicles that follows much of the route of the historic Henness Pass Road.
■ Trail passes many historic stage stop sites.
■ Fishing and camping at Stampede Reservoir, Milton Reservoir, and Jackson Meadow Reservoir.

History

Henness Pass Road developed when transportation routes to the newfound wealth of the West were at a crucial stage. The few settlements along proposed corridors stood to catch the passing lucrative trade. Many vied, many invested, and many indulged in tall promotions, but few lasted. Henness Pass was one of the more notable east-west routes that drew heavy traffic over the northern reaches of the Sierra Nevada. The route was less challenging to stagecoaches and freight wagons than some proposed trails, yet in the long run, it lost out to a more favored route through El Dorado County to the south.

D. B. Scott surveyed this wagon road in 1855, in a bid by interested parties to attract overland emigrants to the Middle and North Yuba Rivers and the various towns in Yuba and Nevada Counties. Patrick Henness and his associate Jackson may have discovered the pass in 1850, or earlier in 1849. The promoted route would take travelers west from the Truckee River, on the California border, across the mountains to Camptonville. Construction of the wagon road took place in 1861.

From 1860 to 1868, Henness Pass Road was heavily used by stagecoaches and freighters because of the 1859 discovery of the Comstock lode at Virginia City, then in Utah Territory, and because it was before the completion of the Central Pacific Railroad. It became necessary to regulate traffic flow at times. Freight haulers could travel during the day, while stagecoaches were restricted to travel at night. Mountain House, 2,000 feet above Goodyears Bar and the present route of California 49, was a welcome sight to miners and travelers alike. Dan T. Cole built an inn on this spectacular ridge in 1860. By 1890, this popular stopping point had grown to a three-story guesthouse with a dance hall and dining room. Many such roadhouse establishments sprang up along this wagon road over the decades. Cornish House, Moore's Stage Station and hotel, Sleighville House, and Sardine Valley House are just some of the names that linger along this historic wagon road.

Verdi, Nevada, at the eastern end of the road, was the site of the first train robbery in the West. In November 1870, school superintendent John Chapman led a band of six men to the town, where they boarded the Central Pacific, still in its first year of operation. They took over the train and uncoupled the cars, keeping just the engine and express car, which carried more than $40,000 in gold. They abandoned the train farther south, in the Truckee River Canyon and made off with the loot. The unhitched railcars coasted downhill to the abandoned engine. The train continued to Truckee to report the daring robbery. All members of the gang were caught within two days, before they had time to spend the money.

Description

Henness Pass Road is a long scenic trail that passes a number of historic sites through a variety of scenery. In its entirety, the trail is suit-

A short hike off Henness Pass Road leads to waterfalls in the Middle Yuba River's Box Canyon

Sierra Buttes can be seen to the north of Henness Pass Road

able for high-clearance vehicles. The forest service has a marked auto tour for the route, with numbered stops at points of interest. The trail described below follows part of this route, but it diverges onto smaller trails and spurs that more closely reflect the original wagon road.

The trail leaves Verdi, Nevada, and crosses the Truckee River and California state line before climbing along a graded dirt road to First Summit—the first point on the auto tour. The trail passes through the 7,310-acre area of the Crystal Burn Fire of August 1994. Currently, the area is being reforested. At First Summit passenger vehicles can follow a graded road around the side of the ridge, but high-clearance vehicles can descend into Dog Valley to pass one of the campsites used by emigrants. The trail rejoins the main graded road via a series of small, formed trails at Second Summit. Northern Sierra #22: Boca Ridge and Verdi Peak Trail touches here before veering off again.

Immediately south of the trail, Stampede Reservoir is a good place to camp and fish for kokanee salmon and rainbow, brown, or Mackinaw trout. There is a boat launch 2 miles west of Stampede Dam on the south side of the lake. The route passes the small Davies Creek USFS Campground. Other campgrounds can be found to the south along CR 270, which travels down the eastern side of the reservoir. Dirt tracks lead to the water's edge at several points, but these are for day-use only; camping is restricted to developed campgrounds.

The auto tour marks a number of historic stage stop sites along the original route. Most of these are nothing more than sites, but they show how busy the road must have been in earlier times. The stop at Kyburz Flat, immediately east of California 89, is a great place to take a break. A short, handicap-accessible boardwalk leads around the site of Moore's Stage Station. The Kyburz Petroglyph is on the south side of the road. It is broken into three pieces—the picture in the brochure shows it in one piece. Take care not to inadvertently walk over it. The petroglyph consists of many small pecks in the rock and is best viewed late in the day when the angle of the sun makes the pockets stand out clearly. A short spur leads to Wheelers Sheep Camp, where an old Basque oven is now protected by a new wooden lean-to. The oven is functional, but those wishing to use it are asked to contact the forest service first. The camp has a couple picnic tables set in the shade and a spring at the south end of Kyburz Flat.

West of Kyburz Flat, the trail joins paved California 89 before turning off onto paved FR 07 and heading toward Jackson Meadow Reservoir. The original Henness Pass Road continues straight ahead at this point and crosses private property to travel down to the site of a bridge over the Little Truckee River. The old bridge, washed out in the 1980s, has not been rebuilt. A spur from the original trail accesses the bridge from the west side of the Little Truckee River along a county road. This spur passes through private property, but you can see an old line shack standing on the west side of the road. The timber building contains a cookhouse, covered verandah, and upstairs bunkhouse.

The main route crosses Little Truckee Summit, the nexus of a popular network of snowmobile trails. From the summit, you can access popular winter destinations such as Jackson Meadow Reservoir, Meadow Lake, Mount Lola, and Haypress Valley. There are three marked, groomed snowmobile routes that total approximately 90 miles. Overnight camping is permitted at Little Truckee Summit between November 16 and April 14.

The main route then turns off the paved road onto graded dirt roads that run slightly south of paved FR 07. The spur to the Little Truckee River bridge leads off from this point. The route passes through Perazzo Meadows and fords the shallow Perazzo Canyon Creek. Just south of the trail, some waterfalls on the Little Truckee River make for a pleasant stop.

Henness Pass (6,920 feet) is located on paved FR 07 east of Jackson Meadow Reservoir. Those taking two days to travel the trail may wish to take advantage of the forest service campgrounds west of the pass around Jackson Meadow Reservoir. The developed campgrounds are close to the lake and offer plenty of shade and lake views. Black bears are common in the area, and some of the campgrounds offer bear-proof boxes for food storage. (Be advised: Use them.) Jackson Meadow Reservoir is popular with anglers, who fish for rainbow and brown trout. The next reservoir along the trail, Milton Lake, is much smaller and has a few backcountry campsites along its shores. The lake has a two pan-size trout limit; larger trout must be released to provide natural control of non-game fish that otherwise threaten to overwhelm the trout.

The graded road offers many spectacular vistas along its length. Possibly the most spectacular views, north over the Sierra Buttes, can be glimpsed along the next section of trail. These rugged buttes are prominently displayed on the far side of the North Yuba River. A worthwhile spur leads to the south from here to the Gates of the Antipodes and overlooks the deep Box Canyon No. 1 on the Middle Yuba River. The narrow, little-used spur leads partway down the side of the ridge and finishes at a collapsed two-story log cabin. The origins of the cabin are unknown, but it is likely that it was associated with mining since long-abandoned and collapsed shafts are nearby. The cabin may have been a halfway point for miners traveling the long route up from the river. The spur travels a narrow, rough shelf road that is rated a 4 for difficulty. The turnaround at the end is tight; longer vehicles may wish to turn on the switchback 0.1 miles before the end. The coordinates of the cabin are GPS: N39°31.51' W120°40.06'.

The Henness Pass route splits into two shortly after the spur. The lower, paved road takes travelers out to California 49 via Forest City. The upper road is still graded dirt, and travels past the site of Mountain House and continues along the ridge tops to finish on California 49 in Camptonville.

A final worthwhile stop near the end of the trail can be found 7 miles south on California 49. The 100-foot-long Oregon Creek Covered Bridge, located a short distance north of North San Juan, stands at the confluence of Oregon Creek and the Middle Yuba River. A day-use picnic area near the bridge makes for a wonderful stop.

Current Road Information

Tahoe National Forest
Sierraville Ranger District
317 South Lincoln Street
Sierraville, CA 96126
(530) 994-3401

Tahoe National Forest
Yuba River Ranger District
15924 Highway 49
Camptonville, CA 95922
(530) 288-3231

Map References

BLM   Reno (NV), Portola, Truckee,
       Yuba City
USFS Toiyabe National Forest, Tahoe
       National Forest
USGS 1:24,000 Verdi (NV), Dog
       Valley, Sardine Peak, Sierraville,
       Independence Lake, Webber Peak,
       Sattley, English Mtn., Haypress
       Valley, Sierra City, Downieville,
       Alleghany, Pike, Camptonville
       1:100,000 Reno (NV), Portola,
       Truckee, Yuba City
Maptech CD-ROM: High Sierra/Tahoe
Nevada Atlas & Gazetteer, p. 42
Northern California Atlas & Gazetteer,
     pp. 71, 81, 70, 80, 79
California Road & Recreation Atlas,
     pp. 61, 60

Route Directions

▼ 0.0   From the intersection of Third Street and Bridge Street in Verdi, just off I-80 in Nevada, zero trip meter and turn northwest onto Bridge Street, which is signposted to Dog Valley Road.
3.7 ▲   Trail ends in Verdi, NV in the center of town. Turn left for I-80 and Reno.
      GPS: N39°31.14′ W119°59.28′

▼ 0.4 SO Cross over Truckee River on bridge.

3.3 ▲ SO Cross over Truckee River on bridge.
▼ 0.6 BR Bear right onto Dog Valley Road.
3.1 ▲ BL Bear left onto Bridge Street.
▼ 0.7 SO Crystal Peak Cemetery on right.
3.0 ▲ SO Crystal Peak Cemetery on left.
      GPS: N39°31.50′ W119°59.86′

▼ 0.9 SO California state line. Road is now Sierra County Road 868. Remain on Dog Valley Road (Henness Pass Road).
2.8 ▲ SO Nevada state Line.
      GPS: N39°31.49′ W120°00.00′

▼ 1.5 SO Road turns to graded dirt. Enter Toiyabe National Forest. Road is now marked as 002. Seasonal closure gate.
2.2 ▲ SO Seasonal closure gate. Road is now paved. Leaving Toiyabe National Forest.
▼ 3.0 SO Track on right; then track on left.
0.7 ▲ SO Track on right; then track on left.
▼ 3.7 SO Track on left is Northern Sierra #22: Boca Ridge and Verdi Peak Trail (FR 074). Information board on right and track on right. Zero trip meter.
0.0 ▲   Continue to the southeast.
      GPS: N39°32.91′ W120°02.28′

▼ 0.0 BR First Summit (auto tour stop 22). Bear right onto graded road 002 following signs to Dog Valley. Graded road on left is 027 to Stampede Dam via Second Summit. Proceed west on lower, graded road. Several tracks on right. Passenger vehicles should bear left via 027 at this point and rejoin the main trail in 2.5 miles at Second Summit.
3.0 ▲ SO First Summit (auto tour stop 22). Several tracks on left; then graded road on right is 027 to Stampede Dam; then track on left at information board. Track on right is Northern Sierra #22: Boca Ridge and Verdi Peak Trail (FR 074). Zero trip meter.
▼ 0.7 BL Bear left onto 012A. Track straight ahead is 002 and track on right is 010, which goes 0.4 miles into Dog Valley to a marker commemorating early travelers along this route. The marker post

is located on the left of track 010, on the far side of the creek at GPS: N39°33.09' W120°02.63'. It can be hard to spot.

2.3 ▲ SO Bear right onto 002 and head uphill. Track on left is 002 and track straight ahead is 010, which goes 0.4 miles into Dog Valley to a marker commemorating early travelers along this route. The marker post is located on the left of track 010, on the far side of the creek at GPS: N39°33.09' W120°02.63'. It can be hard to spot.
GPS: N39°32.91' W120°02.99'

▼ 0.9 SO Cross through Dog Creek; then track on left.
2.1 ▲ SO Track on right; then cross through Dog Creek.

▼ 1.4 TL T-intersection with trail 012. Camping area on left.
1.6 ▲ BR Camping area on right. Turn right onto 012A.
GPS: N39°32.64' W120°03.60'

▼ 1.5 BR Track on left to campsite.
1.5 ▲ BL Track on right to campsite.

▼ 1.9 TL T-intersection with graded road 009. Turn left; then track on left.
1.1 ▲ TR Track on right; then turn right onto unmarked formed trail 012. Graded road 009 continues straight ahead.
GPS: N39°32.51' W120°04.06'

▼ 3.0 TR Second Summit (auto tour stop 21). Turn right onto 027 and cross cattle guard. Two tracks ahead are both Northern Sierra #22: Boca Ridge and Verdi Peak Trail. Zero trip meter and bear right onto graded road 002, following sign to Boca Reservoir.
0.0 ▲ Continue to the northwest, entering Toiyabe National Forest.
GPS: N39°31.57 W120°04.14'

▼ 0.0 Continue to the south, entering Tahoe National Forest. Track on left and track on right.
1.8 ▲ TL Track on left and track on right. Second Summit (auto tour stop 21). Two tracks on right before and after cattle guard are both Northern Sierra #22: Boca Ridge and Verdi Peak Trail. Zero trip meter and turn left onto small,

The Middle Yuba River flows into Milton Reservoir

unmarked trail 009. Passenger vehicles should remain on main graded road 027 and rejoin the trail in 2.5 miles at First Summit.

▼ 0.6 SO Track on right.
1.2 ▲ SO Track on left.
▼ 1.6 SO Track on right.
0.2 ▲ SO Track on left.
▼ 1.7 SO Track on left.
0.1 ▲ SO Track on right.
▼ 1.8 SO Paved road on left is CR 894 to Stampede Reservoir and I-80. Follow sign for Sardine Valley and zero trip meter. This is auto tour stop 20.
0.0 ▲ Continue to the northeast on CR 860.
  GPS: N39°30.41′ W120°05.47′

▼ 0.0 Continue to the southwest on CR 860.
3.1 ▲ SO Paved road on right is CR 894 to Stampede Reservoir and I-80. Follow sign for Verdi and zero trip meter. This is auto tour stop 20.
▼ 0.2 SO Track on right through gate goes to Camp 21 site.
2.9 ▲ SO Track on left through gate goes to Camp 21 site.
▼ 0.3 SO Cross over Davies Creek twice. Camp in designated sites only.
2.8 ▲ SO Cross over Davies Creek twice.
▼ 0.4 SO Davies Creek USFS Campground on left; then track on left for day use only.
2.7 ▲ SO Track on right for day use only; then Davies Creek USFS Campground on right.
  GPS: N39°30.39′ W120°05.90′

▼ 0.6 BR Graded road on left goes to Stampede Reservoir—day use only.
2.5 ▲ BL Graded road on right goes to Stampede Reservoir—day use only.
▼ 1.5 SO Track on right goes to Camp 21 site. The railroad camp site is at GPS: N39°30.86′ W120°06.44′. Entering Sardine Valley.
1.6 ▲ SO Track on left goes to Camp 21 site. The railroad camp site is at GPS: N39°30.86′ W120°06.44′. Leaving Sardine Valley.
▼ 2.1 BR Track on left.
1.0 ▲ SO Track on right.

GPS: N39°30.52′ W120°07.65′

▼ 3.1 TL Cross over Davies Creek; then graded road ahead goes to California 49. Turn left onto CR 450, following the sign for California 89, and zero trip meter. This is auto tour stop 19.
0.0 ▲ Continue to the south.
  GPS: N39°30.72′ W120°08.54′

▼ 0.0 Continue to the west and cross cattle guard.
5.8 ▲ TR Cattle guard; then T-intersection with CR 860. Graded road on left goes to California 49. Turn right onto CR 860, following the sign for Stampede Reservoir. Zero trip meter and cross over Davies Creek. This is auto tour stop 19.
▼ 1.3 SO Track on left.
4.5 ▲ SO Track on right.
▼ 1.8 SO Graded road on right is CR 650 to Sardine Peak Lookout. Follow sign to California 89. Cross over creek; then track on right. This is auto tour stop 18.
4.0 ▲ SO Track on left; then cross over creek; then graded road on left is CR 650 to Sardine Peak Lookout. This is auto tour stop 18. Follow sign to Stampede Reservoir.
  GPS: N39°30.69′ W120°10.55′

▼ 2.5 SO Track on right.
3.3 ▲ SO Track on left.
▼ 2.7 SO Track on left.
3.1 ▲ SO Track on right.
▼ 3.6 SO Track on right; then track on left is 450-20; then cattle guard; then track on right.
2.2 ▲ SO Track on left; then cattle guard; then track on right is 450-20; then track on left.
  GPS: N39°30.45′ W120°12.53′

▼ 4.1 SO Cross over creek.
1.7 ▲ SO Cross over creek.
▼ 4.7 SO Entering Kyburz Flat.
1.1 ▲ SO Leaving Kyburz Flat.
▼ 4.8 BR Graded road on left is 450-10. Remain on CR 450.

1.0 ▲ BL Graded road on right is 450-10. Remain on CR 450.

▼ 5.3 SO Track on left.

0.5 ▲ SO Track on right.

▼ 5.5 SO Cross over creek.

0.3 ▲ SO Cross over creek.

▼ 5.7 SO Leaving Kyburz Flat. Start of interpretive trail around the old stage stop site on right.

0.1 ▲ SO Entering Kyburz Flat. Start of interpretive trail around the old stage stop site on left.

GPS: N39°30.37' W120°14.49'

▼ 5.8 SO Kyburz Petroglyph on left, marked by a sign. This is auto tour stop 17. Track on right is 450-05, which goes 0.8 miles to Wheelers Sheep Camp (keep right at the only intersection along the spur). Zero trip meter.

0.0 ▲ Continue to the east.

GPS: N39°30.40' W120°14.56'

▼ 0.0 Continue to the west.

2.2 ▲ SO Kyburz Petroglyph on right, marked by a sign. This is auto tour stop 17. Track on left is 450-05, which goes 0.8 miles to Wheelers Sheep Camp (keep right at the only intersection along the spur). Zero trip meter.

▼ 1.0 TR Turn right onto paved California 89. The original Henness Pass Road continues straight ahead at this point, but this is now private property.

1.2 ▲ TL Turn left onto graded dirt CR 450, following sign to Kyburz Flat. The original Henness Pass Road went to the right at this point, but this is now private property.

GPS: N39°30.29' W120°15.69'

▼ 2.2 TL Little Truckee Summit. Turn left onto paved FR 07 following sign to Independence Lake. CR 451 on right. Zero trip meter.

0.0 ▲ Continue to the southeast.

GPS: N39°30.35' W120°16.89'

▼ 0.0 Continue to the south. Treasure Mountain Road (FR 05), a groomed snowmobile trail, on right; then Little Truckee Summit snowmobile trailhead on right.

2.0 ▲ TR Little Truckee Summit snowmobile trailhead on left; then Treasure Mountain Road (FR 05), a groomed snowmobile trail, on left; then 4-way intersection with California 89. Turn right onto paved California 89 following sign for Truckee. CR 451 is straight ahead. Zero trip meter.

▼ 1.4 TL Turn left onto graded dirt road 07-10, following sign to Independence Lake, and cross over aqueduct. This is the start of Northern Sierra #23: Independence Lake Trail.

0.6 ▲ TR Cross over aqueduct; then T-intersection with FR 07. Follow sign to California 89.

GPS: N39°29.54' W120°17.83'

▼ 1.6 SO Cross over Little Truckee River on bridge.

0.4 ▲ SO Cross over Little Truckee River on bridge.

▼ 2.0 SO Auto tour stop 16. Small track on left is a spur that follows the original route of Henness Pass Road to the Little Truckee River bridge. Old route also on right. Zero trip meter.

0.0 ▲ Continue to the west.

GPS: N39°29.45' W120°17.24'

Spur to Little Truckee River Bridge

▼ 0.0 Turn onto small formed trail and head northeast, away from graded gravel road. The turn is opposite auto tour stop 16.

▼ 0.4 TL Track on right; then turn left on graded gravel road. Track continues straight ahead.

GPS: N39°29.69' W120°16.90'

▼ 0.7 SO Track on left is private.

▼ 0.8 SO Old timber building on left is a line shack (there is no access to it because it is on private property).

▼ 0.9 TL Turn left past private property ahead.

▼ 1.0 Trail ends at washed out bridge over the Little Truckee River.

GPS: N39°30.14' W120°16.62'

Continuation of Main Trail

▼ 0.0   Continue to the east.

7.5 ▲   SO Auto tour stop 16. Small track on right
              is a spur that follows the original route
              of Henness Pass Road to the Little
              Truckee River bridge. Old route also on
              left. Zero trip meter.
              GPS: N39°29.45' W120°17.24'

▼ 0.2   TR 4-way intersection. Turn right onto CR
              301, which is a marked snowmobile
              route in winter. Northern Sierra #23:
              Independence Lake Trail, also a
              groomed snowmobile route in winter,
              continues straight ahead.

7.3 ▲   TL 4-way intersection. Turn left onto grad-
              ed road 07-10. Northern Sierra #23:
              Independence Lake Trail, a groomed
              snowmobile route in winter, on right.
              GPS: N39°29.45' W120°17.06'

▼ 1.1   SO Cross over creek.

6.4 ▲   SO Cross over creek.

▼ 1.2   SO Track on right.

6.3 ▲   SO Track on left.

▼ 1.3   SO Site of Davis Station (auto tour stop
              15) on left.

6.2 ▲   SO Site of Davis Station (auto tour stop
              15) on right.
              GPS: N39°29.39' W120°18.38'

▼ 1.5   SO Cattle guard. Entering private property.
              Ignore tracks on left and right for next
              1.4 miles.

6.0 ▲   SO Cattle guard. Leaving private property.

▼ 2.9   SO Cattle guard. Leaving private property.

4.6 ▲   SO Cattle guard. Entering private property.
              Ignore tracks on left and right for next
              1.4 miles.

▼ 3.0   SO Graded road on left; then track on left.

4.5 ▲   SO Track on right; then graded road on right.

▼ 3.3   SO Track on left to Mount Lola Trailhead
              parking area. Mount Lola Trail, for hik-
              ers and equestrians, connects to the
              Pacific Crest National Scenic Trail.

4.2 ▲   SO Track on right to Mount Lola Trailhead
              parking area. Mount Lola Trail, for hik-
              ers and equestrians, connects to the

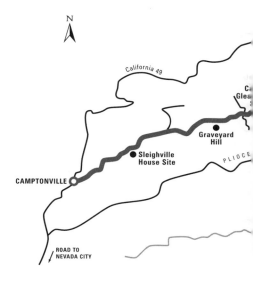

Pacific Crest National Scenic Trail.
              GPS: N39°29.33' W120°20.32'

▼ 3.5   SO Track on left.

4.0 ▲   SO Track on right.

▼ 3.6   SO Cross over Cold Stream on bridge.

3.9 ▲   SO Cross over Cold Stream on bridge.

▼ 4.1   SO Corral on right in Perazzo Meadows.

3.4 ▲   SO Corral on left in Perazzo Meadows.

▼ 5.0   SO Cross through Little Truckee River.

2.5 ▲   SO Cross through Little Truckee River.
              GPS: N39°29.18' W120°22.20'

▼ 5.5   SO 4-way intersection. Track on left and
              track on right are both 07-30.

2.0 ▲   SO 4-way intersection. Track on left and
              track on right are both 07-30.
              GPS: N39°29.16' W120°22.76'

▼ 6.2   SO Track on left goes 0.1 miles to water-
              falls in Little Truckee River Canyon;
              then track on right.

1.3 ▲   SO Track on left; then track on right goes
              0.1 miles to waterfalls in Little Truckee
              River Canyon.

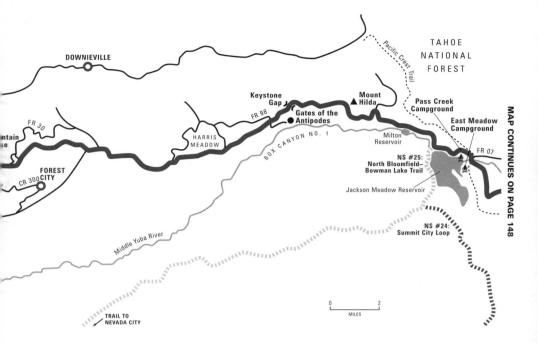

MAP CONTINUES ON PAGE 148

GPS: N39°29.14' W120°23.44'

▼ 7.5 TL Turn left, remaining on dirt road, and zero trip meter. Paved FR 07 is immediately on the right. Marked snowmobile route ends here.

0.0 ▲ Continue to the southeast.
GPS: N39°29.75' W120°24.58'

▼ 0.0 Continue to the southwest.

1.2 ▲ TR Turn right, remaining on dirt road, and zero trip meter. This is a marked snowmobile route in winter. Paved FR 07 is straight ahead.

▼ 0.2 BR Cross over creek; then private property on left.

1.0 ▲ BL Private property on right; then cross over creek.

▼ 1.2 SO Track on left is Northern Sierra #24: Summit City Loop (FR 86). Zero trip meter.

0.0 ▲ Continue to the southeast on CR 301.
GPS: N39°29.46' W120°25.66'

▼ 0.0 Continue to the north, joining Summit City Loop.

2.9 ▲ BL Northern Sierra #24: Summit City Loop (FR 86) leaves on right. Zero trip meter.

▼ 0.4 SO Track on right.

2.5 ▲ BR Track on left.

▼ 0.5 SO California Cooperative Snow Survey Cabin on right.

2.4 ▲ SO California Cooperative Snow Survey Cabin on left.

▼ 0.6 TL T-intersection with paved FR 07. Follow sign to Jackson Meadows, remaining on paved road.

2.3 ▲ TR Turn right onto graded dirt CR 301 following sign to Meadow Lake.
GPS: N39°29.95' W120°25.96'

▼ 0.7 SO Henness Pass (auto tour stop 14).

2.2 ▲ SO Henness Pass (auto tour stop 14).
GPS: N39°30.02' W120°26.12'

▼ 0.8 SO Graded road on left is 07-55 to Jones Valley. Graded road on right goes to Coppin Meadows.

2.1 ▲ SO Graded road on right is 07-55 to Jones Valley. Graded road on left goes to Coppin Meadows.

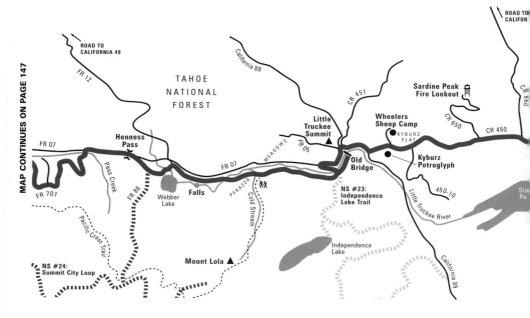

MAP CONTINUES ON PAGE 147

▼ 1.1   TL   Turn left, back onto graded CR 301.
1.8 ▲   TR   T-intersection with paved FR 07.
      GPS: N39°30.10' W120°26.55'

▼ 1.4   SO   Cross through creek.
1.5 ▲   SO   Cross through creek.
▼ 1.7   SO   Track on left.
1.2 ▲   SO   Track on right.
▼ 1.8   SO   Cross over creek.
1.1 ▲   SO   Cross over creek.
▼ 2.6   SO   Track on right.
0.3 ▲   SO   Track on left.
▼ 2.9   TL   Paved FR 07 is immediately to the right. Turn left onto Pass Creek Loop (FR 70) and zero trip meter.
0.0 ▲   Continue to the east. End of snowmobile route.
      GPS: N39°30.35' W120°28.40'

▼ 0.0   Continue to the west. This is a groomed snowmobile route in winter.
7.3 ▲   TR   Turn right onto unmarked, graded CR 301, immediately before paved FR 70, and zero trip meter.
▼ 0.1   SO   Track on right.
7.2 ▲   SO   Track on left.

▼ 0.2   SO   Cross over Pass Creek.
7.1 ▲   SO   Cross over Pass Creek.
▼ 1.4   SO   Track on left is 70-20.
5.9 ▲   SO   Track on right is 70-20.
▼ 2.8   SO   Track on right is 70-30.
4.5 ▲   SO   Track on left is 70-30.
▼ 3.9   SO   Track on left is 70-40; then cross over creek.
3.4 ▲   SO   Cross over creek; then track on right is 70-40.
      GPS: N39°28.91' W120°29.88'

▼ 4.1   SO   Track on right is 70-50.
3.2 ▲   SO   Track on left is 70-50.
▼ 4.6   SO   Track on left is 70-58.
2.7 ▲   SO   Track on right is 70-58.
▼ 4.8   SO   Track on right is 70-60; then cross over creek.
2.5 ▲   SO   Cross over creek; then track on left is 70-60.
▼ 4.9   SO   Track on left is 70-65.
2.4 ▲   SO   Track on right is 70-65.
▼ 5.6   SO   Little Lasier Meadow USFS Horse Camp on right; then hiking and equestrian trail on left joins Pacific Crest Trail in 0.75 miles.

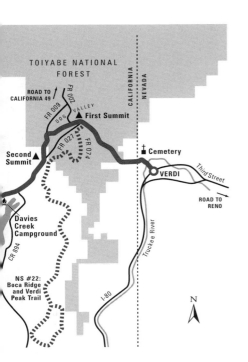

TOIYABE NATIONAL FOREST

ROAD TO CALIFORNIA 49

FR 009
FR 002
FR 027
FR 074

D O G   VALLEY

▲ First Summit

Second Summit ▲

Cemetery

VERDI

Third Street

ROAD TO RENO

Davies Creek Campground

CR 894

Truckee River

NS #22: Boca Ridge and Verdi Peak Trail

I-80

CALIFORNIA
NEVADA

N

1.7 ▲ SO Hiking and equestrian trail on right joins
Pacific Crest Trail in 0.75 miles; then
second entrance to horse camp on left.
GPS: N39°29.31′ W120°30.90′

▼ 5.7 SO Second entrance to horse camp on
right; then cattle guard.
1.6 ▲ SO Cattle guard; then Little Lasier
Meadows USFS Horse Camp on left.

▼ 6.9 TR T-intersection with paved road. Road
on left is 70-80 to East Meadow USFS
Campground. Turn right on paved road
and cross over Pass Creek. Pacific
Crest Trail joins road at this point.
0.4 ▲ TL Cross over Pass Creek; then turn left
on graded dirt FR 70. Paved road continues ahead to East Meadow USFS
Campground. Pacific Crest Trail leaves
road at this point.
GPS: N39°30.14′ W120°31.61′

▼ 7.0 SO Track on right goes to sand pit; then
Pacific Crest Trail leaves on right.
0.3 ▲ BR Pacific Crest Trail joins road from the
left at this point. Track on left goes to
sand pit. Remain on paved road.

▼ 7.3 TL T-intersection with paved FR 07. End
of Pass Creek Loop. Zero trip meter
and follow sign for Jackson Meadow.
0.0 ▲ Continue to the southeast. This is a
groomed snowmobile route in winter.
GPS: N39°30.36′ W120°31.76′

▼ 0.0 Continue to the west. This is a
groomed snowmobile route in winter.
1.4 ▲ TR Turn right onto paved road following
sign to East Meadow USFS
Campground. Zero trip meter.

▼ 0.1 SO Pass Creek USFS Campground and
boat launch on left. Jackson Meadow
Trailer Sanitary Station on right.
1.3 ▲ SO Pass Creek USFS Campground and
boat launch on right. Jackson Meadow
Trailer Sanitary Station on left.

▼ 0.4 SO Aspen Group Camps on right.
1.0 ▲ SO Aspen Group Camps on left.

▼ 0.5 SO Aspen Picnic Ground on left.
0.9 ▲ SO Aspen Picnic Ground on right.

▼ 1.4 SO Jackson Meadow Reservoir on left.
Road on left is Northern Sierra #25:
North Bloomfield–Bowman Lake Trail,
which crosses the dam. This is auto
tour stop 13. Zero trip meter.
0.0 ▲ Continue to the southeast. Road
becomes paved.
GPS: N39°30.59′ W120°33.16′

▼ 0.0 Continue to the northwest. Road turns
to graded dirt.
6.2 ▲ SO Jackson Meadow Reservoir on right.
Road on right is Northern Sierra #25:
North Bloomfield–Bowman Lake Trail,
which crosses the dam. This is auto
tour stop 13. Zero trip meter.

▼ 0.2 SO Look over edge on the left to see old
bridge over the Middle Yuba River.
6.0 ▲ SO Look over edge on the right to see old
bridge over the Middle Yuba River.

▼ 1.5 SO Track on left.
4.7 ▲ SO Track on right.
GPS: N39°31.27′ W120°34.17′

▼ 1.6 SO Track on left.
4.6 ▲ SO Track on right.

▼ 1.7 SO Milton Reservoir on left. This is auto
tour stop 12.

4.5 ▲ SO Milton Reservoir on right. This is auto tour stop 12.

GPS: N39°31.36′ W120°34.45′

▼ 2.2 SO Track on left.
4.0 ▲ SO Track on right.
▼ 2.3 SO Track on left.
3.9 ▲ SO Track on right.
▼ 2.4 SO Track on left; then track on right.
3.8 ▲ SO Track on left; then track on right.
▼ 2.6 SO Track on left goes 0.5 miles to the Milton-Bowman Tunnel. Follow sign to Alleghany.
3.6 ▲ SO Track on right goes 0.5 miles to the Milton-Bowman Tunnel.

GPS: N39°31.49′ W120°35.32′

▼ 2.9 SO Track on right.
3.3 ▲ SO Track on left.
▼ 3.4 SO Track on right.
2.8 ▲ SO Track on left.
▼ 3.6 SO Track on right.
2.6 ▲ SO Track on left.
▼ 3.8 BL Graded road on right; then cross over wash; then track on right.
2.4 ▲ BR Track on left; then cross over creek; then graded road on left.

GPS: N39°31.88′ W120°36.02′

▼ 5.4 SO Track on right is 301-35.
0.8 ▲ SO Track on left is 301-35.

GPS: N39°31.82′ W120°37.22′

▼ 6.0 SO Cattle guard.
0.2 ▲ SO Cattle guard.

GPS: N39°32.24′ W120°37.50′

▼ 6.2 SO Track on left is 301-31 and track on right is 301-30. View on right over Sierra Buttes. Zero trip meter.
0.0 ▲ Continue to the east.

GPS: N39°32.23′ W120°37.78′

▼ 0.0 Continue to the west.
3.4 ▲ SO Track on right is 301-31 and track on left is 301-30. View on left over Sierra Buttes. Zero trip meter.
▼ 2.1 BL Keystone Gap. Two tracks on right at viewpoint.
1.3 ▲ BR Keystone Gap. Two tracks on left at

viewpoint.

GPS: N39°32.25′ W120°39.85′

▼ 2.8 SO Track on left.
0.6 ▲ SO Track on right.
▼ 3.4 SO Graded road on right is FR 98. This is auto tour stop 11. Zero trip meter and follow sign to Alleghany.
0.0 ▲ Continue to the northeast.

GPS: N39°31.49′ W120°40.88′

▼ 0.0 Continue to the southwest.
4.5 ▲ SO Graded road on left is FR 98. This is auto tour stop 11. Zero trip meter and follow sign for Jackson Meadows.
▼ 0.1 SO Track on right; then track on sharp left descends steeply along a little-used shelf road for 1 mile to a collapsed log cabin near the Gates of the Antipodes.
4.4 ▲ BL Track on right descends steeply along a little-used shelf road for 1 mile to a collapsed log cabin near the Gates of the Antipodes; then track on left.

GPS: N39°31.41′ W120°40.98′

▼ 0.2 SO Track on right and track on left.
4.3 ▲ SO Track on right and track on left.
▼ 0.9 SO Track on right.
3.6 ▲ SO Track on left.
▼ 1.1 SO Track and viewpoint on left.
3.4 ▲ SO Track and viewpoint on right.
▼ 1.7 SO Track on right.
2.8 ▲ SO Track on left.
▼ 2.1 SO Track on right to Harris Meadow and Negro Creek; then track on left.
2.4 ▲ SO Track on right; then track on left to Harris Meadow and Negro Creek.

GPS: N39°30.50′ W120°42.81′

▼ 2.4 SO Track on left and track on right.
2.1 ▲ SO Track on left and track on right.
▼ 2.6 SO Track on left.
1.9 ▲ SO Track on right.
▼ 3.0 SO Track on left to the Nixon Mine and track on right. Follow sign to Alleghany.
1.5 ▲ SO Track on right to the Nixon Mine and track on left. Follow sign to Jackson Meadows.

GPS: N39°30.44′ W120°43.81′

▼ 3.5   SO   Track on left and track on right.

1.0 ▲   SO   Track on right and track on left.

▼ 4.5   SO   Graded road on right is FR 98 to Harris Meadow. Join paved road following the sign to Alleghany. Zero trip meter.

0.0 ▲   Continue to the northeast.

GPS: N39°30.05′ W120°45.29′

▬▬▬▬▬▬▬▬▬▬▬▬▬▬▬▬▬▬

▼ 0.0   Continue to the southwest.

4.0 ▲   BR   Paved road ends. Graded road on left is FR 98 to Harris Meadow. Follow sign to Milton Reservoir. Zero trip meter.

▼ 0.3   SO   Track on right.

3.7 ▲   SO   Track on left.

▼ 0.5   SO   Track on left is 301-14.

3.5 ▲   SO   Track on right is 301-14.

▼ 0.8   SO   Track on left is 301-12.

3.2 ▲   SO   Track on right is 301-12.

▼ 1.3   SO   Track on left.

2.7 ▲   SO   Track on right.

▼ 1.7   SO   Graded road on right is 301-8.

2.3 ▲   SO   Graded road on left is 301-8.

GPS: N39°30.14′ W120°46.81′

▬▬▬▬▬▬▬▬▬▬▬▬▬▬▬▬▬▬

▼ 1.8   SO   Graded road on left is FR 84 to Lafayette Ridge Road.

2.2 ▲   SO   Graded road on right is FR 84 to Lafayette Ridge Road.

GPS: N39°30.24′ W120°46.90′

▬▬▬▬▬▬▬▬▬▬▬▬▬▬▬▬▬▬

▼ 1.9   SO   Track on right.

2.1 ▲   SO   Track on left.

▼ 2.0   SO   Track on right is 301-6; then auto tour stop 10 on left. The site itself is set below the road on the left.

2.0 ▲   SO   Auto tour stop 10 on right. The site itself is set below the road on the right. Track on left is 301-6.

GPS: N39°30.33′ W120°47.09′

▬▬▬▬▬▬▬▬▬▬▬▬▬▬▬▬▬▬

▼ 2.5   SO   Track on right.

1.5 ▲   SO   Track on left.

▼ 3.0   SO   Two tracks on left.

1.0 ▲   SO   Two tracks on right.

▼ 3.5   SO   Graded road on right and track on left is 301-2.

0.5 ▲   SO   Graded road on left and track on right is 301-2.

GPS: N39°30.50′ W120°48.61′

▬▬▬▬▬▬▬▬▬▬▬▬▬▬▬▬▬▬

▼ 4.0   TR   Graded road on right is CR 302. Paved road straight ahead is the lower Henness Pass Road. Zero trip meter. This is auto tour stop 9.

0.0 ▲   Continue to the northeast.

GPS: N39°30.47′ W120°49.12′

▬▬▬▬▬▬▬▬▬▬▬▬▬▬▬▬▬▬

▼ 0.0   Continue to the northwest.

4.7 ▲   TL   T-intersection with paved CR 401. The lower Henness Pass Road joins from the right. This is auto tour stop 9. Zero trip meter.

▼ 0.4   SO   Track on left.

4.3 ▲   SO   Track on right.

▼ 1.0   SO   Track on left and track on right.

3.7 ▲   SO   Track on left and track on right.

▼ 1.1   SO   Track on right goes into private property.

3.6 ▲   SO   Track on left goes into private property.

▼ 1.7   SO   Track on right.

3.0 ▲   SO   Track on left.

▼ 2.4   SO   Track on right.

2.3 ▲   SO   Track on left.

▼ 2.9   SO   Track on right.

1.8 ▲   SO   Track on left.

▼ 3.1   SO   Track on left.

1.6 ▲   SO   Track on right.

▼ 3.6   SO   Track on right; then two tracks on left.

1.1 ▲   SO   Two tracks on right; then track on left.

GPS: N39°29.99′ W120°52.36′

▬▬▬▬▬▬▬▬▬▬▬▬▬▬▬▬▬▬

▼ 4.1   SO   Graded road on right is Alpha Colony Road (FR 30) to Ruby Mine; then track on right.

0.6 ▲   SO   Track on left; then graded road on left is Alpha Colony Road (FR 30) to Ruby Mine.

GPS: N39°29.96′ W120°52.92′

▬▬▬▬▬▬▬▬▬▬▬▬▬▬▬▬▬▬

▼ 4.4   TR   T-intersection with CR 300.

0.3 ▲   TL   Turn left on unmarked graded road CR 302.

GPS: N39°29.89′ W120°53.23′

▬▬▬▬▬▬▬▬▬▬▬▬▬▬▬▬▬▬

▼ 4.7   BL   Turnout on right at historical marker for Mountain House; then track on left; then graded road on right. Bear left onto graded road CR 293. Zero trip meter.

0.0 ▲   Continue to the east. Immediately track on right and turnout on left at the historical marker for Mountain House.

▼ 0.0   Continue to the south.

6.2 ▲ BR Graded road on left. Bear right onto CR 300 and zero trip meter.

▼ 0.9 SO Track on left is 293-20. Site of Camp Gleason.

5.3 ▲ SO Track on right is 293-20. Site of Camp Gleason.

GPS: N39°29.60' W120°53.98'

▼ 1.3 SO Spring on right.

4.9 ▲ SO Spring on left.

GPS: N39°29.67' W120°54.25'

▼ 1.6 SO Track on left.

4.6 ▲ SO Track on right.

▼ 2.0 SO Track on right.

4.2 ▲ SO Track on left.

▼ 2.6 SO Track on right is St. Catherine Road (293-18) and track on left is 390.

3.6 ▲ SO Track on right is 390 and track on left is St. Catherine Road (293-18).

GPS: N39°29.59' W120°55.37'

▼ 3.0 SO Track on right is 34-15.

3.2 ▲ SO Track on left is 34-15.

▼ 3.7 SO Graveyard Hill on left; then track on left is 293-14. Site may be the final resting place of a power line worker who died in a snowstorm.

2.5 ▲ SO Track on right is 293-14; then Graveyard Hill on right. Site may be the final resting place of a power line worker who died in a snowstorm.

GPS: N39°29.38' W120°56.37'

▼ 5.8 SO Track on right is Twin Quartz Road (34-13).

0.4 ▲ SO Track on left is Twin Quartz Road (34-13).

GPS: N39°28.97' W120°58.53'

▼ 5.9 SO Track on left is 293-10.

0.3 ▲ SO Track on right is 293-10.

▼ 6.2 SO Track on right is Jouberts Road (34-7); then second track on right is Ditch Road (293-22). Track on left. Zero trip meter.

0.0 ▲ Continue to the northeast.

▼ 0.0   Continue to the southwest.

5.1 ▲ SO Track on right. Track on left is Ditch Road (293-22); then second track on left is Jouberts Road (34-7). Zero trip meter.

▼ 1.5 SO Road on left is 293-4.

3.6 ▲ SO Road on right is 293-4.

GPS: N39°28.28' W121°00.19'

▼ 1.7 SO Track on right is 293-2.

3.4 ▲ SO Track on left is 293-2.

▼ 1.9 BR Site of old stage stop Sleighville House (auto tour stop 3) on left; then bear right past tracks on left that go into private property.

3.2 ▲ BL Bear left past tracks on right that go into private property; then site of old stage stop Sleighville House (auto tour stop 3) on right.

GPS: N39°28.28' W121°00.52'

▼ 2.5 SO Two tracks on right.

2.6 ▲ SO Two tracks on left.

▼ 2.9 SO Track on left.

2.2 ▲ SO Track on right.

▼ 3.2 SO Road becomes paved.

1.9 ▲ SO Road turns to graded dirt.

▼ 3.5 SO Road on right.

1.6 ▲ SO Road on left.

▼ 4.6 BL Mill Street on right. Bear left onto Cleveland Street.

0.5 ▲ SO Mill Street on left.

GPS: N39°27.26' W121°02.67'

▼ 4.9 SO Auto tour stop 2 at historical marker for Camptonville and Lester Allen Pelton—inventor of the Pelton waterwheel.

0.2 ▲ SO Auto tour stop 2 at historical marker for Camptonville and Lester Allen Pelton—inventor of the Pelton waterwheel.

GPS: N39°27.15' W121°03.01'

▼ 5.1 Trail ends at T-intersection with California 49 in Camptonville. Turn left for Nevada City; turn right for Downieville.

0.0 ▲	Trail starts on California 49 at Camptonville. Zero trip meter and turn east on Cleveland Avenue, following sign for Camptonville. The turn is 1.6 miles north of North Yuba USFS Ranger Station. Remain on Cleveland Street. **GPS: N39°27.25′ W121°03.07′**

Boca Ridge and Verdi Peak Trail

STARTING POINT CR 894 at Boca Reservoir, 3.2 miles north of I-80

FINISHING POINT Northern Sierra #21: Henness Pass Road, 3.7 miles west of Verdi, NV

TOTAL MILEAGE 16.9 miles, plus optional 3.5-mile loop and 3-mile spur to Verdi Peak

UNPAVED MILEAGE 16.9 miles, plus optional 3.5-mile loop and 3-mile spur

DRIVING TIME 3 hours (20 minutes extra for 4-rated loop)

ELEVATION RANGE 5,600–8,400 feet

USUALLY OPEN June to November

BEST TIME TO TRAVEL Dry weather

DIFFICULTY RATING 3 for the main trail; 4 for the optional loop

SCENIC RATING 8

REMOTENESS RATING +0

Special Attractions

- Fishing and camping at Boca Reservoir.
- Panoramic views from Verdi Peak Fire Lookout.
- Historic town site of Boca.

View of Stampede Reservoir from the spur trail to Verdi Peak

History

The southern approach to the Verdi Range begins on the eastern shore of Boca Reservoir and makes its way up the slopes of Boca Ridge. The original lake at Boca Reservoir was the scene of great activity during the late nineteenth and early twentieth centuries. Construction of the Central Pacific Railroad between 1866 and 1868 brought thousands of workers to the Sierra Nevada, and Boca was one of many base camps for workers on the grade. The railroad entered the spectacular Truckee Canyon at Boca, Spanish for "mouth."

A lumber mill at Boca supplied railroad ties for the new grade, and a dam ensured a plentiful water supply. The mill also provided timbers for mines and lumber for builders. Once the track was laid past Boca, the town became a stopping point for travelers who enjoyed the hospitality of its three-story hotel. In winter the lake froze, and the lumber company switched gears to harvest ice. Big blocks of ice were insulated in sawdust and shipped to various destinations via the railroad. Saloons did a roaring trade, and Boca gained a reputation for rowdiness and violence. In the late 1880s and early 1890s, the Boca Brewery supplied as many as 30,000 barrels of beer to towns throughout the West. Unfortunately, the brewery burned down just before the turn of the century. It seemed like the town would go on forever; however, the sawmill finally denuded the surrounding mountains and was forced to close in 1908. With no alternative employment, townspeople were forced to walk away from their homes. The final straw for Boca came when its last major employer, the ice foundry, closed in the 1920s.

All that remains of Boca is the small cemetery. The Boca Reservoir we see today was completed in 1940.

Description

This interesting trail close to the Nevada state line travels north from Boca Reservoir to Northern Sierra #21: Henness Pass Road. Immediately after leaving I-80, take a few minutes to look at the old Boca town site and cemetery. There is a short interpretive trail, and although no buildings remain, the old cemetery is mute testimony to the hardships its citizens faced.

The trail starts at Boca Reservoir, opposite the Boca Rest USFS Campground. Set on the lakeshore, this campground has no shade but is popular because of its proximity to the lake. Anglers can fish for rainbow trout (which are stocked annually), brown trout, and kokanee salmon. There is a boat ramp on the southwest shore of Boca Reservoir.

An alternative to the main route begins 0.2 miles from the start of the trail and takes a slightly more circuitous route along a smaller, rougher trail. This alternate 3.5-mile route is rated 4 for difficulty because of loose uneven surfaces and a couple of short, moderately steep climbs. It travels closer to Boca Ridge along designated OHV routes before rejoining the main trail.

The main trail remains 2-rated at this stage, as it climbs around a shelf road, slowly winding toward Verdi Peak. The shelf road is predominantly single vehicle width, but it has plenty of passing places and offers views over low vegetation to Boca and Stampede Reservoirs.

A spur travels 3 miles through curl-leaf mahoganies, stands of aspens, and slopes covered in mule's ears to the Verdi Peak Fire Lookout. The lookout, perched on top of a rock outcrop at 8,445 feet, is in good condition; it has a narrow staircase to the top. The walkway provides 360-degree views: east into Nevada, north over Ladybug Peak and the Verdi Range, northwest over Sardine Valley, and west over Stampede and Boca Reservoirs. The lookout is manned during lightning storms.

Past the spur to Verdi Peak, the trail passes through part of the Crystal Burn Fire of August 1994, when a fire destroyed 7,310 acres. The trail touches Northern Sierra #21: Henness Pass Road before beginning the final 3-rated section that winds along a narrow shelf road around the south side of Beacon Point. This slightly brushy section offers great views into Nevada. Those not wishing to drive this final section can finish on Henness Pass Road.

The main trail is suitable for mountain bikes and forms part of a 28-mile loop from Henness Pass Road that is completed by continuing up the paved road from Boca Reservoir to Stampede Reservoir.

Note that this trail is not accurately shown on topographical maps. The forest service maps are the most accurate for the route described below.

Current Road Information
Tahoe National Forest
Truckee Ranger District
9646 Donner Pass Road
Truckee, CA 96161
(530) 587-3558

Map References
BLM   Truckee, Portola
USFS Tahoe National Forest, Toiyabe National Forest: Carson Ranger District
USGS 1:24,000 Boca, Dog Valley
         1:100,000 Truckee, Portola
Maptech CD-ROM: High Sierra/Tahoe
Northern California Atlas & Gazetteer, pp. 81, 71
California Road & Recreation Atlas, p. 61

Route Directions

▼ 0.0   From CR 894 at Boca Reservoir, 3.2 miles north of the Hirschdale exit of I-80 at Boca, zero trip meter and turn east on FR 72, signposted to Boca Springs and Verdi Peak. The Boca Rest USFS

Verdi Peak Fire Lookout, perched above the Truckee River Canyon

Campground is opposite the turn. Road immediately turns to graded dirt.

0.2 ▲ Trail ends on CR 894 opposite the Boca Rest USFS Campground. Turn left for I-80 and Truckee; turn right for Stampede Reservoir.
GPS: N39°25.14' W120°05.11'

▼ 0.2 SO Track on right is the start of the optional Boca Ridge Loop. Zero trip meter.
0.0 ▲ Continue to the west.
GPS: N39°25.16' W120°04.91'

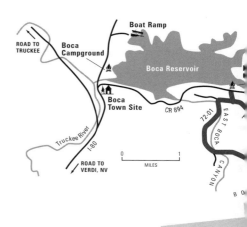

Optional 4-rated Boca Ridge Loop

▼ 0.0 TR Turn right (south) onto 72-01 and pass through seasonal closure gate.
3.5 ▲ TL Seasonal closure gate; then end of optional loop. Turn left onto FR 72 to rejoin the final section of the main trail. Zero trip meter.
▼ 0.1 SO Track on left.
3.4 ▲ SO Track on right.
▼ 0.3 SO Cross through wash; then track on right; then enter East Boca Canyon.
3.2 ▲ SO Leave East Boca Canyon; then track on left; then cross through wash.
▼ 0.5 SO Track on right.
3.0 ▲ SO Track on left.
▼ 1.2 TL Track on left is Verdi OHV Route for 4WDs, ATVs, and motorbikes. Turn left and cross through East Boca Canyon Creek.
2.3 ▲ TR Cross through East Boca Canyon Creek; then T-intersection.
GPS: N39°24.74' W120°03.91'

▼ 1.6 TR OHV route on left.
1.9 ▲ BL OHV route on right.
GPS: N39°25.10' W120°03.85'

▼ 2.1 SO Start of shelf road.
1.4 ▲ SO End of shelf road.
▼ 2.8 SO End of shelf road.
0.7 ▲ SO Start of shelf road.
▼ 2.9 TL Track ahead climbs hill and dead-ends. Turn left onto marked OHV route.
0.6 ▲ TR T-intersection. Track on left climbs hill and dead-ends. Turn right and descend hill.

GPS: N39°25.97' W120°03.55'

▼ 3.5 TR End of Boca Ridge Loop. Turn right onto FR 72 to continue along the main trail. Zero trip meter.
0.0 ▲ Continue to the northeast on alternate loop. Zero trip meter.
GPS: N39°26.08' W120°03.95'

Continuation of Main Trail

▼ 0.0 SO Continue straight (northeast) on FR 72.
1.7 ▲ SO Track on left is the southern end of the optional Boca Ridge Loop. Zero trip meter.
GPS: N39°25.16' W120°04.91'

▼ 0.1 SO Cross through creek on ford.
1.6 ▲ SO Cross through creek on ford.
▼ 0.4 TR Track straight ahead is 72-02, which goes 0.3 miles to Boca Spring USFS Campground. Turn right and pass through seasonal closure gate.
1.3 ▲ TL Seasonal closure gate; then track on right is 72-02, which goes 0.3 miles to Boca Spring USFS Campground.
GPS: N39°25.46' W120°04.58'

▼ 1.5 SO Track on left.
0.2 ▲ SO Track on right.
▼ 1.7 SO Track on right is marked OHV route 72-6. This is the northern end of the alternate 4-rated Boca Ridge Loop. Zero trip meter.

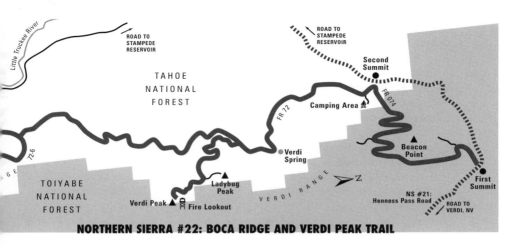

NORTHERN SIERRA #22: BOCA RIDGE AND VERDI PEAK TRAIL

0.0 ▲   Continue to the southwest.
      GPS: N39°26.08' W120°03.95'

▼ 0.0   Continue to the north.
5.8 ▲ SO Track on left is marked OHV route 72-6. This is the start of the alternate 4-rated Boca Ridge Loop. Zero trip meter and continue straight ahead to remain on the main trail; turn sharp left to drive the loop.

▼ 1.7 SO Track on left.
4.1 ▲ SO Track on right.
      GPS: N39°27.11' W120°03.89'

▼ 2.3 SO Track on left is 72-12.
3.5 ▲ SO Track on right is 72-12.
      GPS: N39°27.38' W120°03.81'

▼ 2.6 SO Track on left is 72-16.
3.2 ▲ SO Track on right is 72-16.
▼ 2.7 SO Track on right.
3.1 ▲ SO Track on left.
▼ 3.0 SO Track on left is 72-22.
2.8 ▲ SO Track on right 72-22.
▼ 3.4 SO Track on right goes 1.1 miles to the ridge top.
2.4 ▲ SO Track on left goes 1.1 miles to the ridge top.
      GPS: N39°28.15' W120°03.51'

▼ 4.3 SO Track on left is 72-25.
1.5 ▲ SO Track on right is 72-25.
▼ 5.0 SO Track on left.
0.8 ▲ SO Track on right.

▼ 5.7 SO Track on left.
0.1 ▲ SO Track on right.
▼ 5.8 SO Track on right is 72-28, spur to Verdi Peak. Zero trip meter and follow the sign to Henness Pass Road.
0.0 ▲   Continue to the southwest on FR 72.
      GPS: N39°29.48' W120°03.14'

Spur to Verdi Peak Fire Lookout

▼ 0.0   Proceed to the south on 72-28, following sign to Verdi Peak.
▼ 0.1 SO Seasonal closure gate.
▼ 0.8 SO Track on right.
▼ 1.1 SO Seasonal closure gate.
▼ 1.9 SO Track on left goes 0.4 miles to Ladybug Peak. Continue straight ahead on designated route.
      GPS: N39°28.77' W120°02.72'

▼ 3.0   Spur ends at Verdi Peak Fire Lookout.
      GPS: N39°28.34' W120°02.34'

Continuation of Main Trail

▼ 0.0   Continue to the northeast on FR 72.
3.6 ▲ BR Track on left is 72-28, spur to Verdi Peak. Zero trip meter.
      GPS: N39°29.48' W120°03.14'

▼ 0.5 SO Verdi Spring on right.
3.1 ▲ SO Verdi Spring on left.
      GPS: N39°29.92' W120°03.08'

▼ 0.8   SO   Track on left to camping area.
2.8 ▲   SO   Track on right to camping area.
▼ 1.0   BL   Track on right.
2.6 ▲   BR   Track on left.
▼ 2.1   SO   Track on right alongside power lines.
1.5 ▲   SO   Track on left alongside power lines.
▼ 3.3   SO   Track on left to camping area; then track on right is 72-34.
0.3 ▲   SO   Track on left is 72-34; then track on right to camping area.
GPS: N39°31.35' W120°03.98'

▼ 3.6   TR   Trail touches Northern Sierra #21: Henness Pass Road at Second Summit and the boundary of Toiyabe and Tahoe National Forests. Turn right, immediately before Henness Pass Road, onto FR 074. Do not join Henness Pass Road. Zero trip meter.
0.0 ▲   Continue to the southeast.
GPS: N39°31.57 W120°04.14'

▼ 0.0   Continue to the east.
5.6 ▲   TL   The trail meets Northern Sierra #21: Henness Pass Road at Second Summit and the boundary of Toiyabe and Tahoe National Forests. Turn left onto FR 72, following the sign for Boca Reservoir, and zero trip meter. Do not join Henness Pass Road.
▼ 0.8   SO   Start of shelf road.
4.8 ▲   SO   End of shelf road.
▼ 2.0   SO   End of shelf road.
3.6 ▲   SO   Start of shelf road.
▼ 2.5   TL   Turn left, remaining on FR 074.
3.1 ▲   TR   Track straight ahead. Remain on FR 074.
GPS: N39°31.39' W120°03°08'

▼ 3.0   SO   Start of shelf road.
2.6 ▲   SO   End of shelf road.
▼ 5.1   TR   T-intersection. End of shelf road.
0.5 ▲   TL   Track straight ahead. Remain on FR 074. Start of shelf road.
GPS: N39°32.66' W120°02.72'

▼ 5.3   SO   Track on right.
0.3 ▲   SO   Track on left.
▼ 5.4   SO   Track on right.
0.2 ▲   SO   Track on left.
▼ 5.5   SO   Track on right.

0.1 ▲   SO   Track on left.
▼ 5.6   Trails ends at T-intersection with Northern Sierra #21: Henness Pass Road at First Summit. Turn right for Verdi, NV and I-80; turn left to travel Henness Pass Road.
0.0 ▲   Trail commences on Northern Sierra #21: Henness Pass Road at First Summit, 3.7 miles west of Verdi, NV. Zero trip meter and turn southwest on formed dirt trail FR 074. A USFS information board is opposite the turn.
GPS: N39°32.91' W120°02.28'

Independence Lake Trail

STARTING POINT   Northern Sierra #21: Henness Pass Road (FR 07) at Little Truckee Summit, 1.4 miles west of California 89

FINISHING POINT   California 89, 7 miles north of Truckee

TOTAL MILEAGE   21.5 miles, plus 0.9-miles spur to Independence Lake

UNPAVED MILEAGE   21.3 miles, plus 0.9-mile spur

DRIVING TIME   3 hours

ELEVATION RANGE   6,200–7,600 feet

USUALLY OPEN   April to November

BEST TIME TO TRAVEL   Memorial Day to Labor Day

DIFFICULTY RATING   3

SCENIC RATING   8

REMOTENESS RATING   +0

Special Attractions

■ Fishing and camping at Independence Lake.

■ Lightly traveled trail with spectacular views.

■ Access to a network of backcountry OHV trails.

History

Independence Lake is one of the major reservoirs of the Truckee River Storage Project. This project, from the early 1900s, provides irrigation and drinking water and flood control for the Truckee Meadows region. Independence Creek runs into the Little Truckee River, which flows into the Stampede and Boca Reservoirs, before joining the Truckee River at Truckee Canyon, and continuing to its end in Pyramid Lake, Nevada. The natural basin north of Carpenter Ridge where Independence Lake was established was important to Native Americans whose burial sites are reminders of their presence in this idyllic setting.

Accounts differ as to the year the lake received its name. One story attributes its naming to actress Lola Montez in 1852, and another attributes it to Augustus Moore in 1862. Both accounts agree that the naming occurred on the Fourth of July.

This trail follows many of the late nine-teenth century narrow-gauge railroad grades used by the Sierra Nevada Wood & Lumber Company. Most of the grades and spur lines ended at Hobart Mills, located to the southeast on California 89. Walter Scott Hobart, who founded the company in the 1860s, died in 1892 and the mill site was named for him. Hobart Mills was a liquor-free company town. The company favored hiring married men with families over single men, a policy not unusual for many early Western businesses. The Southern Pacific purchased the lumber company's railroad in 1932, renaming the line Hobart Southern. By 1935, logging activity was winding down as the company depleted timber on its lands. Hobart Mills survived until 1937, making it one of the last major logging companies in the region.

A bronze plaque at the site of Hobart Mills

Independence Lake Trail above the Carpenter Valley

Independence Lake was originally two lakes before dam construction

just north of Prosser Reservoir tells the tale of this once bustling community. One of the locomotives used at Hobart Mills, Shay #14, is still in action today. Built in 1916, Shay #14 now chugs along as part of the rolling stock of the Georgetown Loop Historic Railroad, just west of Denver, Colorado, off of I-70.

Description
The best time to travel this trail is between Memorial Day and Labor Day, when Independence Lake is open to the public. Sierra Pacific Industries, owners of the lake, allows fishing, boating, picnicking, and camping for a small fee.

The trail leaves FR 07 along a graded gravel road, passing one of the original sections of the Henness Pass Road, before the standard drops to a roughly graded road. The spur to Independence Lake begins at an informally marked turn and travels to a fence around the lake. The gate is open when the lake is open to the public. A small fee is charged for driving to the lake area or camping at the informal campground. There is no charge for parking at the gate and walking down to the lake to fish. Visitors must stop and register at the office immediately past the gate. Past the office, an old two-story building on the right was once the hotel for the lumber settlement of Twin Lakes.

The lake has a boat launch and is good for small sailboats, kayaks, as well as small fishing boats. Anglers will find good fishing for trout and salmon, particularly from a boat. Cutthroat trout must be immediately released. Be sure to read the fishing restrictions posted at the entrance. The lake hasn't been stocked since the 1970s.

The main loop continues through Tahoe National Forest along a rough trail that passes several logging areas. The trail turns south at a major intersection toward Sagehen Creek and the Sagehen USFS Campground. The campground has 10 undeveloped sites with vault toilets.

The Sagehen Watershed is the site of several cooperative long-term research projects sponsored by the University of California, the California Department of Forestry and Resource Management, and the National Forest Service. The primary goal of these projects is to determine the responses of plants and animals to timber management practices. Wetland areas around the creek, known as fens, are habitat to a small carnivorous plant.

Some aspens around Sagehen Creek have carvings made by Basque sheepherders, who tended flocks in these regions. The creek has small rainbow, brook, and brown trout, and fishing regulations apply.

Past Sagehen Creek, the trail turns onto a smaller, formed shelf road that is lightly brushy and climbs around the Sagehen Hills. Some of the best views along the trail can be glimpsed south from here over the open meadows of Carpenter Valley and the North Fork of Prosser Creek. The trail rounds a hill and enters into a network of OHV trails that descend through the forest to travel near the south side of Sagehen Creek. In summer, vehicle travel must be limited to existing roads or trails posted as ORV routes. Certain roads are closed all year and others are closed seasonally to protect deer fawning habitat.

The trail finishes on California 89, a short distance north of the Hobart Mills site.

In winter the area is used by snowmobilers; oversnow travel is permitted when there is 12 inches of snowpack. The Prosser Hill Snowmobile Staging Area is south of the trail's end and 3.7 miles north of Truckee. The southern end of the trail along Sagehen Creek is also used by cross-country skiers, although the route is unmarked and ungroomed.

Current Road Information
Tahoe National Forest
Truckee Ranger District
9646 Donner Pass Road
Truckee, CA 96161
(530) 587-3558

Map References
BLM   Truckee
USFS   Tahoe National Forest
USGS 1:24,000   Independence Lake,
       Hobart Mills
      1:100,000 Truckee
Maptech CD-ROM: High Sierra/Tahoe
Northern California Atlas & Gazetteer, p. 81
California Road & Recreation Atlas, p. 61

Route Directions

▼ 0.0   Trail starts on Northern Sierra #21: Henness Pass Road (FR 07) at Little Truckee Summit, 1.4 miles west of the intersection with California 89. Zero trip meter and turn southeast on graded dirt road 07-10, signposted to Independence Lake. Immediately cross over aqueduct on bridge. Trail follows Henness Pass Road for the first 0.7 miles.

3.5 ▲   Cross over aqueduct on bridge; then trail ends at T-intersection with FR 07. Turn right for California 89 and Truckee; turn left for Jackson Meadow Reservoir.
       GPS: N39°29.54′ W120°17.83′

▼ 0.2   SO   Cross over Little Truckee River on bridge.
3.3 ▲   SO   Cross over Little Truckee River on bridge.
▼ 0.5   SO   Henness Pass auto tour stop 16 on right marks a section of the original road bed. Small track on left is a spur along Northern Sierra #21: Henness Pass Road.
3.0 ▲   SO   Henness Pass auto tour stop 16 on left marks a section of the original road bed. Small track on right is a spur along Northern Sierra #21: Henness Pass Road.
       GPS: N39°29.45′ W120°17.24′

▼ 0.7   SO   Graded road on left and right. Track on right is Northern Sierra #21: Henness Pass Road (CR 301).
2.8 ▲   SO   Graded road on left and right. Track on left is Northern Sierra #21: Henness Pass Road (CR 301). Trail follows Henness Pass Road for final 0.7 miles.
       GPS: N39°29.45′ W120°17.06′

▼ 1.1   BR   Track on left; then graded road on left is 07-10. Bear right onto graded road.
2.4 ▲   SO   Graded road on right is 07-10; then track on right.
       GPS: N39°29.16′ W120°16.98′

▼ 1.3   SO   Well-used track on right; then cross through creek.

NORTHERN SIERRA #23: INDEPENDENCE LAKE TRAIL

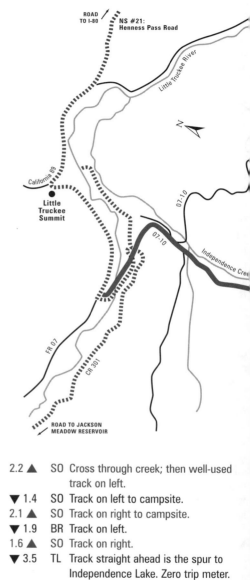

2.2 ▲   SO   Cross through creek; then well-used track on left.
▼ 1.4   SO   Track on left to campsite.
2.1 ▲   SO   Track on right to campsite.
▼ 1.9   BR   Track on left.
1.6 ▲   SO   Track on right.
▼ 3.5   TL   Track straight ahead is the spur to Independence Lake. Zero trip meter.
0.0 ▲   Continue to the north.
       GPS: N39°27.68′ W120°17.48′

Spur to Independence Lake

▼ 0.0   Continue to the south.
▼ 0.1   BL   Track on right.
▼ 0.4   SO   Track on left.
▼ 0.6   SO   Entering Independence Lake fee area. Fee

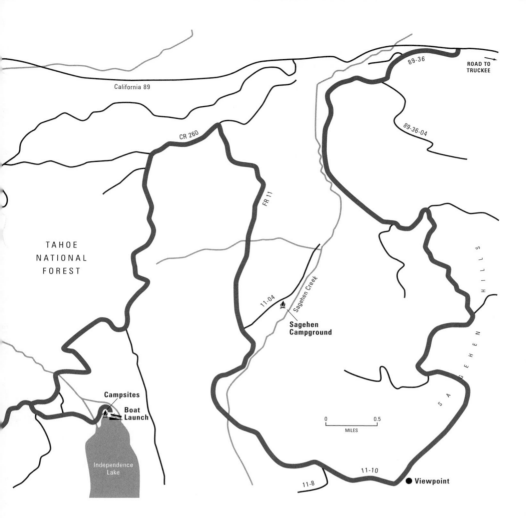

required for driving and camping past this point. Free parking here for day use.

▼ 0.7 SO Cross over lake outlet.

▼ 0.8 SO Track on left and track on right to camping areas.

▼ 0.9 End of trail at Independence Lake.
GPS: N39°27.07′ W120°17.25′

Continuation of Main Trail

▼ 0.0 Continue to the east.

4.6 ▲ TR T-intersection. To the left is the spur to Independence Lake. Zero trip meter.
GPS: N39°27.68′ W120°17.48′

▼ 0.3 SO Track on right; then second track on right for non-motorized use only.

4.3 ▲ SO Track on left for non-motorized use only; then second track on left.

▼ 0.4 SO Track on right; then cross over Independence Creek on bridge; then gate.

4.2 ▲ SO Gate; then cross over Independence Creek on bridge; then track on left.

▼ 1.9 BL Seasonal closure gate; then track on right.

2.7 ▲ BR Track on left; then seasonal closure gate.

▼ 2.1 SO Track on left.

2.5 ▲ SO Track on right.
GPS: N39°27.24′ W120°16.11′

▼ 3.2 SO Track on left is 351-10.

1.4 ▲ SO Track on right is 351-10.

▼ 3.8 SO Track on left.

0.8 ▲ SO Track on right.

▼ 3.9 SO Well-used track on left. Join CR 260.
0.7 ▲ BL Well-used track on right.
GPS: N39°27.57' W120°14.35'

▼ 4.6 TR Gravel road straight ahead. Turn right onto FR 11, following sign to Sagehen Campground. Zero trip meter.
0.0 ▲ Continue to the west.
GPS: N39°27.16' W120°13.80'

▼ 0.0 Continue to the south.
2.6 ▲ TL T-intersection. Turn left onto gravel road. Zero trip meter.
▼ 0.1 SO Seasonal closure gate.
2.5 ▲ SO Seasonal closure gate.
▼ 0.5 SO Track on left.
2.1 ▲ SO Track on right.
▼ 0.8 SO Track on left.
1.8 ▲ SO Track on right.
▼ 1.4 SO Cross over creek.
1.2 ▲ SO Cross over creek.
▼ 2.4 SO Road becomes paved. Track on right is 11-2.
0.2 ▲ SO Track on left is 11-2. Road turns back to graded dirt.
GPS: N39°26.38' W120°15.74'

▼ 2.6 BR Graded road on left is 11-04, which goes 0.5 miles to Sagehen USFS Campground. Zero trip meter. Road turns back to graded dirt.
0.0 ▲ Continue to the north on FR 11.
GPS: N39°26.28' W120°15.81'

▼ 0.0 Continue to the southwest on FR 11.
2.3 ▲ BL Graded road on right is 11-04, which goes 0.5 miles to Sagehen USFS Campground. Zero trip meter. Road is now paved.
▼ 0.5 SO Track on left.
1.8 ▲ SO Track on right.
▼ 0.9 SO Track on right. Follow sign for Carpenter Ridge.
1.4 ▲ SO Track on left.
▼ 1.2 SO Cross over Sagehen Creek on bridge.
1.1 ▲ SO Cross over Sagehen Creek on bridge.
GPS: N39°26.05' W120°16.83'

▼ 1.6 SO Track on left is 11-6.
0.7 ▲ SO Track on right is 11-6.

▼ 2.3 BL Track on right is 11-8, which goes to Carpenter Ridge. In winter it is a cross-country ski route. Follow sign to the Sagehen Hills. Zero trip meter.
0.0 ▲ Continue to the northeast on FR 11.
GPS: N39°25.23' W120°16.88'

▼ 0.0 Continue to the south on 11-10.
5.3 ▲ BR Track on left is 11-8, which goes to Carpenter Ridge. In winter it is a cross-country ski route. Zero trip meter.
▼ 0.9 SO Hike up ridge on right for panoramic views of Carpenter Valley, Red Mountain, and North Fork Prosser Creek.
4.4 ▲ SO Hike up ridge on left for panoramic views of Carpenter Valley, Red Mountain, and North Fork Prosser Creek.
▼ 1.2 BR Track on left.
4.1 ▲ SO Track on right.
▼ 1.3 SO Track on left.
4.0 ▲ SO Track on right.
▼ 1.4 SO Start of shelf road.
3.9 ▲ SO End of shelf road.
▼ 2.1 SO End of shelf road.
3.2 ▲ SO Start of shelf road.
▼ 2.2 BL Track on right is marked as a dead end
3.1 ▲ BR Track on left is marked as a dead end. Bear right onto 11-10.
GPS: N39°24.33' W120°15.44'

▼ 2.5 SO Well-used track on right; then track on left.
2.8 ▲ SO Track on right; then well-used track on left.
GPS N39°24.57' W120°15.44'

▼ 2.7 BR Track on left.
2.6 ▲ BL Track on right.
▼ 3.0 SO Well-used track on left.
2.3 ▲ BL Well-used track on right.
▼ 3.1 SO Views of Stampede Reservoir to the northeast and Prosser Creek Reservoir to the southeast.
2.2 ▲ SO Views of Stampede Reservoir to the northeast and Prosser Creek Reservoir to the southeast.
▼ 3.6 SO Track on right.
1.7 ▲ SO Track on left.
GPS: N39°24.52' W120°14.68'

▼ 4.0	SO	Track on right.
.3 ▲	SO	Track on left.
▼ 4.9	BL	Track on right.
▌.4 ▲	BR	Track on left.
▼ 5.3	BL	Track on right is OHV route. Zero trip meter and pass through seasonal closure gate.
▌.0 ▲		Continue to the southwest.
		GPS: N39°25.41′ W120°14.08′

▼ 0.0		Continue to the northwest.
▌.2 ▲	BR	Seasonal closure gate; then track on left is OHV route. Zero trip meter.
▼ 0.1	SO	Track on left.
▌.1 ▲	SO	Track on right.
▼ 1.2	SO	Seasonal closure gate to protect deer fawning habitat.
▌.0 ▲	SO	Seasonal closure gate to protect deer fawning habitat.
▌1.3	SO	Track on right.
▌.9 ▲	SO	Track on left.
▌2.2	SO	Well-used track on right is 89-36-04.
▌.0 ▲	SO	Well-used track on left is 89-36-04.
		GPS: N39°26.03′ W120°12.67′

▌2.6	SO	Track on left through seasonal closure gate.
▌.6 ▲	BL	Track on right through seasonal closure gate.
		GPS: N39°25.91′ W120°12.25′

▼ 3.1	TL	Track straight ahead continues 1.6 miles to closure gate. Information board at intersection.
▌.1 ▲	TR	T-intersection in front of information board.
▼ 3.2		Seasonal closure gate; then trail ends at T-intersection with California 89. Turn left for Sierraville; turn right for Truckee.
▌.0 ▲		Trail commences on California 89, 1.7 miles north of Hobart USFS Work Center and 7 miles north of Truckee. Zero trip meter and turn west on graded trail 89-36 and pass through seasonal closure gate. There is a Penny Pines sign at the intersection.
		GPS: N39°25.53′ W120°12.01′

Summit City Loop

STARTING POINT Northern Sierra #25: North Bloomfield–Bowman Lake Trail, 3 miles south of Northern Sierra #21: Henness Pass Road

FINISHING POINT Northern Sierra #21: Henness Pass Road (FR 07), 2 miles west of Webber Lake

TOTAL MILEAGE 17.1 miles, plus 2.2-mile spur to Baltimore Lake and 5.9-mile spur to White Rock Lake

UNPAVED MILEAGE 17.1 miles, plus spurs

DRIVING TIME 5 hours (including both spurs)

ELEVATION RANGE 6,200–7,900 feet

USUALLY OPEN April to November

BEST TIME TO TRAVEL April to November

DIFFICULTY RATING 3 (spurs are rated 5 and 4 respectively)

SCENIC RATING 9

REMOTENESS RATING +0

Special Attractions

■ Trail passes five lakes and reservoirs that offer excellent backcountry camping and fishing.

■ Historic site of Summit City and its cemetery.

■ Trail is a groomed snowmobile route in winter.

History

The site of Summit City, a busy mining town of the 1860s, is on the western shore of Meadow Lake. Henry Hartley staked the Excelsior mining claim here in June 1863, and a settlement, originally called Excelsior, had a population of 600 by 1864. Word of the find leaked out and as news traveled, the strike became richer and richer. Concerns about a production drop in Nevada's Comstock Lode quickly drew thousands of miners to what many were calling Little Comstock. In 1866, postal authorities approved the name Meadow Lake for the town's post office. Living conditions at 7,400 feet were far from easy in the winter. Residents often scrambled out of their houses through upstairs windows, and snow depths reached levels that required digging tunnels between houses.

Miners staked claims by the thousands, stamp mills were built, and the population climbed to more than 4,000. Schools, breweries, saloons, and stores flourished in this boom town from the mid to late 1860s. The settlement of Hudsonville, on the far side of Meadow Lake, attracted miners to its entertainment houses.

The winter of 1867–68 brought record levels of snow, trapping thousands. Communication with the outside world was restricted, but the legendary Snowshoe Thompson, a Norwegian emigrant who made his own oak skis, kept up mail delivery to the community.

Though gold-bearing ore kept prospectors interested, extracting it was the real battle. Most gave up as the years went on, leaving only 60 residents in Summit City by 1869. Henry Hartley never gave up. He stayed on into the 1870s, living a hermit's life at the ghost town he truly believed in. Hartley's tombtone in Summit City Cemetery recounts his dream: that he, like his town, would be resurrected to live another day.

Description

Summit City Loop is an easy to moderate trail that passes five very different lakes as well as the historic site of Summit City.

The trail begins on Northern Sierra #25: North Bloomfield–Bowman Lake Trail, 3 miles south of Jackson Meadow Reservoir. The uneven formed trail travels through a mix of forest and small meadows. The first two lakes—Catfish and Tollhouse—are small lakes set in granite basins and surrounded by firs. Some excellent backcountry campsites can be found on the shores of both lakes. Anglers will enjoy fishing in the small lakes as well as in Jackson Meadow Reservoir. French Lake is a short distance off the trail. Vehicle travel is permitted for the first 0.3 miles, but you must hike the remaining distance to the lake. Mountain bikes are permitted to travel the entire way to the lake.

The historic Summit City Cemetery is a short distance off the main trail. Graves are marked by steel crosses, and there is a large monument to

Summit City's founder Henry Hartley. Opposi[te] the graveyard on the other side of the trail, fou[n] dations of the town's brickworks can be seen in [a] clearing. Be careful and tread lightly in th[e] area—the old bricks are very fragile. Summ[it] City's site is on the shores of Meadow Lake an[d] is indicated by a historical marker.

The old town site is the starting point f[or] the very difficult Fordyce Jeep Trail (an e[x] treme hardcore trail for modified, sho[rt] wheel-base vehicles only) and also the start [of] the 5-rated spur toward Baltimore Lake. Th[e] spur travels 2.2 miles southwest along loo[se] uneven rock before finishing on a saddle [a] short distance from Baltimore Lake. Frenc[h] Lake can be seen to the north from here. Th[e] lakes themselves are in an area that prohibi[ts] motorized vehicles. Mountain bikers, hiker[s] and equestrians can descend to the thick[ly] forested basin of Baltimore Lake. The hikin[g] trail continues over a saddle to a group [of] four lakes known as Beyer Lakes.

Past Summit City, the trail becomes grade[d] and the standard improves slightly, passing [a] number of designated campsites on the shore[s] of Meadow Lake. From the ridge above Mead[ow] Lake, excellent views open up over th[e] granite dome landscape, with Fordyce Lake i[n] the distance.

The second spur, to White Rock Lake, [is] rated a 4 for difficulty. This rating is due t[o] the final section that winds down to campsit[es] along the lake's edge. This lake, surrounded b[y] high, pale-colored granite and ringed by fir[s] is among the prettiest in the area. The cam[p] sites at the lake have no facilities.

Past the spur to White Rock Lake, the tra[il] is a graded gravel road maintained by the fo[r] est service that finishes on paved FR 07, [x] miles west of Webber Lake.

The main loop is a groomed snowmobi[le] route in winter and is marked with orange a[r] rows high on the trees.

Current Road Information

Tahoe National Forest
Sierraville Ranger District
317 South Lincoln Street
Sierraville, CA 96126
(530) 994-3401

A short section of slickrock on the Baltimore spur trail

Map References

BLM   Truckee
USFS   Tahoe National Forest
USGS   1:24,000   English Mtn., Webber Peak
       1:100,000   Truckee
Maptech CD-ROM: High Sierra/Tahoe
Northern California Atlas & Gazetteer,
       pp. 80, 81
California Road & Recreation Atlas,
       pp. 60, 61

Route Directions

▼ 0.0   Trail begins on Northern Sierra #25:
           North Bloomfield–Bowman Lake Trail,
           3 miles south of Northern Sierra #21:
           Henness Pass Road. Zero trip meter
           and turn southeast on graded road
           (called Meadow Lake Road on some
           maps), following sign to Catfish Lake
           and Meadow Lake. Cross over creek.
6.6 ▲   Cross over creek; then trail ends at T-
           intersection with Northern Sierra #25:
           North Bloomfield–Bowman Lake Trail.
           Turn right for Jackson Meadow
           Resevoir; turn left for Nevada City.
           GPS: N39°28.44' W120°33.73'

▼ 0.3   SO   Track on left.
6.3 ▲   SO   Track on right.
▼ 0.5   SO   Track on right goes 0.5 miles to
             Catfish Lake.
6.1 ▲   SO   Track on left goes 0.5 miles to
             Catfish Lake.
             GPS: N39°28.34' W120°33.16'

▼ 1.1   SO   Cross over creek.
5.5 ▲   SO   Cross over creek.
▼ 1.3   SO   Track on left.
5.3 ▲   SO   Track on right.
▼ 1.4   SO   Corral on left.
5.2 ▲   SO   Corral on right.
▼ 1.6   SO   Track on right; then cross over creek.
5.0 ▲   SO   Cross over creek; then track on left.
▼ 2.3   SO   Track on right.
4.3 ▲   SO   Track on left.
▼ 2.5   SO   Cross through French Creek.
4.1 ▲   SO   Cross through French Creek.
             GPS: N39°27.10' W120°31.98'

NORTHERN SIERRA #24: SUMMIT CITY LOOP

▼ 3.7   SO   Cross through meadow.
2.9 ▲   SO   Cross through meadow.
▼ 3.8   SO   Well-used but unmarked track on right
             goes 1.6 miles to French Lake.
             Motorized vehicle use prohibited after
             0.3 miles.
2.8 ▲   SO   Well-used but unmarked track on left
             goes 1.6 miles to French Lake.
             Motorized vehicle use prohibited after
             0.3 miles.
             GPS: N39°26.15' W120°31.40'

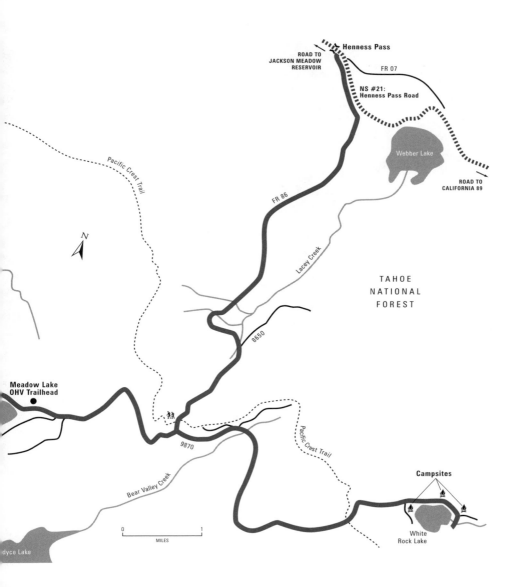

▼ 4.0   SO   Track on right.
2.6 ▲   SO   Track on left.

▼ 4.1   SO   Track on left. Tollhouse Lake on right.
2.5 ▲   SO   Track on right. Tollhouse Lake on left.

        GPS: N39°26.07′ W120°31.02′

▼ 4.2   SO   Cross through creek.
2.4 ▲   SO   Cross through creek.

▼ 4.6   BR   Track on left. Follow sign to
                    Meadow Lake.

2.0 ▲   BL   Track on right.

        GPS: N39°25.68′ W120°30.65′

▼ 5.1   BR   Track on left.
1.5 ▲   BL   Track on right.

▼ 5.2   SO   Track on right; then track on left.
1.4 ▲   SO   Track on right; then track on left.

▼ 5.4   SO   Small lake on right.
1.2 ▲   SO   Small lake on left.

        GPS: N39°25.41′ W120°30.66′

▼ 5.5   SO   Track on left.
1.1 ▲   SO   Track on right.

▼ 5.7   SO   Turnout on right.

Setting up camp at Meadow Lake

0.9 ▲	SO	Turnout on left.
▼ 5.8	SO	Track on right.
0.8 ▲	SO	Track on left.
▼ 6.0	SO	Track on right.
0.6 ▲	SO	Track on left.
		GPS: N39°24.84′ W120°30.52′

▼ 6.1	SO	Unmarked track on left to Summit City Cemetery. Remains of the brickworks are in the small clearing opposite.
0.5 ▲	SO	Unmarked track on right to Summit City Cemetery. Remains of the brickworks are in the small clearing opposite.
		GPS: N39°24.78′ W120°30.50′

▼ 6.6	TL	Track on right is the spur to Baltimore Lake and also leads toward Excelsior Mine and Fordyce Lake. Site of Summit City is marked by a sign. Zero trip meter.
0.0 ▲		Continue to the west-southwest.
		GPS: N39°24.58′ W120°30.13′

Spur to Baltimore Lake

▼ 0.0		At the sign for Summit City, turn south-southwest. Immediately bear right at fork in trail. Track on left is the start of the Fordyce Jeep Trail. Tracks on right to campsites.
▼ 0.2	BR	Track on left goes to Excelsior Mine.
		GPS: N39°24.51′ W120°30.30′

▼ 1.4	SO	Hard-to-spot track on right goes 0.3 miles to mine and is rated 6 for difficulty.
		GPS: N39°23.68′ W120°31.18′

▼ 1.6	BL	Track on right goes 0.1 miles to saddle. No motorized vehicles allowed past the saddle. Hikers and mountain bikers can climb along the old trail to Baltimore Lake.
		GPS: N39°23.58′ W120°31.21′

▼ 2.1	SO	Trail climbs slickrock.
		GPS: N39°23.27′ W120°31.23′

▼ 2.2   Trail ends just east of Baltimore town site at an overlook of Fordyce Lake. Trail is little used by vehicles past this point.
GPS: N39°23.25′ W120°31.23′

Continuation of Main Trail

▼ 0.0   Continue to the north. Immediately track on right and track on left.
4.1 ▲   TR   Track on right and track on left. Track straight ahead is the spur to Baltimore Lake and also leads toward Excelsior Mine and Fordyce Lake. Turn right in front of the Summit City sign, following the sign to Tollhouse Lake. Zero trip meter.
GPS: N39°24.58′ W120°30.13′

▼ 0.1   SO   Track on right to designated campsite. Many tracks on right to campsites for the next 1.2 miles.
4.0 ▲   SO   Track on left to designated campsite. End of designated campsites.

▼ 0.8   SO   Track on left.
3.3 ▲   SO   Track on right.
▼ 0.9   SO   Track on left.
3.2 ▲   SO   Track on right.
▼ 1.3   SO   End of designated camping area.
2.8 ▲   SO   Start of designated camping area. Many tracks on left to designated campsites for the next 1.2 miles.

▼ 1.5   BR   Graded road on left is parking area for Meadow Lake OHV Trail; then track on left.
2.6 ▲   BL   Track on right; then graded road on right is parking area for Meadow Lake OHV Trail.
GPS: N39°25.20′ W120°28.87′

▼ 1.7   SO   Track on left; then track on right.
2.4 ▲   SO   Track on left; then track on right.
▼ 1.8   SO   Track on right.
2.3 ▲   SO   Track on left.
▼ 2.1   BL   Track on right is 84305.
2.0 ▲   BR   Track on left is 84305.
GPS: N39°25.21′ W120°28.18′

▼ 3.6   SO   Track on left.
0.5 ▲   SO   Track on right.
▼ 4.1   SO   Start of FR 86. Graded road on right is spur to White Rock Lake. Zero trip meter.

0.0 ▲   Continue to the northwest. Road becomes rougher.
GPS: N39°25.35′ W120°26.86′

Spur to White Rock Lake

▼ 0.0   Turn southeast on graded road 9870, following sign to White Rock Lake. Immediately track on right.
▼ 0.8   BR   Well-used track on left; then small track on left. Cross over Bear Valley Creek.
GPS: N39°25.52′ W120°26.12′

▼ 1.2   BL   Well-used track on right at sign for Deer Zone D-3.
▼ 3.5   SO   Cross through wash.
▼ 3.6   SO   Track on right.
GPS: N39°24.71′ W120°24.51′

▼ 4.2   BL   Track on right; then Pacific Crest Trail crosses.
GPS: N39°25.04′ W120°24.13′

▼ 4.9   BL   Trail forks. Left goes to campsites (for high-clearance vehicles only) and right goes 0.3 miles to campsites.
GPS: N39°25.24′ W120°23.43′

▼ 5.2   SO   Many campsites along the edge of White Rock Lake.
GPS: N39°25.30′ W120°23.09′

▼ 5.7   SO   Track on left; then cross through creek.
GPS: N39°25.23′ W120°22.67′

▼ 5.9   Trail ends at lakeshore.
GPS: N39°25.12′ W120°22.68′

Continuation of Main Trail

▼ 0.0   Continue to the northeast, following sign to Webber Lake. Road improves.
6.4 ▲   SO   End of FR 86. Graded road on left is spur to White Rock Lake. Follow sign to Meadow Lake and zero trip meter.
GPS: N39°25.35′ W120°26.86′

▼ 0.2   SO   Pacific Crest Trail crosses.
6.2 ▲   SO   Pacific Crest Trail crosses.

View of Fordyce Dam at the end of the Baltimore spur trail

▼ 0.4   SO   Track on right.
6.0 ▲   SO   Track on left.
▼ 1.4   SO   Track on right is 8650; then cross over
             Lacey Creek.
5.0 ▲   SO   Cross over Lacey Creek; then track
             on left is 8650.
▼ 2.2   SO   Cross over creek.
4.2 ▲   SO   Cross over creek.
▼ 2.5   SO   Cross over creek.
3.9 ▲   SO   Cross over creek.
▼ 2.8   SO   Formed road on right is 9840; then
             track on right.
3.6 ▲   SO   Track on left; then formed road on left
             is 9840.
             GPS: N39°27.14′ W120°26.44′

▼ 3.8   SO   Track on left.
2.6 ▲   SO   Track on right.
▼ 5.0   SO   Seasonal closure gates.
1.4 ▲   SO   Seasonal closure gates.
▼ 5.8   SO   Graded road on right is Northern Sierra
             #21: Henness Pass Road (CR 301).
             Trail follows Henness Pass Road for
             final 0.6 miles.

0.6 ▲   BR   Graded road on left is eastern continu-
             ation of Northern Sierra #21: Henness
             Pass Road (CR 301).
             GPS: N39°29.41′ W120°25.70′

▼ 6.2   SO   Track on right.
0.2 ▲   SO   Track on left.
▼ 6.4   Trail ends at T-intersection with paved
             FR 07, part of Northern Sierra #21:
             Henness Pass Road, at Henness Pass.
             Turn right for California 89; turn left for
             Jackson Meadow Reservoir.
0.0 ▲   Trail commences on paved Northern
             Sierra #21: Henness Pass Road (FR
             07) at Henness Pass, 2 miles west of
             Webber Lake. Zero trip meter and turn
             southwest on graded dirt road CR 301,
             following the sign to White Rock Lake
             and Meadow Lake. Turn is immediate-
             ly west of county mile marker 9.47.
             Trail follows Henness Pass Road for
             first 0.6 miles.
             GPS: N39°29.90′ W120°26.00′

North Bloomfield–Bowman Lake Trail

STARTING POINT California 49 in Nevada City, 0.3 miles west of California 20

FINISHING POINT Northern Sierra #21: Henness Pass Road at Jackson Meadow Reservoir

TOTAL MILEAGE 40.7 miles

UNPAVED MILEAGE 30.7 miles

DRIVING TIME 5 hours

ELEVATION RANGE 2,000–6,600 feet

USUALLY OPEN Year-round

BEST TIME TO TRAVEL Dry weather

DIFFICULTY RATING 2

SCENIC RATING 9

REMOTENESS RATING +0

Special Attractions

- Bowman Lake and Jackson Meadow Reservoir.
- Malakoff Diggins State Park.
- Historic town of Graniteville and Graniteville Cemetery.

History

Traveling the North Bloomfield–Bowman Lake Trail offers an opportunity to follow in the footsteps of miners from a time long gone, but not quite forgotten. Nevada City, at the start of the trail, may seem busy nowadays, but try to imagine the scene in 1850, when 10,000 gold-hungry men and boys tried to make this newly constructed camp their home. On the northwest side of Sugarloaf Mountain is the site of Allan's Foundry, the first manufacturing site of the renowned Pelton waterwheel. Lester Allan Pelton's wheel revolutionized hydraulic mining by harnessing nearly all the energy of water. The first wheel was used in the highly productive North Star Mine in Grass Valley, which produced $33 million in gold by 1928. The invention opened the door for the hydroelectric power industry.

Establishing wagon roads to the mines was of utmost importance, but it was quite a challenge in country cut by steep canyons. The first bridge to the Malakoff Diggins was built in the 1850s at Edwards Crossing over the South Yuba River. Today's high-arched steel bridge, built in 1904, is the fourth bridge at this location.

The settlement of Lake City, also known as Painesville, was settled in 1853, east of the Malakoff Diggins. By 1857, more than 300 people lived at the site. No buildings survive, but a sign marks the location of Bridget Waldron's livery stable.

The drive downhill to Malakoff Diggins is an eye-opener on how hydraulic mining changed the landscape. Between the 1850s and 1880s gold miners channeled creeks high in the mountains to create enough pressure for hydraulic operations at lower elevations. High-powered water jets directed by giant monitor nozzles collapsed hillsides so that dirt and rocks could be washed for gold. An estimated $3.5 million worth of gold was extracted from this vicinity. By 1884, farmers had managed to lobby a ban on hydraulic mining because silt and mud buried fields and changed the flow of downstream rivers and waterways. The site of North Bloomfield (see page 179), on the edge of Malakoff Diggins, has an excellent selection of miners' dwellings, stores, and a museum.

Farther to the northeast the trail passes the site of Quinn Ranch, a former stage stop called Shand that was no doubt a welcome sight to travelers. From here they went to Graniteville, formerly known as Eureka. Today, the site is a far cry from its gold mining days of the 1860s. Surface mines were worked as early as 1850, though these played out by the end of the decade. A return to lode mining rekindled the town in the mid 1860s. Hotels, stores, a blacksmith shop, and several saloons operated until the 1870s.

Picturesque Bowman Lake, set below Quartz Hill, was an important water source for some of the mining communities at lower elevations. The dam was built on the old Bowman Ranch. Bowman House, just below the dam, was at the junction of two important wagon roads. The early route up through Eureka (Graniteville), on past Marsh Mill (operated by Charles Marsh), to Bowman House was an alternative to the Henness Pass Road. The Pacific Turnpike Road, also known as Culbertson's Road, joined in from the south at this point. From here these separate routes headed northeast to Jackson's Meadow, nowadays Jackson Meadow Reservoir.

Description

This easy, graded road travels from Nevada City past the northern shore of Bowman Lake to finish on Northern Sierra #21: Henness Pass Road at Jackson Meadow Reservoir.

From Nevada City, the trail drops steeply along a small paved road to cross over the South Yuba River at Edwards Crossing. The South Yuba Trail, an enjoyable hike along the South Yuba River, crosses the road at this point. This moderate trail is 15 miles long and takes hikers east to Washington. The river is stocked yearly with rainbow trout. The road turns to graded dirt after the bridge, and it climbs to the top of the ridge, where Northern Sierra #26: Alleghany Trail heads off to the north. The main trail bears east and passes the developed South Yuba BLM Campground, which has 16 campsites in a shaded gully at the site of some old mine workings. A small fee is charged.

The trail enters Malakoff Diggins State Park, once the site of some of the most prosperous and active hydraulic mining ventures in California. You can view the mine face and see the massive changes in the landscape caused by hydraulic mining. Many of the original buildings from the settlement of North Bloomfield can also be seen in the park. The park has a campground and a few cabins in the main part of town. There is plenty to see and do in the park, and many people choose to make it an overnight stop along the trail. There are several short and interesting hiking trails, including the 3-mile Rim Trail around the perimeter of the Malakoff Diggins, and the 3-mile Diggins Trail through the works.

Continuing east through Tahoe National Forest, the trail passes Snowtent Spring, a flowing cold-water spring with an informal camping area behind it. Northern Sierra #26: Alleghany Trail rejoins shortly before Graniteville and the historic Graniteville Cemetery, which is a short distance west of the settlement. There are no services in Graniteville, but the settlement has some wonderful old, historic houses that are used as summer homes.

Past Graniteville, the trail drops in standard to become a roughly graded dirt road. It winds past oaks, manzanitas, and firs to Bowman Lake, a popular destination for outdoor enthusiasts. The trail drops in standard again—this section of road is not maintained by the forest service. A wonderful selection of backcountry campsites is scattered along the lakeshore among large granite boulders and firs. There is an informal boat launch, and both boat and shore anglers will enjoy fishing for brown and rainbow trout. The lake is stocked annually with fingerlings.

As the trail leaves the lakeshore, additional camping areas can be found, including the Bowman Lake Campground, where there are a couple of scattered tables, and the more maintained Jackson Creek USFS Campground. Note that the Bowman Lake Campground does not appear on the Tahoe National Forest map.

The trail ends at the intersection with Northern Sierra #21: Henness Pass Road at Jackson Meadow Reservoir.

Current Road Information

Tahoe National Forest
Yuba River Ranger District
15924 Highway 49
Camptonville, CA 95922
(530) 288-3231

Map References

BLM   Yuba City, Truckee, Portola
USFS   Tahoe National Forest
USGS   1:24,000   Nevada City, North
        Bloomfield, Pike, Alleghany,
        Graniteville, English Mtn.,
        Haypress Valley
        1:100,000 Yuba City, Truckee,
        Portola
Maptech CD-ROM: High Sierra/Tahoe
Northern California Atlas & Gazetteer,
        pp. 79, 80, 70
California Road & Recreation Atlas,
        pp. 65, 60

One of Graniteville's historic buildings

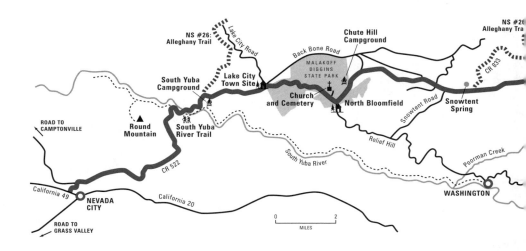

Route Directions

▼ 0.0   From the intersection of California 49 and California 20 at Nevada City, exit the divided road onto California 49, following sign for Downieville. Proceed 0.3 miles west; then zero trip meter and turn north on paved North Bloomfield Road (CR 522). Remain on paved North Bloomfield Road, ignoring turns to the left and right.

8.5 ▲   Trail ends at T-intersection with California 49 in Nevada City.
GPS: N39°16.16′ W121°01.19′

▼ 0.5   TR   T-intersection. Remain on North Bloomfield Road, following sign for South Yuba Campground. Lake Vera Road is on the left.

8.0 ▲   TL   Lake Vera Road is straight ahead. Turn left, remaining on North Bloomfield Road.

▼ 7.1   SO   South Yuba Trail (hiking) to Round Mountain on left; then cross over South Yuba River on bridge. Road turns to graded dirt.

1.4 ▲   SO   Road becomes paved. Cross over South Yuba River on bridge; then South Yuba Trail (hiking) to Round Mountain on right.
GPS: N39°19.78′ W120°59.04′

▼ 7.2   SO   Hiking access on right to river and continuation of the South Yuba Trail.

1.3 ▲   SO   Hiking access on left to river and continuation of the South Yuba Trail.

▼ 8.0   SO   Track on left.

0.5 ▲   SO   Track on right.

▼ 8.5   BR   Graded road on left is Northern Sierra #26: Alleghany Trail (Grizzly Hill Road). Zero trip meter and remain on North Bloomfield Road, following sign to Malakoff Diggins State Park.

0.0 ▲   Continue to the south.
GPS: N39°20.48′ W120°58.50′

▼ 0.0   Continue to the northeast.

5.3 ▲   BL   Graded road on right is Northern Sierra #26: Alleghany Trail (Grizzly Hill Road). Zero trip meter.

▼ 0.2   SO   Track on right into South Yuba BLM Campground and access to South Yuba Trail.

5.1 ▲   SO   Track on left into South Yuba BLM Campground and access to the South Yuba Trail.

▼ 0.6   SO   Track on left.

4.7 ▲   SO   Track on right.

▼ 0.9   SO   Track on left and track on right.

4.4 ▲   SO   Track on left and track on right.

▼ 1.4   SO   Track on right.

3.9 ▲   SO   Track on left.

▼ 1.6   SO   Track on right.

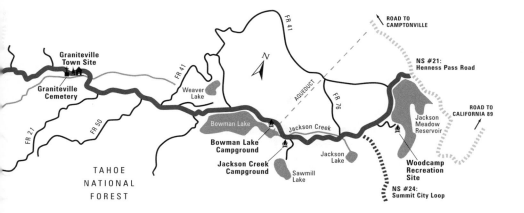

3.7 ▲	SO	Track on left.	
▼ 2.1	SO	Track on right.	
3.2 ▲	SO	Track on left.	
▼ 2.3	SO	Site of Lake City on both sides of the road; then track on left.	
3.0 ▲	SO	Track on right; then site of Lake City on both sides of the road.	
		GPS: N39°21.49′ W120°56.52′	

▼ 2.4	BR	Lake City Road on left; then Back Bone Road on left. Remain on North Bloomfield Road, following sign for Malakoff Diggins. Enter Malakoff Diggins State Park.
2.9 ▲	TL	Back Bone Road on right; then Lake City Road on right. Remain on North Bloomfield Road and exit state park.
		GPS: N39°21.54′ W120°56.47′

▼ 3.2	SO	Rim Trail (hiking) to campground on left.
2.1 ▲	SO	Rim Trail (hiking) to campground on right.
		GPS: N39°21.92′ W120°55.87′

▼ 3.7	SO	Diggins Loop Trail access on left.
1.6 ▲	SO	Diggins Loop Trail access on right.
▼ 3.9	SO	Humbug Trail (hiking) on right.
1.4 ▲	SO	Humbug Trail (hiking) on left.
		GPS: N39°21.92′ W120°55.35′

▼ 4.0	SO	Cross over North Bloomfield Drain Tunnel.
1.3 ▲	SO	Cross over North Bloomfield Drain Tunnel.

▼ 4.5	SO	Road becomes paved. Two cabins on right; then Diggins overlook and historical marker on left.
0.8 ▲	SO	Diggins overlook and historical marker on right; then two cabins on left. Road turns to graded dirt.
▼ 5.0	SO	Track on left to cemetery. Then St. Columncille's Catholic Church on left and Le Du Mine overlook on right.
0.3 ▲	SO	Le Du Mine overlook on left and St. Columncille's Catholic Church on right. Then track on right to cemetery.
		GPS: N39°22.00′ W120°54.26′

▼ 5.1	SO	Track on left; then China Garden on right.
0.2 ▲	SO	China Garden on left; then track on right.
▼ 5.3	SO	North Bloomfield. Zero trip meter at the intersection of North Bloomfield Road and Relief Hill Road.
0.0 ▲		Continue to the southwest, following sign for Nevada City.
		GPS: N39°22.08′ W120°53.95′

▼ 0.0		Continue to the northeast, following sign for Graniteville.
5.4 ▲	SO	North Bloomfield. Zero trip meter at the intersection of North Bloomfield Road and Relief Hill Road.
▼ 0.2	SO	Picnic area at Blair Lake on right.
5.2 ▲	SO	Picnic area at Blair Lake on left.
▼ 0.6	SO	Blair Trail (hiking) crosses road. Paved

road on left goes to Chute Hill Campground—run by the Malakoff Diggins State Historic Park.

4.8 ▲ SO Paved road on right goes to Chute Hill Campground—run by the Malakoff Diggins State Historic Park. Blair Trail (hiking) crosses road.

▼ 1.3 SO Paved road continues to the left. Continue straight ahead onto graded dirt road.

4.1 ▲ SO Paved road enters from right. Continue straight ahead and join paved road.
GPS: **N39°23.17' W120°53.68'**

▼ 3.6 BR Track on right; then bear right and join graded road, following sign for Graniteville.

1.8 ▲ BL Graded road continues straight ahead. Bear left onto graded road; then track on left.
GPS: **N39°23.75' W120°51.40'**

▼ 4.1 SO Track on right and graded road on left.

1.3 ▲ SO Track on left and graded road on right.

▼ 4.5 SO Track on right is Snowtent Road to Relief Hill.

0.9 ▲ SO Track on left is Snowtent Road to Relief Hill.
GPS: **N39°23.73' W120°50.43'**

▼ 4.6 SO Track on left is 522-2.

0.8 ▲ SO Track on right is 522-2.

▼ 5.1 SO Track on right and track on left; then second track on left.

0.3 ▲ SO Track on right; then second track on right and track on left.

▼ 5.2 SO Snowtent Spring and camping area on left.

0.2 ▲ SO Snowtent Spring and camping area on right.
GPS: **N39°23.98' W120°49.71'**

▼ 5.4 SO Road on right is Robbins Ranch Road. Track on left is Northern Sierra #26: Alleghany Trail (CR 833) signposted to Moores Flat and Bucks Ranch. Zero trip meter.

0.0 ▲ Continue to the southwest.
GPS: **N39°24.09' W120°49.52'**

▼ 0.0 Continue to the northeast.

6.0 ▲ SO Road on left is Robbins Ranch Road. Track on right is Northern Sierra #26: Alleghany Trail (CR 833) signposted to Moores Flat and Bucks Ranch. Zero trip meter.

▼ 0.3 SO Track on right.

5.7 ▲ SO Track on left.

▼ 0.4 SO Track on right.

5.6 ▲ SO Track on left.

▼ 1.7 SO Track on left and track on right.

4.3 ▲ SO Track on left and track on right.

▼ 2.7 SO Track on left; then track on right.

3.3 ▲ SO Track on left; then track on right.

▼ 3.1 SO Graded road on right.

2.9 ▲ SO Graded road on left.

▼ 3.2 SO Track on left.

2.8 ▲ SO Track on right.

▼ 3.6 SO Track on left.

2.4 ▲ SO Track on right.

▼ 3.7 SO Track on right.

2.3 ▲ SO Track on left.

▼ 4.1 SO Track on left and track on right.

1.9 ▲ SO Track on right and track on left.

▼ 4.4 SO Track on left.

1.6 ▲ SO Track on right.

▼ 4.8 SO Track on left.

1.2 ▲ SO Track on right.

▼ 4.9 SO Track on right.

1.1 ▲ SO Track on left.

▼ 5.1 SO Graded road on left is S2248.

0.9 ▲ SO Graded road on right is S2248.
GPS: **N39°26.29' W120°45.31'**

▼ 5.8 SO Graniteville Cemetery on right. Track on left.

0.2 ▲ SO Graniteville Cemetery on left. Track on right.
GPS: **N39°26.38' W120°44.71'**

▼ 6.0 SO Entering Graniteville. Historical marker and public telephone on left. Zero trip meter.

0.0 ▲ Continue to the southwest.
GPS: **N39°26.35' W120°44.49'**

▼ 0.0 Continue to the northeast.

7.0 ▲ SO Leaving Graniteville. Historical marker and public telephone on right. Zero trip meter.

NORTH BLOOMFIELD AND MALAKOFF DIGGINS

The virtually deserted town of North Bloomfield is within the boundaries of Malakoff Diggins State Historic Park, northeast of Nevada City. Three prospectors first discovered gold near Humbug Creek in 1851. By 1853, the hamlet of Humbug had sprung up along the creek. When Humbug's population merited a post office in 1857, residents decided to change the image of their town with a new name. They voted June 1, 1857, and chose Bloomfield. The post office added "North" to the name to distinguish it from a Sonoma County settlement of the same name.

Before long, North Bloomfield had some 1,700 residents, eight saloons, five hotels, two breweries, two churches, a daily freight service, and a variety of other services. The Malakoff Mine was North Bloomfield's economic base, and it used hydraulic mining to extract gold. Entire hillsides were blasted away with high-pressure streams of water, turning dirt and rock into muddy, debris-filled streams that were directed through sluices, which caught the gold. The rest of the mud was carried through an 8,000-foot

North Bloomfield hotel

tunnel and dumped into the South Yuba River. Operated by the North Bloomfield Gravel Mining Company, the Malakoff Mine was the largest hydraulic mining operation in the world. Its gigantic operation created a huge canyon, which can now be seen in the Malakoff Diggins State Historic Park.

In order to manage its operations, the North Bloomfield Gravel Mining Company aided in the construction of the world's first long-distance telephone line, stretching from French Corral through North Bloomfield to Bowman Lake.

Hydraulic mining was extremely profitable, but proved devastating to streams, filling them with sediment, and burying cropland. The process was banned in 1884, and the end of hydraulic mining was also the end of North Bloomfield. People abandoned the town, and today it is the headquarters for the state park and residence for a number of park employees. Several of its mining-era buildings, including the schoolhouse, are still standing, and others have been reconstructed. The pharmacy, saloon, and general store have been refurbished and appear to be ready for business. A museum has exhibits illustrating the town's history. The Malakoff Diggins State Historic Park also has picnic areas and campgrounds, hiking trails, and a beautiful reservoir.

Edwards Crossing bridges the South Yuba River

▼ 0.5   SO   Track on left. Leaving Graniteville.

6.5 ▲   SO   Track on right. Entering Graniteville.

▼ 0.8   SO   Track on left; then cross over Poorman Creek on bridge.

6.2 ▲   BL   Cross over Poorman Creek on bridge; then bear left past track ahead.

▼ 1.0   SO   Track on left.

6.0 ▲   SO   Track on right.

▼ 1.6   SO   Track on left.

5.4 ▲   SO   Track on right.

▼ 1.8   TL   Graded road on right is FR 21 to Washington. Bear left onto graded road. Immediately track on left.

5.2 ▲   TR   Track on right; then turn right onto unmarked graded road. Track ahead goes to Washington.
          GPS: N39°26.24′ W120°43.17′

▼ 2.8   SO   Track on left and track on right.

4.2 ▲   SO   Track on left and track on right.

▼ 3.4   SO   Graded road on right is FR 50.

3.6 ▲   SO   Graded road on left is FR 50.
          GPS: N39°26.64′ W120°41.69′

▼ 3.9   SO   Graded road on left is Pinoli Ridge Road (FR 41) to Jackson Meadow Reservoir.

3.1 ▲   SO   Graded road on right is Pinoli Ridge Road (FR 41) to Jackson Meadow Reservoir.
          GPS: N39°26.62′ W120°41.07′

▼ 4.3   BR   Graded road on left; then seasonal closure gate.

2.7 ▲   SO   Seasonal closure gate; then graded road on right.
          GPS: N39°26.65′ W120°40.63′

▼ 5.3 SO Track on right.

1.7 ▲ SO Track on left.

▼ 5.4 TL Seasonal closure gate; then T-intersection. Track on right goes to base of the dam wall.

1.6 ▲ TR Track ahead goes to base of the dam wall. Turn right and pass through seasonal closure gate.

GPS: N39°26.80' W120°39.54'

▼ 6.0 SO Track on right.

1.0 ▲ SO Track on left.

▼ 6.2 SO Track on left. Bowman Lake on right.

0.8 ▲ SO Track on right. Road is now marked as FR 18.

▼ 6.3 SO Two tracks on right give access to Bowman Lake.

0.7 ▲ SO Two tracks on left give access to Bowman Lake.

▼ 7.0 SO Well-used, unmaintained track on left and track on right to campsite. Zero trip meter.

0.0 ▲   Continue to the southwest.

GPS: N39°27.32' W120°38.60'

▼ 0.0 SO Continue to the northeast.

5.5 ▲ SO Well-used, unmaintained track on right and track on left to campsite. Zero trip meter.

▼ 1.4 SO Campsites on right.

4.1 ▲ SO Campsites on left.

▼ 1.5 SO Leaving shore of Bowman Lake.

4.0 ▲ SO Trail starts to follow alongside Bowman Lake.

▼ 1.7 SO Track on right to campsites.

3.8 ▲ SO Track on left to campsites.

▼ 1.9 SO Track on right to Bowman Lake Campground; then cross over Milton Reservoir to Bowman Lake Tunnel Aqueduct. Many tracks on right to camping areas for the next 0.6 miles.

3.6 ▲ SO Cross over the Milton Reservoir to Bowman Lake Tunnel Aqueduct. Track on left to Bowman Lake Campground.

GPS: N39°27.64' W120°36.62'

▼ 2.2 SO Track on right. Last access point to Bowman Lake.

3.3 ▲ SO Track on left. First access point to Bowman Lake.

▼ 2.5 SO Cross over Jackson Creek.

3.0 ▲ SO Cross over Jackson Creek. Many tracks on left to camping areas for the next 0.6 miles.

▼ 2.6 SO Cross over Jackson Creek; then Jackson Creek USFS Campground on right. Track on right goes to Sawmill Lake.

2.9 ▲ SO Track on left goes to Sawmill Lake. Jackson Creek USFS Campground on left; then cross over Jackson Creek.

GPS: N39°27.47' W120°36.04'

▼ 2.9 SO Track on right.

2.6 ▲ SO Track on left.

▼ 3.5 SO Track on right.

2.0 ▲ SO Track on left.

▼ 3.8 SO Track on right.

1.7 ▲ SO Track on left.

▼ 4.0 SO Track on right.

1.5 ▲ SO Track on left.

▼ 4.9 SO Graded road on left is Austin Meadows Road (FR 76).

0.6 ▲ SO Graded road on right is Austin Meadows Road (FR 76).

GPS: N39°28.15' W120°34.34'

▼ 5.5 SO Graded road on right is Northern Sierra #24: Summit City Loop. Zero trip meter.

0.0 ▲   Continue to the southwest.

GPS: N39°28.44' W120°33.73'

▼ 0.0   Continue to the north.

3.0 ▲ BR Graded road on left is Northern Sierra #24: Summit City Loop. Zero trip meter.

▼ 0.4 SO Entering Jackson Meadow Recreation Area; then track on left.

2.6 ▲ SO Track on right; then leaving Jackson Meadow Recreation Area.

▼ 0.6 SO Road becomes paved.

2.4 ▲ SO Road turns to graded dirt.

▼ 0.7 SO Paved road on right goes to Woodcamp Recreation Sites—camping, picnicking, and boat launch. Road turns back to graded dirt.

2.3 ▲ SO Road is now paved. Paved road on left goes to Woodcamp Recreation Sites—camping, picnicking, and boat launch.

▼ 2.1   SO   Graded road on left is FR 41 to Round
             Valley. Follow sign to Jackson
             Meadow Dam. Road is now paved.
0.9 ▲   SO   Graded road on right is FR 41 to Round
             Valley. Follow sign to Bowman Lake.
             Road turns to graded dirt.
             GPS: N39°30.11' W120°33.62'

▼ 2.7   SO   Start to cross Jackson Meadow Dam.
0.3 ▲   SO   Leave dam.
▼ 3.0   Trail ends at T-intersection with
             Northern Sierra #21: Henness Pass
             Road. Turn right for California 89; turn
             left for Milton Reservoir.
0.0 ▲   Trail commences on Northern Sierra
             #21: Henness Pass Road at Jackson
             Meadow Reservoir. Zero trip meter and
             turn southwest on unmarked paved
             road and start to cross the dam.
             GPS: N39°30.59' W120°33.16'

NORTHERN SIERRA #26

Alleghany Trail

STARTING POINT Northern Sierra #25: North
   Bloomfield–Bowman Lake Trail, 8.5
   miles north of Nevada City
FINISHING POINT Northern Sierra #25: North
   Bloomfield–Bowman Lake Trail, 6 miles
   west of Graniteville
TOTAL MILEAGE 31.1 miles
UNPAVED MILEAGE 28.8 miles
DRIVING TIME 5 hours
ELEVATION RANGE 2,200–4,800 feet
USUALLY OPEN April to November
BEST TIME TO TRAVEL Dry weather
DIFFICULTY RATING 4
SCENIC RATING 10
REMOTENESS RATING +1

Special Attractions
- Historic town of Alleghany.
- Two long shelf road descents to the Middle
  Yuba River.
- Trout fishing in the Middle Yuba River.

History
Traveling the Alleghany Trail gives an insight
into how impenetrable this deep canyon
country would have been to Indians and
prospectors alike. The influx of gold-hungry
miners opened up this region in the early
1850s. Smiths Flat, founded in 1851, was the
first mining camp in this locale. Kanaka Flat,
Wet Ravine, Cumberland, and Kanaka City
all followed within a few months. In 1853, J.
McCormick and Perry Bonham, from Al-
legheny, Pennsylvania, started the Alleghany
Mine. By 1856, the town of Alleghany was
laid out. A post office was established the following year, having moved from Chips Flat
on the south side of Kanaka Creek. Mines
were popping up all over; many had colorful
names such as Brush Creek, Gold Canyon,
Ireland, and the Kate Hardy Mine, which had
a covered bridge over the Oregon Creek. Other mines along this trail are the Oriental
Mine, Yellow Jacket Mine, and of course the
Sixteen-to-One Mine.

In 1855, John Thomas Bradbury was digging in his backyard in Alleghany when he
hit a quartz outcrop. He started a tunnel and
discovered what would become one of the
richest and longest lasting mines in the West,
the Sixteen-to-One Mine. H. L. Johnson, a
schoolteacher from Ohio, took over the
Tightner Mine, just northeast of the Sixteen-
to-One and immediately struck it rich. In
1916, it became evident that these two mines
were tapping into the same vein. Johnson
built one of the finest houses in town, sold
his mine for $550,000, and moved to Berke-
ley. The Tightner Mine stayed in business for
nearly 60 years.

Hotels, saloons, stores, schools, churches,
boardwalks, and brass bands all had their day
in Alleghany. Sadly, fires were a constant enemy for this community, perched on the side
of Kanaka Creek Canyon. Two-story hotels
were destroyed and rebuilt even before the
turn of the twentieth century. In 1933, a fire
burned many of the remaining wooden
buildings in town.

Alleghany Trail follows a memorable section of the Tyler Foote Grade, a narrow wagon road from Nevada City to Alleghany.

The old Kanaka Creek bridge in Allegany is now overgrown

Completed over a period of six months in 1913, the road was financed by Mr. Foote, a mine owner in Grass Valley, to the tune of $85,000. Italian stonemasons were employed by the contractor to construct the high stone embankment walls needed to get around the tight curves of the cliff above the Middle Yuba River. These painstakingly hand-built retaining walls are still in place today and are clearly visible as you drive along the canyon walls. The hair-raising stagecoach trip from Nevada City to Alleghany could take as long as two days. Some newcomers refused to invest in the town after they traveled this frightening single-lane route.

If this old road seems manageable today, imagine how it was when it was even narrower, and then try to imagine delivering six tons of winter supplies in an early truck and trailer through several feet of snow. Sam Bidwell delivered mail using a canvas-covered Dodge Power Wagon pickup, fitted with chains during winter. At times Sam was forced to use a diesel Caterpillar bulldozer to get the groceries and mail through deep snow on Tyler Foote Road.

Description

This trail starts and finishes on Northern Sierra #25: North Bloomfield–Bowman Lake Trail, crossing the Middle Yuba River twice and traveling through the historic settlement of Alleghany, site of one of the oldest operating gold mines in California.

The trail leaves North Bloomfield–Bowman Lake Trail 8.5 miles north of Nevada City along a well-graded road. It heads north through Tahoe National Forest, passing through the settlement of Columbia Hill before making a steep descent along a roughly graded, single-lane shelf road to Foote Crossing. The road widens in enough places so that passing is not a problem. The Middle Yuba River flows through the deep canyon; this descent and the subsequent climb up the far side offer incredible views over the river. There are some good swimming holes at Foote Crossing but no camping spots. Anglers can fish for brown and rainbow trout. The road becomes slightly wider as it climbs

away from Foote Crossing on the north side of the river. Stunning views over jagged granite ridges continue on this side of the river.

The trail follows a graded dirt road through the forest, winding above Kanaka Creek to Alleghany. Some of the area is privately owned, and a number of mining claims are scattered along the trail. If you plan to pan or prospect in this potentially rich area, be sure you are not inadvertently trespassing on somebody else's claim. Check with the U.S. Forest Service office in Nevada City for current regulations.

The trail joins paved Main Street to travel through Alleghany. Many old structures remain: both residential and commercial buildings connected with the local mining industry. The original office of the Sixteen-to-One Mine stands on Miners Street, a short distance past the mine itself, which continues to turn a profit to this day. There is no gas in Alleghany, but there is a bar and a small café.

The route leaves town along Kanaka Creek Road and crosses over Kanaka Creek on a new bridge. The original bridge is below the road to the right. An old stamp mill can be seen beside the bridge, covered in vegetation.

Past the creek, the trail takes on more of a 4WD character. It climbs steeply up loose, scrabbly soil away from the creek and passes through Chips Flat, the site of the region's original post office, onto Lafayette Ridge. Dropping once again to the Middle Yuba River, the trail passes close to Plumbago and the Plumbago Mine, both still operational and currently owned by the Sixteen-to-One Mining Company. This part of the trail should not be attempted in wet weather; steep grades, a narrow shelf road, and a surface that turns extremely greasy make this section very dangerous when wet. The shelf road here is narrow with few passing places as it descends to Gold Canyon.

There are some pleasant campsites tucked alongside the river on either side of the bridge over the Middle Yuba. There is also a great swimming hole 0.1 mile northwest of the bridge. Once over the bridge, the trail becomes lumpy with embedded and loose boulders—this section is often rearranged when the river floods.

Italian stonemasons constructed this shelf road to Alleghany

Drivers should exercise care and watch their vehicle's underbody in a couple of spots. However, it should be well within the capabilities of most stock SUVs or 4WD pickups.

The trail climbs steeply from the river to rejoin Northern Sierra #25: North Bloomfield–Bowman Lake Trail. The road becomes graded and travels through some private property and logging areas.

This trail is suitable for mountain bikers, although it is a punishing ride even for the fittest.

Current Road Information
Tahoe National Forest
Yuba River Ranger District
15924 Highway 49
Camptonville, CA 95922
(530) 288-3231

Map References
BLM   Truckee
USFS   Tahoe National Forest

USGS 1:24,000   North Bloomfield, Pike, Alleghany
        1:100,000 Truckee
Maptech CD-ROM: High Sierra/Tahoe
Northern California Atlas & Gazetteer,
        pp. 79, 80
California Road & Recreation Atlas,
        pp. 65, 60

Route Directions

▼ 0.0   From Northern Sierra #25: North
           Bloomfield–Bowman Lake Trail, 8.5
           miles north of Nevada City, zero trip
           meter and turn left (northwest) onto
           Grizzly Hill Road, following the sign for
           North Columbia. North Bloomfield—
           Bowman Lake Trail bears northeast at
           this point along North Bloomfield Road
           and heads toward Malakoff Diggins.
3.1 ▲   Trail ends back on Northern Sierra
           #25: North Bloomfield–Bowman Lake

Trail. Turn left to visit Malakoff Diggins and Bowman Lake; continue straight ahead for Nevada City.
GPS: N39°20.48′ W120°58.50′

▼ 0.1   SO   Graded road on left is Mountain Springs Road.
3.0 ▲   SO   Graded road on right is Mountain Springs Road.
▼ 0.8   SO   Road on right is Jennet Trail.
2.3 ▲   SO   Road on left is Jennet Trail.
▼ 1.5   SO   Track on left and track on right.
1.6 ▲   SO   Track on left and track on right.
▼ 2.1   SO   Cross over Spring Creek.
1.0 ▲   SO   Cross over Spring Creek.
▼ 2.3   BL   Graded road on right; then track on left.
0.8 ▲   BR   Track on right; then graded road on left. Bear right, following sign to South Yuba Campground and Trail.
GPS: N39°22.12′ W120°58.45′

▼ 2.9   SO   Road becomes paved.
0.2 ▲   SO   Road turns to graded dirt.
▼ 3.1   TR   T-intersection with paved Tyler Foote Crossing Road (CR 613). Zero trip meter.
0.0 ▲   Continue to the east.
GPS: N39°22.37′ W120°59.18′

▼ 0.0   Continue to the north.
3.1 ▲   TL   Turn left onto paved Grizzly Hill Road and zero trip meter.
▼ 0.2   SO   Graded road on right is Lake City Road.
2.9 ▲   SO   Graded road on left is Lake City Road.
▼ 1.2   TL   Turn left onto graded dirt Tyler Foote Crossing Road at Columbia Hill. Cruzon Grade Road continues straight ahead.
1.9 ▲   TR   T-intersection with paved road at Columbia Hill. Cruzon Grade Road on left. Remain on Tyler Foote Crossing Road. Road is now paved.
GPS: N39°23.23′ W120°58.50′

▼ 1.6   SO   Track on right.
1.5 ▲   SO   Track on left.
▼ 1.9   SO   Track on right.
1.2 ▲   SO   Track on left.
▼ 2.0   SO   Track on left.
1.1 ▲   SO   Track on right.

▼ 2.6   SO   Track on left; then cross over Grizzly Creek. Private road on right and track on left.
0.5 ▲   SO   Private road on left and track on right. Cross over Grizzly Creek; then track on right.
GPS: N39°24.16′ W120°57.85′

▼ 3.1   BL   Two tracks on left; then graded road on right is Grizzly Ridge Road (FR 37). Zero trip meter and bear left onto S191, following sign to Foote Crossing.
0.0 ▲   Continue to the southeast past two tracks on right. End of shelf road.
GPS: N39°24.38′ W120°58.17′

▼ 0.0   Continue to the west. Start to descend shelf road to Foote Crossing.
5.8 ▲   BR   Graded road on left is Grizzly Ridge Road (FR 37). Zero trip meter and bear right, following sign for Graniteville Road.
▼ 0.9   SO   Track on left.
4.9 ▲   BL   Track on right.
▼ 2.2   SO   Hiking trail on left goes down to river.

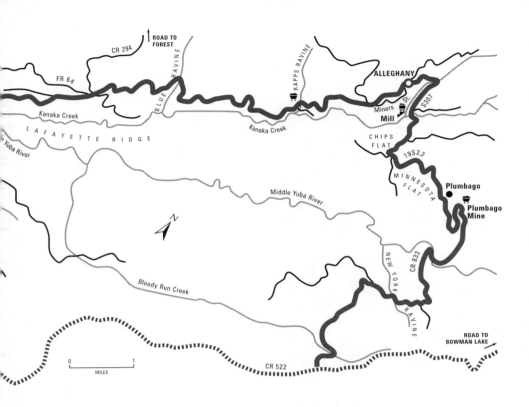

3.6 ▲ SO Hiking trail on right goes down to river.
        GPS: N39°25.00′ W120°57.25′

▼ 2.3 SO Cross over the Middle Yuba River on
            bridge at Foote Crossing. Track on left
            after bridge is a hiking trail that goes
            past mining claim and adit.
3.5 ▲ SO Track on right is a hiking trail that goes
            past mining claim and adit. Cross over
            the Middle Yuba River on bridge at
            Foote Crossing.
        GPS: N39°25.00′ W120°57.07′

▼ 2.6 SO Hiking trail on right to river on left-hand
            bend.
3.2 ▲ SO Hiking trail on left to river on right-hand
            bend.
▼ 5.3 SO Track on left. End of shelf road.
0.5 ▲ SO Start of shelf road. Track on right.
        GPS: N39°25.88′ W120°55.85′

▼ 5.8 SO Graded road on left is FR 64 to Squirrel
            Creek; then second graded road on left
            is CR 294 to the town of Forest. Zero

trip meter and follow sign to Alleghany.
Track on right.
0.0 ▲   Continue to the southwest.
        GPS: N39°26.11′ W120°55.31′

▼ 0.0   Continue to the northeast.
6.8 ▲ SO Track on left. Graded road on right is
            CR 294 to the town of Forest; then
            second graded road on right is FR 64
            to Squirrel Creek. Zero trip meter and
            follow sign to Foote Crossing.
▼ 0.8 SO Track on right.
6.0 ▲ SO Track on left.
▼ 1.1 SO Track on right and track on left.
5.7 ▲ SO Track on left and track on right.
        GPS: N39°26.59′ W120°54.58′

▼ 1.9 SO Cross over Blue Ravine.
4.9 ▲ SO Cross over Blue Ravine.
        GPS: N39°26.88′ W120°54.09′

▼ 4.9 SO Mine on left.
1.9 ▲ SO Mine on right.
        GPS: N39°27.25′ W120°52.09′

Old Ophir Mine five-stamp mill north of Kanaka Creek bridge

▼ 5.0 BL Cross over Rapps Ravine; then two tracks on right.
1.8 ▲ BR Two tracks on left; then cross over Rapps Ravine.
▼ 5.2 SO Track on left. Start of shelf road.
1.6 ▲ SO End of shelf road. Track on right.
▼ 6.2 SO Cross over creek.
0.6 ▲ SO Cross over creek.
▼ 6.8 SO 4-way intersection with paved roads on the edge of Alleghany. Zero trip meter and cross Miners Street; then bear right to join Main Street.
0.0 ▲ Continue to the south.
GPS: N39°27.84' W120°50.84'

▼ 0.0 Continue to the north. Remain on Main Street through town.
3.2 ▲ SO Bear left off Main Street; then 4-way intersection with Miners Street. Zero trip meter and continue straight ahead to join Foote Crossing Road. Road is now graded dirt.
▼ 0.5 SO Road on right is Miners Street.
2.7 ▲ BR Road on left is Miners Street.
▼ 0.7 SO Volunteer fire department on right down Plaza Street.
2.5 ▲ SO Volunteer fire department on left down Plaza Street.
▼ 0.8 TR Turn right on Kanaka Creek Road (S307), immediately after the post office.
2.4 ▲ TL T-intersection with Main Street. Enter Alleghany past post office on left.
GPS: N39°28.38' W120°50.53'

▼ 0.9 SO Road turns to graded dirt.
2.3 ▲ SO Road is now paved.
▼ 1.4 SO Cross over creek.
1.8 ▲ SO Cross over creek.
▼ 2.0 SO Old mill remains on right on far side of canyon.
1.2 ▲ SO Old mill remains on left on far side of canyon.
▼ 2.1 TR Graded road on left.
1.1 ▲ TL Graded road on right.
GPS: N39°27.98' W120°50.23'

▼ 2.2 SO Cross over Kanaka Creek on bridge. Start of shelf road.

1.0 ▲ SO End of shelf road. Cross over Kanaka Creek on bridge.
▼ 2.4 SO Track on left.
0.8 ▲ SO Track on right.
▼ 2.8 SO Track on right; then track on left. End of shelf road.
0.4 ▲ SO Track on right; then track on left. Start of shelf road.
▼ 2.9 SO Track on left.
0.3 ▲ SO Track on right.
▼ 3.0 BL Chips Flat. Track on right. Follow sign for OHV trail.
0.2 ▲ SO Chips Flat. Track on left.
GPS: N39°27.40' W120°50.16'

▼ 3.2 TR Track on right; then second track on right signposted to Minnesota Flat; then immediately turn right onto third track on right (19S23, CR S200) signposted to German Bar. Zero trip meter.
0.0 ▲ Continue to the southwest.
GPS: N39°27.30' W120°50.16'

▼ 0.0 Continue to the east.
6.8 ▲ TL T-intersection. Zero trip meter. Turn left; then immediately track on left signposted to Minnesota Flat. Continue straight ahead following sign for Malone Orchard; then immediately track on left.
▼ 0.7 SO Track on right.
6.1 ▲ SO Track on left.
▼ 1.7 SO Plumbago on left—private property.
5.1 ▲ SO Plumbago on right—private property.
GPS: N39°27.10' W120°48.96'

▼ 1.8 SO Track on left.
5.0 ▲ SO Track on right.
▼ 1.9 SO Start of shelf road descending to the Middle Yuba River.
4.9 ▲ SO End of shelf road.
▼ 2.8 BR Track on left to Plumbago Mine.
4.0 ▲ BL Track on right to Plumbago Mine.
GPS: N39°27.07' W120°48.73'

▼ 4.0 SO Track on left. End of shelf road.
2.8 ▲ BL Bear left, following sign to Alleghany. Start of shelf road.
▼ 4.1 SO Turnout on left; then cross over the Middle Yuba River on bridge. Road is

now CR 833.

2.7 ▲ SO Cross over the Middle Yuba River on bridge; then turnout on right.
GPS: N39°26.22′ W120°48.73′

▼ 4.3 SO Campsite on right. There are mining claims around the river. Start of shelf road.
2.5 ▲ SO End of shelf road. Campsite on left. There are mining claims around the river.
▼ 5.3 SO Cross over creek.
1.5 ▲ SO Cross over creek.
▼ 5.5 BR Track on left. End of shelf road.
1.3 ▲ BL Track on right. Start of shelf road.
▼ 5.8 SO Track on left.
1.0 ▲ SO Track on right.
GPS: N39°25.64′ W120°48.53′

▼ 6.2 SO Track on left; then track on right.
0.6 ▲ SO Track on left; then track on right.
▼ 6.4 SO Cross over creek in New York Ravine.
0.4 ▲ SO Cross over creek in New York Ravine.
▼ 6.8 SO Unmarked graded road on right. Zero trip meter.
0.0 ▲ Continue to the east.
GPS: N39°25.60′ W120°49.33′

▼ 0.0 Continue to the west past track on left.
2.3 ▲ BR Track on right; then unmarked graded road on left. Bear right onto unmaintained road CR 833. Zero trip meter.
▼ 0.3 SO Track on right.
2.0 ▲ SO Track on left.
▼ 0.5 SO Track on right.
1.8 ▲ SO Track on left.
▼ 1.8 SO Cross over Bloody Run Creek.
0.5 ▲ SO Cross over Bloody Run Creek.
GPS: N39°24.44′ W120°49.41′

▼ 2.1 SO Track on left.
0.2 ▲ SO Track on right.
▼ 2.3 Trail ends at 4-way intersection with Northern Sierra #25: North Bloomfield–Bowman Lake Trail (CR 522). Robbins Ranch Road is straight ahead. Turn left for Bowman Lake; turn right to return to Nevada City.
0.0 ▲ Trail commences on Northern Sierra #25: North Bloomfield–Bowman

Lake Trail (CR 522), 6 miles west of Graniteville. Zero trip meter and turn north onto CR 833 at the sign for Moores Flat and Bucks Ranch. Robbins Ranch Road is opposite the start of the trail.
GPS: N39°24.09′ W120°49.52′

Sierra Buttes Trail

STARTING POINT FR 93, 0.3 miles south of Packer Lake Saddle
FINISHING POINT Sierra Buttes Road, 1 mile west of Sierra City
TOTAL MILEAGE 6.6 miles, plus 1.2-mile spur to Sierra Buttes Fire Lookout
UNPAVED MILEAGE 6.6 miles, plus 1.2-mile spur
DRIVING TIME 1.75 hours, plus 1 hour round-trip for hike to the lookout
ELEVATION RANGE 4,200–7,700 feet
USUALLY OPEN July to November
BEST TIME TO TRAVEL Dry weather
DIFFICULTY RATING 5
SCENIC RATING 10
REMOTENESS RATING +0

Special Attractions

■ Long section of narrow shelf road with views of Sierra Buttes and the North Yuba River Valley.
■ Moderately strenuous hike to the Sierra Buttes Fire Lookout.
■ Access to a network of 4WD trails and many lakes for fishing and camping.

History

The volcanic Sierra Buttes rise about 4,500 feet above the old mining town of Sierra City. Sierra Buttes Mine, on the south face of the buttes, was one of the earliest mines in this vicinity. Starting operations in the early 1850s, it was a big employer in the area and produced more than $17 million in gold by the time it closed in 1937. Stamp mills, flumes, and boarding houses came and went over the decades.

Lower Sardine Lake, visible to the northeast from the Sierra Buttes Fire Lookout, was

The long shelf road to Sierra City is narrow with limited passing places

Permanent snow on the northern face of the Sierra Buttes above Upper Sardine Lake

the headwater dam for the flume and ditch that delivered water around the steep slope of the buttes to the Sierra Buttes Mine. The lake was also the site of the Young America Mine, which operated from 1884 to 1893, producing an average of $20,000 to $30,000 in gold a month. Watt Hughes, part owner of the mine, built a sizable house in nearby Sierra City, which is now the Holly House Bed & Breakfast.

By 1858, Sierra City had evolved from a number of dispersed mining camps into a lively town on the banks of the North Yuba River, where miners had their choice of several bars and saloons. Thompson's Saloon, Capital Hotel, Phelan's Saloon, Socarracco Hotel, Rose's Hotel, and Carrollo Saloon were just a few of the establishments that catered to thirsty miners.

Description

The prominent volcanic peaks of Sierra Buttes, visible for miles around, are one of the most distinctive geological features in the northern Sierra Nevada. As you approach the buttes, the forest service's small lookout can be seen perched precariously on the uppermost peak (8,587 feet). Although no longer used for spotting fires, the lookout is now one of the most popular hiking destinations in the region. On warm summer weekends, it is not unusual to see 30 or more hikers admiring the views from the lookout platform.

Most hikers reach the lookout from the Sierra Buttes Trailhead near the start of this trail. For those with a high-clearance 4WD, there is a second option. The Sierra Buttes OHV Trail travels along a well-used, roughly graded trail for 2.6 miles to a spur to the lookout. The spur immediately starts to climb to the northeast, averaging a consistent slope of about 20 degrees. The surface is uneven, but apart from a few patches of rock and embedded boulders, it is smooth though loose in places. Most of the spur travels through the forest, but a few areas open up and provide views over low vegetation. A spectacular campsite 0.4 miles along the spur offers breathtaking, panoramic views. The spur ends for vehicles after 1.2

miles. Park your vehicle and hike the remaining distance to the lookout. The trail is easy to follow, and it ascends a series of switchbacks, first as a foot trail, then joining the old road to the peak. Allow an hour round-trip for the hike, not including time spent at the top. The final ascent to the lookout climbs three flights of metal grating stairs that were affixed to the rock in 1964 by five forest service employees.

The lookout platform provides 360-degree views. To the north are the Sardine Lakes and Sand Pond, with Volcano Lake to the northeast and Packer Lake and Gold Valley to the northwest. On a clear day, you can see as far north as Lassen Peak and Mount Shasta. To the east is the Sierra Valley, an important summer range for foothill ranchers. To the south you can see Jackson Meadow Reservoir and the deep cut of the North Yuba River, about 3,000 feet below. The small burned area to the west is the result of the August 1978 Cap Fire above Downieville.

The main trail continues toward Sierra City, passing the turn to the Monumental Mine before making the long shelf road descent to the valley floor. Passing places are extremely limited along the narrow road, especially near the northern end. The final 1.3 miles are maintained by Sierra County and are wide enough for two vehicles to pass with care.

Current Road Information

Tahoe National Forest
Yuba River Ranger District
15924 Highway 49
Camptonville, CA 95922
(530) 288-3231

Map References

BLM   Portola
USFS   Tahoe National Forest; Plumas
       National Forest
USGS   1:24,000 Sierra City
       1:100,000 Portola
Maptech CD-ROM: High Sierra/Tahoe
Northern California Atlas & Gazetteer, p. 70
California Road & Recreation Atlas, p. 60
Other: Lakes Basin, Sierra Buttes and

Plumas Eureka State Park
Recreation Guide, Plumas National
Forest OHV Map—Summer Use

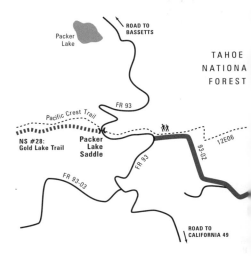

Route Directions

▼ 0.0   From the intersection of FR 93-03 and FR 93, 11 miles north of California 49, continue 0.4 miles east. Zero trip meter and turn southeast on small graded road 93-02, following sign to Sierra Buttes Lookout. Coming from the east, the trail starts 0.3 miles south of Packer Lake Saddle.

2.6 ▲   Trail ends at intersection with paved FR 93. Continue straight ahead for Packer Lake and Northern Sierra #28: Gold Lake Trail; turn left for California 49.
         GPS: N39°36.86′ W120°39.94′

▼ 0.2 SO Sierra Buttes Trailhead. Sierra Buttes Trail (12E06) on left for hikers to fire lookout and Pacific Crest Trail. Continue straight ahead, following sign for Sierra Buttes OHV Trail.

2.4 ▲ SO Sierra Buttes Trailhead. Sierra Buttes Trail (12E06) on right for hikers to fire lookout and Pacific Crest Trail.
           GPS: N39°36.70′ W120°39.86′

▼ 0.7 SO Track on right.
1.9 ▲ SO Track on left.
▼ 0.9 SO Track on left.
1.7 ▲ SO Track on right.
▼ 1.4 SO Remains of Holmes Cabin on right. Track on right; then track on left is 93-21.
1.2 ▲ SO Track on right is 93-21; then track on left. Remains of Holmes Cabin on left.
           GPS: N39°36.10′ W120°40.52′

▼ 1.8 SO Track on right is 93-22. Trail is now a formed dirt trail.
0.8 ▲ SO Track on left is 93-22. Trail is now a graded dirt road.
           GPS: N39°35.81′ W120°40.23′
▼ 2.3 SO Spring on left.
0.3 ▲ SO Spring on right.
           GPS: N39°35.52′ W120°40.04′

▼ 2.6 BR Track on left is 93-23, spur to Sierra

NORTHERN SIERRA #27: SIERRA BUTTES TRAIL

           Buttes Fire Lookout. Track straight ahead is a dead end. Follow sign to Sierra City. Zero trip meter.
0.0 ▲   Continue to the northwest.
           GPS: N39°35.26′ W120°40.01′

Spur to Sierra Buttes Fire Lookout

▼ 0.0   Head northeast on 93-23.
▼ 0.2 BR Track on left.
▼ 0.4 SO Campsite with spectacular view on right; then track on left rejoins. Pacific Crest Trail crosses.
           GPS: N39°35.32′ W120°39.67′

▼ 1.2   End of vehicle trail. Hiking trail from the Sierra Buttes Trailhead comes in from the northwest and continues east along a steep 0.8-mile trail to the lookout.
           GPS: N39°35.73′ W120°39.18′

Continuation of Main Trail

▼ 0.0   Continue to the south.
4.0 ▲ BL Track on right is a dead end; then second track on right is 93-23, spur to the Sierra Buttes Lookout. Zero trip meter.
           GPS: N39°35.26′ W120°40.01′

▼ 0.5 SO Track on left; then track on right.

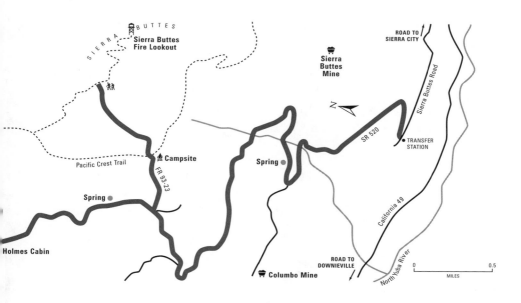

3.5 ▲   BR   Bear right, following the sign to Sierra Buttes; then track on right.

          GPS: N39°35.06' W120°40.39'

▼ 0.6   SO   Track on left. Track on right goes 0.3 miles to viewpoint. Trail starts to descend single-lane shelf road.

3.4 ▲   SO   End of shelf road. Track on left goes 0.3 miles to viewpoint. Track on right.

▼ 1.5   SO   Cross over creek.

2.5 ▲   SO   Cross over creek.

▼ 1.6   SO   Track on right.

2.4 ▲   SO   Track on left.

▼ 1.8   SO   Cross over creek.

2.2 ▲   SO   Cross over creek.

▼ 2.3   SO   Cross over creek.

1.7 ▲   SO   Cross over creek.

▼ 2.4   SO   Spring on right.

1.6 ▲   SO   Spring on left.

          GPS: N39°34.65' W120°39.39'

▼ 2.6   BL   Track on right rejoins in 0.1 miles.

1.4 ▲   BR   Track on left rejoins.

▼ 2.7   BL   Track on right rejoins; then well-used track on right goes to Columbo Mine. Start of county-maintained road.

1.3 ▲   BR   Well-used track on left goes to Columbo Mine; then track on left rejoins in 0.1 miles. Follow sign to Sierra Buttes. End of county-main-

tained road.

          GPS: N39°34.59' W120°39.63'

▼ 3.0   SO   Cross over creek.

1.0 ▲   SO   Cross over creek.

          GPS: N39°34.56' W120°39.30'

▼ 4.0   Trail ends at the Sierra City Transfer Station. Turn left for California 49 and Sierra City.

0.0 ▲   From Main Street in Sierra City, zero trip meter and turn northwest onto Butte Street. Proceed 0.1 miles and turn left onto Sierra Buttes Road, following sign for Buttes Lookout. Proceed 1 mile to the Sierra City Transfer Station and the start of the trail. Zero trip meter and turn east on graded dirt Sierra Buttes Road (SR 520). Start of shelf road.

          GPS: N39°34.03' W120°39.10'

Steep ascent to Sierra Buttes Fire Lookout

Gold Lake Trail

STARTING POINT FR 93 at Packer Lake Saddle, 1.5 miles west of Packer Lake
FINISHING POINT Gold Lake Road at Gold Lake, 9 miles south of Graeagle
TOTAL MILEAGE 6.4 miles
UNPAVED MILEAGE 5.9 miles
DRIVING TIME 1.5 hours
ELEVATION RANGE 6,400–7,200 feet
USUALLY OPEN July to November
BEST TIME TO TRAVEL Dry weather
DIFFICULTY RATING 5
SCENIC RATING 9
REMOTENESS RATING +0

Special Attractions

- Lakes Basin Petroglyphs and Lakes Basin Campground near the northern end of the trail.
- Fantastic camping along the shores of Gold Lake.
- Moderately challenging trail that passes by or near a number of lakes.

History

Maidu Indians used this area for about a thousand years, and Paleo-Indians may have frequented the area as much as 8,000 to 10,000 years earlier. Petroglyphs north of Gold Lake offer a link to these early people; however, the meaning of these carvings is still very much open to debate.

In the late 1850s a lodge catered to tourists at Gold Lake. In 1913, the road to Gold Lake was put through, providing much easier access to the scenic lake.

Packer Lake, near the southern end of the trail, was a resting point along a pack trail. By 1926, a lakeside lodge was attracting a growing number of visitors. Several cabins and a number of platforms for seasonal tents were added as demand grew. Activities such as fishing, boating, horseback riding, and hiking drew people seeking to escape the heat of the Central Valley in summer.

Description

This short, moderately rated trail takes drivers with high-clearance 4WDs directly past two lakes, with another three less than 0.5 miles from the main trail and accessible by vehicle. The trail, initially marked as Deer Lake Road, leaves from Packer Lake Saddle. It quickly becomes a 4WD trail as it travels onto the ridge top. The Pacific Crest National Scenic Trail runs close to the vehicle trail on top of the ridge. Spectacular views from the ridge include Gold Valley and Craycroft Ridge to the west. The deep blue Deer Lake, nestled in a rocky basin and surrounded by firs, can be seen some 350 feet below to the east. Deer Lake is one of the few bodies of water where it is possible to catch eastern brook trout. It can be reached by a steep 0.3-mile descent.

From Deer Lake, the single-lane trail is marked as Summit OHV Trail and travels through loose, deep soils. Some steep downhill sections are interspersed with loose off-camber slopes and tight maneuvers through the trees. At the shadier, more enclosed Summit Lake, the trail swings east toward Gold Lake. Other OHV trails lead off from here—west to Gold Valley and north to Oakland Pond. The main route enters Plumas National Forest and the Lakes Basin Recreation Area and descends to the edge of Gold Lake. Camping within the recreation area is limited to designated sites only, but campers need not worry. One of the prettiest forest service campgrounds is located on the southeastern shore of Gold Lake. Because it can only be reached by 4WD vehicles, it is often quiet, providing campers with their choice of 16 lakeside campsites, most with picnic tables and fire rings. The campground has a pit toilet but no other facilities. Backcountry campsites can also be found at Summit Lake and on the ridge above Deer Lake.

Lakes Basin is one of the prime fishing areas in Plumas National Forest, with nearly 50 small glacial lakes and many coldwater trout streams. Gold Lake is a prime destination where anglers can fish for Mackinaw, brook, brown, and rainbow trout. The area is stocked every two years with several thousand rainbow and brook trout.

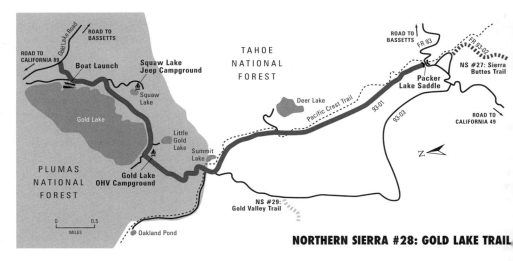

NORTHERN SIERRA #28: GOLD LAKE TRAIL

From the campground, the main trail follows along the southern shore of Gold Lake, where it earns its difficulty rating of 5. You will have to crawl over some embedded rocks and boulders and along loose sections of rubble. This is the most challenging and slowest section of the trail. Although slow and requiring care, the rock crawling should be within the capabilities of most high-clearance 4WDs, even full size or extra long ones. Several day-use areas along this stretch will appeal to picnickers, anglers, or those just wanting to relax by the lake.

Another side trail leads 0.5 miles to a designated camping area at Squaw Lake. The trail then follows the paved road past busier camping areas and a boat launch to finish on Gold Valley Road. A point of interest near the Lakes Basin Campground, a short distance from the end of the trail, is a group of large boulders covered with petroglyphs, weathered and faint with age but still discernible. To reach the petroglyphs from the end of the trail, proceed north on Gold Lake Road for 2.3 miles; then turn southwest, following the sign to Lakes Basin Campground. Pass the campground and follow the sign for Elwell Lodge. The petroglyphs are 0.4 miles from Gold Lake Road on the right, at coordinates GPS: N39º41.95' W120º39.61'.

Current Road Information
Tahoe National Forest

Yuba River Ranger District
15924 Highway 49
Camptonville, CA 95922
(530) 288-3231

Plumas National Forest
Beckwourth Ranger District
23 Mohawk Road / PO Box 7
Blairsden, CA 96103
(530) 836-2575

Map References
BLM   Portola
USFS   Plumas National Forest; Tahoe
        National Forest
USGS 1:24,000   Sierra City, Gold Lake
        1:100,000 Portola
Maptech CD-ROM: High Sierra/Tahoe
Northern California Atlas & Gazetteer, p. 70
California Road & Recreation Atlas, p. 60
        (incomplete)
Other: Lakes Basin, Sierra Buttes and
        Plumas Eureka State Park
        Recreation Guide; Plumas National
        Forest OHV Map—Summer Use

Route Directions

▼ 0.0   From paved FR 93 at Packer Lake
        Saddle, 5.7 miles west of Gold Lake
        Road and Bassetts and 1.5 miles west
        of Packer Lake, zero trip meter at 4-
        way intersection and turn north on

unmaintained road, signposted Deer
Lake Road (93-01). Northern Sierra
#27: Sierra Buttes Trail commences
0.3 miles south of the saddle.

2.0 ▲ Trail ends on paved FR 93 at Packer
Lake Saddle. Turn left for Packer Lake,
Gold Lake Road, and Bassetts; continue
straight ahead 0.3 miles south to travel
Northern Sierra #27: Sierra Buttes Trail.
GPS: N39°37.17′ W120°39.98′

▼ 0.8 SO Track on right. Follow the OHV trail sign.
1.2 ▲ SO Track on left.
GPS: N39°37.88′ W120°40.20′

▼ 1.7 SO Track on right to campsite; then Deer
Lake visible below trail on the right.
Pacific Crest Trail runs parallel with the
route at this point.
0.3 ▲ SO Deer Lake is visible below trail on the
left. Pacific Crest Trail runs parallel
with the route at this point. Track on
left to campsite.

GPS: N39°38.63′ W120°40.33′

▼ 1.9 SO Pacific Crest Trail crosses.
0.1 ▲ SO Pacific Crest Trail crosses.

▼ 2.0 SO Track on right is Deer Lake OHV Trail,
which descends 0.3 miles to Deer
Lake. Zero trip meter and follow the
sign for Summit OHV Trail. Pacific
Crest Trail crosses at the intersection.
0.0 ▲ Continue to the southwest.
GPS: N39°38.85′ W120°40.24′

▼ 0.0 Continue to the north.
1.1 ▲ SO Track on left is Deer Lake OHV Trail,
which descends 0.3 miles to Deer
Lake. Zero trip meter. Pacific Crest Trail
crosses at the intersection.

▼ 1.1 SO Track on left goes 1.2 miles to the
southern end of Northern Sierra #29:
Gold Valley Trail. Zero trip meter.
Summit Lake is on the right.
0.0 ▲ Continue to the south.
GPS: N39°39.66′ W120°40.52′

Sierra Buttes, seen from the ridge-top trail

Gold Lake in the Lakes Basin Recreation Area

▼ 0.0   Continue to the northeast.

1.3 ▲   BL   Track on right goes 1.2 miles to the southern end of Northern Sierra #29: Gold Valley Trail. Zero trip meter and follow the sign to Deer Lake OHV Trail. Summit Lake is on the left.

▼ 0.1   SO   Track on left is a marked OHV trail that goes to Oakland Pond. Follow sign to Little Gold Lake and enter Plumas National Forest and Lakes Basin Recreation Area. Camping is allowed in designated sites only.

1.2 ▲   SO   Track on right is a marked OHV trail to Oakland Pond. Leaving Plumas National Forest and Lakes Basin Recreation Area. Dispersed camping is permitted past this point.

▼ 0.2   SO   Pacific Crest Trail crosses.

1.1 ▲   SO   Pacific Crest Trail crosses.

▼ 0.3   BL   Track on right.

1.0 ▲   BR   Track on left.

        GPS: N39°39.81' W120°40.38'

▼ 0.7   SO   Track on left; then cattle guard.

0.6 ▲   SO   Cattle guard; then track on right.

▼ 0.8   SO   Track on right to private property.

0.5 ▲   BR   Track on left to private property. Follow sign to Summit Lake.

▼ 1.2   BR   Start of Gold Lake OHV Campground. Private property on left. Bear right and follow around the lakeshore.

0.1 ▲   BL   End of designated camping area. Private property on right. Bear left away from the lake.

        GPS: N39°40.27' W120°39.98'

▼ 1.3   SO   Track on right goes 0.25 miles to Little Gold Lake. Zero trip meter.

0.0 ▲   Continue to the west.

        GPS: N39°40.18' W120°39.87'

▼ 0.0   Continue to the east.

2.0 ▲   SO   Track on left goes 0.25 miles to Little Gold Lake. Zero trip meter and follow sign to Summit Lake.

▼ 0.3   SO   Leaving Gold Lake OHV Campground.

1.7 ▲   SO   Entering Gold Lake OHV Campground.

▼ 0.4   SO   Day-use area on left.

1.6 ▲   SO   Day-use area on right.

▼ 0.5   SO   Track on left to lakeshore is for day use only.

1.5 ▲   SO   Track on right to lakeshore is for day use only.

▼ 0.7   SO   Track on left to lakeshore is for day use only.

1.3 ▲   SO   Track on right to lakeshore is for day use only.
        GPS: N39°40.31' W120°39.19'

▼ 1.0   SO   Turnout on left provides foot access to beach.

1.0 ▲   SO   Turnout on right provides foot access to beach.

▼ 1.1   BL   Track on right to Squaw Lake and Squaw Lake Jeep Campground.

0.9 ▲   SO   Track on left to Squaw Lake and Squaw Lake Jeep Campground.
        GPS: N39°40.39' W120°38.86'

▼ 1.5   TR   Parking area straight ahead provides foot access to the lake. Turn right onto paved road.

0.5 ▲   TL   Parking area on right provides foot access to lake. Turn left, following the sign for Little Gold Lake and Summit Lake. Trail is now designated OHV Route 60 (21N93) for 4WDs, ATVs, and motorbikes—rated black. Trail is now a rough, formed trail.

▼ 1.6   SO   Track on left to boat launch and unde-veloped campground.

0.4 ▲   SO   Track on right to boat launch and unde-veloped campground.

▼ 2.0   Trail finishes on Gold Lake Road. Turn left for the Lakes Basin Petroglyphs and Graeagle; turn right for Bassetts and California 49.

0.0 ▲   From Gold Lake Road, 6 miles north of Bassetts and California 49, zero trip meter and turn southwest onto paved road, following sign for Gold Lake Boat Launch Facility. Trail runs along the southern shore of Gold Lake.
        GPS: N39°40.78' W120°38.42'

Gold Valley Trail

STARTING POINT CR A14, immediately south of Johnsville

FINISHING POINT FR 93-03, 6.2 miles north of the intersection with FR 93

TOTAL MILEAGE 15.4 miles

UNPAVED MILEAGE 14.2 miles

DRIVING TIME 4 hours

ELEVATION RANGE 5,200–7,200 feet

USUALLY OPEN July to November

BEST TIME TO TRAVEL July to November

DIFFICULTY RATING 6

SCENIC RATING 9

REMOTENESS RATING +1

Special Attractions

■ Plumas Eureka State Park and historic Johnsville.

■ Panoramic ridge-top trail with views of the Lakes Basin Recreation Area and Spencer Lake.

■ Remains of the Four Hills Mine.

■ Challenging section through Gold Valley.

History

Gold Valley Trail begins just south of Johnsville at the Plumas Eureka State Park Museum. The open-air museum, established in 1959, offers insight on life in a gold min-ing community during the latter half of the nineteenth century.

Mohawk Mill is at the base of Eureka Peak, called Gold Mountain during the early mining days. This gigantic mill cost nearly $50,000 to construct in 1876 and contained a whopping 60 stamps, capable of processing 5,000 pounds of ore in a single day. A muse-um is housed in what was formerly a miners' bunkhouse.

This trail makes its way up a hand-built wagon road that led to many mining camps farther up Jamison Creek. Grass Lake, south-east of the trail past the Jamison Mine, was the site of a fish camp for an outfit based in Johnsville. Because of the difficult terrain, everything that went to the camp had to be

By 1888, the Eureka Mine had tunneled a mile into the mountain

taken in by pack mules. All that remains today at the site are foundations.

The Four Hills, Willoughby, and Empire are prominent mines passed as you proceed up and over the range toward Pauley Creek. People packed in supplies to these mines from Downieville. In those days it was a day's trip with a fully laden mule; today it is an afternoon's mountain bike ride through what was called Devils Den.

An Englishman named Hunt operated the Four Hills Mine. He would make his way over the mountains into Sierra City for supplies and a rewarding whiskey and soda. On one of his infrequent visits to the Upper Hotel, the bartender accidentally gave him whiskey and something from a cream soda bottle. Hunt went mad after taking his first gulp, screaming that he'd been poisoned. He was almost right. It seems someone had accidentally left the local remedy for bed bugs, a common problem in those days, in a soda bottle behind the counter. Hunt survived, but he was not as amused as the hotel staff and clientele. Hunt's Four Hills Mine went

on to produce almost half a million dollars worth of gold. The mine buildings remained well into the twentieth century, until a local youth blasted them to bits. The kid was spotted by a cowboy tending cattle in Gold Valley and ended up in jail.

Description

The trail starts in Johnsville at the Plumas Eureka State Park office and museum. Before starting the trail, the Johnsville Cemetery, a short distance north just off the main street in Johnsville, is well worth a visit. The state park has an open-air display of mining artifacts and the Mohawk Mill can be seen on the slope below Eureka Peak from the south side of the museum parking lot.

The first mile of the trail is paved because it leads to the park's developed campground. The trail runs around the southeastern side of Eureka Peak along Jamison Creek, with Mount Washington to the south. Sections of hand-stacked rock wall that support this section of shelf road were built by miners. Irene Falls, a series of small falls on Jamison Creek, are immediately west of the undeveloped Ross Camp.

The trail briefly joins a graded gravel road on its way to the site of A-Tree Camp, passing the head of the deep Florentine Canyon before turning onto a small formed trail that climbs steeply to the ridge top. This ridge offers some of the most scenic vistas along the trail, which winds through a landscape of bare broken granite, scattered fir trees, and slopes covered with mule's ears. To the north is the Lakes Basin Recreation Area, with the glacial Wades, Rock, and Jamison Lakes 600 feet below. Spencer Lakes and the Sierra Buttes are visible to the south. The trail follows the southern boundary of the recreation area, which is also the boundary separating Tahoe and Plumas National Forests. It passes the remains of the Four Hills Mine. Deep shafts and surface workings are scattered about on several levels; concrete footings of what might have been a mill can also be seen.

The trail is rated a 4 for difficulty as far as the mine because of some moderately loose and rocky climbs and because the deep, dusty surface makes traction difficult. The section from Four Hills Mine to Hawley Lake is rated a 5 for difficulty. It winds down to the lake along a steep, loose, and moguled slope. If you intend to retrace your route to Johnsville, be sure you can climb back up the hill before beginning the descent. The trail only gets more difficult from here.

Near Hawley Lake the trail passes through Camp Nejedly, private property deeded to the Boy Scouts of America in 1964. In addition to use by the scouts, the camp regularly hosts mentally and physically impaired children. Local four-wheel-drive clubs help transport campers into the area. The Boy Scouts of America require a permit to camp at the lake.

Wade, Rock, and Jamison Lakes

Past the camp, the trail quickly earns its difficulty rating of 6. Those without high-clearance and sturdy tires, or those driving full-size vehicles should consider turning back. The difficulty comes from steep loose descents and a rocky surface. Watch your vehicle's underbody on some of the tight maneuvers. You will have to ride large boulders to avoid underbody damage. Full-size vehicles are likely to find some of the turns through trees and rocks too tight for comfort; this section is best suited for compact and sub-compact vehicles.

As the trail enters Gold Valley, it becomes lightly brushy, crossing and re-crossing Pauley Creek. However, the bushes here are softer and more forgiving on paintwork or clothing than the brittle manzanitas found throughout much of Northern California. This brushy section goes for approximately 0.6 miles. Rock hounds may enjoy hunting for pyrite around the creek.

The trail re-enters the forest and continues to wind past the OHV trailheads to Pauley Creek and Smiths Lake. There are a few more loose and rocky climbs, but none as difficult to negotiate as the ones at the north end of Gold Valley. This section is heavily used by mountain bikers, who are shuttled up from Downieville to take advantage of the exhilarating downhill runs back to the town via Pauley Creek Trail, Butcher Ranch Trail, 3rd Divide Trail, or 2nd Divide Trail. Butcher Ranch Trail is excellent for spring wildflower viewing. In winter the section south of Hawley Lake is an ungroomed snowmobile trail.

The trail finishes at the intersection with 93-03, 6.2 miles north of paved FR 93. The intersection is not well marked, but it is well used and has an OHV sign past the turn.

Current Road Information

Plumas National Forest
Beckwourth Ranger District
23 Mohawk Road / PO Box 7
Blairsden, CA 96103
(530) 836-2575

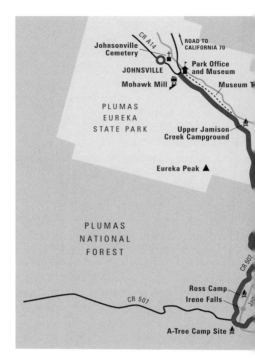

Map References

BLM   Portola
USFS   Plumas National Forest; Tahoe
       National Forest
USGS   1:24,000   Johnsville, Gold Lake,
       Mt. Fillmore
       1:100,000 Portola
Maptech CD-ROM: High Sierra/Tahoe
Northern California Atlas & Gazetteer, p. 70
California Road & Recreation Atlas, p. 60
Other: Plumas National Forest OHV
       Map—Summer Use; Lakes Basin,
       Sierra Buttes and Plumas Eureka
       State Park Recreation Guide

Route Directions

▼ 0.0   From CR A14 immediately south of
         Johnsville, zero trip meter and turn south-
         west on small paved road at the Plumas
         Eureka State Park office and museum.
         Trail begins through the parking lot.
4.5 ▲   Trail ends at the Plumas Eureka State
         Park office and museum immediately
         south of Johnsville. Turn right for
         California 70 and Portola.

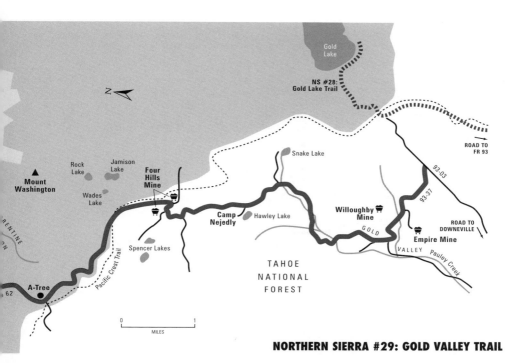

GPS: N39°45.42' W120°41.82'

▼ 0.1 SO Campground and Museum Trail for hikers on left.

4.4 ▲ SO Campground and Museum Trail for hikers on right.

▼ 0.3 SO Emigrant Trail marker on right.

4.2 ▲ SO Emigrant Trail marker on left.

▼ 1.1 SO Upper Jamison Creek Campground on left.

3.4 ▲ SO Upper Jamison Creek Campground on right.

GPS: N39°44.55' W120°42.38'

▼ 1.2 SO Road turns to graded dirt. Sections of shelf road for the next 2.6 miles.

3.3 ▲ SO Road is now paved. End of shelf road.

▼ 2.0 SO Turnout on left. Exiting Plumas Eureka State Park into Plumas National Forest.

2.5 ▲ SO Exiting Plumas National Forest into Plumas Eureka State Park. Turnout on right.

GPS: N39°44.25' W120°43.21'

▼ 2.1 SO Track on left. Road is now designated OHV Route 36B for 4WDs, ATVs and motorbikes—rated green.

2.4 ▲ SO Track on right.

▼ 2.3 SO Track on left.

2.2 ▲ SO Track on right.

▼ 2.6 SO Track on left to campsite.

1.9 ▲ SO Track on right to campsite.

▼ 3.8 SO End of shelf road.

0.7 ▲ SO Sections of shelf road for the next 2.6 miles.

▼ 3.9 SO Track on left.

0.6 ▲ SO Track on right.

▼ 4.0 SO Track on left.

0.5 ▲ SO Track on right.

▼ 4.1 SO Ross Camp—unimproved USFS camping area—on left.

0.4 ▲ SO Ross Camp—unimproved USFS camping area—on right.

GPS: N39°44.08' W120°45.03'

▼ 4.2 SO Track on left to Irene Falls on Jamison Creek.

0.3 ▲ SO Track on right to Irene Falls on Jamison Creek.

▼ 4.5 TL T-intersection. CR 507 (OHV Route 36) continues to the right. Turn left, following sign to A-Tree and Four Hills Mine, and zero trip meter. Trail is now

The Mohawk Stamp Mill, constructed in 1877

designated OHV Route 62 for 4WDs, ATVs, and motorbikes—rated green.

0.0 ▲ Continue to the east.

GPS: N39°44.10′ W120°45.35′

▼ 0.0 Continue to the south.

2.0 ▲ TR Graded road continues ahead. Turn right and join CR 507 (OHV Route 36) for 4WDs, ATVs, and motorbikes—rated green. Zero trip meter.

▼ 0.1 SO A-Tree Road Camp—unimproved USFS camping area—on right; then cross over Jamison Creek on bridge; then track on right.

1.9 ▲ SO Track on left; then cross over Jamison Creek on bridge; then A-Tree Road Camp—unimproved USFS camping area—on left.

▼ 2.0 TL Graded road bears right toward A-Tree. Stay on the upper road. Turn left onto OHV Route 62 for 4WDs, ATVs, and motorbikes—rated blue. Zero trip meter. Pacific Crest Trail crosses at this intersection.

0.0 ▲ Continue to the north.

GPS: N39°42.92′ W120°44.64′

▼ 0.0 Continue to the southeast.

3.1 ▲ TR T-intersection with graded road. To the left goes toward A-Tree. Turn right and zero trip meter. Pacific Crest Trail crosses at this intersection.

▼ 1.5 SO Turnout on right.

1.6 ▲ SO Turnout on left.

GPS: N39°42.44′ W120°43.52′

▼ 1.8 SO Pacific Crest Trail crosses. To the left goes into the Lakes Basin Recreation Area to Wade Lake, Mount Washington, and Grass Lake.

1.3 ▲ SO Pacific Crest Trail crosses. To the right goes into the Lakes Basin Recreation Area to Wade Lake, Mount Washington, and Grass Lake.

GPS: N39°42.49′ W120°43.19′

▼ 2.0 TL Spencer Lakes to the right. Turn left for a spectacular viewpoint over Wade Lake, Rock Lake, and Jamison Lake.

1.1 ▲ TR Rejoin main trail. Spencer Lakes to the left.

GPS: N39°42.43′ W120°43.07′

▼ 2.2 TL Rejoin main trail; then Pacific Crest Trail leaves to the left.

0.9 ▲ TR Pacific Crest Trail joins on the right; then turn right for a spectacular viewpoint over Wade Lake, Rock Lake, and Jamison Lake.

GPS: N39°42.34′ W120°42.94′

▼ 2.8 SO Remains of Four Hills Mine on left and right. Track on left.

0.3 ▲ SO Track on right. Remains of Four Hills Mine on left and right.

GPS: N39°41.90′ W120°42.66′

▼ 2.9 BR Track on left toward Mud Lake.

0.2 ▲ BL Track on right toward Mud Lake.

GPS: N39°41.79′ W120°42.66′

▼ 3.1 TL Track on right to the bottom of the Four Hills Mine; then well-used trail continues straight ahead to Spencer Lakes. There is a jeep and motorbike sign on a tree, but no other markings. The Four Hills Mine mill site is at the intersection. Zero trip meter.

0.0 ▲ Continue to the west. Track on left to the bottom of the Four Hills Mine.

GPS: N39°41.86′ W120°42.75′

▼ 0.0 Continue to the south.

1.2 ▲ TR T-intersection. Well-used track on left goes to Spencer Lakes. Zero trip meter and turn right up hill. The intersection is unmarked. The Four Hills Mine mill site is at the intersection.

▼ 0.3 SO Track on right.

0.9 ▲ SO Track on left.

GPS: N39°41.66′ W120°42.81′

▼ 0.8 SO Entering Camp Nejedly—private property.

0.4 ▲ SO Leaving Camp Nejedly.

GPS: N39°41.33′ W120°42.56′

▼ 1.2 SO Hawley Lake on right. Track on right to lakeshore. Zero trip meter.

0.0 ▲		Continue to the north.
		GPS: N39°41.04′ W120°42.47′

▼ 0.0		Continue to the south, following sign to Gold Valley.
3.1 ▲	SO	Hawley Lake on left. Track on left to lakeshore. Zero trip meter.
▼ 0.2	SO	Leaving Camp Nejedly.
2.9 ▲	SO	Entering Camp Nejedly—private property.
▼ 0.6	SO	Cross through creek.
2.5 ▲	SO	Cross through creek.
▼ 0.7	SO	Cross through creek.
2.4 ▲	SO	Cross through creek.
▼ 0.8	TR	Track on right; then immediately turn right and cross over Pauley Creek. Track on left goes to Snake Lake.
2.3 ▲	TL	Cross over Pauley Creek; then track on right goes to Snake Lake. Turn left and immediately pass track on left.
		GPS: N39°40.64′ W120°41.94′

▼ 0.9	TL	Track on right. Trail can be slightly brushy for the next 0.6 miles.
2.2 ▲	TR	Track on left.
▼ 1.1	SO	Cross through creek twice.
2.0 ▲	SO	Cross through creek twice.
▼ 1.2	SO	Cross over creek twice.
1.9 ▲	SO	Cross over creek twice.
▼ 1.3	SO	Entering Gold Valley.
1.8 ▲	SO	Leaving Gold Valley.
		GPS: N39°40.28′ W120°42.12′

▼ 1.4	SO	Cross through creek twice.
1.7 ▲	SO	Cross through creek twice.
▼ 1.5	SO	Cross through Pauley Creek.
1.6 ▲	SO	Cross through Pauley Creek. Trail can be slightly brushy for the next 0.6 miles.
		GPS: N39°40.19′ W120°42.28′

▼ 1.6	SO	Track on right.
1.5 ▲	SO	Track on left.
		GPS: N39°40.17′ W120°42.34′

▼ 1.7	SO	Track on left to campsite by small cascades. Trail standard has improved to a 4.
1.4 ▲	SO	Track on right to campsite by small cascades. Trail enters the 6-rated section.

▼ 1.8	SO	Cross through creek.
1.3 ▲	SO	Cross through creek.
▼ 2.2	SO	Cross through Pauley Creek.
0.9 ▲	SO	Cross through Pauley Creek.
		GPS: N39°39.84′ W120°42.61′

▼ 2.3	SO	Track on right.
0.8 ▲	SO	Track on left.
▼ 2.9	TL	T-intersection with small formed trail. There is an OHV trail sign after the turn.
0.2 ▲	TR	Track continues straight ahead. Follow OHV marker on the tree.
		GPS: N39°39.34′ W120°42.45′

▼ 3.1	SO	Track on right is Pauley Creek Trail to Smith Lake. (Sign is high on the tree and hard to spot.) Zero trip meter and continue up the hill.
0.0 ▲		Continue to the north.
		GPS: N39°39.19′ W120°42.42′

▼ 0.0		Continue to the south.
1.5 ▲	SO	Track on left is Pauley Creek Trail to Smith Lake. (Sign is high on the tree and hard to spot.) Zero trip meter.
▼ 0.6	SO	Cross through creek.
0.9 ▲	SO	Cross through creek.
▼ 0.8	SO	Track on right to Empire Mine—private property.
0.7 ▲	BR	Track on left to Empire Mine—private property.
		GPS: N39°39.12′ W120°41.85′

▼ 1.5		Trail ends at T-intersection with 93-03. Turn left to intersect with Northern Sierra #28: Gold Lake Trail; turn right to exit to Downieville.
0.0 ▲		Trail commences on 93-03, 6.2 miles north of the intersection with FR 93, which in turn is 11 miles north of California 49. Zero trip meter and turn southwest on formed trail 93-37, marked with a mountain bike sign "Downieville Downhill," and also marked to Gold Valley. After the turn, the route is marked to OHV trails: Gold Valley, Pauley Creek, and Smith Lake.
		GPS: N39°39.02′ W120°41.13′

Poker Flat OHV Trail

STARTING POINT California 49, on the western edge of Downieville

FINISHING POINT La Porte Road at North Star Junction, 2.5 miles north of Strawberry Valley

TOTAL MILEAGE 41.5 miles

UNPAVED MILEAGE 41.5 miles

DRIVING TIME 8 hours

ELEVATION RANGE 3,000–6,400 feet

USUALLY OPEN May to October

BEST TIME TO TRAVEL Dry weather

DIFFICULTY RATING 5

SCENIC RATING 10

REMOTENESS RATING +1

Special Attractions

■ Long trail that passes many pioneer mining settlements and cemeteries.

■ Site of Poker Flat.

■ Steep, challenging grades to and from Poker Flat.

■ Panoramic views from Saddleback Fire Lookout.

History

Poker Flat OHV Trail follows a well-used miners' trail from the 1850s. Fortune seekers established Downieville, on the banks of the turbulent North Yuba River, in 1849. Among the eager arrivals was a Scot named William Downie. His leadership qualities in the town's formative years may have been the reason why his name was adopted for the camp known previously as The Forks. The far-flung outpost flourished in no time, gaining a somewhat boisterous reputation.

The steep trail that leads out of Downieville passes a site known as Red Ant. The forest service had a station at the top of the thousand-foot climb from the North Yuba River. Every morning during fire season, a ranger would climb to the lookout on top of Red Ant Mountain and return in the evening to a cabin at Red Ant. The lookout on Saddleback Mountain had not yet been

built. Just north of Red Ant are the remains of the Monte Cristo Mine. The Monte Cristo Hotel was just below the road at a small intersection.

The town of Fir Cap, also called Fir Cap Diggings, was situated on the flat northwest of the Telegraph Mine. A post office established there in 1869 was discontinued in 1886.

The site of Poker Flat, established in the early 1850s, has always been a difficult place to reach. The steep grades on both sides of Canyon Creek were as dangerous for pack mules then as they are for vehicles today. A packer hauling a dead man out of town on one of his mules commented, "They're not bad to pack out, you know. You've got to be gruesome. If the relatives see the guy draped over the saddle, tied down and gurgling, they holler, you know."

The steep trail out of Poker Flat on the north side of Canyon Creek was built in the 1890s. A fallen tree was often tied to the back of wagons descending the trail to act as a brake. Come winter, this part of the Sierra Nevada saw its fair share of snow, which was often too deep and dangerous for laden mules, forcing packers to carry goods in and out on their backs. They tied rope around wooden skis to provide grip on the steep trails.

At one time Poker Flat supported several stores, a Masonic Hall, numerous saloons, a blacksmith, a jeweler, butcher shops, and three hotels, and the town's population approached 2,000. A fire in 1859 destroyed much of the town, but most residents stayed and rebuilt. A school was established in 1863 for children from town and the surrounding mining camps.

Howland Flat, also referred to as Table Rock, is one of a series of mining camps that developed along the northern side of Port Wine Ridge. Queen City, St. Louis, Pine Grove, and Scales are just a few others. Howland Flat's post office was established in 1857 and was discontinued in 1922. The town had numerous stores, a theater, a bakery, a brewery, and several busy saloons. The mining town reached a peak of 1,500 residents, and most worked at nearby hydraulic, placer, and drift mines. An estimated $14 million worth of ore was extracted during the life of the mines.

Another mining camp along the trail, Port Wine, allegedly was named for a cask of port wine discovered near the settlement. Ironically, the town was described as sober and religious. Large-scale hydraulic mining washed away most of the original town.

Description

Poker Flat OHV Trail leaves California 49 from the western edge of Downieville. The well-marked, formed CR 509 immediately starts to climb away from the North Yuba River along a shelf road. The trail, initially suited for high-clearance 2WD vehicles, climbs into Tahoe National Forest and travels below the flat-topped Fir Cap. An OHV trail rated more difficult by the forest service runs over the top of Fir Cap, providing excellent views from the summit. This trail can be very brushy.

The short trail to Saddleback Fire Lookout is a worthwhile detour from the main route. Rated 3 for difficulty, this narrow shelf road offers views east to the Sierra Buttes and beyond. It ends at a fire lookout, built in 1933, that is still manned during the summer. You can usually climb up to the tower, perched on an outcrop of rock, with permission from the lookout. Panoramic views from the tower include Tahoe and Plumas National Forests and great views of the Sierra Buttes. On a clear day you can just make out the shape of the lookout on Sierra Buttes (See Northern Sierra #27: Sierra Buttes Trail, page 190). Table Rock and Pilot Peak are visible to the north.

Back on the main trail, you will pass the start of Northern Sierra #31: Chimney Rock OHV Trail before reaching the spur to the volcanic Devils Postpile. The main trail then descends steeply along Grizzly Ridge to the historic settlement of Poker Flat. The 2-mile descent is steep and loose, narrow at times, with an uneven surface and poor traction. Two-wheel-drive vehicles should not attempt this part of the trail. Much of the land

at Poker Flat is privately owned, and there are active mining claims all along Canyon Creek. If you want to try your hand at gold panning, be sure to get permission from the mining claimant. The BLM's Folsom field office is the best place to find this information; the phone number is (916) 985-4474. The BLM's website can also tell you what you need to know.

The lumpy crossing over Canyon Creek is rearranged almost every year by spring runoff, but it is normally passable with a high-clearance 4WD. The open area of Poker Flat OHV Campground on the north side of Canyon Creek has a few tables and fire rings.

The historical marker for Poker Flat is next to one of the few surviving timber buildings; wildfires have burned the area on two separate occasions. A track continues farther east along Canyon Creek to various mining claims. The main trail swings north and starts to climb the steep, loose Wild Steer Surveys Route. The grade is more or less constant, averaging 20 degrees. At times it travels through cuttings, where runoff and years of traffic, both wagon and vehicle, have eroded the roadbed 10 to 15 feet into the surrounding hillside. The surface is loose and scrabbly with patches of fist-size rubble interspersed with a fine loose surface. Low range 4WD and a slow, steady pace will carry most vehicles safely to the top. Vehicles traveling downhill may need to reverse at times because passing places are scarce.

Watch out for piles of rocks at the intersection at the top of the climb, where 22N43 leads away in a small clearing. Miners working at Poker Flat would weigh their pickups down with rocks from the creek to give them traction for the climb up the steep grade. At the top of the climb, they would dump the rocks, creating the piles you see today. The steep descent and ascent on either side of Poker Flat gives the trail its difficulty rating of 5.

From the top of the northern climb, the trail becomes easier and is rated between a 2 and 3 for the remainder of the route. This section passes through one historic mining

Old wooden building on Poker Flat

Miners from Sicily, England, and Russia rest in St. Louis Cemetery

settlement after another. The first settlement is Howland Flat, where little remains. Only a few old buildings and a cemetery with graves dating from the late nineteenth century remain at Potosi. Please respect the gravesites. Note that most of the area is held under mining lease and that the cabins and structures along the way are privately owned. The cabins of the Wink Eye Mine are not in use, but they are still private property.

A popular 19-mile mountain bike trail, the Howland Flat Loop, joins this trail at Howland Flat and leaves it at Queen City. The full loop travels through La Porte and Lake Delahunty and is rated most difficult by the forest service.

The trail passes north of Sugarloaf Hill and starts to run along Port Wine Ridge. A side trail, 21N69, just north of Queen City travels east above Canyon Creek past the site of Wahoo, the Monumental Mine, and on to the Pacific Mine. Hydraulic mining eroded the hillsides here, and flumes and aqueducts along the trail are reminders of the area's long history of mining.

After crossing over Cedar Grove Ravine, the sites of Queen City and Port Wine are reached. Foundations and the ruins of a few old buildings are all that remain of these mining towns. Port Wine's cemetery is a short distance from the main trail, with many old graves lying in secluded spots.

Scales is now a privately-owned site. The Scales Cemetery, just east of the settlement, has many headstones that reflect the hardships of early mining life; many of the deceased were victims of accidents and women who died during childbirth.

The final section of the trail is narrow and runs around the edge of a hillside; it is lightly brushy in places and can be avoided by taking paved FR 30, which intersects the trail in several places. The paved road takes a more circuitous route to exit to Strawberry Valley. The trail finishes north of Strawberry Valley on La Porte Road, 0.7 miles north of the turnoff to Strawberry USFS Campground, which is on the edge of the now silted up Sly Creek Reservoir.

Current Road Information

Tahoe National Forest
Yuba River Ranger District
15924 Highway 49
Camptonville, CA 95922
(530) 288-3231

Plumas National Forest
Beckwourth Ranger District
23 Mohawk Road / PO Box 7
Blairsden, CA 96103
(530) 836-2575

Map References

BLM   Portola, Chico
USFS   Tahoe National Forest; Plumas
       National Forest
USGS   1:24,000   Downieville, Mt.
       Fillmore, La Porte, Goodyears Bar,
       Strawberry Valley
       1:100,000 Portola, Chico
Maptech CD-ROM: High Sierra/Tahoe
Northern California Atlas & Gazetteer,
       pp. 70, 69
California Road & Recreation Atlas, p. 60
Other: Plumas National Forest OHV
       Map—Summer Use

Route Directions

▼ 0.0		From California 49, on the western edge of Downieville, zero trip meter and turn northwest on dirt road. Climb up the hillside, following sign to Chimney Rock Trail and Poker Flat OHV Trail. Road is a single-lane shelf road.
7.6 ▲		Trail finishes on California 49 on the western edge of Downieville.
		GPS: N39°33.49' W120°49.99'

▼ 0.8	SO	Cross over creek in Coyote Ravine.
6.8 ▲	SO	Cross over creek in Coyote Ravine.
▼ 1.9	BR	Cross over creek; then track on left.
5.7 ▲	SO	Track on right; then cross over creek.
▼ 2.0	SO	Track on left; then track on right.
5.6 ▲	SO	Track on left; then track on right.
▼ 2.3	SO	Track on right.
5.3 ▲	SO	Track on left.
▼ 2.8	BR	Track on left; then road forks. The lower road is Oak Ranch Road. Take

the upper of the two roads, which is
unmarked. Track on right.

4.8 ▲   SO Track on left; then track on right is Oak
Ranch Road; then track on right.
GPS: N39°34.48' W120°51.53'

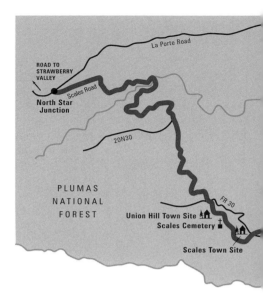

▼ 3.5   SO Track on right.
4.1 ▲   SO Track on left.
▼ 3.7   SO Slightly cleared area is the site of
Red Ant.
3.9 ▲   SO Slightly cleared area is the site of
Red Ant.
GPS: N39°35.18' W120°51.50'

▼ 4.4   SO Track on right is the start of Fir Cap
OHV Trail, which goes 0.3 miles to an
unmarked graveyard on the right of the
trail. Coordinates of the graves are
N39°35.66' W120°51.31'.
3.2 ▲   SO Track on the left is the start of Fir Cap
OHV Trail, which goes 0.3 miles to an
unmarked graveyard on the right of the
trail. Coordinates of the graves are
N39°35.66' W120°51.31'.
GPS: N39°35.70' W120°51.44'

▼ 4.7   SO Cabin on left and track on left at the
Monte Cristo Mine.
2.9 ▲   SO Cabin on right and track on right at the
Monte Cristo Mine.
GPS: N39°35.87' W120°51.53'

▼ 5.3   SO Track on left into the White Bear Mine.
2.3 ▲   SO Track on right into the White Bear Mine.
GPS: N39°36.27' W120°51.48'

▼ 5.8   SO Track on left.
1.8 ▲   SO Track on right.
▼ 6.3   SO Track on left to Telegraph Diggings.
1.3 ▲   BL Track on right to Telegraph Diggings.
GPS: N39°36.85' W120°51.91'

▼ 6.5   SO Track on left.
1.1 ▲   SO Track on right.
▼ 7.6   BR Track on right is Fir Cap OHV Trail (25-
23-2); then track on left is 25-19 and
second track on left is FR 25 to Devils
Postpile. Bear right onto 25-23 following sign to Saddleback Lookout and
Poker Flat. Zero trip meter.

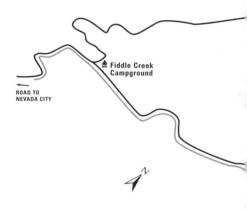

0.0 ▲   Continue to the east.
GPS: N39°37.82' W120°51.74'

▼ 0.0   Continue to the northwest.
2.3 ▲   BL Track on right is FR 25 to Devils
Postpile and second track on right is
25-19; then track on left is Fir Cap OHV

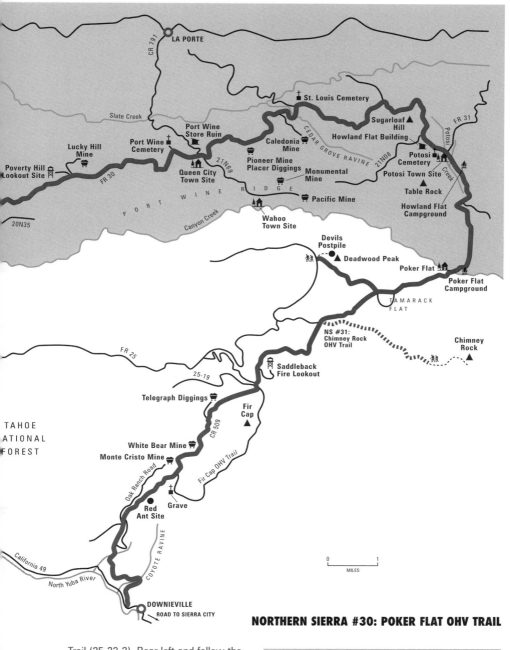

CR 791

LA PORTE

St. Louis Cemetery

Slate Creek

Sugarloaf Hill

FR 31

Port Wine Store Ruin

Howland Flat Building

Potosi

Lucky Hill Mine

Port Wine Cemetery

Caledonia Mine

Potosi Cemetery

Poverty Hill Lookout Site

FR 30

21N69

Pioneer Mine Placer Diggings

CEDAR GROVE RAVINE

21N08

Potosi Town Site

Queen City Town Site

Monumental Mine

Table Rock

20N35

P O R T   W I N E   R I D G E

Pacific Mine

Howland Flat Campground

Canyon Creek

Wahoo Town Site

Devils Postpile

Deadwood Peak

Poker Flat

Poker Flat Campground

TAMARACK FLAT

FR 25

NS #31: Chimney Rock OHV Trail

Chimney Rock

25-19

Saddleback Fire Lookout

Telegraph Diggings

Fir Cap

TAHOE NATIONAL FOREST

CR 509

White Bear Mine

Monte Cristo Mine

Oak Ranch Road

Fir Cap OHV Trail

Grave

Red Ant Site

COYOTE RAVINE

0   1
MILES

California 49

North Yuba River

DOWNIEVILLE
ROAD TO SIERRA CITY

NORTHERN SIERRA #30: POKER FLAT OHV TRAIL

Trail (25-23-2). Bear left and follow the sign to Downieville. Zero trip meter.

▼ 0.4 SO Track on right goes 0.7 miles up a 3-rated track to Saddleback Lookout.

1.9 ▲ SO Track on left goes 0.7 miles up a 3-rated track to Saddleback Lookout.
GPS: N39°38.02′ W120°52.00′

▼ 1.2 SO Track on left. Follow sign to Chimney Rock Trail.

1.1 ▲ SO Track on right.
GPS: N39°38.57′ W120°51.84′

▼ 1.8 SO Track on left.

0.5 ▲	SO	Track on right.
▼ 2.3	BL	Track on right is Northern Sierra #31:Chimney Rock OHV Trail. Track on left. Zero trip meter and bear left, following sign to Poker Flat OHV Trail.
0.0 ▲		Continue to the southeast.

GPS: N39°39.33' W120°51.76'

▼ 0.0		Continue to the northwest.
1.8 ▲	SO	Track on left is Northern Sierra #31: Chimney Rock OHV Trail. Track on right. Zero trip meter.
▼ 0.7	TR	T-intersection with roughly graded road. Follow sign to Poker Flat OHV Trail.
1.1 ▲	TL	Graded road continues ahead. Turn sharp left and climb up hill on smaller unmarked trail. There is a sign for Poker Flat OHV Trail at the intersection.

GPS: N39°39.82' W120°51.60'

▼ 0.8	SO	Turnout on left.
1.0 ▲	SO	Turnout on right.
▼ 1.2	SO	Track on right.
0.6 ▲	SO	Track on left.
▼ 1.4	SO	Track on left.
0.4 ▲	SO	Track on right.
▼ 1.7	SO	Track on left.
0.1 ▲	SO	Track on right.
▼ 1.8	SO	Track on left is the spur to the Devils Postpile. Zero trip meter and follow the sign to Poker Flat OHV Trail. Track on right is Tamarack OHV Trail.
0.0 ▲		Continue to the south. End of climb.

GPS: N39°40.47' W120°51.37'

Spur to Devils Postpile

▼ 0.0		Proceed west at the start of the OHV part of the trail.
▼ 0.1	SO	Track on right.
▼ 0.2	SO	Track on right.
▼ 0.4	BL	Track on right goes 0.6 miles north of Deadwood Peak.

GPS: N39°40.40' W120°51.83'

▼ 1.7		Hiking trail on right is Devils Postpile Trail (10E26); then track on left.

GPS: N39°40.09' W120°52.89'

Continuation of Main Trail

▼ 0.0		Continue to the north and start descent to Poker Flat.
2.1 ▲	SO	Track on right is the spur to the Devils Postpile. Zero trip meter. Track on left is Tamarack OHV Trail.

GPS: N39°40.47' W120°51.37'

▼ 0.4	SO	Cross through creek; then track on left to Deadwood Mine.
1.7 ▲	SO	Track on right to Deadwood Mine; then cross through creek.

GPS: N39°40.65' W120°51.15'

▼ 0.5	SO	Track on right.
1.6 ▲	SO	Track on left.
▼ 0.8	SO	Start of shelf road.
1.3 ▲	SO	End of shelf road.
▼ 1.2	SO	End of shelf road.
0.9 ▲	SO	Start of shelf road.
▼ 1.7	SO	Track on right.
0.4 ▲	BR	Track on left.

GPS: N39°41.46' W120°50.62'

▼ 1.8	BL	Trail forks coming into Poker Flat. Track on right goes to mining claims and Blind Street.
0.3 ▲	BR	Leaving Poker Flat. Track on left goes to mining claims and Blind Street.

GPS: N39°41.51' W120°50.60'

▼ 1.9	BR	Track on left and track on right to private property. End of descent. Cross through Canyon Creek; then track on left. Entering Plumas National Forest on north side of creek.
0.2 ▲	BL	Track straight ahead. Bear left and cross through Canyon Creek; then track on right and track on left to private property. Entering Tahoe National Forest on south side of creek. Start to climb away from Poker Flat.

GPS: N39°41.57' W120°50.69'

▼ 2.0	SO	Poker Flat OHV Campground on right at the confluence of Grizzly Creek and Canyon Creek.
0.1 ▲	SO	Poker Flat OHV Campground on left at the confluence of Grizzly Creek and Canyon Creek.

GPS: N39°41.65' W120°50.62'

▼ 2.1   TL   Old building on right; then turn left up the hill. Track continues ahead along Canyon Creek. Zero trip meter.

0.0 ▲   Continue to the southwest.

GPS: N39°41.67' W120°50.55'

▼ 0.0   Continue to the northwest and start to climb away from Poker Flat.

1.9 ▲   TR   T-intersection in front of old building in Poker Flat. Track on left goes along Canyon Creek. Zero trip meter.

▼ 0.5   SO   Cross over creek.

1.4 ▲   SO   Cross over creek.

▼ 1.6   SO   Track on right.

0.3 ▲   SO   Track on left.

▼ 1.8   BR   Track on left.

0.1 ▲   BL   Track on right.

▼ 1.9   SO   Well-used track on right. Zero trip meter. End of climb from Poker Flat. Note the piles of rocks at the intersection used by miners coming up the hill.

0.0 ▲   Continue to the south on FR 32 and start to descend to Poker Flat.

GPS: N39°42.58' W120°51.60'

▼ 0.0   Continue to the north.

6.1 ▲   SO   Well-used track on left. Continue onto FR 32 following the sign for Poker Flat OHV Campground. Zero trip meter.

View of Fir Cap from Saddleback Lookout

Note the piles of rocks at this intersection used by miners coming up the hill.

▼ 0.2   SO Cross over creek.
5.9 ▲   SO Cross over creek.
▼ 0.7   SO Howland Flat USFS Campground on right.
5.4 ▲   SO Howland Flat USFS Campground on left.
        GPS: N39°42.93' W120°52.16'

▼ 1.0   SO Cross over creek on bridge; then track on left to old mining remains.
5.1 ▲   SO Track on right to old mining remains; then cross over creek on bridge.
▼ 1.2   BL Track on right is FR 31—rated black. Bear left and cross over Potosi Creek. This is the site of Potosi.
4.9 ▲   BR Potosi town site. Cross over Potosi Creek; then track on left is FR 31—rated black. Bear right onto FR 32 for 4WDs, ATVs, and motorbikes—rated blue.
        GPS: N39°43.02' W120°52.67'

▼ 1.3   SO Two old cabins on right at Wink Eye Mine.
4.8 ▲   SO Two old cabins on left at Wink Eye Mine.
        GPS: N39°43.01' W120°52.80'

▼ 1.4   SO Track on right; then Potosi Cemetery on left.
4.7 ▲   SO Potosi Cemetery on right; then track on left.
        GPS: N39°42.94' W120°52.88'

▼ 1.7   SO Track on right.
4.4 ▲   SO Track on left.
▼ 1.8   SO Track on left. Remains of a Howland Flat stone building with circular well out back on left; then cross over creek.
4.3 ▲   SO Cross over creek; then remains of a Howland Flat stone building with circular well out back on right; then track on right.
        GPS: N39°42.87' W120°53.28'

▼ 1.9   SO Track on left is 21N08.
4.2 ▲   SO Track on right is 21N08.
▼ 2.1   SO Track on right.
4.0 ▲   SO Track on left.
▼ 2.2   SO Cross over creek. Trail is passing through an area where hydraulic mining took place. Sugarloaf Hill is on the left.
3.9 ▲   SO Trail is passing through an area where hydraulic mining took place. Cross over creek. Sugarloaf Hill is on the right.
▼ 2.3   SO Track on left.
3.8 ▲   SO Track on right.
▼ 2.5   SO Cross over creek. Slate Creek Ravine is on the right.
3.6 ▲   SO Cross over creek. Slate Creek Ravine is on the left.
▼ 2.9   SO Two tracks on right.
3.2 ▲   SO Two tracks on left.
▼ 3.0   SO Track on left to Debi D Mine.
3.1 ▲   SO Track on right to Debi D Mine.
        GPS: N39°43.15' W120°53.99'

▼ 3.8   SO Two tracks on right.
2.3 ▲   SO Two tracks on left.
▼ 4.0   SO Track on left and track on right.
2.1 ▲   SO Track on left and track on right.
▼ 4.8   SO Track on left.
1.3 ▲   SO Track on right.
▼ 5.1   SO Track on left and track on right.
1.0 ▲   SO Track on left and track on right.
▼ 5.4   SO Track on left.
0.7 ▲   SO Track on right.
▼ 5.5   SO Track on right.
0.6 ▲   SO Track on left.
▼ 5.6   SO Track on right.
0.5 ▲   SO Track on left.
▼ 5.7   SO Track on left.
0.4 ▲   SO Track on right.
▼ 5.8   SO Track on right.
0.3 ▲   SO Track on left.
▼ 5.9   SO Track on right is 21N96.
0.2 ▲   SO Track on left is 21N96.
        GPS: N39°41.86' W120°55.70'

▼ 6.0   SO Unmarked track on right goes 0.1 miles to St. Louis Cemetery. Coordinates of cemetery are N39°41.86' W120°55.82'.
0.1 ▲   SO Unmarked track on left goes 0.1 miles to St. Louis Cemetery. Coordinates of cemetery are N39°41.86' W120°55.82'.
▼ 6.1   BL Wide graded track on right. Zero trip meter.

0.0 ▲		Continue to the north. End of shelf road.

GPS: N39°41.70' W120°55.79'

▼ 0.0		Continue to the south on FR 31. Start of shelf road.
3.4 ▲	BR	Wide graded track on left. Zero trip meter.
▼ 0.3	SO	Cross over Cedar Grove Ravine on bridge.
3.1 ▲	SO	Cross over Cedar Grove Ravine on bridge.
▼ 0.4	SO	Spring on left.
3.0 ▲	SO	Spring on right.

GPS: N39°41.51' W120°55.66'

▼ 0.6	SO	Track on left.
2.8 ▲	SO	Track on right.
▼ 0.7	SO	Track on left is 21N55 to Caledonia Mine.
2.7 ▲	SO	Track on right is 21N55 to Caledonia Mine.
▼ 1.4	SO	Track on left; then cross over creek.
2.0 ▲	SO	Cross over creek; then track on right.
▼ 1.5	SO	Track on right.
1.9 ▲	SO	Track on left.
▼ 1.6	SO	Two tracks on right.
1.8 ▲	SO	Two tracks on left.
▼ 1.7	SO	Track on left.
1.7 ▲	SO	Track on right.
▼ 1.9	SO	Track on right into old hydraulic mining area is now private.
1.5 ▲	SO	Track on left into old hydraulic mining area is now private.

GPS: N39°40.75' W120°55.85'

▼ 2.0	SO	Track on left into Pioneer Mine Placer Diggings; then Pioneer Mine Trail crosses over Deacon Long Ravine.
1.4 ▲	SO	Pioneer Mine Trail crosses over Deacon Long Ravine; then track on right into Pioneer Mine Placer Diggings.

GPS: N39°40.63' W120°55.93'

▼ 2.4	SO	Track on left; then track on right is 21N58.
1.0 ▲	SO	Track on left is 21N58; then track on right.

GPS: N39°40.47' W120°56.27'

▼ 2.5	SO	Track on left is 21N69, which goes 2.4 miles to the Pacific Mine site. Access varies.
▼ 0.9 ▲	SO	Track on right is 21N69, which goes 2.4 miles to the Pacific Mine site. Access varies.

GPS: N39°40.39' W120°56.33'

▼ 2.9	SO	Track on right.
0.5 ▲	SO	Track on left.
▼ 3.2	SO	Cross over Pats Gulch. Spring on left.
0.2 ▲	SO	Spring on right. Cross over Pats Gulch.
▼ 3.3	SO	Track on left is 21N12.
0.1 ▲	SO	Track on right is 21N12.
▼ 3.4	SO	Well-used track on right is CR 791. Zero trip meter.
0.0 ▲		Continue to the north on FR 31 for 4WDs and motorbikes.

GPS: N39°39.90' W120°56.41'

▼ 0.0		Continue to the south on FR 30 for 4WDs and motorbikes—rated green.
6.4 ▲	SO	Well-used track on left is CR 791. Zero trip meter.
▼ 0.2	SO	Cross over creek.
6.2 ▲	SO	Cross over creek.
▼ 0.3	SO	Track on left. Part of Queen City site on right and up the track on left.
6.1 ▲	SO	Track on right. Part of Queen City site on left and up the track on right.
▼ 0.5	SO	Track on left; then second track on left and track on right. Port Wine store ruin is on the left.
5.9 ▲	SO	Track on left and track on right; then second track on right. Port Wine store ruin is on the right.

GPS: N39°39.65' W120°56.80'

▼ 0.7	BL	Track on right is 21N59, which goes 0.1 miles to Port Wine Cemetery. A historical board marks the intersection.
5.7 ▲	BR	Track on left is 21N59, which goes 0.1 miles to Port Wine Cemetery. A historical board marks the intersection.

GPS: N39°39.65' W120°56.93'

▼ 0.8	SO	Dam on left.
5.6 ▲	SO	Dam on right.
▼ 1.9	SO	Track on right is 21N48Y.
4.5 ▲	SO	Track on left is 21N48Y.
▼ 2.4	SO	Cross over creek.
4.0 ▲	SO	Cross over creek.

▼ 3.4 SO Track on right is 21N48Y to Lucky Hill Mine site. Remain on FR 30.

3.0 ▲ SO Track on left is 21N48Y to Lucky Hill Mine site. Remain on FR 30.
GPS: N39°38.17′ W120°57.94′

▼ 3.5 SO Track on right goes to Poverty Hill lookout site.

2.9 ▲ SO Track on left goes to Poverty Hill lookout site.

▼ 4.8 SO Track on left.

1.6 ▲ SO Track on right.

▼ 5.4 BR Three tracks on left and old cabin on left; then track on left.

1.0 ▲ BL Track on right; then old cabin on right and three tracks on right.
GPS: N39°36.76′ W120°58.63′

▼ 5.5 SO Track on left.

0.9 ▲ SO Track on right.

▼ 5.9 SO Track on right.

0.5 ▲ SO Track on left.

▼ 6.0 BL Well-used track on right is CR 691. Remain on FR 30.

0.4 ▲ BR Well-used track on left is CR 691. Remain on FR 30.
GPS: N39°36.35′ W120°58.97′

▼ 6.4 SO 4-way intersection. Track on left is 20N35 and paved road on right is FR 30 (CR 690). Zero trip meter.

0.0 ▲ Continue to the north, joining FR 30 (CR 690).
GPS: N39°36.03′ W120°59.12′

▼ 0.0 Continue to the south on unmarked CR 590.

7.2 ▲ SO 4-way intersection. Track on right is 20N35 and paved road on left is FR 30 (CR 690). Zero trip meter.

▼ 0.1 SO Cross over Rock Creek on bridge.

7.1 ▲ SO Cross over Rock Creek on bridge.

▼ 0.2 SO Track on left and track on right.

7.0 ▲ SO Track on left and track on right.

▼ 0.4 SO Track on left.

6.8 ▲ SO Track on right.

▼ 0.7 SO Scales town buildings on right are now private property.

6.5 ▲ SO Scales town buildings on left are now private property.

GPS: N39°35.89′ W120°59.53′

▼ 0.9 SO Scales Cemetery on left. Hydraulic mining pit is behind it.

6.3 ▲ SO Scales Cemetery on right. Hydraulic mining pit is behind it.
GPS: N39°35.89′ W120°59.74′

▼ 1.0 TR Track straight ahead goes to mine diggings.

6.2 ▲ TL T-intersection. Track on right goes to mine diggings.
GPS: N39°35.84′ W120°59.84′

▼ 1.2 SO Track on right; then cross over Rock Creek twice on bridge; then track on right.

6.0 ▲ SO Track on left; then cross over Rock Creek twice on bridge; then track on left.

▼ 1.5 SO Track on left. Site of Union Hill.

5.7 ▲ SO Track on right. Site of Union Hill.

▼ 1.7 SO Cross over paved FR 30 (CR 690).

5.5 ▲ SO Cross over paved FR 30 (CR 690).
GPS: N39°35.92′ W121°00.30′

▼ 2.3 SO Track on left.

4.9 ▲ SO Track on right.
GPS: N39°35.80′ W121°00.69

▼ 2.9 BR Track on left.

4.3 ▲ BL Track on right.
GPS: N39°35.97′ W121°01.06′

▼ 3.2 SO Track on left.

4.0 ▲ SO Track on right.

▼ 3.7 BR Track on left.

3.5 ▲ BL Track on right.
GPS: N39°36.11′ W121°01.61′

▼ 3.8 SO Cross over gravel FR 30. Track on right is 21N11F. Continue straight across and swing around to the southwest.

3.4 ▲ SO Cross over gravel FR 30. Track on left is 21N11F.
GPS: N39°36.18′ W121°01.56′

▼ 4.6 SO Track on left is 20N30 and track on right is 20N63A.

2.6 ▲	SO	Track on right is 20N30 and track on left is 20N63A.

GPS: N39°36.49' W121°02.31'

▼ 5.1	SO	Track on left and track on right are both 20N28.
2.1 ▲	SO	Track on left and track on right are both 20N28.
▼ 6.1	SO	Track on left and track on right are both 20N28.
1.1 ▲	SO	Track on left and track on right are both 20N28.

GPS: N39°36.01' W121°03.07'

▼ 7.2	BL	Bear left and cross over Slate Creek on two bridges. Track on right after bridges goes to Slate Creek Reservoir. Zero trip meter.
0.0 ▲		Continue to the north.

GPS: N39°36.74' W121°03.29'

▼ 0.0		Continue to the southeast. Start of shelf road.
2.7 ▲	BR	Track on left. Zero trip meter and cross over Slate Creek on two bridges.
▼ 0.6	SO	Cross over creek.
2.1 ▲	SO	Cross over creek.
▼ 1.0	SO	End of shelf road.
1.7 ▲	SO	Start of shelf road.
▼ 2.0	SO	Track on right and track on left.
0.7 ▲	SO	Track on right and track on left.
▼ 2.1	SO	Track on right; then track on left.
0.6 ▲	SO	Track on right; then track on left.
▼ 2.4	BR	Track on left.
0.3 ▲	BL	Track on right.
▼ 2.5	SO	Track on left.
0.2 ▲	SO	Track on right.
▼ 2.7		North Star Junction. Trail finishes at T-intersection with paved La Porte Road. Turn left for Strawberry Valley; turn right for La Porte.
0.0 ▲		Trail begins at North Star Junction on paved La Porte Road, 0.7 miles north of Strawberry USFS Campground. Zero trip meter and turn northeast onto graded dirt Scales Road. There is a street sign at the intersection.

GPS: N39°35.27' W121°04.59'

Chimney Rock OHV Trail

STARTING POINT Northern Sierra #30: Poker Flat OHV Trail, 9.9 miles north of Downieville
FINISHING POINT Chimney Rock Trailhead
TOTAL MILEAGE 2.4 miles (one-way)
UNPAVED MILEAGE 2.4 miles
DRIVING TIME 20 minutes (one-way)
ELEVATION RANGE 6,000–6,600 feet
USUALLY OPEN April to October
BEST TIME TO TRAVEL Dry weather
DIFFICULTY RATING 4
SCENIC RATING 9
REMOTENESS RATING +0

Special Attractions

- Short, challenging spur from the longer Northern Sierra #30: Poker Flat OHV Trail.
- Very popular mountain bike route.
- Easy hiking trail to Chimney Rock.

History

Chimney Rock (6,698 feet) is one of a series of striking peaks that rises sharply from the northern end of Craycroft Ridge. Needle Point, Rattlesnake Peak, Gibraltar, Tennessee Mountain, Saddleback Mountain, and the aptly named Cloud Splitter form a ring of peaks around Chimney Rock. Deep ravines, canyons, and valleys separate these cone-like spires. Present-day visitors enjoy this striking landscape, but it was a navigation nightmare for miners of the late nineteenth and early twentieth centuries.

A string of pack trails ran through the canyons and up the ridges to reach various mining camps across the mountains. Craycroft Ridge Trail was one of the major pack trails running north from Downieville. It ran from the Gold Bluff Mine, one of the earliest lode mines, all the way up the ridge past Needle Point and Rattlesnake Peak, and on to Sunnyside Meadow. Sheepherders drove their flocks up this trail to reach the pastures and spring at Sunnyside,

Nelson Creek. A fork to the northeast took pack trains down to McRae Meadow and additional mining camps.

Many of the surrounding pack trails are overgrown nowadays. However, with a keen eye, experienced hikers or horseback riders can follow these old supply routes, once the sole domain of packers and their trusted mules.

Description

Chimney Rock OHV Trail is a short detour from Northern Sierra #30: Poker Flat OHV Trail that leads to the Chimney Rock Trailhead.

The first 1.5 miles of Chimney Rock OHV Trail are suitable for any high-clearance vehicle; the final 0.9 miles give the trail its difficulty rating of 4. This part is best suited for compact and mid-size SUVs. Full-size SUVs and pickups may find the shelf road a little too narrow for safety. Steep grades and a very loose, friable surface make it very easy for vehicles to loose traction and grind to a stop on the return trip. Two-wheel-drive vehicles should not attempt the difficult final mile.

The OHV trail ends at the Chimney Rock Trailhead. From here, a well-defined, narrow trail for hikers and mountain bikers runs around the side of the mountain and zigzags up to Chimney Rock. The huge volcanic rock, a little more than 1 mile from the trailhead, measures approximately 12 feet in diameter and 25 feet in height. The trail eventually connects to the Empire Creek Trail. Hikers or bikers who can arrange a pickup can continue via Empire Creek Canyon on the long trip to Downieville.

Current Road Information

Tahoe National Forest
Yuba River Ranger District
15924 Highway 49
Camptonville, CA 95922
(530) 288-3231

Map References

BLM   Portola
USFS Tahoe National Forest; Plumas
       National Forest

then known as Sheep Ranch. The narrow trail also passed the Craycroft Mine and the Garibaldi Cabin, named for its first occupant.

Getting supplies and mail to these camps proved to be quite a challenge for packers, who were quite often a miner's only contact with the outside world. It was important for packers to stop a while and have a meal with the camp residents. An observant packer knew if he was welcome or if he should move on; some lone miners could hardly afford to feed themselves, never mind a hungry visitor.

Other pack trails went to mining camps north of Chimney Rock. A trail leading out of Poker Flat wound up Tennessee Ravine to the Tennessee Mine, where small-scale hydraulic mining continued into the 1910s (even though it was outlawed in 1884). The trail continued up the East Fork of Canyon Creek to the Gibraltar Mine. From there it zigzagged up the side of Rattlesnake Peak to the old Craycroft Ridge Trail. The trail continued north toward Gibraltar by way of the Cowell Mine, where it connected with a trail at the head of

USGS 1:24,000 Mt. Fillmore
    1:100,000 Portola
Maptech CD-ROM: High Sierra/Tahoe
Northern California Atlas & Gazetteer, p. 70
California Road & Recreation Atlas, p. 60
    (incomplete)
Other: Plumas National Forest OHV
    Map—Summer Use

Route Directions

▼ 0.0   From Northern Sierra #30: Poker Flat OHV Trail, 9.9 miles north of Downieville, zero trip meter and proceed north on formed trail following sign to Chimney Rock Trail.

          GPS: N39°39.33′ W120°51.76′

▼ 0.5 SO Track on left.

▼ 0.6 SO Track on right; then two tracks on left.

▼ 1.5 SO Bunker Hill. Bunker Democrat Channel Mine sign on tree. High-clearance 4WDs only past this point.

          GPS: N39°40.00′ W120°50.45′

▼ 2.4   Trail ends at the Chimney Rock Trailhead.

          GPS: N39°40.24′ W120°49.49′

View from the hiking trail to Chimney Rock

The off-camber approach to Chimney Rock can be loose

Forbestown to Feather Falls Trail

STARTING POINT Forbestown Road, 1.1 miles northwest of Forbestown

FINISHING POINT FR 27, on the eastern edge of Feather Falls

TOTAL MILEAGE 18.1 miles

UNPAVED MILEAGE 17.3 miles

DRIVING TIME 2 hours

ELEVATION RANGE 900–3,400 feet

USUALLY OPEN April to November

BEST TIME TO TRAVEL Dry weather only

DIFFICULTY RATING 4

SCENIC RATING 7

REMOTENESS RATING +1

Special Attractions

- Sunset Hill Fire Lookout.
- Fishing at Ponderosa Reservoir.
- Long, winding forest trail with a moderately difficult, 4-rated section.
- Forbestown Cemetery.

History

Old Forbestown dates back to the early days of California's gold rush. Ben F. Forbes and James D. Forbes, emigrants from Wisconsin, were among the first to prospect and invest at this location. Ben prospected in Forbes Ravine (now called Forbestown Ravine), opened a trading post, and later opened a post office to cater to the influx of miners. James built the United States Hotel and began the first stagecoach service from Oroville to the boomtown of Forbestown.

Forbestown was a supply center for the surrounding communities of New York Flat and Ohio. By the late 1850s, more than 2,000 people had moved to the town, which by that time boasted a number of hotels and saloons, a blacksmith, a library, and a Masonic Hall. A fire in 1861 burned down most of the town, but the settlers rebuilt.

In 1885, the appropriately named Gold Bank Mine was established at the junction of Mosquito Gulch and Forbestown Ravine,

northeast of town. Harry P. Stow owned the mine, and his mansion reflected his wealth. For the next two decades, the mine brought prosperity to Forbestown. After ores played out in 1904, many employees left town.

Forbestown went through a series of revivals into the late 1930s, most revolving around the re-worked Gold Bank Mine. Sadly, the town center was unable to survive and has faded with time. All that remains today is the Masonic Hall established in 1854, one of the oldest in California, and the cemetery. Several hundred headstones tell tales of times long since forgotten. The headstone of young Elish belongs to a boy killed in a cave-in on the banks of the nearby Feather River.

Feather Falls was predominantly a company town—bare spaces indicate the sites where buildings once stood. A concrete vault on the main street is all that is left of the old company headquarters.

Description

Two worthwhile features of this trail are just off the main route near the southern end. The Sunset Hill Fire Lookout, 0.5 miles west of the start of the trail, is still manned during summer. The gate is normally open when there is a lookout on duty, and you can often climb up the tower with the lookout's permission. Constructed in the 1960s, the tower is not one of the most important in the region. Its view is perpendicular to the surrounding ridges with only one face visible, which makes it of limited use in spotting fires. However it does offer great views of Lake Oroville, Bloomer Mountain, and Mooretown Ridge.

Historic Forbestown Cemetery, 0.6 miles east of the start down Old Forbestown Road, has graves dating to the late 1880s. The Forbestown Lodge was built in 1854 and stands near the cemetery. Coordinates of the lodge are GPS: N39º31.57' W121º16.66'.

The main trail descends well-graded forest roads to the small Ponderosa Reservoir, which is surrounded by firs and formed by a dam on the South Fork of the Feather River. No gas-powered boats are allowed on the reservoir. There are a couple of pleasant picnic spots with limited shade. This section follows the

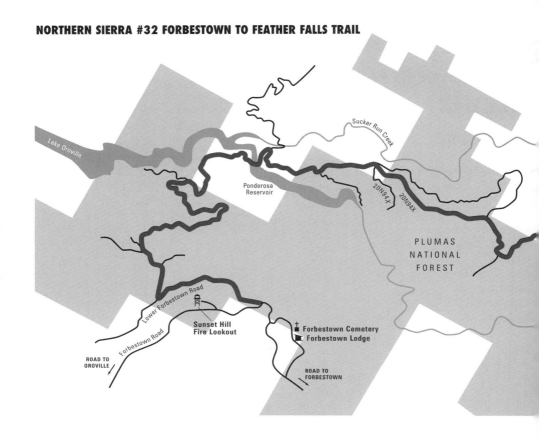

old Ponderosa Way, a firebreak road put in by the Civilian Conservation Corps. (For more on the Ponderosa Way, see Northern Sierra #42: Ponderosa Way, page 286.)

Once on the north side of the river, the trail swiftly turns to 4WD only, climbing formed trail 20N94X toward the ridge. This section should only be attempted in dry weather; deep ruts attest to the greasy and friable nature of the trail's surface. 4WD will be needed to negotiate the ruts, which account for the 4 rating of this trail.

On top of the ridge, the trail enters forest owned by Sierra Pacific Industries. Logging may restrict access at times, but the route primarily follows county and forest roads to finish on A Line Road, 0.3 miles east of Feather Falls. No camping or campfires are permitted on Sierra Pacific Industries land.

This route is not shown in its entirety on topographical or forest maps.

Current Road Information

Plumas National Forest
Beckwourth Ranger District
23 Mohawk Road / PO Box 7
Blairsden, CA 96103
(530) 836-2575

Map References

BLM   Chico
USFS   Plumas National Forest (incomplete)
USGS   1:24,000   Forbestown, Clipper Mills
    1:100,000   Chico
Maptech CD-ROM: High Sierra/Tahoe
Northern California Atlas & Gazetteer,
    pp. 69, 68
California Road & Recreation Atlas,
    p. 60 (incomplete)
Other: Plumas National Forest OHV
    Map—Summer Use

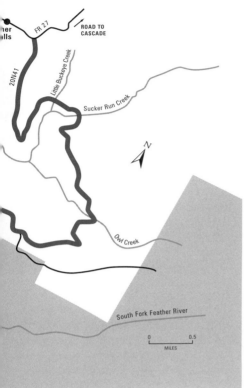

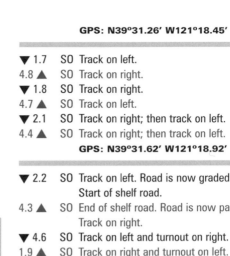

GPS: N39°31.26' W121°18.45'

▼ 1.7   SO   Track on left.
4.8 ▲   SO   Track on right.
▼ 1.8   SO   Track on right.
4.7 ▲   SO   Track on left.
▼ 2.1   SO   Track on right; then track on left.
4.4 ▲   SO   Track on right; then track on left.
        GPS: N39°31.62' W121°18.92'

▼ 2.2   SO   Track on left. Road is now graded dirt.
             Start of shelf road.
4.3 ▲   SO   End of shelf road. Road is now paved.
             Track on right.
▼ 4.6   SO   Track on left and turnout on right.
1.9 ▲   SO   Track on right and turnout on left.
▼ 5.0   SO   Two tracks on left.
1.5 ▲   SO   Two tracks on right.
        GPS: N39°32.49' W121°18.79'

▼ 6.0   SO   Track on right.
0.5 ▲   SO   Track on left.
▼ 6.4   BL   Turnout on right. Cross over Ponderosa
             Reservoir Dam. End of shelf road.
0.1 ▲   BR   Cross over Ponderosa Reservoir Dam.
             Turnout on left. Start of shelf road.
▼ 6.5   TL   T-intersection on north side of dam.
             Track on right goes to campsite.
             Zero trip meter.
0.0 ▲   Continue to the southwest.
        GPS: N39°32.99' W121°18.14'

▼ 0.0   Continue to the west.
3.8 ▲   TR   Track continues straight ahead to
             campsite. Zero trip meter and turn
             right toward Ponderosa Reservoir Dam.
▼ 0.2   TR   Two tracks on left, track straight
             ahead, and small track on sharp right.
             Turn right onto larger graded road and
             start to climb up the hill.
3.6 ▲   TL   Two tracks straight ahead, track on
             right, and small track on left. Turn left
             onto larger graded road.
        GPS: N39°33.15' W121°18.16'

▼ 1.1   BL   Track on right.
2.7 ▲   SO   Track on left.
▼ 2.1   SO   Two gated tracks on left and two
             tracks straight ahead, second of which
             is 20N94X. Major track on right also.

Route Directions

▼ 0.0   From Forbestown Road, 1.1 miles
             northwest of Forbestown, 0.5 miles
             northeast of Sunset Hill Fire Lookout,
             zero trip meter and turn southwest on
             graded dirt Lower Forbestown Road.
             Immediately track on right.
6.5 ▲   Track on left; then trail ends on
             paved Forbestown Road. Turn right for
             Sunset Hill Fire Lookout and Oroville;
             turn left for Forbestown Cemetery
             and Challenge.
        GPS: N39°31.73' W121°17.23'

▼ 0.8   SO   Track on left.
5.7 ▲   SO   Track on right.
▼ 1.4   TR   Graded road continues straight ahead.
             Road is now paved.
5.1 ▲   TL   Graded road continues straight ahead.
             Road is now graded dirt.

Continue straight ahead onto 20N94X, which heads up the hill.

1.7 ▲ SO Major track on left, track on right, and two gated tracks straight ahead. Continue straight ahead on major ungated trail, heading downhill.
GPS: N39°33.56′ W121°16.82′

▼ 2.9 SO Two tracks on right.
0.9 ▲ SO Two tracks on left.
▼ 3.1 BL Track on right.
0.7 ▲ SO Track on left.
GPS: N39°33.41′ W121°15.83′

▼ 3.8 BR End of climb. Well-used track on left. Zero trip meter.
0.0 ▲ Continue downhill to the south.
GPS: N39°33.57′ W121°15.24′

▼ 0.0 Continue to the east.

7.8 ▲ BL Track continues to the right. Zero trip meter.
▼ 0.3 SO Track on left under power lines.
7.5 ▲ SO Track on right under power lines.
▼ 0.6 BL Track on right.
7.2 ▲ BR Track on left.
GPS: N39°33.31′ W121°14.85′

▼ 0.9 SO Track on right under power lines.
6.9 ▲ SO Track on left under power lines.
▼ 1.0 SO Track on right in cleared area.
6.8 ▲ SO Track on left in cleared area.
▼ 1.1 SO Track on right.
6.7 ▲ SO Track on left.
▼ 1.3 SO Gate.
6.5 ▲ SO Gate.
GPS: N39°33.78′ W121°14.34′

▼ 1.5 SO Track on left and track on right.
6.3 ▲ SO Track on left and track on right.

Ponderosa Reservoir

<table>
<thead>
<tr><th></th><th></th><th></th></tr>
</thead>
<tbody>
<tr><td>▼ 1.7</td><td>BR</td><td>Well-used track on left.</td></tr>
<tr><td>6.1 ▲</td><td>BL</td><td>Well-used track on right.</td></tr>
</tbody>
</table>

GPS: N39°33.88′ W121°14.00′

<table>
<tbody>
<tr><td>▼ 1.9</td><td>SO</td><td>Track on left and track on right.</td></tr>
<tr><td>5.9 ▲</td><td>SO</td><td>Track on left and track on right.</td></tr>
<tr><td>▼ 2.5</td><td>SO</td><td>Track on left; then gate.</td></tr>
<tr><td>5.3 ▲</td><td>SO</td><td>Gate; then track on right.</td></tr>
</tbody>
</table>

GPS: N39°33.86′ W121°13.22′

<table>
<tbody>
<tr><td>▼ 2.8</td><td>BL</td><td>Track on right.</td></tr>
<tr><td>5.0 ▲</td><td>BR</td><td>Track on left.</td></tr>
</tbody>
</table>

GPS: N39°33.94′ W121°13.01′

<table>
<tbody>
<tr><td>▼ 3.1</td><td>SO</td><td>Track on left and track on right.</td></tr>
<tr><td>4.7 ▲</td><td>SO</td><td>Track on left and track on right.</td></tr>
<tr><td>▼ 3.3</td><td>SO</td><td>Track on left.</td></tr>
<tr><td>4.5 ▲</td><td>SO</td><td>Track on right.</td></tr>
<tr><td>▼ 3.4</td><td>SO</td><td>Cross over Owl Creek; then track on right.</td></tr>
<tr><td>4.4 ▲</td><td>SO</td><td>Track on left; then cross over Owl Creek.</td></tr>
<tr><td>▼ 4.0</td><td>SO</td><td>Track on right.</td></tr>
<tr><td>3.8 ▲</td><td>BR</td><td>Track on left.</td></tr>
</tbody>
</table>

GPS: N39°34.56′ W121°13.50′

<table>
<tbody>
<tr><td>▼ 4.5</td><td>SO</td><td>Track on left.</td></tr>
<tr><td>3.3 ▲</td><td>SO</td><td>Track on right.</td></tr>
<tr><td>▼ 4.8</td><td>BR</td><td>Track on left.</td></tr>
<tr><td>3.0 ▲</td><td>BL</td><td>Track on right.</td></tr>
<tr><td>▼ 5.1</td><td>SO</td><td>Cross over Sucker Run Creek on bridge.</td></tr>
<tr><td>2.7 ▲</td><td>SO</td><td>Cross over Sucker Run Creek on bridge.</td></tr>
</tbody>
</table>

GPS: N39°35.11′ W121°13.88′

<table>
<tbody>
<tr><td>▼ 5.5</td><td>SO</td><td>Cross over Little Buckeye Creek.</td></tr>
<tr><td>2.3 ▲</td><td>SO</td><td>Cross over Little Buckeye Creek.</td></tr>
</tbody>
</table>

GPS: N39°35.10′ W121°14.28′

<table>
<tbody>
<tr><td>▼ 6.4</td><td>SO</td><td>Gate.</td></tr>
<tr><td>1.4 ▲</td><td>SO</td><td>Gate.</td></tr>
</tbody>
</table>

GPS: N39°34.57′ W121°14.39′

<table>
<tbody>
<tr><td>▼ 7.1</td><td>BR</td><td>Track on right.</td></tr>
<tr><td>0.7 ▲</td><td>BR</td><td>Track on left.</td></tr>
<tr><td>▼ 7.6</td><td>SO</td><td>Gate; then track on right under power lines.</td></tr>
<tr><td>0.2 ▲</td><td>SO</td><td>Track on left under power lines; then gate.</td></tr>
<tr><td>▼ 7.8</td><td></td><td>Trail ends at T-intersection with paved A Line Road (FR 27). Turn left for Feather Falls; turn right for Cascade.</td></tr>
</tbody>
</table>

<table>
<tbody>
<tr><td>0.0 ▲</td><td></td><td>Trail begins on paved FR 27, 0.2 miles north of the intersection of A Line Road (FR 27) and B Line Road on the eastern edge of Feather Falls. Zero trip meter and turn southeast on formed dirt road marked 20N41.</td></tr>
</tbody>
</table>

GPS: N39°35.58′ W121°14.86′

Milsap Bar Trail

STARTING POINT FR 94, 10.7 miles northeast of FR 27

FINISHING POINT Oroville–Quincy Highway at the Brush Creek USFS Work Center

TOTAL MILEAGE 15.5 miles

UNPAVED MILEAGE 15.1 miles

DRIVING TIME 1.5 hours

ELEVATION RANGE 1,800–4,200 feet

USUALLY OPEN April to November

BEST TIME TO TRAVEL Dry weather

DIFFICULTY RATING 2

SCENIC RATING 9

REMOTENESS RATING +0

Special Attractions

- Excellent fishing at Milsap Bar.
- Riverside camping and swimming in the Middle Fork of the Feather River.
- Access to Big Bald Rock Trailhead for hikers.
- Historic Cascade Bar near the start of the trail.

History

Milsap Bar Trail commences deep within Plumas National Forest on the edge of Mountain Spring House Ridge, some 2,300 feet above the Middle Fork of the Feather River. The site of old Mountain Spring House, 700 feet above the trail's starting point, has panoramic views of the forest. From the ridge-top house, one old pack trail ran west down Mountain Spring House Ridge and another, called Hansons Bar Trail, ran to the north; both dropped steeply to the river. You can still hike the Hansons Bar Trail to the sites of Graves Cabin and Kennedy

Cabin, 1.7 miles upstream on the Middle Fork. All of these old pack trails are now within the Middle Fork Feather Wild & Scenic River Reserve. The reserve, established in October 1968, stretches a total of 77 miles along this river canyon. Feather Falls is in the Feather Falls Scenic Area, some 8 miles downstream from Milsap Bar Bridge. With a 640-foot-drop, Feather Falls is the sixth highest in the United States.

The entire region surrounding the trail on the south side of the river was the scene of extensive logging in the first half of the twentieth century. The Feather River Pine Mills, known as Hutchinson Lumber Company prior to 1927, had a far-reaching network of logging roads, and the company built a new sawmill at the town of Feather Falls in 1939.

Construction of the Oroville Dam to the west spelled doom for the industry here. Rising lake waters submerged the outgoing railroad to Oroville known as the Feather Falls Railway. The old Hutchinson Lumber Company locomotive #3 pulled its last trainload out of Feather Falls on March 19, 1965.

Cascade is east along Cascade Creek, a short distance from the start. The settlement is now the Cascade Resort, a collection of summer cabins and home of the Cascade Bar. This small log cabin at the edge of a meadow on Cascade Creek boasts the oldest continually operating liquor license in California and has been trading since 1876. The bar is open from April to December; if a bartender is not on hand, ring the triangle on the front verandah and someone will open the bar for you. You will not only get a beverage at the Cascade Bar, but a slice of California history as well. The two-story dwelling next to the Cascade Bar was once a popular lodging house. An Indian named Williams opened a trading post here in 1876, a business he operated until he was hanged in Feather River for allegedly cheating in a game of chance.

Description

The trail leaves FR 94, 10.7 miles northeast of Feather Falls. It is unsigned at first, but marked FR 62 a short distance past the start. The trail immediately starts to descend a shelf road through a mix of forest, winding down the side of the valley toward the Middle Fork of the Feather River. The trail surface is uneven enough to require a high-clearance vehicle.

A small forest service campground sits alongside the Middle Fork of the Feather River at Milsap Bar. There is currently no fee for camping there. The campground is popular with anglers because Milsap Bar offers some of the best rainbow trout fishing in the region.

On the north side of the river, the trail climbs a moderate grade to join Oroville-Quincy Highway, passing some private property at the upper end.

Near the end of the trail a spur leads to the Big Bald Rock Trailhead, a hiking trail that goes up to the open granite dome. The trail ends on Oroville–Quincy Highway at the Brush Creek Work Center.

Current Road Information

Plumas National Forest
Beckwourth Ranger District
23 Mohawk Road / PO Box 7
Blairsden, CA 96103
(530) 836-2575

Map References

BLM   Chico
USFS   Plumas National Forest
USGS   1:24,000   Cascade, Brush Creek
      1:100,000   Chico
Maptech CD-ROM: High Sierra/Tahoe
Northern California Atlas & Gazetteer,
      pp. 68, 69
California Road & Recreation Atlas, p. 59
Other: Plumas National Forest OHV
      Map—Summer Use

Route Directions

▼ 0.0   From Feather Falls, travel east on paved road FR 27 (A Line Road) for 7 miles. Turn left (north) onto FR 94, following the sign for Milsap Bar, and proceed 8 miles. A signposted detour here takes you to the historic Cascade Bar. From there, retrace your route back to FR 94 and proceed north for an additional 2.7 miles (a total of 10.7

Cascade Bar has the oldest liquor license in California

miles from FR 27). Zero trip meter and turn northwest on graded dirt FR 62.

7.9 ▲ Trail ends at FR 94. Turn right and follow above directions, in reverse, to Cascade Bar and Feather Falls.

GPS: N39°42.38' W121°12.93'

▼ 0.4 SO Track on right goes 1.7 miles to Hansons Bar Trailhead. Corral on left. Main trail is now marked FR 35 for 4WDs, ATVs, and motorbikes.

7.5 ▲ SO Track on left goes 1.7 miles to Hansons Bar Trailhead. Corral on right.

GPS: N39°42.66' W121°13.08'

▼ 2.3 SO Start of shelf road.
5.6 ▲ SO End of shelf road.
▼ 5.8 SO Cross over creek.
2.1 ▲ SO Cross over creek.

GPS: N39°43.11' W121°14.79'

▼ 7.2 SO Crooked Bar visible below—identified by a bend in the river.
0.7 ▲ SO Crooked Bar visible below—identified by a bend in the river.
▼ 7.4 SO Track on right goes out toward

NORTHERN SIERRA #33: MILSAP BAR TRAIL

Crooked Bar.
0.5 ▲ SO Track on left goes out toward Crooked Bar.

GPS: N39°42.85' W121°16.08'

▼ 7.9 SO Road becomes paved. Track on sharp left goes into Milsap Bar USFS Campground. Zero trip meter.
0.0 ▲ Continue to the southeast.

GPS: N39°42.53' W121°16.14'

Milsap Bar Trail

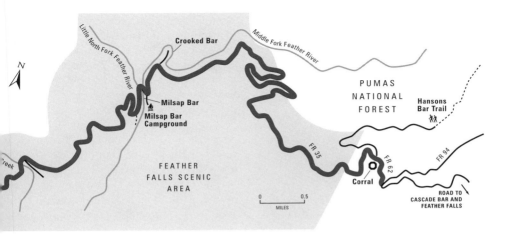

▼ 0.0   Continue to the northwest.

7.6 ▲   BL   Road returns to graded dirt. Track on right goes into Milsap Bar USFS Campground. Zero trip meter.

▼ 0.1   SO   Cross over Middle Fork Feather River on bridge at confluence of Little North Fork Feather River.

7.5 ▲   SO   Cross over Middle Fork Feather River on bridge at the confluence of Little North Fork Feather River.
     GPS: N39°42.58′ W121°16.19′

▼ 0.2   SO   Road turns to graded dirt.

7.4 ▲   SO   Road is now paved.

▼ 0.4   SO   Hiking trail to river on left.

7.2 ▲   SO   Hiking trail to river on right.

▼ 3.0   SO   Cross over creek; then track on left.

4.6 ▲   SO   Track on right; then cross over creek.
     GPS: N39°41.53′ W121°17.37′

▼ 3.1   SO   Cross over Indian Creek.

4.5 ▲   SO   Cross over Indian Creek.

▼ 4.0   SO   End of shelf road.

3.6 ▲   SO   Start of shelf road.

▼ 4.6   SO   Track on left.

3.0 ▲   SO   Track on right.
     GPS: N39°40.84′ W121°18.45′

▼ 5.0   SO   Track on left; then second track on left and track on right.

2.6 ▲   SO   Track on left and track on right; then second track on right.

▼ 5.2   SO   Track on right.

2.4 ▲   SO   Track on left.

▼ 5.4   SO   Track on left.

2.2 ▲   SO   Track on right.

▼ 5.6   SO   Track on left is 21N49; then track on right.

2.0 ▲   SO   Track on left; then track on right is 21N49.
     GPS: N39°41.02′ W121°19.17′

▼ 6.2   SO   Kaelin Road on left.

1.4 ▲   BL   Kaelin Road on right.

▼ 6.3   SO   Two tracks on right.

1.3 ▲   SO   Two tracks on left.

▼ 7.2   TR   T-intersection with paved Bald Rock Road. Track on left goes 3.3 miles to Big Bald Rock Trailhead.

0.4 ▲   TL   Paved road ahead goes 3.3 miles to Big Bald Rock Trailhead. Turn left onto graded dirt FR 62 (22N62, OHV Route 1) for 4WDs, ATVs, and motorbikes— rated green. Follow the sign to Milsap Bar Campground.
     GPS: N39°41.08′ W121°20.55′

▼ 7.6   Trail ends at T-intersection with Oroville–Quincy Highway at the Brush Creek USFS Work Center. Turn right for Bucks Lake; turn left for Oroville.

0.0 ▲   Trail commences on the Oroville– Quincy Highway, 24 miles south of Bucks Lake at the Brush Creek USFS Work Center. Zero trip meter and turn south on paved Bald Rock Road.
     GPS: N39°41.41′ W121°20.29′

Three Lakes Trail

STARTING POINT FR 33 at Lower Bucks Lake, 2.8 miles north of Oroville-Quincy Highway

FINISHING POINT Three Lakes

TOTAL MILEAGE 10 miles (one-way)

UNPAVED MILEAGE 10 miles

DRIVING TIME 1 hour (one-way)

ELEVATION RANGE 5,000–6,200 feet

USUALLY OPEN May to November

BEST TIME TO TRAVEL May to November

DIFFICULTY RATING 3

SCENIC RATING 9

REMOTENESS RATING +0

Special Attractions

- Excellent fishing in Lower Bucks Lake and Three Lakes.
- Hiking access to the Pacific Crest National Scenic Trail and the Bucks Lake Wilderness.
- A hundred miles of groomed snowmobile trails in the Bucks Lake region.

History

Bucks Lake, formerly Buck's Ranch, was named for Horace "Buck" Bucklin. Natives of New York, Bucklin and his partner Francis Walker settled here in the autumn of 1850. Buck's Ranch lay along what became the Oroville to Quincy stage and express route and served as the supply center for outlying mining camps. The property changed hands several times and eventually had a hotel.

The Feather River Power Company established Bucks Lake in the late 1920s as part of the Bucks Creek Hydroelectric Power Project. The project involved constructing Bucks Lake Dam, Lower Bucks Lake Dam, Three Lakes Dam, Milk Ranch Creek Conduit, Grizzly Creek Forebay Dam, aqueducts, lengthy penstocks, an incline railway, and finally the Bucks Creek Powerhouse on the Feather River.

A narrow-gauge railroad was built to move the huge amounts of material across this mountainous terrain. Contractor H. H.

Boomer used a Bucyrus steam-driven shovel to load rock onto railcars. The massive steam shovel, built by the Bucyrus Erie firm of South Milwaukee, took nine men to operate. It was a forerunner of today's gigantic Ruston Bucyrus earthmoving machinery. Upon reaching the construction site, rock was offloaded by tipping the railcars sideways. It took approximately 326,000 cubic yards of rock to complete Bucks Lake Dam. Little of the narrow-gauge railroad is visible today.

The shelf road to Three Lakes sits on top of the Milk Ranch Creek Conduit. This lengthy underground pipe boosts Lower Bucks Lake with waters from Three Lakes.

Description

The trail to Three Lakes travels a long shelf road built to service the aqueduct connecting Three Lakes to Lower Bucks Lake, part of the Pacific Gas & Electric's hydroelectric power scheme. For the most part, the 2-rated trail is suitable for high-clearance 2WDs. However, the final couple of miles where the trail leaves the level grade of the aqueduct and climbs to Three Lakes is loose, rough, and requires 4WD.

The trail leaves from the western side of Bucks Lake, which has excellent fishing for kokanee salmon and Mackinaw and rainbow trout. Lower Bucks Lake is renowned for its silver salmon. There are developed campgrounds around Bucks Lake and Lower Bucks Lake; these pleasant, shaded lakeside sites are the best places to camp along the trail. The campsites along Lower Bucks Lake are limited to self-contained RVs; tent camping is restricted to sites on Bucks Lake.

The graded trail traverses a level grade on the side of Bald Eagle Mountain. Many small creeks spill over the trail; for the most part they have concrete fords to prevent the trail from washing away. The vehicle trail ends at the Pacific Crest National Scenic Trail, where it enters the Bucks Lake Wilderness. The hiking trail to Kellogg Lake and Rich Bar leaves the Pacific Crest National Scenic Trail a short distance east of the trailhead. Three Lakes are visible from the trailhead. Water levels fluctuate because of hydroelectric use. A couple of

Lower Bucks Lake, excellent for catching silver salmon

small, rocky campsites can be found at the end of the trail, but these are not as pleasant as the campgrounds at Bucks Lake. Anglers will enjoy fishing for brook and golden trout at Three Lakes.

In winter, snowmobilers and cross-country skiers use the trail system around Bucks Lake and Little Bucks Lake. The area, with 100 miles of groomed trails and an annual snowfall of 75 inches, is one of the most popular snowmobile trail systems in the state.

Current Road Information

Plumas National Forest
Mt. Hough Ranger District
39696 Highway 70
Quincy, CA 95971
(530) 283-0555

Map References

BLM   Chico
USFS Plumas National Forest
USGS 1:24,000   Bucks Lake, Storrie
       1:100,000 Chico
Maptech CD-ROM: High Sierra/Tahoe
Northern California Atlas & Gazetteer, p. 69
California Road & Recreation Atlas, p. 60
Other: Plumas National Forest OHV
      Map—Summer Use

NORTHERN SIERRA #34: THREE LAKES TRAIL

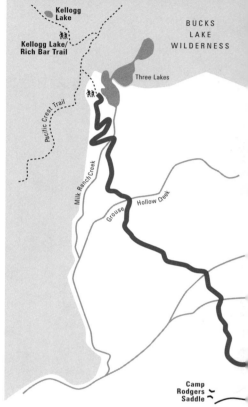

Route Directions

▼ 0.0   From Oroville–Quincy Highway on the western edge of Bucks Lake, zero trip meter and turn north on FR 33 following the sign to Lower Bucks Lake. Proceed 2.8 miles north; then zero trip meter and turn northwest on the graded dirt FR 24 (24N24, OHV Route 10) for 4WDs, ATVs, and motorbikes—rated blue. The route is signed to Lower Bucks and Three Lakes. The trail immediately passes along the north shore of Lower Bucks Lake, passing through Lower Bucks USFS Campground.
      GPS: N39°53.89' W121°12.30'

▼ 0.3 SO Cross over creek. Hiking trail on right.
▼ 1.0 BR Track on left to final lakeside campsite.

    Bear right, through seasonal closure gate, remaining on OHV Route 10.
      GPS: N39°54.17' W121°13.17'

▼ 1.4 SO Dam on left. Start of shelf road.
▼ 2.7 SO Cross over Bear Ravine.
      GPS: N39°54.98' W121°13.55'

▼ 3.5 SO Cross through creek.
      GPS: N39°55.53' W11°13.90'

▼ 3.6 SO Cross through creek.
▼ 4.2 SO Cross through Slide Ravine.
▼ 5.0 BR Track on left is 24N35. Remain on marked OHV Route 10 and zero trip meter.
      GPS: N39°55.73' W121°15.03'

▼ 0.0   Continue to the west.
▼ 0.5 SO Radio tower on left. Views to the west

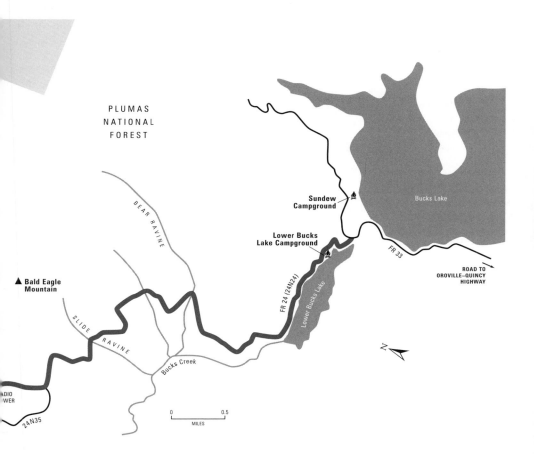

PLUMAS
NATIONAL
FOREST

BEAR RAVINE

SLIDE RAVINE

Bald Eagle Mountain

Bucks Creek

RADIO TOWER

24N35

FR 24 (24N24)

Lower Bucks Lake

Bucks Creek

Sundew Campground

Lower Bucks Lake Campground

Bucks Lake

FR 33

ROAD TO OROVILLE–QUINCY HIGHWAY

N

0   0.5
MILES

look down Bucks Creek to North Fork Feather River.

▼ 1.0 SO Camp Rodgers Saddle on left. Views on left to North Fork Feather River and Rock Creek Dam, set below Ben Lomond.
▼ 1.6 SO Cross through creek.
▼ 1.9 SO Cross through creek.
▼ 3.2 SO Cross through Grouse Hollow Creek.
      GPS: N39°57.72′ W121°14.25′

▼ 3.9 SO Cross through Milk Ranch Creek. Trail starts to climb.
      GPS: N39°58.05′ W121°13.72′

▼ 4.9 BL Pull-in on right.
▼ 5.0   Trail ends at Three Lakes and the Pacific Crest Trailhead on the edge of the Bucks Lake Wilderness. The Kellogg Lake/Rich Bar Trail leads off of

the Pacific Crest Trail just east of the trailhead. Three Lakes are a short distance through the trees to the east.
      GPS: N39°58.28′ W121°13.34′

NORTHERN SIERRA #35

Grizzly Ridge Trail

STARTING POINT CR 207 at Taylorsville, 4.6 miles east of California 89

FINISHING POINT Lake Davis Road (CR 112), 5 miles north of Portola

TOTAL MILEAGE 43.8 miles, plus 3.1-mile spur to Crystal Lake, 1.5-mile spur to Grizzly Peak, and 1.1-mile spur to Argentine Rock

UNPAVED MILEAGE 43.6 miles, plus spurs

DRIVING TIME 6 hours

ELEVATION RANGE 3,600–7,400 feet
USUALLY OPEN July to late November
BEST TIME TO TRAVEL June to November
DIFFICULTY RATING 2, spurs are rated 3 and 4
SCENIC RATING 9
REMOTENESS RATING +0

Special Attractions

■ Fossil shell impressions near Taylorsville.
■ Mount Hough Fire Lookout, Smith Peak Fire Lookout, and the site of the Argentine Rock Fire Lookout.
■ Crystal Lake and Lake Davis.

History

Taylorsville, at the start of the trail, honors Jobe Terrill Taylor, identified as the town's founder. Taylor passed through the vicinity in 1850 and returned in 1852 to settle. The Maidu who lived here were apparently peaceful, thus making the area attractive to settlers. There are two points of interest near Taylorsville. The first, a site for fossil shell casts, is near the Taylorsville Campground. From the start of the trail, continue east through Taylorsville for 0.7 miles to a T-intersection at the Taylorsville Campground and Rodeo Grounds. Turn left (north) and travel 0.1 miles. The reddish and greenish shale on the east side of the road has imprints of shells left behind by receding waters of an ancient lake. The second site, the Taylorsville Cemetery, is on the east side of town. Turn south on Cemetery Street, and the cemetery will be on the left. It contains graves of many pioneers, including that of founder Jobe Terrill Taylor.

Maidu Indians continue to live in what is now called Indian Valley. The Worldmaker, as Maidu elders tell the story, made the country safe by clearing it of man-killers. Monster Snake Pool and Canoe Hammering Point feature in Maidu stories. Monster Snake Pool was supposedly formed by a giant snake, and some Maidu refused to swim in the lake because they did not wish to disturb the sleeping snake. Canoe Hammering Point, off to the north, was home to a man-eating monster who hammered all day long on a wooden canoe until Worldmaker tricked the monster into showing him his

weapons. Worldmaker grabbed one of the weapons and cut off the monster's head, ridding the valley of the threat to the Maidu.

Mount Hough commands excellent views over Indian Valley and beyond, making it an obvious choice for a fire lookout. The first lookout was built around 1916, and the present lookout was built in the late 1980s.

Walker Mine, at an elevation of 6,000 feet on the northern side of Grizzly Ridge, was a major copper mining operation established after the turn of the twentieth century. J. R. Walker and two associates staked claims here based on a mining engineer's report. The mine employed nearly 600 men at its peak, and the settlement at the mine had more than 60 private houses, 4 bunkhouses, and more than 100 company houses as well as a motion picture hall, hospital, schools, service station, and more. The mine had 13 levels and yielded an estimated 167 million tons of copper during its working life. The extremely large tailings pond and concrete mill site have been declared a toxic site, and the mine has long been involved in pollution issues.

Winter was a force to be dealt with by residents at the Walker Mine settlement. There was literally no escape once cold weather set in. Snow depths made travel via horse, carriage, or foot impossible. The truly desperate tried to use the 9-mile aerial tramway that had buckets loaded with ore. Tension towers spanning great distances across canyons had no clearance for passengers on top of outward-bound ore, winds could blow them off of their perch, and they could freeze before reaching the end. Tram riders, men familiar with the workings of the tramway, would search for and try to rescue those who tried to flee. They endured hours of freezing conditions and would typically find victims in the deep snow below the tramway.

Description

Grizzly Ridge Trail is a long, scenic road in Plumas National Forest that winds past three fire lookouts and a small, pretty lake before finishing at Lake Davis. Part of the route is included in the national forest's network of

Walker Mine mill

OHV trails, so ATVs and motorbikes also use the trail. In winter, cross-country skiers and snowmobilers enjoy the trail, especially around Lake Davis and up to the Smith Peak Fire Lookout.

The trail leaves Taylorsville up the China Grade, an easy climb that leads swiftly to the top of Grizzly Ridge. The shelf road has sporadic views of Indian Valley and Mount Jura. The trail follows the eastern boundary of the Mount Hough State Game Reserve. A very worthwhile 4-rated spur leads to the Mount Hough Fire Lookout and continues to Crystal Lake. The lookout is manned during fire season, and you may climb up to the tower with permission from the lookout on duty. The view encompasses Indian Valley, Lake Almanor, Round Lake, Mount Jura, Grizzly Peak, and the town of Quincy. Hang-gliders

use Mount Hough as a launch site. There is no platform, and the launch site is considered moderately difficult. The spur continues to Crystal Lake, a small lake set in a natural rock bowl. The final, steep descent to the lake is what gives the spur its 4 difficulty rating. One campsite can be found among the trees on the lakeshore.

Back on the main trail, the route continues through the forest along Grizzly Ridge. A second spur leads toward the top of Grizzly Peak, stopping below the summit on the east side. Most of this spur is rated a 4 for difficulty. The recommended turnaround point is given in the route directions. Although the trail continues 0.2 miles past this point, the difficulty rating increases to 5 because of the steep, loose slope and off-camber side slope. In addition, there is no safe place to turn around. There are only narrow turning points that put a vehicle crossways on a steep slope, thus risking rolling over.

The third spur is 5 miles farther along the ridge. This one goes a short distance to the closed Argentine Rock Fire Lookout. Rated a 3 for difficulty, the spur finishes below the lookout, which is perched high on the outcropping of Argentine Rock. From here, Grizzly Ridge can be seen to the north and south, and the Middle Fork of the Feather River and Sierra Buttes can be seen to the south. The small USFS campground of Bradys Camp is near Argentine Rock. The camp is near a stream at the edge of a small meadow renowned for the pitcher plants growing in marshy areas. The campground currently has no fee and limited facilities, but it makes a pleasant overnight stop.

From Argentine Rock, the trail continues through the forests on the north side of Grizzly Ridge. The standard of the road varies between small, formed trails and wider graded dirt roads. The trail detours slightly to pass the Walker Mine; work is currently underway to restore the area. The mill remains can be seen from the road below the site.

Past the Walker Mine, the route briefly intersects the Beckwourth Trail near Emigrant Creek. From here the trail stays below Grizzly Ridge and passes beside Summit Marsh. The wide meadows with Little Grizzly Creek running through them are a particularly pretty part of the trail. These meadows and Grizzly Ridge are both deer fawning habitat.

Smith Peak Fire Lookout, perched high above Lake Davis, offers a panoramic view that includes much of the route just traveled. Visitors are welcome between 9:30 A.M. and 6:00 P.M. when the lookout is manned during fire season. You will need to hike the final 0.2 miles up to the lookout, but the view is well worth the climb.

The trail finishes on the edge of the Lake Davis Recreation Area. The reservoir was developed for recreation rather than hydroelectric use, and it is stocked annually with rainbow, German brown, and lake trout. Bullhead are also regularly caught. Hunting in season for mule deer, waterfowl, and quail is permitted in the recreation area. Camping is limited to developed campgrounds only, normally open from late April to late October. The lake is also used for picnicking, jet skiing, swimming, and boating. There are four boat launches on the lake, and an 18.4-mile mountain bike loop runs around the lake. In winter it is used for ice fishing, snowmobiling, and cross-country skiing.

With the exception of the spurs, the trail is suitable for high-clearance 2WDs in dry weather. In wet weather, it is best avoided because of easily damaged, greasy sections. The trail closes naturally with snowfall; it is normally open from July to November, but exact dates vary each year.

Current Road Information

Plumas National Forest
Beckwourth Ranger District
23 Mohawk Road / PO Box 7
Blairsden, CA 96103
(530) 836-2575

Plumas National Forest
Feather River Ranger District
875 Mitchell Avenue
Oroville, CA 95965
(530) 534-6500

Map References

BLM   Susanville, Portola
USFS   Plumas National Forest
USGS   1:24,000   Taylorsville, Crescent
       Mills, Spring Garden, Mt. Ingalls,
       Grizzly Valley, Blairsden, Portola
       1:100,000 Susanville, Portola
Maptech CD-ROM: Shasta Lake/Redding;
       High Sierra/Tahoe
Northern California Atlas & Gazetteer,
       pp. 60, 59, 70
California Road & Recreation Atlas, p. 60
Other: Plumas National Forest OHV
       Map—Summer Use

Route Directions

▼ 0.0   From California 89, turn east on paved road to Taylorsville (CR 207) and proceed 4.6 miles. On the western edge of Taylorsville, zero trip meter and turn

Mount Hough Fire Lookout

south on graded dirt road marked
China Grade. Trail immediately follows
along the Mount Hough State Game
Refuge boundary (on the right) along
CR 208.

5.1 ▲ Trail ends on CR 207, immediately
west of Taylorsville. Turn left to exit to
California 89.

GPS: N40°04.53′ W120°50.50′

▼ 0.4 BL Track on right.
4.7 ▲ SO Track on left.
▼ 0.9 SO Two tracks on right and track on left.
4.2 ▲ SO Two tracks on left and track on right.
▼ 1.1 SO Track on right.
4.0 ▲ SO Track on left.
▼ 2.5 SO Track on left; then graded road on right
to California 89. Continue straight past
two more tracks on left.
2.6 ▲ BR Two tracks on right; then graded road
on left to California 89. Bear right following sign to Taylorsville; then track
on right.

GPS: N40°03.03′ W120°51.09′

▼ 5.1 SO Track on sharp right is FR 403 (OHV
Route 51) for 4WDs, ATVs, and motor-
bikes—rated green. This is the spur to
Mount Hough Fire Lookout and Crystal
Lake. Zero trip meter.

0.0 ▲ Continue to the north on CR 208.

GPS: N40°01.57′ W120°51.63′

Spur to Mount Hough Fire Lookout and Crystal Lake

▼ 0.0 Proceed northwest on FR 403 (OHV
Route 51).
▼ 0.5 SO Track on right.
▼ 0.6 SO Track on right.
▼ 1.6 SO Track on right.
▼ 2.3 SO Track on right.
▼ 2.4 BL Track on right goes 0.3 miles to Mount
Hough Fire Lookout. Track is now
marked 403N11; then track on right.

GPS: N40°02.80' W120°53.29'

▼ 2.5 SO Track on left; then track on right.
▼ 2.7 TR Track continues straight ahead. Turn sharp right and start the 4-rated descent.
GPS: N40°03.05' W120°53.36'

▼ 3.1 Spur ends at Crystal Lake. There is one campsite in the trees by the lake's edge.
GPS: N40°02.95' W120°53.07'

Continuation of Main Trail

▼ 0.0 Continue to the south, joining FR 403.
5.3 ▲ BR Track on left is FR 403 (OHV Route 51) for 4WDs, ATVs, and motorbikes— rated green. This is the spur to Mount Hough Fire Lookout and Crystal Lake. Zero trip meter.
GPS: N40°01.57' W120°51.63'

▼ 0.9 TL Turn left onto unmarked track in a clearing before Tollgate Creek. This is Rhinehart Meadow. Leaving boundary of the Mount Hough State Game Reserve.

4.4 ▲ TR T-intersection with larger trail. Trail now follows along boundary of the Mount Hough State Game Reserve on the left. This clearing is Rhinehart Meadow.
GPS: N40°00.82' W120°51.54'

▼ 2.6 TL T-intersection with 25N10Y.
2.7 ▲ TR Turn right onto unmarked track. There is a marker opposite the intersection for 25N10Y.
GPS: N40°01.14' W120°50.22'

▼ 3.1 SO Track on left is 25N29K.
2.2 ▲ SO Track on right is 25N29K.
▼ 4.7 SO Track on right.
0.6 ▲ SO Track on left.
▼ 5.1 SO Track on left. Taylor Rock on right.
0.2 ▲ SO Track on right. Taylor Rock on left.
GPS: N40°00.33' W120°48.79'

▼ 5.3 SO King Solomon Saddle. Track on right is 25N18. Then track on left, also 25N18, is the spur to Grizzly Peak (OHV Route 52) for 4WDs, ATVs, and motorbikes— rated blue. Zero trip meter.
0.0 ▲ Continue to the west on 25N29 (OHV Route 52)—rated green.

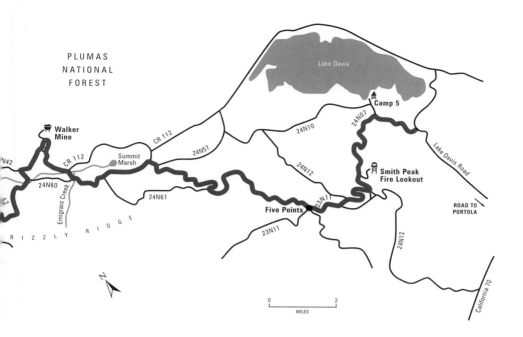

GPS: N40°00.28' W120°48.63'

Spur to Grizzly Peak

▼ 0.0   Turn north on 25N18.

▼ 0.3   BR Track on left. Remain on OHV Route 52.

▼ 0.7   SO Track on right.
         GPS: N40°00.53' W120°48.11'

▼ 1.0   SO Track on left.

▼ 1.5   Spur ends below Grizzly Peak. Trail
         continues for 0.2 miles, but it becomes
         5-rated with dangerous turning places.
         This is the last safe turning point.
         Views south overlook Grizzly Mountain.
         GPS: N40°00.85' W120°47.70'

Continuation of Main Trail

▼ 0.0   Continue to the east on 25N29 (OHV
         Route 52)—rated green.

4.6 ▲   SO King Solomon Saddle. Track on right is
         25N18, the spur to Grizzly Peak (OHV
         Route 52) for 4WDs, ATVs, and motor-
         bikes—rated blue. Track on left is also
         25N18. Zero trip meter.
         GPS: N40°00.28' W120°48.63'

▼ 3.0   SO Track on left.

1.6 ▲   SO Track on right.

▼ 4.2   SO Track on right.

0.4 ▲   SO Track on left.

▼ 4.6   BL Track on right is 25N29, spur to
         Argentine Rock. Zero trip meter.

0.0 ▲   Continue to the northwest on 25N29
         (OHV Route 52).
         GPS: N39°57.83' W120°45.50'

Spur to Argentine Rock

▼ 0.0   Turn south on 25N29, following the sign
         to Squirrel Creek and California 70.

▼ 0.6   BR Track on left goes 0.1 miles to Bradys
         Camp USFS Campground and contin-
         ues to California 70. (Turn left again
         immediately after the intersection, fol-
         lowing sign to the campground.) To
         continue to Argentine Rock, bear right
         up unmarked road that climbs the hill.
         GPS: N39°57.37' W120°45.35'

▼ 0.8   SO Track on right.

▼ 1.1   Trail ends immediately below the
         closed Argentine Rock Fire Lookout.

Continuation of Main Trail

▼ 0.0   Continue to the east on 24N19 (OHV Route 52).

2.0 ▲   BR   Track on left is 25N29, spur to Argentine Rock. Zero trip meter.

GPS: N39°57.83' W120°45.50'

▼ 2.0   TR   T-intersection with 25N42A.

0.0 ▲   TL   Immediately after last intersection, 25N42A continues straight ahead. Turn left onto 24N19 (OHV Route 52) for 4WDs, ATVs, and motorbikes—rated blue.

GPS: N39°56.91' W120°43.76'

▼ 2.0   TL   4-way intersection immediately after last intersection. Straight ahead is 24N19. To the right is OHV Route 52 for 4WDs, ATVs, and motorbikes—rated green. Turn left onto 25N42 (OHV Route 61) for 4WDs, ATVs, and motor-bikes—rated green. Zero trip meter.

0.0 ▲   Continue to the west.

GPS: N39°56.89' W120°43.75'

▼ 0.0   Continue to the north.

8.1 ▲   TR   4-way intersection. Track on left is 24N19. Straight ahead is OHV Route 52 for 4WDs, ATVs, and motorbikes—rated green. Turn right onto 25N42A and zero trip meter.

▼ 0.8   SO   Track on right.

7.3 ▲   BR   Track on left.

▼ 1.4   BR   Track on left is 24N08X.

6.7 ▲   BL   Track on right is 24N08X.

▼ 2.0   SO   Track on left.

6.1 ▲   SO   Track on right.

▼ 2.3   SO   Track on right is 24N94Y and track on left is 25N42F.

5.8 ▲   SO   Track on left is 24N94Y and track on right is 25N42F.

▼ 3.4   SO   Track on left is 24N42J.

4.7 ▲   SO   Track on right is 24N42J.

GPS: N39°57.39' W120°42.65'

▼ 4.2   SO   Track on right is 25N42D.

3.9 ▲   SO   Track on left is 25N42D.

▼ 6.2   BL   Track on right is 24N60, signposted to Emigrant Creek. Bear left onto 25N42.

1.9 ▲   BR   Track on left is 24N60, signposted to Emigrant Creek. Bear right and join 25N42 (OHV Route 61).

GPS: N39°57.26' W120°41.29'

▼ 6.8   TR   T-intersection. To the left is 25N42 (CR 112). Turn right and join CR 112.

1.3 ▲   TL   Track straight ahead is 25N42 (CR 112).

GPS: N39°57.64' W120°41.39

▼ 8.0   SO   Track on right.

0.1 ▲   SO   Track on left.

▼ 8.1   TR   Track on left goes 0.2 miles to remains of the Walker Mine mill—concrete buildings and tailings. Turn sharp right, following sign to Lake Davis, and zero trip meter.

0.0 ▲   Continue to the southwest on the lower track.

GPS: N39°57.80' W120°39.97'

▼ 0.0   Continue to the south on the upper track.

4.3 ▲   TL   Track straight ahead goes 0.2 miles to remains of the Walker Mine mill—concrete buildings and tailings. Turn sharp left, following sign to Genesee, and zero trip meter.

▼ 0.2   SO   Track on right to Genesee. Continue straight ahead on CR 112.

4.1 ▲   BR   Track on left to Genesee. Bear right on 24N09, following sign to Nye Meadows and Mount Ingalls.

GPS: N39°57.70' W120°40.14'

▼ 1.3   SO   Track on right to Walker Mine tailings; then cattle guard.

3.0 ▲   BR   Cattle guard; then track on left to Walker Mine tailings.

▼ 1.4   TR   CR 112 continues straight ahead. Turn right onto 24N60 and cross over Little Grizzly Creek, following sign to Emigrant Creek.

2.9 ▲   TL   Cross over Little Grizzly Creek; then T-intersection with CR 112.

GPS: N39°56.85' W120°40.00'

▼ 1.7   TL   T-intersection. To the right is OHV Route 61 to Cascade Creek. Emigrant

Creek is immediately to the right. Turn left onto 24N57, following sign to Paradise Creek. The northwest corner of the intersection has a Beckwourth Trail marker in the trees.

2.6 ▲   TR   OHV Route 61 goes straight ahead to Cascade Creek. Emigrant Creek is straight ahead. The northwest corner of the intersection has a Beckwourth Trail marker in the trees.

GPS: N39°56.60′ W120°40.04′

▼ 2.4   SO   Track on right.
1.9 ▲   SO   Track on left.

GPS: N39°56.17′ W120°39.57′

▼ 2.7   BL   Track on right is 24N58, which goes 2 miles to Grizzly Ridge. Bear left on 24N57.
1.6 ▲   SO   Track on left, also 24N58, goes 2 miles to Grizzly Ridge.

GPS: N39°56.18′ W120°39.21′

▼ 2.8   SO   Track on right is also 24N58.
1.5 ▲   SO   Track on left is 24N58.
▼ 3.8   SO   Cattle guard.
0.5 ▲   SO   Cattle guard.
▼ 4.1   SO   Track on left is 24N57B.
0.2 ▲   SO   Track on right is 24N57B. Continue on OHV Route 61.

GPS: N39°55.79′ W120°37.79′

▼ 4.2   SO   Track on right is 24N11X; then track on left.
0.1 ▲   SO   Track on right; then track on left is 24N11X.
▼ 4.3   TR   Well-used track on left is 24N85Y. Summit Marsh on left. Zero trip meter.
0.0 ▲   Continue to the southwest, remaining on OHV Route 61.

GPS: N39°55.79′ W120°35.56′

▼ 0.0   Continue to the south, remaining on OHV Route 61.
3.4 ▲   TL   Track straight ahead is 24N85Y. Summit Marsh is straight ahead. Zero trip meter.
▼ 0.3   SO   Track on left is 24N57.
3.1 ▲   SO   Track on right is 24N57.
▼ 2.4   SO   Track on left is 24N85YB.

1.0 ▲   SO   Track on right is 24N85YB.

GPS: N39°54.39′ W120°36.58′

▼ 3.1   SO   Track on right is 24N61. Continue straight ahead on 25N85Y (OHV Route 61).
0.3 ▲   SO   Track on left is 24N61. Continue straight ahead on 25N85Y (OHV Route 61).

GPS: N39°54.20′ W120°36.58′

▼ 3.4   TL   Turn left, remaining on 24N85Y, following the sign to Smith Peak. OHV Route 61 continues straight ahead and becomes 24N97 to Happy Valley. Zero trip meter.
0.0 ▲   Continue to the west.

GPS: N39°54.03′ W120°36.29′

▼ 0.0   Continue to the northeast.
6.6 ▲   TR   T-intersection with OHV Route 61. OHV Route 61 continues to the left and becomes 24N97 to Happy Valley. Turn right following sign to Grizzly Creek, remaining on 24N85Y and joining OHV Route 61 for 4WDs, ATVs, and motorbikes—rated green. Zero trip meter.
▼ 0.1   SO   Track on left is 24N89Y.
6.5 ▲   SO   Track on right is 24N89Y rejoining.
▼ 1.9   SO   Track on left is 24N89Y rejoining.
4.7 ▲   BL   Track on right is 24N89Y.
▼ 3.9   TL   4-way intersection with 23N11 at Five Points. To the right goes to Happy Valley. Note that the track signed to Smith Peak no longer goes there and should be ignored.
2.7 ▲   TR   4-way intersection at Five Points. Straight ahead is the continuation of 23N11 to Happy Valley. Turn right on 23N26X, following sign to Grizzly Ridge. Note that the track signed to Smith Peak (on left) no longer goes there and should be ignored.

GPS: N39°52.25′ W120°34.33′

▼ 4.8   SO   Track on right is 23N26X.
1.8 ▲   SO   Track on left is 23N26X.
▼ 5.1   TR   Track on left is 24N12. Turn right onto 24N12.
1.5 ▲   TL   Turn left on 23N11. 24N12 continues straight ahead.

▼ 6.6   TL   4-way intersection. 24N12 continues straight ahead. Track on right is 23N82. Track on left is 24N07. Turn left, following sign to Smith Peak Fire Lookout, and zero trip meter.

0.0 ▲   Continue to the northwest.

GPS: N39°51.61' W120°32.37'

▼ 0.0   Continue to the northeast. Trail now runs along the edge of the Smith Peak State Game Refuge.

4.4 ▲   TR   4-way intersection. Straight ahead is 23N82. Track on left is 24N12. Zero trip meter and turn right onto 24N12, following sign to Lake Davis.

▼ 0.8   SO   Track on right is 24N07A, which goes 1.1 miles to Smith Peak Fire Lookout.

3.6 ▲   SO   Track on left is 24N07A, which goes 1.1 miles to Smith Peak Fire Lookout.

GPS: N39°52.13' W120°32.33'

▼ 1.4   SO   Track on left.
3.0 ▲   SO   Track on right.
▼ 1.9   BR   Track on left is 23N88.
3.5 ▲   BL   Track on right is 23N88.
▼ 2.1   BL   Track on right.
2.3 ▲   BR   Track on left.
▼ 2.6   SO   Track on right is 24N07C and track on left is 24N07B.
1.8 ▲   SO   Track on left is 24N07C and track on right is 24N07B.

GPS: N39°52.81' W120°31.40'

▼ 2.8   SO   Entering Lake Davis Recreation Area.
1.6 ▲   SO   Leaving Lake Davis Recreation Area.
▼ 2.9   TR   T-intersection with gravel road 24N10. Follow sign to Portola. Exiting Smith Peak State Game Refuge. Lake Davis is opposite.
1.5 ▲   TL   Turn left onto graded dirt road 24N07. Trail follows along boundary of the Smith Peak State Game Refuge.

GPS: N39°53.20' W120°30.61'

▼ 3.2   SO   Two tracks on right.
1.2 ▲   SO   Two tracks on left.
▼ 3.5   SO   Track on right; then gravel road on left to Eagle Point Fishing Access.

0.9 ▲   SO   Gravel road on right to Eagle Point Fishing Access; then track on left.

GPS: N39°52.71' W120°30.29'

▼ 4.2   SO   Track on right is 23N15Y. Road becomes paved.
0.2 ▲   SO   Track on left is 23N15Y. Road turns to graded dirt.
▼ 4.3   BR   Track on left joins main road. Follow sign to Portola.
0.1 ▲   BL   Track on right rejoins main road. Follow sign to Smith Peak.
▼ 4.4   Trail ends at T-intersection with Lake Davis Road (CR 112, 23N06). Turn right for Portola.
0.0 ▲   Trail begins on Lake Davis Road (CR 112, 23N06), 5 miles north of Portola. Zero trip meter and turn northwest on paved road, following sign for Camp 5 and boat ramp. To reach the start of the trail from California 70, follow the sign for Lake Davis and turn north up West Street, which turns into Joy Street, and finally into Lake Davis Road. From California 70, it is 5 miles to the start of the trail.

GPS: N39°52.24' W120°29.89'

NORTHERN SIERRA #36

Diamond Mountains Trail

STARTING POINT Frenchman Lake Road (FR 176), 1.2 miles north of California 70 and Chilcoot

FINISHING POINT Forest Road 24N01 at the north end of Frenchman Lake

TOTAL MILEAGE 22 miles, plus 0.6-mile spur to Crystal Peak

UNPAVED MILEAGE 22 miles, plus 0.6-mile spur

DRIVING TIME 3 hours

ELEVATION RANGE 5,200–7,600 feet

USUALLY OPEN April to November

BEST TIME TO TRAVEL Dry weather

DIFFICULTY RATING 4

SCENIC RATING 9

REMOTENESS RATING +1

Frenchman Lake

Special Attractions

- Boating, fishing, and camping at Frenchman Lake.
- Spectacular Diamond Mountains.
- Access to other OHV routes in the area.

History

Diamond Mountains Trail begins just north of the settlement of Chilcoot and the historic Beckwourth Pass, both of which are along the Beckwourth Emigrant Trail. Chilcoot, established in about 1900, was likely named for Alaska's Chilkoot Pass on the overland trail from Skagway to the headwaters of the Yukon River in the Yukon Territory, Canada. The Chilkoot Trail was used in 1897 during the Klondike gold rush.

Chilcoot, California, is just west of the pass discovered by African-American mountain man James Pierson Beckwourth in the spring of 1850. Like many prospectors of that era, Beckwourth was taken with tales of a gold lake, reportedly somewhere in the northern part of the state. Though he never found his gold lake, he did discover a pass that was an al-

ternative to passes farther south. The route needed little improvement, and at 5,228 feet, it was the lowest to cross the Sierra Nevada. Beckwourth promoted the route from Truckee Meadows (now Reno, Nevada), up and over his gentle pass, on to the American Valley (now Quincy), and then to Bidwell's Bar. Bidwell's Bar is now submerged under the waters of Lake Oroville. Beckwourth's route was open by late 1851, and he led the first group of settlers along his trail to Marysville, south of Bidwell's Bar.

As more emigrant trains came his way in 1852, Beckwourth set up a trading post and hotel at his War Horse Ranch, just west of the present-day town of Beckwourth. Beckwourth's trading post was a welcome sight for westbound emigrants, who could stock up on basic supplies and see a friendly face. A restored cabin at the northern end of Sierra Valley is representative of the original trading post and is now open to visitors. Beckwourth's trail received considerably less use by the mid-1850s, as other trails to the south were becoming more popular.

Description

Diamond Mountains Trail, on the northeastern edge of the Sierra Nevada, offers interesting contrast to the many trails that travel through the range's pine and fir forests. The granitic Diamond Mountains are just south of the Honey Lake Fault.

The trail leaves the eastern edge of the wide Sierra Valley—an old lakebed caught between volcanic and granitic mountain ranges now used extensively by ranchers as a summer pasture. The sandy trail travels north toward the southern end of the Diamond Mountains. The predominant vegetation is sagebrush and junipers, with small pines becoming more prevalent as the trail climbs through spectacular scenery.

The first part of the trail is a single track with patches of loose, deep sand. This section partly accounts for the difficulty rating of 4. As the trail meanders through the range, it joins larger roads, some of which form the OHV trail shown on the Plumas National Forest OHV Map—Summer Use.

After passing a small, open valley, the seldom-used trail leaves the OHV route behind and starts to climb toward Crystal Peak and Adams Peak. This section can be lightly brushy because it is not used much. It also has loose surfaces and some short rocky sections to contend with.

Near Crystal Peak, a bunch of trails wind around the mountain at different levels, making navigation confusing; GPS coordinates will help you follow the correct route. There are some forest markers, but many intersections are unsigned. The trail joins OHV Route 76, which leads to within 0.6 miles of Crystal Peak. From there, a short rough 4-rated spur leads to the top of the peak and excellent views of Long Valley, Honey Lake, and Adams Peak.

The main trail remains on OHV Route 76 and starts to descend to Frenchman Lake. The main trail appears little used at first, but it soon turns into a well-defined, formed trail. The descent twists past granite boulders to cross Galeppi Creek before continuing to Frenchman Lake, a short distance south of the Salmon Egg Shoal Fishing Access point.

Frenchman Lake, at the headwaters of the Feather River, was created in 1962 for recreation and offers many outdoor activities in summer and winter. Summer fun includes camping, hiking, picnicking, fishing, water skiing, and boating (there are two boat launches at the lake). Anglers can catch rainbow and German brown trout, and hunters can find mule deer and waterfowl. Camping is permitted in developed campgrounds only, which are normally open from late April to October. In winter, the lake is used for ice fishing, cross-country skiing, and snowmobiling. A mountain bike trail coincides with this route from Chilcoot to Crystal Peak. The 10.5-mile bike trail is rated more difficult and takes approximately two hours each way.

Current Road Information

Plumas National Forest
Feather River Ranger District
875 Mitchell Avenue
Oroville, CA 95965
(530) 534-6500

Map References

BLM   Portola
USFS   Plumas National Forest
USGS   1:24,000   Chilcoot, Beckwourth
       Pass, Constantia, Frenchman Lake
       1:100,000 Portola
Maptech CD-ROM: High Sierra/Tahoe
Northern California Atlas & Gazetteer, p. 71
California Road & Recreation Atlas,
       p. 61 (incomplete)
Other: Plumas National Forest OHV
       Map—Summer Use

Route Directions

▼ 0.0   From California 70 at Chilcoot, 5.6 miles west of US 395 and Hallelujah Junction, zero trip meter and turn north on paved Frenchman Lake Road (FR 176, CR 284), following the sign to Frenchman Lake. Proceed 1.2 miles to the start of the trail. Zero trip meter and turn east (right) on the formed sandy trail marked 24N88 (OHV Route 74) for 4WDs, ATVs, and motorbikes—

View of Adams Peak from the trail

rated green. The trail crosses private property for the first 0.3 miles.

5.0 ▲ Trail ends on paved Frenchman Lake Road (FR 176, CR 284). Turn right for Frenchman Lake; turn left for California 70 and Chilcoot.

GPS: N39°48.92′ W120°08.23′

▼ 0.3 SO Fence line. Entering BLM land.
4.7 ▲ SO Fence line. The trail crosses private property from here to the finish.

▼ 0.4 BL Track on right.
4.6 ▲ SO Track on left.

▼ 0.7 SO Track on right; then gate; then track on left and track on right along fence line.
4.3 ▲ SO Track on left and track on right along fence line; then gate; then track on left.

▼ 1.0 SO Track on right is 23N62. Entering Plumas National Forest.
4.0 ▲ SO Leaving Plumas National Forest. Track on left is 23N62.

GPS: N39°49.46′ W120°07.47′

▼ 1.2 BR Track continues ahead. Bear right onto 23N67 (OHV Route 74).
3.8 ▲ TL Track on right. Turn left onto 24N88.

GPS: N39°49.68′ W120°07.48′

▼ 1.9 BL Track on right.
3.1 ▲ BR Track on left.

▼ 2.2 BR Track on left goes 0.4 miles to a spring.
2.8 ▲ SO Track on right goes 0.4 miles to a spring.

GPS: N39°50.02′ W120°07.05′

▼ 3.2 SO Track on left.
1.8 ▲ SO Track on right.

▼ 3.4 SO Track on right is 23N62.
1.6 ▲ SO Track on left is 23N62.

GPS: N39°50.79′ W120°06.81′

▼ 4.4 SO Track on left.
0.6 ▲ SO Track on right.

▼ 4.7 BL Track on right. Follow marker for OHV Route 74.
0.3 ▲ BR Track on left. Follow marker of OHV Route 74.

GPS: N39°51.79′ W120°06.94′

▼ 5.0 TR T-intersection with formed trail 24N44. OHV Route 74 goes left at this point. Ahead is a small valley. Zero trip meter.
0.0 ▲ Continue to the east.

GPS: N39°52.02′ W120°07.06′

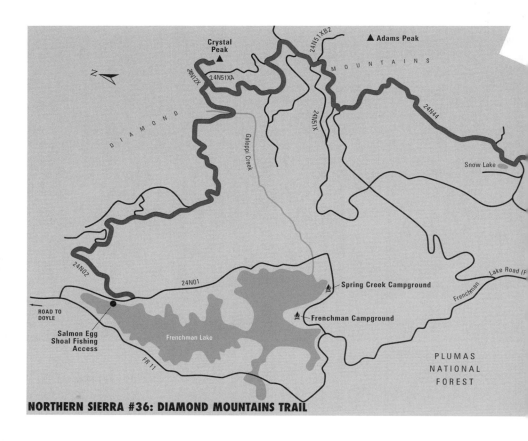

NORTHERN SIERRA #36: DIAMOND MOUNTAINS TRAIL

▼ 0.0   Continue to the northwest.
6.6 ▲   TL   Trail continues to the right around a small valley. Turn left, following marker for OHV Route 74. Zero trip meter.

▼ 0.3   SO   Track on left to the edge of Snow Lake, which is often dry in summer.
6.3 ▲   SO   Track on right to the edge of Snow Lake, which is often dry in summer.

▼ 0.7   SO   Track on right.
5.9 ▲   SO   Track on left.

▼ 1.1   SO   Wire gate.
5.5 ▲   SO   Wire gate.
       GPS: N39°52.77′ W120°07.00′

▼ 2.6   SO   Cross through creek; then track on left.
4.0 ▲   SO   Track on right; then cross through creek.
       GPS: N39°53.77′ W120°06.68′

▼ 3.2   SO   Saddle. Adams Peak is to the northeast.
3.4 ▲   SO   Saddle. Adams Peak is to the northeast.
       GPS: N39°54.13′ W120°06.67′

▼ 3.9   SO   Trail passes through private property.
2.7 ▲   SO   Exit private property.

▼ 4.2   SO   Exit private property.
2.4 ▲   SO   Trail passes through private property.

▼ 4.3   SO   Cross through creek; then track on right.
2.3 ▲   SO   Track on left; then cross through creek.

▼ 4.4   TR   Track continues straight ahead. Turn right up well-used track.
2.2 ▲   TL   T-intersection with 24N44.
       GPS: N39°54.60′ W120°07.42′

▼ 4.5   SO   Track on left and track on right. Continue straight ahead, bearing right then left. Proceed north past second track on left.
2.1 ▲   SO   Track on right; then track on left and track on right. Continue straight ahead to the south.

▼ 4.6   SO   Track on left and track on right.
2.0 ▲   SO   Track on left and track on right.
       GPS: N39°54.70′ W120°07.36′

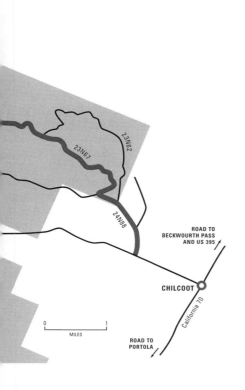

▼ 6.3 SO Track on right. Rejoining 24N51X.
0.3 ▲ BR Track on left.
▼ 6.6 TL Track continues straight ahead. Turn
left onto well-used, unmarked track
and zero trip meter.
0.0 ▲ Continue to the southeast.
GPS: N39°55.78′ W120°06.63′

▼ 0.0 Continue to the southwest.
2.8 ▲ TR Track on left. Zero trip meter.
▼ 0.5 SO Track on right is 24N51XA (OHV Route
75) for 4WDs, ATVs, and motorbikes—
rated green.
2.3 ▲ SO Track on left is 24N51XA (OHV Route
75) for 4WDs, ATVs, and motorbikes—
rated green.
GPS: N39°55.82′ W120°07.10′

▼ 1.1 SO Two tracks on right; then collapsed
wooden building on left.
1.7 ▲ SO Collapsed wooden building on right;
then two tracks on left.
▼ 1.2 TR Track continues straight ahead. Turn
right and continue north on 24N12X
(OHV Route 75).
1.6 ▲ TL T-intersection. Proceed east on
24N51X (OHV Route 75).
GPS: N39°55.59′ W120°07.58′

▼ 2.0 SO Track on left.
0.8 ▲ SO Track on right.
▼ 2.8 TL Track on right is 24N12X (OHV Route
76), spur to Crystal Peak—rated blue.
Zero trip meter and turn left, also onto
OHV Route 76—rated green.
0.0 ▲ Continue to the southeast.
GPS: N39°56.51′ W120°07.82′

Spur to Crystal Peak

▼ 0.0 Proceed east on 24N12X (OHV Route 76).
▼ 0.1 SO Track on right is OHV Route 75—rated
green.
▼ 0.6 Track on left to diggings and views
over Doyle, Long Valley, and north to
Honey Lake. Then trail ends at small
loop around Crystal Peak.
GPS: N39°56.54′ W120°07.45′

▼ 5.7 SO Track on right is 24N51XB2 toward
Adams Peak.
0.9 ▲ BR Track on left is 24N51XB2 toward
Adams Peak. Remain on 24N51XB.
GPS: N39°55.19′ W120°06.74′

▼ 5.8 TR T-intersection with 24N51X.
0.8 ▲ TL 24N51X continues straight ahead.
Turn sharp left onto 24N51XB.
GPS: N39°55.23′ W120°06.83′

▼ 6.1 BL Track on right. Bear left onto 24N55X.
0.5 ▲ SO Track on left. Continue straight ahead
onto 24N51X.
GPS: N39°55.41′ W120°06.70′

▼ 6.2 TR Track continues ahead. Turn right onto
unmarked track.
0.4 ▲ TL T-intersection with unmarked, well-
used track.
GPS: N39°55.49′ W120°06.73′

▼ 0.0   Continue to the west and immediately bear left, following marker for 24N02 (OHV Route 76). Track on right goes 0.2 miles to cabin.

7.6 ▲   TR   Track on left goes 0.2 miles to cabin; then track straight ahead is 24N12X (OHV Route 76), spur to Crystal Peak—rated blue. Zero trip meter and turn right onto 24N02 (OHV Route 75).
            GPS: N39°56.51′ W120°07.82′

▼ 0.7   TR   Track continues ahead. Turn right and cross over Galeppi Creek; then track on left. Bear right, remaining on OHV Route 76.

6.9 ▲   TL   Track straight ahead. Turn left and cross over Galeppi Creek; then track on right. Turn left again, remaining on OHV Route 76.
            GPS: N39°56.14′ W120°08.28′

▼ 1.6   SO   Track on right.
6.0 ▲   SO   Track on left.
▼ 3.5   SO   Track on right.
4.1 ▲   SO   Track on left.
            GPS: N39°56.02′ W120°10.14′

▼ 4.5   SO   Track on right.
3.1 ▲   BR   Track on left.
▼ 5.6   SO   Track on right. Remain on OHV Route 76.
2.0 ▲   BR   Track on left. Remain on OHV Route 76.
            GPS: N39°57.08′ W120°11.44′

▼ 5.9   SO   Cattle guard.
1.7 ▲   SO   Cattle guard.
▼ 6.1   BL   Track on right.
1.5 ▲   BR   Track on left.
▼ 7.2   SO   Track on right.
0.4 ▲   BR   Track on left.
▼ 7.5   SO   Track on left is 24N07X. Remain on OHV Route 76.
0.1 ▲   BL   Track on right is 24N07X. Remain on OHV Route 76.
▼ 7.6   Cattle guard; then trail ends at T-intersection with graded 24N01 at the north end of Frenchman Lake. Turn left for Chilcoot; turn right for Doyle.
0.0 ▲   Trail begins on graded road 24N01 at the north end of Frenchman Lake,

0.2 miles south of Salmon Egg Shoal Fishing Access and 1.5 miles south of the intersection with FR 11. Zero trip meter and turn northeast on formed dirt trail 24N02 (OHV Route 76) for 4WDs, ATVs, and motorbikes—rated blue.
GPS: N39°56.24′ W120°12.10′

NORTHERN SIERRA #37

Thompson Peak Trail

STARTING POINT   CR 208, 4.6 miles south of US 395 and Janesville

FINISHING POINT   Richmond Road (CR 203), 3 miles south of Susanville

TOTAL MILEAGE   28.9 miles, plus 9.1-mile loop past Wemple Cabin and 2.5-mile spur to Thompson Peak

UNPAVED MILEAGE   25.3 miles, plus spurs

DRIVING TIME   5 hours

ELEVATION RANGE   4,200–7,700 feet

USUALLY OPEN   May to November

BEST TIME TO TRAVEL   Dry weather

DIFFICULTY RATING   2

SCENIC RATING   9

REMOTENESS RATING   +0

Special Attractions

■ Excellent views from two fire lookouts along the northwestern end of the Diamond Mountains.

■ Raptor viewing in spring and fall from Thompson Peak.

History

Thompson Peak Trail offers excellent views east over the Honey Lake Valley as it climbs through the Diamond Mountains. Honey Lake Valley was an important corridor to settlers making their way west. The Lassen Trail, just to the west, had such a bad reputation that it was nicknamed the Horn Route because it was so difficult, dangerous, and slow that emigrants might as well have taken the sea route around Cape Horn. A number of parties had to be rescued from Peter Lassen's torturous route. Many chose to bear south on

Thompson Peak Fire Lookout on the ridge of the Diamond Mountains

the Beckwourth Trail and others went north to Oregon. This meant that much of northeastern California missed out on emigrant trade, a valuable asset to developing communities.

William B. Nobles sought to correct this in 1851. The following year, with $2,000 from businessmen in Shasta, he set out to find an alternate route to Lassen's. His trail left the Lassen Trail at what is now Black Rock, Nevada, bearing southwest to the northern reaches of Honey Lake. From there, Noble's trail followed the Susan River through present-day Susanville and continued northwest, through Nobles Pass in what is now Lassen National Forest, to rejoin the Lassen Trail near Bogard Station on present-day California 44. Noble's trail was faster and much easier, and it succeeded in drawing most wagon trains bound for California north of the Mother Lode.

Isaac Roop built a log cabin close to the Susan River in the summer of 1854 and developed a trading post known as Roop's House. At the trading post, emigrants along the Nobles Trail could rest up, water their stock, and take on provisions for the rest of their journey. After a gunfight in 1863 known as the Sagebrush War, the cabin became known as Roop's Fort. Roop's establishment, located in central Susanville, is now open to visitors. In time, the Nobles Trail became an important freight route through the mountains.

Description

Thompson Peak Trail is generally suitable for high-clearance 2WDs in dry weather. Drivers of passenger vehicles can usually make it to the Wemple Cabin, but they will find the remainder of the trail too rough, especially the final climb to Thompson Peak. The trail is a snowmobile route in winter. The main snowmobile route is rated easy, with the spur to Thompson Peak rated moderate.

The trail leaves CR 208 south of Janesville and is initially well signed to Thompson Peak. The graded, lightly graveled road travels through Plumas National Forest. A loop near the start of the trail leads to the Wemple

Cabin, set in a small meadow. The wooden two-story cabin and adjacent corral are in good order.

A second spur leads to the Thompson Peak Fire Lookout. The road to the lookout is rough enough to require a high-clearance vehicle. The lookout is perched atop the rocky spine of the Diamond Mountains; the steep slopes drop dizzyingly to Long Valley and Honey Lake. The lookout is manned during fire season, and you are normally welcome to climb up to the tower with permission from the lookout on duty. The square concrete building next to the lookout is a former radar site. From the lookout, there are views over Susanville to the north, Shaffer Mountain to the northeast, and Honey Lake to the east. The fire lookout on Red Rock can be seen to the northwest and the fire lookout on Smith Peak is visible to the south. On a clear day, the distinctive shape of the Sierra Buttes can just be seen on the horizon to the south.

In addition to serving as a fire lookout, the peak is noted as an observation point for spring and fall raptor migrations. Warm air rising from Honey Lake creates thermals that the birds use to gain the altitude necessary to carry them over mountains and the Modoc Plateau to the north. Commonly seen raptors include prairie falcons, Swainson's hawks, peregrine falcons, bald eagles, golden eagles, red-tailed hawks, northern goshawks, and ospreys. White pelicans and sandhill cranes also migrate past this area. In fall, large flocks of sandhill cranes can often be seen on their way to the Central Valley. Hanggliders also use the thermal lift of the scarp slope; a hangglider launch site is on the northern face of the cliff.

The Sierra Army Depot borders Honey Lake to the east of Thompson Peak. The army detonates outdated ordnance in the Honey Lake region. Detonations often happen twice a day at a black area visible from the Thompson Peak Fire Lookout.

The main trail continues through the northern end of the Diamond Mountains, skirting the northern end of Wildcat Ridge. The volcanic cap of the ridge can be seen to he right; bare, jagged peaks form the very edge of the escarpment that drops down to Honey Lake Valley. Many small meadows, usually ringed by aspens, can be seen along the trail. One such meadow is the site of Wheeler Sheep Camp, a Basque sheepherders' regional base.

Approaching the Red Rock Fire Lookout, the trail enters a more open landscape composed of loose volcanic slopes. The lookout, built in the 1940s, stands on the northern end of the Diamond Mountains. Like the one on Thompson Peak, the lookout is manned during fire season, and you can normally climb to the tower with permission from the lookout on duty. From the tower, you can see Smith Peak and the fire lookout on Mount Hough to the south, with Taylorsville and the Indian Valley to the southwest. To the north is Lassen Peak, and on a clear day, you can see as far as Mount Shasta. Antelope Lake is to the southeast, and Diamond Mountain is immediately to the northeast.

Past the lookout, the road gradually descends toward Susanville, following Gold Run Creek for much of the way and joining CR 204. The trail ends 3 miles south of Susanville at the intersection with CR 203. Much of this trail is impassable in wet weather and should not be attempted then.

Current Road Information

Plumas National Forest
Mt. Hough Ranger District
39696 Highway 70
Quincy, CA 95971
(530) 283-0555

Bureau of Land Management
Eagle Lake Field Office
2950 Riverside Drive
Susanville, CA 96130
(530) 257-0456

Red Rock Spring

Wemple Cabin sits beside Antelope Creek

Map References

BLM   Susanville
USFS Plumas National Forest; Lassen
       National Forest
USGS 1:24,000 Antelope Lake,
       Janesville, Diamond Mtn., Susanville
       1:100,000 Susanville
Maptech CD-ROM: Shasta Lake/Redding
Northern California Atlas & Gazetteer, p. 60
California Road & Recreation Atlas, pp. 60, 54

Route Directions

▼ 0.0   From US 395 at Janesville, proceed
         south on CR 208 for 4.6 miles to the
         start of the trail. Zero trip meter and
         turn southeast on wide graded road
         28N02, following the sign to
         Thompson Lookout.

1.3 ▲   Trail ends at T-intersection with paved
         CR 208. Turn right for Antelope Lake;

turn left for Janesville and US 395.
GPS: N40°14.65' W120°31.02'

▼ 0.5 BR Track on left; then graded road on left is 28N26. Remain on 28N02.

0.8 ▲ BL Graded road on right is 28N26; then track on right. Remain on 28N02.

▼ 0.7 SO Track on left is 28N02E.

0.6 ▲ SO Track on right is 28N02E.

▼ 0.9 SO Track on right is 28N02B.

0.4 ▲ SO Track on left is 28N02B.

▼ 1.0 SO Track on right.

0.3 ▲ SO Track on left.

▼ 1.1 SO Track on left is 28N02G.

0.2 ▲ SO Track on right is 28N02G.

▼ 1.3 SO Track on left is 27N04, the loop past Wemple Cabin. Zero trip meter and follow sign to Thompson Lookout.

0.0 ▲ Continue to the northeast.
GPS: N40°14.25' W120°31.70'

Loop past Wemple Cabin

▼ 0.0 Turn southeast on 27N04.

▼ 0.4 TR Track on left is 27N04 to Murdock Crossing. Turn right onto 27N46, following sign to Wemple Cabin.
GPS: N40°13.95' W120°31.90'

▼ 0.9 SO Track on left is 27N60, which is the end of the loop.
GPS: N40°13.82' W120°32.32'

▼ 1.8 SO Track on left.

▼ 2.0 SO Track on right; then cross over Antelope Creek.

▼ 2.9 SO Track on left is 27N46A.
GPS: N40°13.39' W120°33.68'

▼ 4.4 BL Track on right is 27N46. Bear left onto 27N61.
GPS: N40°12.58' W120°34.13'

▼ 4.6 SO Track on left.

▼ 5.1 SO Two tracks on right.

▼ 5.3 SO Track on left; then cross over Antelope Creek; then track on right.

▼ 5.4 TL Track straight ahead is 27N60. Zero trip meter and turn left onto unmarked trail 27N60.

GPS: N40°12.00' W120°33.39'

▼ 0.0 Continue to the northeast. Wemple Cabin can be seen in the meadow on the left.

▼ 0.1 SO Track on left.

▼ 0.8 SO Track on right. Follow sign to US 395.

▼ 1.8 SO Track on right.

▼ 2.1 SO Track on right.

▼ 2.3 SO Track on left.

▼ 2.4 SO Track on right is 27N37.
GPS: N40°13.53' W120°32.47'

▼ 2.8 End of loop. Turn right and travel 0.9 miles back to the main trail.
GPS: N40°13.82' W120°32.32'

Continuation of Main Trail

▼ 0.0 Continue to the southwest.

1.2 ▲ SO Track on right is 27N04, the loop past Wemple Cabin. Zero trip meter and follow sign to Janesville.
GPS: N40°14.25' W120°31.70'

▼ 0.8 SO Track on right is 28N02F.

0.4 ▲ SO Track on left is 28N02F.

▼ 1.2 BL Track on right is 28N02A, spur to Thompson Peak Fire Lookout. Zero trip meter.

0.0 ▲ Continue to the southeast on 28N02.
GPS: N40°14.31' 120°32.89'

Spur to Thompson Peak Fire Lookout

▼ 0.0 Proceed northwest on 28N02A.

▼ 0.3 SO Track on left is 28N14. Remain on 28N02A. Trail is marked as a snowmobile route—rated blue.

▼ 2.5 Spur ends at Thompson Peak Fire Lookout.
GPS: N40°15.66' 120°33.37'

Continuation of Main Trail

▼ 0.0 Continue to the west on 28N02.

3.5 ▲ BR Track on left is 28N02A, spur to Thompson Peak Fire Lookout. Zero trip meter.
GPS: N40°14.31' 120°32.89'

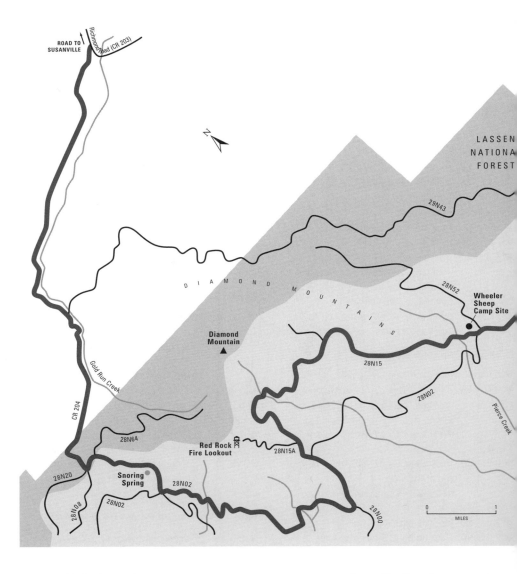

▼ 0.3	SO	Cattle guard.
3.2 ▲	SO	Cattle guard.
▼ 0.7	SO	Track on right is 28N02H.
2.8 ▲	SO	Track on left is 28N02H.
▼ 1.7	SO	Track on left.
1.8 ▲	SO	Track on right.
▼ 2.4	SO	Track on left.
1.1 ▲	SO	Track on right.

GPS: N40°14.78' W120°35.02'

▼ 3.5	BL	Cross over Boulder Creek; then track on left to Lowe Flat; then graded road on right is the continuation of 29N43

to Susanville. Zero trip meter and bear left onto 29N43, following sign to Antelope Lake. Also small track on left.

0.0 ▲		Continue to the southeast. Track on right to Lowe Flat; then cross over Boulder Creek.

GPS: N40°15.41' W120°35.85'

▼ 0.0		Continue to the west.
3.6 ▲	BR	Small track on right; then graded road on left is continuation of 29N43 to Susanville. Zero trip meter and bear

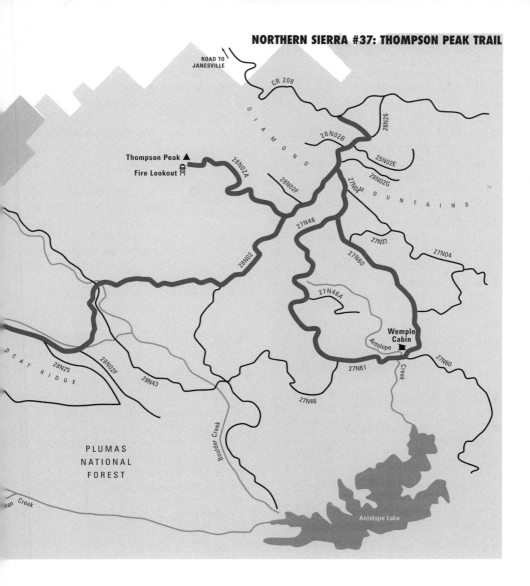

right onto 28N02, following sign to Janesville.

▼ 0.5 BR Graded road on left is 29N43 to Antelope Lake. Bear right onto 28N02, following the sign to Red Rock.

3.1 ▲ SO Graded road on right is 29N43. Follow the sign to Janesville.

GPS: N40°15.20′ W120°36.22′

▼ 0.9 SO Track on left.

2.7 ▲ SO Track on right.

▼ 1.0 SO Track on right is 28N02C.

2.6 ▲ SO Track on left is 28N02C.

▼ 1.2 SO Track on right; then cross over creek; then track on left is 29N02F.

2.4 ▲ SO Track on right is 29N02F; then cross over creek; then track on left.

▼ 1.7 SO Track on left is 28N25.

1.9 ▲ SO Track on right is 28N25.

GPS: N40°15.49′ W120°37.12′

▼ 2.5 SO Cattle guard.

1.1 ▲ SO Cattle guard.

▼ 2.6 SO Track on left is 28N35.

1.0 ▲ SO Track on right is 28N35.

▼ 3.0   SO   Track on right is 28N02P.
0.6 ▲   SO   Track on left is 28N02P.
▼ 3.1   SO   Cross over creek.
0.5 ▲   SO   Cross over creek.
▼ 3.3   SO   Track on left is 28N26X.
0.3 ▲   SO   Track on right is 28N26X.
▼ 3.5   BL   Track on right is 28N52. Follow sign to Red Rock Lookout.
0.1 ▲   BR   Track on left is 28N52. Follow sign to Lowe Flat.
         GPS: N40°16.49′ W120°38.37′

▼ 3.6   BR   Track on left is 28N02. Follow the sign to Red Rock Lookout and zero trip meter. The flat on the right is the site of Wheeler Sheep Camp.
0.0 ▲   Continue to the southeast on 28N02.
         GPS: N40°16.55′ W120°38.54′

▼ 0.0   Continue to the north on 28N15.
5.1 ▲   BL   Track on right is 28N02. Follow the sign to Lowe Flat. The flat on the left is the site of Wheeler Sheep Camp. Zero trip meter.
▼ 0.2   SO   Track on right.
4.9 ▲   SO   Track on left.
▼ 0.3   SO   Cross over Pierce Creek.
4.8 ▲   SO   Cross over Pierce Creek.
▼ 0.4   BL   Track on right; then cross over creek.
4.7 ▲   BR   Cross over creek; then track on left.
         GPS: N40°16.75′ W120°38.90′

▼ 0.7   SO   Track on left.
4.4 ▲   SO   Track on right.
▼ 0.8   SO   Track on right.
4.3 ▲   SO   Track on left.
▼ 2.1   SO   Track on right.
3.0 ▲   SO   Track on left.
▼ 2.7   SO   Track on right.
2.4 ▲   SO   Track on left.
▼ 3.1   SO   Track on left.
2.0 ▲   SO   Track on right.
▼ 3.3   SO   Cross over creek.
1.8 ▲   SO   Cross over creek.
▼ 3.4   SO   Cross over creek.
1.7 ▲   SO   Cross over creek.
         GPS: N40°17.95′ W120°41.02′

▼ 3.6   SO   Track on left; then spring on left.
1.5 ▲   SO   Spring on right; then track on right.

         GPS: N40°17.81′ W120°41.19′

▼ 3.8   TR   Track on left.
1.3 ▲   TL   Track on right.
▼ 4.1   SO   Track on right; then cross over Indian Creek.
1.0 ▲   SO   Cross over Indian Creek; then track on left.
▼ 4.9   SO   Track on right.
0.2 ▲   SO   Track on left.
▼ 5.1   SO   Track on right is 28N15A, which goes 1.4 miles to Red Rock Fire Lookout. Zero trip meter.
0.0 ▲   Continue to the north.
         GPS: N40°17.28′ W120°41.90′

▼ 0.0   Continue to the south.
5.2 ▲   SO   Track on left is 28N15A, which goes 1.4 miles to Red Rock Fire Lookout. Zero trip meter.
▼ 0.4   SO   Graded road on left is 28N02.
4.8 ▲   BL   Graded road on right is 28N02. Bear left onto 28N15.
         GPS: N40°16.97′ W120°41.89′

▼ 1.2   BR   Graded road on left is 28N00.
4.0 ▲   BL   Graded road on right is 28N00.
         GPS: N40°16.23′ W120°42.00′

▼ 1.9   SO   Cross over creek.
3.3 ▲   SO   Cross over creek.
▼ 2.5   SO   Cross over creek.
2.7 ▲   SO   Cross over creek.
▼ 4.1   SO   Track on left.
1.1 ▲   SO   Track on right.
▼ 4.5   SO   Cross over creek.
0.7 ▲   SO   Cross over creek.
▼ 5.2   TR   4-way intersection. Straight ahead goes to Moonlight Valley. Track on left goes to Greensville. Follow sign to Susanville and zero trip meter.
0.0 ▲   Continue to the east on 28N02.
         GPS: N40°18.12′ W120°44.06′

▼ 0.0   Continue to the north.
9.0 ▲   TL   4-way intersection. Straight ahead goes to Greensville. Track on right goes to Moonlight Valley. Zero trip meter and follow sign to Red Rock Lookout.

RAPTOR VIEWING

Hawks, like eagles and kites, are powerful raptors common throughout Northern California. These birds perch in trees and on telephone poles overlooking open meadows and grasslands with a sit-and-wait hunting technique; then they swoop down on their prey, ripping it apart with their hooked beak and sharp talons. They also dive on prey. Their diet ranges from small rodents to medium-size birds, amphibians, and reptiles.

Red-shouldered hawk

Sharp-shinned hawk

Female harrier

Cooper's hawk

The red-tailed hawk is a large bird that reaches lengths of about 24 inches and has a wingspan more than twice its length. The red-tailed hawk goes through several color phases, which can make identification difficult. Generally, the bird has dark upperparts, light underparts, and a red tail. Females are larger than males. They hawks like open country, fields, and mixed woodlands, and they normally make their nests in trees; bulkily constructed with sticks, the nests are usually added to each year. Both parents incubate the eggs but only the female raises the young.

Northern harriers are slender hawks with long tails and wings and range from 16 to 24 inches in length. The male is gray with black wingtips; the female is larger and brown with a streaked underside. They both have white rump bands at the base of the tail and a disc-shaped ruff of feathers that give an owl-like face. This facial disc, like that of some owls, serves as a sound-gathering feature to assist in the pursuit of prey. The northern harrier actively hunts, flying close to the ground, looking for motion and listening for the squeak of mice and other small animals in the ground cover below. In fact, because of this behavior, the harrier may be the easiest hawk for novices to identify because no other hawk routinely flies so close to the ground. It cruises over fields and meadows, seemingly grazing the grasses with its belly. Northern harriers are found in almost any type of open country—including open fields, wet meadows, marshes, and alpine meadows. They nest on raised mounds on the ground in tall vegetation, with shelters made of grass and sticks.

Cooper's hawks are also fairly common in Northern California, especially when migrants from outside California winter over. They are grayer in color and smaller than red-tailed hawks, with a rounded tail. They prefer woodlands. The largest hawk in California is the red-shouldered hawk, primarily found along the coast. From tip of the beak to the end of the tail, red-shouldered hawks can measure more than 3 feet. The back and head are pale brown, underparts are orange with buff bars, wings are black and white, and the tail is black with white bands. Another hawk of Northern California is the sharp-shinned hawk, a smaller raptor with rounded wings and a long tail. Both hawks have gray backs and heads and rusty bellies and faces.

▼ 0.5   SO   Track on right and Snoring Spring on left; then track on left.

8.5 ▲   SO   Track on right; then Snoring Spring on right and track on left.

GPS: N40°18.49' W120°43.85'

▼ 1.3   BL   Track on right is 28N64.

7.7 ▲   BR   Track on left is 28N64.

▼ 1.6   TR   4-way intersection. To the left is 28N08 and straight ahead is 28N20. Turn right onto unmarked CR 204.

7.4 ▲   TL   4-way intersection. Straight ahead is 28N08 and track on right is 28N20. Turn left onto the major road.

GPS: N40°19.05' W120°44.55'

▼ 1.7   SO   Track on left.

7.3 ▲   SO   Track on right.

▼ 2.0   SO   Track on left.

7.0 ▲   SO   Track on right.

▼ 3.0   SO   Track on left. Trail is now following along Gold Run Creek.

6.0 ▲   SO   Track on right.

▼ 4.0   SO   Track on right.

5.0 ▲   SO   Track on left.

▼ 4.3   SO   Road on right.

4.7 ▲   BR   Road on left.

GPS: N40°20.51' W120°42.80'

▼ 4.8   SO   Two tracks on left.

4.2 ▲   SO   Two tracks on right.

▼ 5.4   SO   Road becomes paved. Remain on Gold Run Road, ignoring turns to the left and right.

3.6 ▲   SO   Road turns to graded dirt.

▼ 9.0   Trail ends at T-intersection with Richmond Road (CR 203). Turn left for Susanville.

0.0 ▲   Trail commences on Richmond Road (CR 203), 3 miles south of Susanville. Richmond Road is initially called Weatherlow Street as it leaves Main Street at the stoplight. Zero trip meter and turn southwest on the paved Gold Run Road (CR 204). Remain on the paved road, ignoring turns to the left and right for 3.6 miles.

GPS: N40°22.65' W120°39.20'

Belfast Petroglyphs Trail

STARTING POINT CR A27, 10 miles east of Susanville

FINISHING POINT US 395, 18 miles south of Ravendale

TOTAL MILEAGE 19.7 miles

UNPAVED MILEAGE 19.7 miles

DRIVING TIME 3 hours

ELEVATION RANGE 4,100–4,600 feet

USUALLY OPEN April to December

BEST TIME TO TRAVEL Spring and fall, in dry weather

DIFFICULTY RATING 3

SCENIC RATING 8

REMOTENESS RATING +1

Special Attractions

■ Belfast Petroglyphs and other petroglyphs near Balls Canyon.

■ Wildlife watching at Biscar National Cooperative Wildlife Management Area.

■ Remote, lightly traveled trail.

History

Belfast Petroglyphs Trail leads off from the historic Nobles Trail on the northern edge of the Honey Lake Valley. This old trail, founded by William H. Nobles in 1852, was developed to draw westbound emigrants to Shasta City, far off to the northwest. This alternative to the Lassen Trail made its way southwest via Honey Lake, up the Susan River, through present-day Susanville, and continued northwest past Lassen Peak along the route of present-day California 44.

The Belfast Petroglyphs are in a region shared among the Maidu, generally from the Sierra Nevada; the Paiute, from the Great Basin to the east; and the Modoc from the north. Petroglyphs in this area may depict visions seen by shamans; however, the true meaining of these images remains a mystery. We can only marvel at such indecipherable work left behind by those who came before us.

Belfast Petroglyphs on the dark boulders above Willow Creek

Description

Belfast Petrolglyphs Trail is a remote, lightly used trail that travels through an arid volcanic landscape with rough lava boulders and sagebrush. The trail leaves CR A27 along a maintained, graded dirt county road initially marked Belfast Road. Past Belfast, the trail narrows and crosses private ranchland before entering BLM land. A short distance from the trail, the Belfast Petroglyphs can be found along basalt boulders overlooking Willow Creek. The site is not marked, but it is easy to find; a turnout marks the spot. Follow the trail approximately 100 yards to a drop-off above Willow Creek. Many of the carvings have been badly eroded by the elements. The more sheltered ones or those on dark rocks are easier to see.

The main trail swings east at this point and joins a formed single track that travels across the wide sagebrush-covered valley on the western side of Shaffer Mountain. The rough trail surface is littered with sharp volcanic rocks. It is not difficult, just very slow going. Taking the trail at high speeds might cause tire damage and will certainly shake passengers about. Hikers may find additional petro-

glyphs at various points along or slightly away from the trail.

The trail drops steeply from a rise, down a rocky pinch that will require some care. In the valley, the trail has a smooth sandy surface with some deep sand traps. It passes beside Shaffer Well before briefly entering the Biscar National Cooperative Wildlife Management Area. A track leads 0.1 miles to the dam of Biscar Reservoir, a good spot for viewing waterfowl. This area, and the trail in general, offers excellent opportunities to view golden eagles, prairie falcons, red-tailed hawks, chukars, and pronghorn antelope.

The trail becomes a graded dirt road and crosses the Southern Pacific Railroad at the old Karlo Siding, before swinging east to cross Secret Creek and finish on US 395. In wet weather the trail becomes impassable because the dry, friable soils quickly turn to deep, gooey mud.

Current Road Information

Bureau of Land Management
Eagle Lake Field Office
2950 Riverside Drive
Susanville, CA 96130
(530) 257-0456

NORTHERN SIERRA #38: BELFAST PETROGLYPHS TRAIL

Map References

BLM   Susanville, Eagle Lake
USGS 1:24,000 Litchfield, Petes Valley,
          Karlo, Five Springs
          1:100,000 Susanville, Eagle Lake
Maptech CD-ROM: Shasta Lake/Redding
Northern California Atlas & Gazetteer,
          pp. 60, 61, 51
California Road & Recreation Atlas, p. 55
Other: BLM Recreation Guide for
          Northeastern California and
          Northwestern Nevada

Route Directions

▼ 0.0   From Susanville, proceed south on US 395
              to the edge of town and turn east onto CR
              A27. Proceed 10 miles to the start of the
              trail. Zero trip meter and turn north on
              graded dirt Belfast Road (CR 246).

4.5 ▲   Trail ends at T-intersection with paved
              Center Road (CR A27). Turn right for
              Susanville; turn left for Litchfield.
              GPS: N40°24.07′ W120°27.03′

▼ 2.6 SO Track on left is Nett Road.
1.9 ▲ SO Track on right is Nett Road.
▼ 2.8 SO Belfast. Cross over Willow Creek
              on bridge.
1.7 ▲ SO Belfast. Cross over Willow Creek
              on bridge.
▼ 2.9 BL Road on right. Bear left past the "End
              of County Maintenance" sign and pass
              through gate.

1.6 ▲ SO Gate; then road on left.
              GPS: N40°26.65′ W120°27.03′

▼ 3.1 BR Track on left; then track on right.
1.4 ▲ BL Track on left; then track on right.
▼ 3.7 SO Pass through fence line. Road is
              marked 26032.
0.8 ▲ SO Pass through fence line.
▼ 4.5 BR Cattle guard; then bear right onto
              small, formed trail marked 26039 and
              zero trip meter. From the turnout on
              left, the Belfast Petroglyphs are 100
              yards along a track to the left. Park
              at the turnout and walk the short dis-
              tance west to where the gorge drops
              down to the creek.
0.0 ▲   Continue to the south and cross cattle
              guard.
              GPS: N40°28.06′ W120°26.83′

▼ 0.0   Continue to the northeast.
7.2 ▲ TL T-intersection. From the turnout on
              right, the Belfast Petroglyphs are 100
              yards along the track to the right. Park
              at the turnout and walk the short dis-
              tance west to where the gorge drops
              down to the creek. Zero trip meter.
▼ 1.5 BL Track on right toward Balls Canyon.
5.7 ▲ BR Track on left toward Balls Canyon.
              GPS: N40°28.39′ W120°25.31′

▼ 3.8 SO Well-used track on left goes to Butte Well.
3.4 ▲ SO Well-used track on right goes to Butte Well.
              GPS: N40°29.86′ W120°23.57′

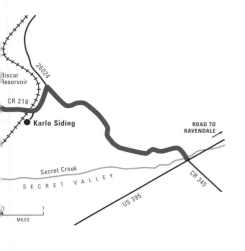

▼ 4.9 SO Pass through wire gate.
2.3 ▲ SO Pass through wire gate.
GPS: N40°30.12′ W120°22.33′

▼ 5.4 SO Trail passes close to the edge of Balls
            Canyon.
1.8 ▲ SO Trail passes close to the edge of Balls
            Canyon.
▼ 6.0 SO Pass through wire gate.
1.2 ▲ SO Pass through wire gate.
▼ 6.2 SO Short rough drop off of rise.
1.0 ▲ SO Short rough climb up rise.
            GPS: N40°30.43′ W120°20.91′

▼ 7.2 SO 4-way intersection. Track on left goes
            to Shaffer Well. Track on right is 26030.
            Zero trip meter and follow sign to Karlo.
0.0 ▲   Continue to the south on 26039.
            GPS: N40°31.20′ W120°20.55′

▼ 0.0   Continue to the northeast on 26039.
1.8 ▲ SO 4-way intersection. Track on right goes
            to Shaffer Well. Track on left is 26030.
            Zero trip meter and follow sign to
            Belfast.

The trail along Balls Canyon, northwest of Schaffer Mountain

▼ 1.3   SO   Track on left.
0.5 ▲   SO   Track on right.
▼ 1.7   SO   Cattle guard.
0.1 ▲   SO   Cattle guard.
        GPS: N40°32.52′ W120°19.70′

▼ 1.8   TR   Track on left enters the Biscar National
             Cooperative Wildlife Management
             Area and goes 0.1 miles to a dam.
             Zero trip meter and cross through
             Snowstorm Creek wash.
0.0 ▲   Continue to the southeast. Road is
             now a formed trail.
        GPS: N40°32.65′ W120°19.72′

▼ 0.0   Continue to the northeast on CR 216.
             Road is now graded dirt.
6.2 ▲   TL   Cross through Snowstorm Creek wash;
             then track straight ahead enters the
             Biscar National Cooperative Wildlife
             Management Area and goes 0.1 miles
             to a dam. Zero trip meter.
▼ 0.2   SO   Track on right to cabin.
6.0 ▲   SO   Track on left to cabin.
▼ 0.9   BL   Cross over railroad; then track on right
             to Karlo Siding.
5.3 ▲   BR   Track on left to Karlo Siding; then cross
             over railroad.
        GPS: N40°33.18′ W120°18.88′

▼ 1.7   BR   Track on left is 26024; then cross cat-
             tle guard over creek.
4.5 ▲   BL   Cross cattle guard over creek; then
             track on right is 26024.
        GPS: N40°33.77′ W120°19.13′

▼ 6.1   SO   Cross over Secret Creek.
0.1 ▲   SO   Cross over Secret Creek.
▼ 6.2   Cattle guard; then trail ends at intersec-
             tion with US 395. Turn left for Ravendale;
             turn right for Susanville. Track opposite is
             Shinn Ranch Road (CR 345).
0.0 ▲   Trail commences on US 395 at mile marker
             92, 18 miles south of Ravendale. Zero trip
             meter and turn west on graded dirt road.
             Cross cattle guard and follow the sign to
             Karlo Road and wildlife viewing area.
             Shinn Ranch Road (CR 345) is opposite.
        GPS: N40°35.04′ W120°14.98′

Antelope Mountain and Crater Lake Trail

STARTING POINT CR A-1, 2.2 miles north of
Christie USFS Campground
FINISHING POINT California 44, 0.1 miles
southeast of Bogard USFS Work Station
TOTAL MILEAGE 15.6 miles, plus 3.8-mile spur
to Antelope Mountain Fire Lookout and
4.8-mile spur to Crater Lake
UNPAVED MILEAGE 15.6 miles, plus spurs
DRIVING TIME 3 hours
ELEVATION RANGE 5,300–7,600
USUALLY OPEN May to December
BEST TIME TO TRAVEL May to December
DIFFICULTY RATING 1
SCENIC RATING 9
REMOTENESS RATING +0

Special Attractions

■ Panoramic views from Antelope Mountain
Fire Lookout
■ Fishing and camping at Crater and Eagle
Lakes.
■ Trail intersects with the historic Nobles
and Lassen Trails.

Description

Eagle Lake and Honey Lake are part of the
Basin and Range province of the Great
Basin. Both Eagle and Honey Lakes are
remnants of an ancient glacial lake called
Lake Lahontan. Eagle Lake, the second
largest natural lake in the state, has no outlet, and it is well known for having excellent
angling opportunities, mainly for Eagle
Lake trout. Most closely related to rainbow
trout, these fish have adapted to Eagle Lake's
alkaline water and thrive where introduced
species do not. One reason for their survival
is that the fish are extremely long lived;
some have been estimated to be 11 years
old. They spawn in Pine Creek, but dry conditions often mean that they cannot do so
annually. Evolution has favored the long-
lived fish that are able to spawn later in life.

Antelope Mountain Fire Lookout

Eagle Lake trout are extremely fast growing, and a 4-year-old can be more than 22 inches long and weigh 4 pounds. Attempts to introduce game fish have repeatedly failed. Since 1956, the California Department of Fish and Game has successfully stocked Eagle Lake trout in other lakes across the state. As many as 200,000 are planted in various lakes each year, primarily for sport fishing.

Bird-watchers at Eagle Lake may see some of the 95 species known to be in the lake's vicinity, including bald eagles, golden eagles, pelicans, and ospreys. Hunting for mule deer and waterfowl (in season) are also popular activities around the lake.

The trail begins just west of Eagle Lake and travels through Lassen National Forest along a graded road toward Antelope Mountain Fire Lookout. A spur heads south to the modern lookout, which is manned during fire season; visitors are normally welcome to climb up to the tower with permission from the lookout on

duty. Views from the top include Eagle Lake to the northeast, volcanic Lassen Peak to the west, and the open area of Pine Creek Valley to the southwest. Whaleback Mountain and Logan Mountain are to the north, with Antelope Valley beyond them. On a clear day, the snow-covered peak of Mount Shasta can be seen way off to the northwest.

Back on the main trail, the road swiftly descends to cross the Pine Creek Valley. The valley previously had a large Indian population, with many villages and campsites in this fertile hunting and fishing ground. Today, the trail winds around the edge of the valley and passes many backcountry campsites tucked into the trees. Part of the trail follows an old lumber railroad grade, long since abandoned, put in to carry felled trees to mill.

A second spur from the main trail leads 4.8 miles to Crater Lake, which is set in a volcanic crater. The lake has a pretty, developed USFS campground by the shore with scattered firs and aspens providing shade; a fee is charged. A small boat ramp enables you to get out onto the lake in small motorboats or rowboats. The main trail ends on California 44, a short distance south of Bogard Work Station and 28 miles northeast of Susanville. Bogard was an important rest stop for travelers along the Lassen and Nobles Trails, which crossed this route a short distance from the national scenic byway of California 44.

The entire trail, including the spurs to Antelope Mountain and Crater Lake, is a groomed snowmobile route in winter, classed as easiest. The Bogard snowmobile area at the end of the trail has 80 miles of groomed, designated snowmobile trails along forest roads, all rated easy.

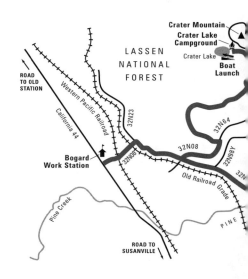

Current Road Information

Lassen National Forest
Eagle Lake Ranger District
477-050 Eagle Lake Road
Susanville, CA 96130
(530) 257-4188

Map References

BLM   Eagle Lake, Burney
USFS   Lassen National Forest
USGS   1:24,000   Pikes Point, Antelope
       Mtn., Pine Creek Valley, Harvey Mtn.
       1:100,000   Eagle Lake, Burney
Maptech CD-ROM: Shasta Lake/Redding
Northern California Atlas & Gazetteer,
       pp. 50, 49
California Road & Recreation Atlas, p. 54
Other: BLM Recreation Guide for
       Northeastern California and
       Northwestern Nevada (incomplete)

Route Directions

▼ 0.0   From CR A-1 just west of Eagle Lake,
           7.3 miles south of the intersection with
           Spalding Tract Road and 2.2 miles north
           of Christie USFS Campground, zero trip
           meter and turn west on graded dirt FR
           21, following sign for Antelope Lookout.
           Immediately track on left.
4.4 ▲   Track on right; then trail ends on paved
           CR A-1 on the western side of Eagle

Lake. Turn left for Adin and California 139; turn right for Susanville.
           GPS: N40°36.08′ W120°50.89′

▼ 0.9   SO   Track on left is 32N75.
4.5 ▲   SO   Track on right is 32N75.
▼ 1.7   SO   Track on left.
2.7 ▲   SO   Track on right.
▼ 1.8   SO   Track on right is 33N38; then cattle guard.
2.6 ▲   SO   Cattle guard; then track on left is 33N38.
           GPS: N40°36.98′ W120°52.40′

▼ 2.1   SO   Track on left is 32N69 and track on right is 32N90Y.
2.3 ▲   SO   Track on right is 32N69 and track on left is 32N90Y.
           GPS: N40°37.15′ W120°52.65′

▼ 2.4   SO   Track on right is 33N31 to Prison Springs. Remain on FR 21, following the sign to Antelope Lookout.
2.0 ▲   SO   Track on left is 33N31 to Prison Springs. Remain on FR 21.
           GPS: N40°37.20′ W120°52.92′

▼ 2.5   SO   Track on left.
1.9 ▲   SO   Track on right.
▼ 3.3   SO   Track on right.
1.1 ▲   SO   Track on left.

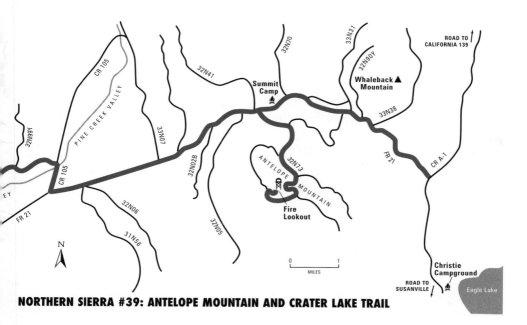

NORTHERN SIERRA #39: ANTELOPE MOUNTAIN AND CRATER LAKE TRAIL

▼ 3.7   SO Track on right is 32N70.
0.7 ▲   SO Track on left is 32N70.
▼ 3.9   SO Track on left is 32N02C.
0.5 ▲   SO Track on right is 32N02C.
▼ 4.0   SO Summit Camp on right—undeveloped
            USFS camping area.
0.4 ▲   SO Summit Camp on left—undeveloped
            USFS camping area.
        GPS: N40°37.18' W120°54.71'

▼ 4.4   SO Track on left is 32N73, spur to
            Antelope Mountain Fire Lookout. Track
            on right is 32N41. Zero trip meter.
0.0 ▲   Continue to the northeast.
        GPS: N40°37.07' W120°55.12'

Spur To Antelope Mountain Fire Lookout

▼ 0.0   Proceed southeast on 32N73, following
            sign to Antelope Lookout.
▼ 0.7   SO Track on left.
▼ 1.5   SO Track on right.
▼ 2.1   BR Two tracks on left.
        GPS: N40°35.85' W120°53.99'

▼ 2.9   TR Track on left; then track continues straight
            ahead. Turn right onto well-used track.
        GPS: N40°35.52' W120°53.92'

▼ 3.7   SO Track on left.
▼ 3.8   Spur ends at Antelope Mountain Fire
            Lookout.
        GPS: N40°35.56' W120°54.57'

Continuation of Main Trail

▼ 0.0   Continue to the southwest.
4.9 ▲   SO Track on right is 32N73, spur to
            Antelope Mountain Fire Lookout. Track
            on left is 32N41. Zero trip meter.
        GPS: N40°37.07' W120°55.12'

▼ 0.2   SO Track on left is 32N05.
4.7 ▲   SO Track on right is 32N05.
▼ 0.5   SO Track on right.
4.4 ▲   SO Track on left.
▼ 0.9   SO Track on left is 32N02B.
4.0 ▲   SO Track on right is 32N02B.
▼ 1.4   SO Track on left and track on right.
3.5 ▲   SO Track on left and track on right.
▼ 2.2   SO Track on right.
2.7 ▲   SO Track on left.
▼ 2.4   SO Cattle guard. Entering Pine Creek Valley.
2.5 ▲   SO Cattle guard. Leaving Pine Creek Valley.
▼ 2.5   SO Graded road on right is 33N07 to Champs
            Flat. Follow sign to California 44.
2.4 ▲   SO Graded road on left is 33N07 to Champs
            Flat. Follow sign to Eagle Lake.

Aspens and firs ring Crater Lake

GPS: N40°35.88′ W120°57.31′

▼ 3.5   SO   Track on left.
1.4 ▲   SO   Track on right.
▼ 3.9   SO   Track on left.
1.0 ▲   SO   Track on right.
▼ 4.2   SO   Two tracks on left—first is 32N06, second is 31N56.
0.7 ▲   SO   Two tracks on right—first is 31N56, second is 32N06.
▼ 4.9   TR   FR 21 continues straight ahead. Zero trip meter and turn sharp right onto CR 105.
0.0 ▲   Continue to the northeast.
  GPS: N40°35.09′ W120°59.74′

▼ 0.0   Continue to the north.
4.5 ▲   TL   T-intersection with FR 21. Zero trip meter and turn sharp left, following sign to Eagle Lake.
▼ 0.6   TL   Cross over Pine Creek; then cattle guard; then turn left on 32N07, following sign for Bogard Station.

3.9 ▲   TR   T-intersection with CR 105. Turn right and cross over cattle guard; then cross over Pine Creek.
  GPS: N40°35.64′ W120°59.63′

▼ 1.5   SO   Track on right is 32N99Y.
3.0 ▲   SO   Track on left is 32N99Y.
▼ 1.8   SO   Cattle guard.
2.7 ▲   SO   Cattle guard.
▼ 1.9   SO   Track on right. Many tracks on right to backcountry campsites along the edge of the valley.
2.6 ▲   SO   Track on left.
▼ 3.2   SO   Track on left.
1.3 ▲   SO   Track on right.
▼ 3.7   SO   Track on right is 32N98Y.
0.8 ▲   SO   Track on left is 32N98Y.
▼ 3.8   SO   Track on left.
0.7 ▲   SO   Track on right.
▼ 4.5   SO   4-way intersection. Track on left. Graded road on right is 32N08, spur to Crater Lake. Zero trip meter and join the graded road.

0.0 ▲		Continue to the east on 32N07, following the sign to CR 105. Many tracks on left to backcountry campsites along the edge of the valley.

GPS: N40°35.43' W121°03.52'

Spur to Crater Lake

▼ 0.0		Proceed northeast on 32N08, following sign to Crater Lake.
▼ 1.0	BL	Track on right is 32N64.
▼ 4.3	SO	Track on right is 32N63Y, which travels a small loop around Crater Mountain and gives a view of the lake from above.

GPS: N40°37.53' W121°02.21'

▼ 4.6	SO	Enter Crater Lake USFS Campground.
▼ 4.8		Spur ends at boat ramp on Crater Lake.

GPS: N40°37.54' W121°02.63'

Continuation of Main Trail

▼ 0.0		Continue to the west, following sign to California 44.
1.8 ▲	SO	4-way intersection. Track on right. Graded road on left is 32N08, spur to Crater Lake. Zero trip meter.

GPS: N40°35.43' W121°03.52'

▼ 0.7	SO	Track on right is 32N07E.
1.1 ▲	SO	Track on left is 32N07E.
▼ 1.0	BL	Track on right is 32N23; then cross over hard-to-distinguish railroad grade. Road is now 32N08.
0.8 ▲	BR	Cross over hard-to-distinguish railroad grade; then track on left is 32N23. Road is now 32N07.
▼ 1.3	SO	Bogard Well on left.
0.5 ▲	SO	Bogard Well on right.
▼ 1.5	SO	Cattle guard; then cross over Western Pacific Railroad.
0.3 ▲	SO	Cross over Western Pacific Railroad; then cattle guard.
▼ 1.6	SO	Lassen and Nobles Trails cross road.
0.2 ▲	SO	Lassen and Nobles Trails cross road.

GPS: N40°35.29' W121°05.04'

▼ 1.8		Track on right; then trail ends at T-intersection with California 44. Turn left for Susanville; turn right for Old Station.

0.0 ▲		Trail commences on California 44, 0.1 miles southeast of the Bogard USFS Work Station, rest area, and snowmobile trailhead, 28 miles northwest of Susanville. Zero trip meter and turn north on graded road 32N08 at the sign for Crater Lake Campground. Immediately track on left.

GPS: N40°35.19' W121°05.26'

Susan River to Juniper Lake Trail

STARTING POINT Mooney Road (CR A-21), 4.1 miles south of California 44

FINISHING POINT Juniper Lake Road (CR 318), 6.2 miles north of Chester

TOTAL MILEAGE 35.7 miles, plus 5.6-mile spur to Juniper Lake

UNPAVED MILEAGE 35.7 miles, plus 5.6-mile spur

DRIVING TIME 5 hours

ELEVATION RANGE 5,000–7,000 feet

USUALLY OPEN May to December

BEST TIME TO TRAVEL May to December

DIFFICULTY RATING 2

SCENIC RATING 9

REMOTENESS RATING +0

Special Attractions

- Fishing and camping at Silver, Echo, and Juniper Lakes.
- Lassen Volcanic National Park.
- Hiking access to the Caribou Wilderness and trails within Lassen Volcanic National Park.
- Long, meandering forest trail for vehicles, mountain bikes, and horses in summer and snowmobiles in winter.

History

This route passes Mount Harkness (8,045 feet) in Lassen Volcanic National Park near the end of the trail. The summit is approximately 1,300 feet above picturesque Juniper

Lake, and the climb to it is an enjoyable hike, with the added attraction of visiting an historic lookout. This cone-shaped mountain was chosen as a fire lookout site back in 1930.

The task of getting materials and food up the mountain was left to the capable operator of a Fordson Tractor, who used a sled to transport the goods in winter. Obtaining sufficient water during fire season was an ongoing problem. The lookouts shoveled spring snow into a 1,000-gallon tank and let it melt. This offered a very basic water supply for the coming season. In time, attempts to drop water by air also proved to be rather laborious. Like many others, this lookout tower dropped out of regular service in the late 1970s when aerial surveillance compensated for the reduced number of lookouts, though many forestry officials were unhappy with such coverage. The U.S. Forest Service and the National Park Service reintroduced fire spotters at the aging tower for a period in the late 1980s.

Description

Susan River to Juniper Lake Trail is a pleasant drive through Lassen National Forest. Along the way, it passes small lakes, shady campgrounds, and beautiful forest scenery to finish in the southeast corner of Lassen Volcanic National Park. Although much of the trail is suitable for passenger vehicles, some rough spots require high-clearance.

The trail leaves CR A-21 south of California 44 and follows the good graded road to Silver Lake. Two developed campgrounds are set among the trees, back from the lake's edge; the Silver Beach Picnic Area and a small boat launch are set directly on the water's edge. Much of Silver Lake's shoreline is taken up by vacation homes.

Past Silver Lake, the trail passes above small Betty Lake, visible below the trail, and then alongside Shotoverin Lake. Later, Echo Lake and the small, but heavily used campground beside it can be found a short distance north of the main trail.

Past Echo Lake, the trail turns off FR 10 and travels to Hay Meadow and a hiking trailhead into the Caribou Wilderness. From here, hikers and equestrians can reach many of the small mountain lakes within the wilderness, including Evelyn, Long, and Triangle Lakes. Some pleasant, walk-in backcountry campsites are near the trailhead around the edge of Hay Meadow.

The vehicle trail travels along roads established primarily for logging, following a loop out of Lassen National Forest into Pacific Gas & Electric–owned forest and then back into Lassen National Forest. Camping is prohibited in PG&E forest except at designated campgrounds. Back in the national forest, the trail travels along Last Chance Creek, which drains south to Lake Almanor—visible from several points along the trail. Last Chance Creek is fed by four springs, so it has good flow throughout the summer.

A worthwhile spur leads 4.8 miles north to Juniper Lake in Lassen Volcanic National Park. From here, several hiking trails penetrate farther into the park, taking hikers to destinations such as Cameron Meadows, Snag Lake, Cinder Cone, and Horseshoe Lake. A very pleasant developed campground can be found on the south side of the lake, with views across the water to Lassen Peak. The hiking trail to Mount Harkness starts at the campground and climbs 1.9 miles to the old fire lookout at the peak. The lookout's cabin is currently being restored by the National Park Service. Allow three hours for the round-trip hike.

From Silver Lake to Last Chance Creek, the trail is a groomed snowmobile route in winter. It is part of the system of groomed trails accessed from the Bogard Staging Area.

Current Road Information

Lassen National Forest
Almanor Ranger District
PO Box 767
Chester, CA 96020
(530) 258-2141

Lassen Volcanic National Park
PO Box 100
Mineral, CA 96063
(530) 595-4444

Last Chance Creek

Map References

BLM   Lake Almanor, Burney
USFS Lassen National Forest
USGS 1:24,000 Swain Mtn., Bogard
      Buttes, Red Cinder, Chester,
      Mt. Harkness
      1:100,000 Lake Almanor, Burney
Maptech CD-ROM: Shasta Lake/Redding
Northern California Atlas & Gazetteer,
      pp. 59, 49
California Road & Recreation Atlas, p. 54
      (incomplete)
Other: A Guide to the Ishi, Thousand Lakes,
      & Caribou Wilderness (incomplete)

Route Directions

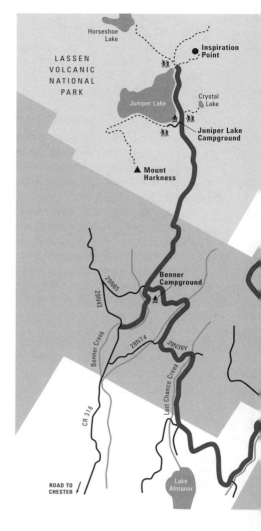

▼ 0.0   From California 44, 24 miles northeast
            of Susanville, zero trip meter and turn
            south on paved Mooney Road (CR A-
            21), following the sign to Silver Lake
            and Westwood. Proceed 4.1 miles to
            the start of the trail. Zero trip meter
            and turn west on Silver Lake Road.
4.7 ▲   Trail ends at intersection with paved
            Mooney Road (CR A-21). Turn left for
            California 44 and Susanville; turn right
            for Westwood.
            GPS: N40°29.43′ W121°04.49′

▼ 0.6   SO Track on right. Many campsites on
            the Susan River on left.
4.1 ▲   SO Track on left.
▼ 1.2   SO Track on right.
3.5 ▲   SO Track on left.
▼ 2.2   SO Track on right.
2.5 ▲   SO Track on left.
▼ 2.6   SO Track on right.
2.1 ▲   SO Track on left.
▼ 3.5   SO Track on right.
1.2 ▲   SO Track on left.
▼ 3.6   SO Cross over the Susan River; then track
            on left.
1.1 ▲   SO Track on right; then cross over the
            Susan River. Many campsites on the
            Susan River on right.
            GPS: N40°29.98′ W121°08.08′

▼ 4.7   BL FR 10 goes to the right and left.
            Entering Silver Lake Recreation Area.

            To the right goes to North Shore,
            Caribou Wilderness, and Silver Bowl
            USFS Campground. Zero trip meter
            and bear left, following the sign to East
            Shore and Rocky Knoll Campground.
0.0 ▲   Continue to the southeast on Silver
            Lake Road.
            GPS: N40°29.96′ W121°09.15′

▼ 0.0   Continue to the southwest.
3.1 ▲   BR FR 10 continues to the left and goes
            to North Shore, Caribou Wilderness,
            and Silver Bowl USFS Campground.
            Leaving Silver Lake Recreation Area.
            Zero trip meter.

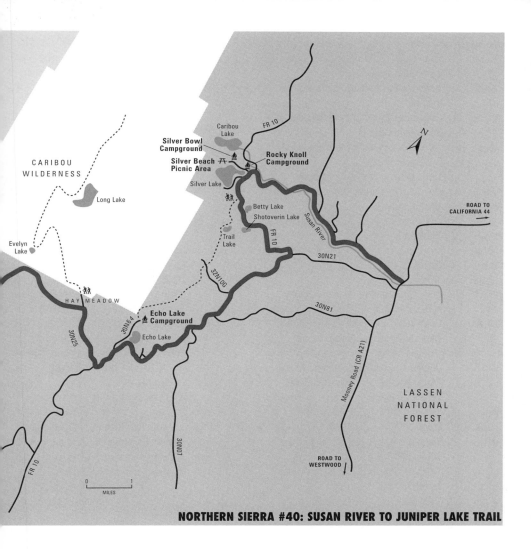

NORTHERN SIERRA #40: SUSAN RIVER TO JUNIPER LAKE TRAIL

▼ 0.1   TL   4-way intersection. Silver Beach Picnic Area is straight ahead and Rocky Knoll USFS Campground is on the right. Turn left, remaining on FR 10 and following the sign to California 36.

3.0 ▲   TR   4-way intersection. Road on left goes 0.1 miles to Silver Beach Picnic Area. Rocky Knoll USFS Campground is straight ahead. Turn right, following the sign for CR A-21.
    GPS: N40°29.92' W121°09.28'

▼ 0.3   TL   4-way intersection. Track straight ahead goes to East Shore and track on right goes into picnic area. Turn left following

the sign to Echo Lake, remaining on FR 10.

2.8 ▲   TR   4-way intersection. Track on left goes to East Shore and track straight ahead goes into picnic area. Turn right, following sign to the campground.
    GPS: N40°29.80' W121°09.33'

▼ 0.8   SO   Trail on right goes to Trail Lake, Echo Lake, and Heckles Ranch for hikers, equestrians, and mountain bikers.

2.3 ▲   SO   Trail on left goes to Trail Lake, Echo Lake, and Heckles Ranch for hikers, equestrians, and mountain bikers.
    GPS: N40°29.40' W121°09.19'

▼ 1.2   SO   Betty Lake is a short distance below the road to the left.

1.9 ▲   SO   Betty Lake is a short distance below the road to the right.

▼ 1.6   SO   Two tracks on right go to the edge of Shotoverin Lake.

1.5 ▲   SO   Two tracks on left go to the edge of Shotoverin Lake.

    GPS: N40°28.95′ W121°08.65′

▼ 2.0   SO   Track on right.

1.1 ▲   SO   Track on left.

▼ 2.5   SO   Track on right.

0.6 ▲   SO   Track on left.

▼ 3.0   SO   Track on left.

0.1 ▲   SO   Track on right.

▼ 3.1   TR   Major graded road on left is 30N21. Zero trip meter.

0.0 ▲   Continue to the northwest on FR 10.

    GPS: N40°28.86′ W121°07.32′

▼ 0.0   Continue to the southwest on FR 10.

6.2 ▲   TL   Major graded road ahead is 30N21. Zero trip meter.

▼ 0.6   SO   Track on left is 32N10M.

5.6 ▲   SO   Track on right is 32N10M.

▼ 1.3   SO   Track on right is 32N10L; then track on left is 32N10H.

4.9 ▲   SO   Track on right is 32N10H; then track on left is 32N10L.

▼ 1.5   SO   Track on right.

4.7 ▲   SO   Track on left.

▼ 1.8   SO   Cross over creek.

4.4 ▲   SO   Cross over creek.

▼ 1.9   SO   Track on right is 32N10G.

4.3 ▲   SO   Track on left is 32N10G.

▼ 2.4   SO   Major graded road on left is 30N81 to CR A-21.

3.8 ▲   SO   Major graded road on right is 30N81 to CR A-21.

    GPS: N40°27.09′ W121°08.29′

▼ 3.0   SO   Graded road on left is 30N07, which goes to Swain Mountain Staging Area on CR A-21, also marked as a mountain bike and snowmobile route. Track on right is 30N57. Continue on FR 10, following the sign to the Caribou Wilderness.

3.2 ▲   SO   Graded road on right is 30N07, which goes to Swain Mountain Staging Area on CR A-21, also marked as a mountain bike and snowmobile route. Track on left is 30N57. Continue on FR 10, following the sign to Silver Lake.

    GPS: N40°26.66′ W121°08.52′

▼ 4.5   SO   Track on right.

1.7 ▲   SO   Track on left.

▼ 4.7   SO   Track on right is 32N10T.

1.5 ▲   SO   Track on left is 32N10T.

▼ 5.6   TL   4-way intersection. Track on right is 30N64, which goes 0.6 miles to Echo Lake and Echo Lake USFS Campground. Track straight ahead is 30N65. Remain on FR 10 (32N10), following the sign to Caribou Wilderness.

0.6 ▲   TR   4-way intersection. Track on left is 30N65. Track straight ahead is 30N64, which goes 0.6 miles to Echo Lake and Echo Lake USFS Campground. Remain on FR 10 (32N10), following the sign to Silver Lake.

    GPS: N40°25.52′ W121°10.02′

▼ 6.2   TR   Track on left; then paved road ahead goes to California 36. Zero trip meter and turn right onto graded road 30N25, following sign to the Caribou Wilderness.

0.0 ▲   Continue to the northeast past track on right.

    GPS: N40°25.08′ W121°10.14′

▼ 0.0   Continue to the northwest.

1.4 ▲   TL   T-intersection with FR 10. Paved road on right goes to California 36. Zero trip meter and turn left, following the sign to Silver Lake.

▼ 0.1   SO   Track on right; then cross over creek; then track on left.

1.3 ▲   SO   Track on right; then cross over creek; then track on left.

▼ 0.7   SO   Track on left.

0.7 ▲   SO   Track on right.

▼ 0.9   SO   Track on left.

0.5 ▲   SO   Track on right.

▼ 1.1   SO   Track on right.

0.3 ▲   SO   Track on left.

▼ 1.4 TL Track continues 0.2 miles straight ahead to Hay Meadow Trailhead. Zero trip meter.
0.0 ▲ Continue to the east.
GPS: N40°25.91′ W121°11.06′

▼ 0.0 Continue to the south on well-used unmarked trail.
9.2 ▲ TR T-intersection. To the left goes 0.2 miles to Hay Meadow Trailhead. Zero trip meter.

▼ 0.3 SO Track on right to Hay Meadow; then cross through Bailey Creek; then track on left.
8.9 ▲ SO Track on right; then cross through Bailey Creek; then track on left to Hay Meadow.

▼ 0.4 SO Track on right.
8.8 ▲ SO Track on left.
▼ 1.2 SO Track on left.
8.0 ▲ SO Track on right.
GPS: N40°25.90′ W121°12.24′

▼ 1.5 TR Turn right at T-intersection with graded road; then track on left.
7.7 ▲ TL Track on right; then graded road continues straight ahead.
GPS: N40°26.05′ W121°12.54′

▼ 1.9 SO Track on left.
7.3 ▲ SO Track on right.
▼ 2.3 SO Track on left.
6.9 ▲ SO Track on right.
▼ 2.5 SO Track on left.
6.7 ▲ SO Track on right.
▼ 2.9 SO Track on left.
6.3 ▲ SO Track on right.
▼ 3.4 SO Track on left.
5.8 ▲ SO Track on right.
GPS: N40°25.55′ W121°14.01′

▼ 4.2 SO Track on right.
5.0 ▲ SO Track on left.
▼ 4.4 SO Track on left.
4.8 ▲ SO Track on right.
▼ 5.3 SO Track on left and track on right.

Juniper Lake, at the end of the spur in Lassen Volcanic National Park

3.9 ▲ SO Track on left and track on right.
▼ 6.8 BL Track on right.
2.4 ▲ BR Track on left.
▼ 6.9 SO Track on right; then track on left.
2.3 ▲ SO Track on right; then track on left.
▼ 7.9 SO Well-used graded road on left.
1.3 ▲ SO Well-used graded road on right.

GPS: N40°23.44′ W121°12.31′

▼ 8.0 SO Cross over Mud Creek; then track on left.
1.2 ▲ SO Track on right; then cross over Mud Creek.

GPS: N40°23.57′ W121°12.22′

▼ 8.6 SO Well-used track on right.
0.6 ▲ BR Well-used track on left.
▼ 8.9 SO Track on left.
0.3 ▲ SO Track on right.
▼ 9.2 TR 4-way intersection. Track straight ahead is the continuation of 30N72 to California 36. Zero trip meter.
0.0 ▲ Continue to the northwest.

GPS: N40°22.67′ W121°11.34′

▼ 0.0 Continue to the south.
4.7 ▲ TL 4-way intersection. Track on right and left is 30N72. To the right goes to California 36. Zero trip meter and follow the sign to Mud Creek Rim.
▼ 0.3 SO Track on right.
4.4 ▲ SO Track on left.
▼ 0.7 SO Cross over Mud Creek.
4.0 ▲ SO Cross over Mud Creek.

GPS: N40°22.67′ W121°12.06′

▼ 0.8 SO Track on right.
3.9 ▲ BR Track on left.
▼ 0.9 SO Track on right.
3.8 ▲ SO Track on left.
▼ 1.6 SO Track on right.
3.1 ▲ SO Track on left.
▼ 1.7 SO Track on right.
3.0 ▲ SO Track on left.
▼ 1.8 SO Track on right.
2.9 ▲ SO Track on left.
▼ 1.9 SO Track on left and corral on left.
2.8 ▲ SO Track on right and corral on right.
▼ 2.2 TR Graded road on left.
2.5 ▲ TL Road swings right. Turn left onto graded road.

GPS: N40°21.42′ W121°11.99′

▼ 2.6 SO Track on right.
2.1 ▲ SO Track on left.
▼ 3.5 SO Track on left and track on right.
1.2 ▲ SO Track on left and track on right.
▼ 3.6 SO Track on right.
1.1 ▲ SO Track on left.
▼ 4.6 SO Track on right.
0.1 ▲ SO Track on left.
▼ 4.7 TR 4-way intersection. Track on left on left-hand bend is 90L; also road continues straight ahead. Zero trip meter
0.0 ▲ Continue to the east.

GPS: N40°21.81′ W121°13.82′

▼ 0.0 Continue to the northwest up hill on trail marked with logging marker 140K.
5.1 ▲ TL 4-way intersection. Track straight ahead is 90L. Zero trip meter.
▼ 0.2 SO Track on right.
4.9 ▲ SO Track on left.
▼ 0.8 BR Track on left.
4.3 ▲ SO Track on right.
▼ 1.7 TL T-intersection. Turn left onto 29N36Y and cross over Last Chance Creek.
3.4 ▲ TR Cross over Last Chance Creek; then track continues straight ahead.

GPS: N40°23.19′ W121°14.37′

▼ 2.8 TR T-intersection with 29N74. To the left joins Juniper Lake Road in 1 mile. Turn right, also signed to Juniper Lake Road.
2.3 ▲ TL Road continues ahead to rejoin Juniper Lake Road. Turn left onto unmarked road at the signpost for Juniper Lake Road.

GPS: N40°23.15′ W121°15.29′

▼ 3.8 SO Cross over a tributary of Benner Creek; then track on right.
1.3 ▲ SO Track on left; then cross over a tributary of Benner Creek.
▼ 3.9 BL Two tracks on right.
1.2 ▲ BR Two tracks on left.
▼ 4.8 SO Track on left.
0.3 ▲ SO Track on right.
▼ 5.1 TL 4-way intersection. Juniper Lake Road is to the left and right. Straight ahead is 29N65. Zero trip meter. Spur to Juniper Lake is to the right.

| 0.0 ▲ | | Continue to the northeast on graded road. |
| | | **GPS: N40°23.91' W121°16.27'** |

Spur to Juniper Lake

▼ 0.0		Turn northwest on graded Juniper Lake Road.
▼ 0.2	SO	Track on left.
▼ 0.5	SO	Track on left.
▼ 1.9	SO	Cattle guard. Entering Lassen Volcanic National Park—no firearms or hunting camps permitted in the park.
		GPS: N40°25.41' W121°16.54'

| ▼ 4.2 | SO | Park fee station; then track on left goes 0.4 miles to Juniper Lake Campground and Mount Harkness Hiking Trail. Follow sign to Snag Lake and Horseshoe Lake. |
| | | **GPS: N40°27.07' W121°17.57'** |

| ▼ 4.5 | SO | Hiking trail on right goes 0.4 miles to Crystal Lake. |
| | | **GPS: N40°27.27' W121°17.72'** |

| ▼ 5.6 | SO | Hiking trail on right goes 0.6 miles to Inspiration Point; then trail ends at picnic area on the shore of Juniper Lake. Other hiking trails go to Cameron Meadows (1.6 miles), Snag Lake (2.9 miles), Cinder Cone (7.6 miles), Horseshoe Lake (1.4 miles), Lower Twin Lake (5.3 miles), Summit Lake (9 miles), and Warner Valley (9.1 miles). Private cabins are immediately past the end of the road. |
| | | **GPS: N40°28.00' W121°18.47'** |

Continuation of Main Trail

▼ 0.0		Continue to the southeast on graveled Juniper Lake Road.
1.3 ▲	TR	4-way intersection. Juniper Lake Road continues straight ahead and is the spur to Juniper Lake. Track on left is 29N65. Zero trip meter.
		GPS: N40°23.91' W121°16.27'

▼ 0.3	SO	Benner USFS Campground on left.
1.0 ▲	SO	Benner USFS Campground on right.
		GPS: N40°23.71' W121°16.06'

▼ 0.4	SO	Cross over Benner Creek.
0.9 ▲	SO	Cross over Benner Creek.
▼ 0.8	SO	Track on left.
0.5 ▲	SO	Track on right.
▼ 1.3		Trail ends at intersection with graded road 29N42 on right. Bear left on paved road CR 318 to exit to Chester.
0.0 ▲		Trail commences on CR 318, 6.2 miles north of Chester. To reach the start of the trail from California 36, zero trip meter at the northeastern edge of Chester and turn northwest on Feather River Drive. Proceed 0.7 miles and turn right onto Chester– Juniper Lake Road (CR 318), following the sign for Juniper Lake. Proceed 5.5 miles on the paved road to the start of the trail. At the intersection with graded dirt 29N42 on the left, zero trip meter and bear right (northeast) onto graded dirt 28N42, following the sign for Juniper Lake.
		GPS: N40°23.03' W121°16.35'

Humboldt Trail

STARTING POINT California 89, 4 miles south of the intersection with California 36

FINISHING POINT CR 91422 at Jonesville Snowmobile Park, 4.2 miles east of Butte Meadows

TOTAL MILEAGE 20.4 miles

UNPAVED MILEAGE 19.1 miles

DRIVING TIME 2 hours

ELEVATION RANGE 4,600–6,600 feet

USUALLY OPEN May to November

BEST TIME TO TRAVEL May to November

DIFFICULTY RATING 2

SCENIC RATING 8

REMOTENESS RATING +0

Special Attractions

■ Historic route of the Humboldt Trail.

■ Jonesville Snowmobile Park and a network of groomed snowmobile trails in winter.

■ Humboldt Peak and Robbers Roost.

History

The Humboldt Trail travels a section of a longer trail known as the Chico and Humboldt Wagon Road. This route was developed in the early 1860s as a mine supply route that began in Chico and headed northeast across the Sierra Nevada. John Bidwell and associated businessmen vied with others for the contract to build this valuable passage from the Sacramento Valley. Their route was established with the help of the Maidu, a people who knew the footpaths across the Sierra Nevada. The road joined the Nobles Trail in Susanville and was intended for prospectors and supply wagons heading to the diggings of what were the territories of Utah and Washington, today's Nevada and Idaho.

Stage drivers stopped off at the Ruffa Ranch, beside Butt Creek and below Eagle Rocks on the eastern approach to Humboldt Summit, where they could refresh their horses or change teams before making the rough climb to the 6,610-foot summit, more than a thousand feet higher. The basic wagon road was described as having many small summits before the main one. The tiring, dusty route had several switchbacks on either side of the summit and caused a number of high-centers. This was more a reflection of the typical road conditions of the day as opposed to a complaint.

The winding climb passed Robbers Roost near the summit, which was the scene of several stagecoach robberies. Once past the Roost, drivers could breathe a sigh of relief and begin the slow twisting route down the western side of the mountain. Starting in 1866, this road was used as a mail route between Chico and Boise City, Idaho Territory. It also opened new regions for development. Logging increased greatly and settlers took up land in the Jonesville and Butte Meadows areas in the late 1860s and '70s. Large wagons pulled by six or eight oxen hauled lumber to the newly built Woodsum Brothers sawmill below Lomo, north of present-day Yuba City. Come springtime, cattlemen found this a good road on which to drive their herds into the mountain meadows.

Jonesville Stage Stop, beside Jones Creek, grew large enough to support a fine two-story hotel, a welcome sight to weary travelers. People wishing to escape the Central Valley's summer heat also came to cabins and resorts along this mountain road. The historic Jonesville Hotel still stands near the end of the described trail, though it does not operate as a hotel anymore.

Description

Humboldt Trail leaves California 89 on the western shore of Lake Almanor opposite the start of the Lake Almanor Recreation Trail, a 9.7-mile loop for hikers, mountain bikers, and cross-country skiers. The paved loop follows an easy grade and is barrier free. Lake Almanor is a great spot for trout fishing and wildlife viewing for black-tail deer, ospreys, eagles, and waterfowl.

Humboldt Trail is graded dirt all the way, but there are some spots, particularly on the west side of Humboldt Peak, that make it better suited for high-clearance 2WDs. Initially, the trail travels through private forest owned by the Pacific Gas & Electric Company. No camping or fires are allowed along this section. The trail then enters Lassen National Forest at a meadow on Butt Creek, a pretty place with a zigzag pole fence bisecting the meadow.

The trail continues through the forest and passes two parts of the privately owned Ruffa Ranch. The ranch has some old buildings still standing and a collapsed log cabin. In fall, groves of mature aspens provide splashes of gold against a backdrop of the Eagle Peaks to the south and Butt Mountain to the north. The trail climbs to Humboldt Summit, below Humboldt Peak, passing the rocky outcrops of Robbers Roost along the way. A short section of shelf road is only wide enough for a single vehicle. The Pacific Crest National Scenic Trail crosses the summit, traveling 1.5 miles south up a moderately steep grade to Humboldt Peak (7,087 feet), before continuing to the southeast. There is trailhead parking at the summit.

Crossing into Tehama County, the trail descends a wide road toward Jonesville.

Ruffa Ranch buildings

Meadows around Butt Creek

Those wanting a longer drive can loop back to Lake Almanor along the Humbug Summit Road, another historic route that will return you via a selection of forest roads. The main trail ends at the Jonesville Snowmobile Park, a staging area for a network of groomed winter trails. A gate at the snowmobile park closes the road to vehicles from January 1 to March 15.

Current Road Information
Lassen National Forest
Almanor Ranger District
PO Box 767
Chester, CA 96020
(530) 258-2141

Map References
BLM   Lake Almanor
USFS   Lassen National Forest

USGS   1:24,000   Almanor, Humbug
        Valley, Humboldt Peak, Jonesville
        1:100,000 Lake Almanor
Maptech CD-ROM: Shasta Lake/Redding
Northern California Atlas & Gazetteer,
        pp. 58, 59
California Road & Recreation Atlas,
        pp. 60, 59

Route Directions

▼ 0.0   From California 89, 4 miles south of
            the intersection with California 36
            at Chester, zero trip meter and turn
            southwest at the sign for Humboldt
            Trail and Humbug Trail. Road opposite
            goes 0.1 miles to one of the Lake
            Almanor Recreation Trailheads and 0.3
            miles to an archery area in the nation-
            al forest. Immediately track on right

and track on left are both 400A. Trail initially passes through PG&E-owned forest.

4.8 ▲ Track on right and track on left are both 400A; then trail ends at T-intersection with the scenic byway California 89. Turn left for Chester; turn right for Quincy. Road opposite goes 0.1 miles to one of the Lake Almanor Recreation Trailheads and 0.3 miles to an archery area.
GPS: N40°13.64′ W121°12.45′

▼ 0.4 SO Track on right is 461 and track on left.
4.4 ▲ SO Track on left is 461 and track on right.
▼ 0.6 BR Graded road on left is Humbug Trail.
4.2 ▲ BL Graded road on right is Humbug Trail.
GPS: N40°13.13′ W121°12.48′

▼ 0.9 SO Track on left and track on right.
3.9 ▲ SO Track on left and track on right.
▼ 1.0 SO Track on left is 460 and track on right.
3.8 ▲ SO Track on right is 460 and track on left.
▼ 1.5 SO Track on right and track on left are both 450.
3.3 ▲ SO Track on right and track on left are both 450.
▼ 1.8 SO Track on left and track on right.
3.0 ▲ SO Track on left and track on right.
▼ 1.9 SO Track on left is 600 and track on right.
2.9 ▲ SO Track on right is 600 and track on left.
▼ 2.2 SO Track on right.
2.6 ▲ SO Track on left.
▼ 2.5 SO Track on right.
2.3 ▲ SO Track on left.
▼ 2.6 SO Track on right is 145 and track on left.
2.2 ▲ SO Track on left is 145 and track on right.
GPS: N40°12.60′ W121°14.49′

▼ 3.2 SO Track on left and track on right are both 660.
1.6 ▲ SO Track on left and track on right are both 660.
▼ 3.6 SO Track on left and track on right are both 600.
1.2 ▲ SO Track on left and track on right are both 600.
▼ 3.9 SO Track on left is 652 and track on right.
0.9 ▲ SO Track on right is 652 and track on left.
▼ 4.0 SO Track on right goes to Soldier

Meadows USFS Campground and track on left.

0.8 ▲ SO Track on left goes to Soldier Meadows USFS Campground and track on right.
GPS: N40°12.13′ W121°15.68′

▼ 4.3 SO Track on right is 654.
0.5 ▲ SO Track on left is 654.
▼ 4.8 SO Cross over Soldier Creek on bridge; then 4-way intersection. Graded road on left is 27N65 to Humbug Valley and Yellow Creek. Graded road on right is 28N36. Zero trip meter and follow sign for Humboldt Summit. Entering Lassen National Forest.
0.0 ▲ Continue to the east on CR 308 and cross over Soldier Creek on bridge.
GPS: N40°12.05′ W121°16.50′

▼ 0.0 Continue to the west on CR 308.
5.6 ▲ SO 4-way intersection. Graded road on right is 27N65 to Humbug Valley and Yellow Creek. Graded road on left is 28N36. Zero trip meter and follow sign to California 89 and Chester.
▼ 0.4 SO Two tracks on left; then track on right is 27N15.
5.2 ▲ SO Track on left is 27N15; then two tracks on right.
▼ 1.5 SO Track on left.
4.1 ▲ SO Track on right.
▼ 2.1 SO Cattle guard.
3.5 ▲ SO Cattle guard.
▼ 2.3 SO Track on right.
3.3 ▲ SO Track on left.
▼ 2.5 BL Track on right is Shanghai Road (27N16); then track on left.
3.1 ▲ SO Track on right; then track on left is Shanghai Road (27N16).
GPS: N40°11.45′ W121°19.14′

▼ 2.8 BR Graded road on left to corrals.
2.8 ▲ SO Graded road on right to corrals.
▼ 3.0 SO Cross over creek; then tank on left and track on right.
2.6 ▲ SO Track on left and tank on right; then cross over creek.
GPS: N40°11.39′ W121°19.77′

▼ 3.1 SO Cross over Shanghai Creek.

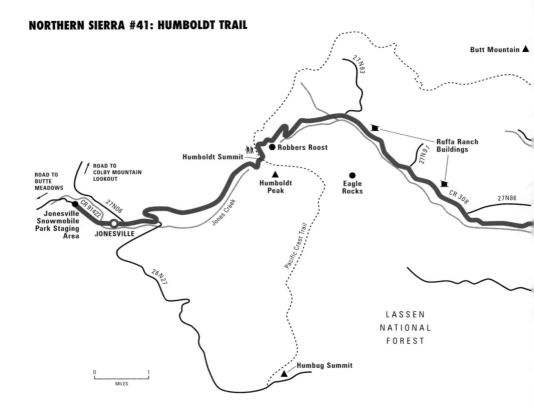

2.5 ▲	SO	Cross over Shanghai Creek.
		GPS: N40°11.31′ W121°19.88′

▼ 4.7	SO	Track on right.
0.9 ▲	SO	Track on left.
▼ 5.6	SO	Graded road on right is 27N86. Zero trip meter.
0.0 ▲		Continue to the southeast.
		GPS: N40°10.31′ W121°22.06′

▼ 0.0		Continue to the northwest.
5.4 ▲	SO	Graded road on left is 27N86. Zero trip meter.
▼ 0.3	SO	Track on right.
5.1 ▲	SO	Track on left.
▼ 0.7	SO	Ruffa Ranch buildings on right.
4.7 ▲	SO	Second group of Ruffa Ranch buildings on left.
		GPS: N40°10.37′ W121°22.82′

▼ 1.3	SO	Track on right is 27N91.
4.1 ▲	SO	Track on left is 27N91.

▼ 2.3	SO	Second section of Ruffa Ranch. Butt Mountain is on the right and Eagle Rocks are on the left.
3.1 ▲	SO	Ruffa Ranch. Butt Mountain is on the left and Eagle Rocks are on the right.
		GPS: N40°10.49′ W121°24.55′

▼ 2.4	SO	Cabins on left and right and collapsed log cabin on right—part of the Ruffa Ranch.
3.0 ▲	SO	Cabins on left and right and collapsed log cabin on left—part of the Ruffa Ranch.
▼ 2.6	SO	Cross over a tributary of Butt Creek.
2.8 ▲	SO	Cross over a tributary of Butt Creek.
▼ 3.0	SO	Graded road on right is 27N93.
2.4 ▲	SO	Graded road on left is 27N93.
▼ 3.1	SO	Cross over creek.
2.3 ▲	SO	Cross over creek.
▼ 3.2	SO	Track on left.
2.2 ▲	SO	Track on right.
▼ 4.1	BR	Track on left.

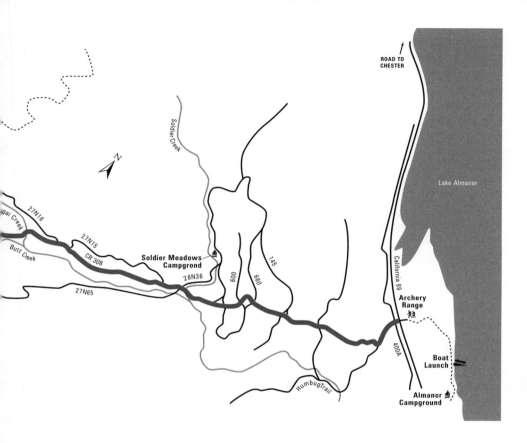

1.3 ▲	BL	Track on right.
▼ 4.9	SO	Start of shelf road to Humboldt Summit.
0.5 ▲	SO	End of shelf road.
▼ 5.4	SO	Entering Tehama County at Humboldt Summit; then Pacific Crest Trail crosses. To the left it climbs toward Humboldt Peak and continues to Cold Spring. Parking area on right. Zero trip meter at summit. End of shelf road.
0.0 ▲		Continue to the north on CR 308.
		GPS: N40°09.13′ W121°26.11′

▼ 0.0		Continue to the southeast on CR 91422.
3.2 ▲	SO	Pacific Crest Trail crosses. To the right it climbs toward Humboldt Peak and continues to Cold Spring. Parking area on left; then entering Plumas County at Humboldt Summit. Zero trip meter. Start of shelf road.
▼ 3.2	SO	Track on left is 26N27 to Humbug Summit and CR 307. Zero trip meter. Road becomes paved.

0.0 ▲		Continue to the north.
		GPS: N40°07.20′ W121°27.30′

▼ 0.0		Continue to the southwest.
1.4 ▲	BL	Track on right is 26N27 to Humbug Summit and CR 307. Zero trip meter and follow sign to Humboldt Summit.
▼ 0.4	SO	Graded road on right is 27N06 to Colby Mountain Lookout. This is Jonesville— private property.
1.0 ▲	SO	Graded road on left is 27N06 to Colby Mountain Lookout. This is Jonesville —private property.
		GPS: N40°06.95′ W121°27.62′

▼ 0.5	SO	Leaving Lassen National Forest.
0.9 ▲	SO	Entering Lassen National Forest.
▼ 0.8	SO	Cross over Jones Creek.
0.6 ▲	SO	Cross over Jones Creek.
		GPS: N40°06.75′ W121°28.05′

▼ 1.4		Trail ends at Jonesville Snowmobile

Park Staging Area. This is the road closure point in winter. Continue straight ahead for Butte Meadows.

0.0 ▲   Trail commences at the Jonesville Snowmobile Park Staging Area, 4.2 miles east of Butte Meadows along CR 91422. This is the road closure point in winter. Zero trip meter at the seasonal closure gate and proceed east along paved CR 91422.

GS: N40°06.81' W121°28.66'

Ponderosa Way

STARTING POINT   California 36, 9 miles west of Mineral

FINISHING POINT   Cohasset Road in Cohasset, 16 miles north of Chico

TOTAL MILEAGE   59 miles, plus 2.4-mile spur to McCarthy Point Lookout

UNPAVED MILEAGE   57 miles, plus 2.4-mile spur

DRIVING TIME   7 hours

ELEVATION RANGE   1,800–4,300 feet

USUALLY OPEN   May to November

BEST TIME TO TRAVEL   Dry weather

DIFFICULTY RATING   3

SCENIC RATING   10

REMOTENESS RATING   +1

Special Attractions

■ Long trail along part of historic firebreak put in by the Civilian Conservation Corps.

■ Dizzying ascents and descents into the deep canyons of Antelope Creek, Mill Creek, and Deer Creek.

■ Fire lookout tower at McCarthy Point can be rented for overnight stays.

History

The official Ponderosa Way Firebreak and Truck Trail was developed after the Great Depression in response to the national unemployment crisis. This ambitious trail promoted by Stuart B. Show was designed to stretch some 700 miles along the west side of the Sierra Nevada, from the Kern River in the south to the Pit River at the northern end of

the range. The intention was to cut a wide path between the lower level oak vegetation and the mixed conifer forests of the higher elevations. This would safeguard the forests from fires that might rage up the mountainsides from the Central Valley.

Although the firebreak and trail were never completed, the Civilian Conservation Corps (CCC) did install several hundred miles of the intended route. A total of 24 CCC camps were involved in the enormous project. Thousands of hours of labor were required to clear steep slopes and move massive amounts of soil and rock by blasting and digging. The CCC also constructed the McCarthy Point Fire Lookout in 1936, reached by a spur from Ponderosa Way. With the outbreak of World War II, fire spotters were given the added duty of looking for enemy aircraft. This precaution was part of the Aircraft Warning Service (AWS), which had observation points that stretched the length of the West Coast. See *California Trails—North Coast Region*, Trail #15 for a more elaborate enemy detection station that was also a vital part of the early warning system. McCarthy Point Fire Lookout was manned until the mid 1960s.

Description

Nowadays, it is impossible to travel the full length of the Ponderosa Way, but this one long section offers a good glimpse of the hand-built road. The trail leaves California 36, 9 miles west of the hamlet of Mineral, which sits on the edge of Battle Creek Meadows, a volcanic caldera formed by the collapse of Mount Maidu.

The trail passes through private subdivisions before descending steeply to cross Paynes Creek. It passes the eastern end of Northern Sierra #43: Hogsback Road, which descends west to Red Bluff. Ponderosa Way continues through the forest and passes undeveloped camping areas before starting to descend into Antelope Canyon, the first of the major east-west running canyons. The volcanic plug of Black Butte is immediately south of the trail at the start of the descent.

The undeveloped South Antelope Camp-

Rock formations along Ponderosa Way

ground, along Antelope Creek, has a few sites in a shady gully beside the creek. Farther south, Northern Sierra #44: Peligreen-Grapevine Jeepway leads off to the west. The main trail continues through Lassen National Forest and privately owned forest maintained by PG&E for timber harvesting. The slow descent along a winding, narrow shelf road follows Mill Creek Rim down to Mill Creek. This is one of the most scenic sections of the drive.

Black Rock, an unusual basalt plug several hundred feet tall, is in Mill Creek; it diverts water around it to form a waterfall and a swimming hole at the bottom. A developed forest service campground at Black Rock has several sites beside Mill Creek among oaks, camphor laurels, and walnut trees.

Past Mill Creek, the trail climbs steeply out of the canyon to a spur that leads 2.4 miles to McCarthy Point Fire Lookout. At The Narrows, the trail drops steeply on either side into separate drainages. This point was well known to early travelers on the Lassen Trail; a historical marker at the spot records some of their thoughts. The lookout is perched at 3,600 feet on the very edge of Mill Creek Canyon's southern rim. It was once used to spot fires in the Mill Creek drainage. In 1994, forest service workers and volunteers restored the lookout. It has a two-room cabin that can sleep eight, a kitchen, and a bathroom. For a small fee, it can be rented for a two-night minimum stay. Contact the Almanor Ranger District for information and reservations. A short walk along a paved trail takes you to the lookout. If the lookout is occupied, please be considerate and leave the occupants alone.

Much of this section of the Ponderosa Way skirts the eastern edge of the Ishi Wilderness. Several hiking trails start along Ponderosa Way and go into the wilderness. One of the most popular is the Deer Creek Trail, a moderate 7-mile hike that offers spectacular views of Deer Creek Canyon and the region's basalt cliffs and spires. Other trails, such as Devils Den, are better suited for more experienced hikers because of steep grades and difficult navigation. Devils Den Trail parallels Deer Creek for 4.5 miles before climbing up to the ridge top. The Moak Trail is an easy 7-mile hike that is excellent for springtime wildflower viewing, but it has little shade and is often uncomfortably hot in summer. Navigation is difficult along this trail because sections of it are poorly defined.

South of the turnoff to McCarthy Point, much of Ponderosa Way passes through PG&E owned forests. Many logging trails branch off to the left and the right. The Lassen Trail follows the main route for a short section and passes the site of Bruff Camp, a stopping point for early emigrants.

The final deep east–west canyon is the one cut by Deer Creek; like the others, it is a fast flowing creek in a rugged canyon. The final section of the trail travels through more privately owned forest, passing the site of the Campbell Fire Lookout, to join gravel Cohasset Road. It ends 16 miles north of Chico in the small settlement of Cohasset.

Current Road Information
Bureau of Land Management
Redding Field Office
355 Hemsted Drive
Redding, CA 96002
(530) 224-2100

Lassen National Forest
Almanor Ranger District
PO Box 767
Chester, CA 96020
(530) 258-2141

Map References
BLM   Lake Almanor, Chico
USFS   Lassen National Forest
USGS   1:24,000   Finley Butte, Panther
       Spring, Barkley Mtn., Devils Parade
       Ground, Cohasset
       1:100,000 Lake Almanor, Chico
Maptech CD-ROM: Shasta Lake/Redding;
       High Sierra/Tahoe
Northern California Atlas & Gazetteer,
       pp. 57, 58, 68
California Road & Recreation Atlas,
       pp. 53, 59
Other: A Guide to the Ishi, Thousand
       Lakes, & Caribou Wilderness

Route Directions

▼ 0.0   From California 36, 9 miles west of Mineral, zero trip meter and turn south on paved CR 707A at the sign for Ponderosa Way. Canyon View Road is opposite the turn. Cross cattle guard and immediately track on left.

8.2 ▲ BL Track on right; then cattle guard. Trail ends at intersection with California 36. Turn right for Mineral; turn left for Red Bluff.
GPS: N40°20.82′ W121°45.77′

▼ 0.1 BL Road on right.
8.1 ▲ BR Road on left.
▼ 0.2 SO Track on left. Remain on paved road, passing through private property.
8.0 ▲ SO Track on right.
▼ 1.0 BL Navion Road on right.
7.2 ▲ BR Navion Road on left.
▼ 1.1 SO Road turns to graded dirt.
7.1 ▲ SO Road becomes paved.
▼ 1.7 SO Cross through Paynes Creek; then track on left.
6.5 ▲ SO Track on right; then cross through Paynes Creek.
GPS: N40°20.35′ W121°46.09′

▼ 1.9 BL Track on right.
6.3 ▲ SO Track on left.
▼ 2.3 SO Cross over creek.
5.9 ▲ SO Cross over creek.
▼ 2.9 SO Track on left.
5.3 ▲ SO Track on right.
▼ 3.6 SO Cross through Chapman Gulch.
4.6 ▲ SO Cross through Chapman Gulch.
GPS: N40°19.65′ W121°46.53′

▼ 4.4 SO Track on right.
3.8 ▲ SO Track on left.
▼ 4.6 SO Track on right.
3.6 ▲ SO Track on left.
▼ 4.8 SO Two tracks on left.
3.4 ▲ SO Two tracks on right.
▼ 5.5 SO Track on right.
2.7 ▲ SO Track on left.
▼ 6.2 SO Cross over Plum Creek.
2.0 ▲ SO Cross over Plum Creek.
▼ 7.7 BR Track on left.
0.5 ▲ BL Track on right.

▼ 7.8 BR Bear right and join paved Plum Creek Road.
0.4 ▲ BL Bear left onto graded dirt Ponderosa Way.
GPS: N40°18.10′ W121°47.70′

▼ 8.2 TL Shake House on left (private property). Paved road ahead is Northern Sierra #43: Hogsback Road. Zero trip meter and turn left onto paved CR 707B (28N29), following the sign for Black Rock.
0.0 ▲   Continue to the northeast on Plum Creek Road. Shake House on right (private property).
GPS: N40°17.87′ W121°48.04′

▼ 0.0   Continue to the east. Immediately track on right.
9.0 ▲ TR Track on left; then T-intersection with paved Plum Creek Road. To the left is Northern Sierra #43: Hogsback Road. Zero trip meter.
▼ 0.1 SO Road turns to graded dirt.
8.9 ▲ SO Road becomes paved.
▼ 0.5 SO Cross over Carter Creek on bridge.
8.5 ▲ SO Cross over Carter Creek on bridge.
▼ 0.9 SO Track on right; then track on left.
8.1 ▲ SO Track on right; then track on left.
▼ 1.0 SO Track on left.
8.0 ▲ SO Track on right.
▼ 1.2 SO Track on left.
7.8 ▲ SO Track on right.
▼ 1.8 SO Track on left.
7.2 ▲ SO Track on right.
▼ 2.9 BR Track on left.
6.1 ▲ BL Track on right.
▼ 3.1 BL Track on right.
5.9 ▲ BR Track on left.
▼ 3.6 SO Cross through North Fork Antelope Creek.
5.4 ▲ SO Cross through North Fork Antelope Creek.
GPS: N40°16.86′ W121°45.81′

▼ 4.1 SO Track on right along Shelton Ridge; then track on left.
4.9 ▲ SO Track on right; then track on left along Shelton Ridge.
▼ 4.3 SO Track on left.
4.7 ▲ SO Track on right.
▼ 4.9 SO Track on left.

The South Fork of Antelope Creek

4.1 ▲	SO	Track on right.
▼ 5.2	SO	Track on left.
3.8 ▲	SO	Track on right.
▼ 5.3	SO	Entering Lassen National Forest.
3.7 ▲	SO	Exiting Lassen National Forest.

GPS: N40°16.34' W121°46.92'

▼ 5.8	SO	Cross over Middle Fork Antelope Creek on bridge.
2.2 ▲	SO	Cross over Middle Fork Antelope Creek on bridge.
▼ 6.8	SO	Camping area on right (no sign) and track on left.
2.2 ▲	SO	Camping area on left (no sign) and track on right.

GPS: N40°16.07' W121°47.32'

▼ 6.9	SO	Track on right.
2.1 ▲	SO	Track on left.
▼ 7.2	SO	Graded road on left is Upper Middle Ridge Road (28N71).
1.8 ▲	SO	Graded road on right is Upper Middle Ridge Road (28N71).

GPS: N40°15.79' W121°46.93'

▼ 7.4	SO	Track on right.
1.6 ▲	SO	Track on left.
▼ 7.5	SO	Black Butte on right, high above South Fork Antelope Creek.
1.5 ▲	SO	Black Butte on left, high above South Fork Antelope Creek.
▼ 8.5	SO	Track on left.
0.5 ▲	SO	Track on right.
▼ 9.0	SO	Track on right into South Antelope USFS Campground. Zero trip meter.
0.0 ▲		Continue to the west.

GPS: N40°15.25' W121°45.42'

▼ 0.0		Continue to the southeast.
3.0 ▲	SO	Track on left into South Antelope USFS Campground. Zero trip meter.
▼ 0.1	SO	Cross over South Fork Antelope Creek on bridge.
2.9 ▲	SO	Cross over South Fork Antelope Creek on bridge.
▼ 1.7	SO	Panther Spring Forest Service Station

on right.

1.3 ▲ SO Panther Spring Forest Service Station on left.

GPS: N40°14.90' W121°46.26'

▼ 2.0 SO Track on right.
1.0 ▲ SO Track on left.

▼ 2.1 SO Track on right is 160P; track on left is 150P; then second track on left is 28N29F.
0.9 ▲ SO Track on right is 28N29F; then track on left is 160P; second track on right is 150P.

▼ 2.2 SO Two tracks on right.
0.8 ▲ SO Two tracks on left.

▼ 3.0 SO Graded road on right is Northern Sierra #44: Peligreen-Grapevine Jeepway (28N57). Zero trip meter at the turn and follow the sign to Mill Creek.
0.0 ▲ Continue to the northwest.

GPS: N40°14.07' W121°46.50'

▼ 0.0 Continue to the southeast.
2.8 ▲ SO Graded road on left is Northern Sierra #44: Peligreen-Grapevine Jeepway (28N57). Zero trip meter at the turn and follow the sign to Panther Springs.

▼ 0.1 SO Track on right.
2.7 ▲ SO Track on left.

▼ 0.2 SO Track on left is 28N29G.
2.6 ▲ SO Track on right is 28N29G.

▼ 0.3 SO Track on right.
2.5 ▲ SO Track on left.

▼ 0.9 SO Track on left is N Line.
1.9 ▲ SO Track on right is N Line.

▼ 1.6 SO Track on left.
1.2 ▲ SO Track on right.

▼ 1.8 SO Track on right is 220P.
1.0 ▲ SO Track on left is 220P.

▼ 2.4 SO Track on left is 230P.
0.4 ▲ SO Track on right is 230P.

GPS: N40°12.94' W121°44.58'

▼ 2.8 SO Track on right is 27N13, which goes 1 mile to Long Point. Zero trip meter and follow the sign to Black Rock.
0.0 ▲ Continue to the northwest.

GPS: N40°12.60' W121°44.58'

▼ 0.0 Continue to the east.
4.7 ▲ SO Track on left is 27N13, which goes 1

mile to Long Point. Zero trip meter and follow the sign to Panther Springs.

▼ 0.7 SO Start of shelf road.
4.0 ▲ SO End of shelf road.

▼ 4.4 SO Well-used track on right.
0.3 ▲ BR Well-used track on left.

GPS: N40°11.07' W121°42.87'

▼ 4.5 SO Cross over creek on bridge.
0.2 ▲ SO Cross over creek on bridge.

▼ 4.7 SO Track on right goes into Black Rock USFS Campground and Mill Creek Trail (4E10), which travels up and down the creek. Zero trip meter.
0.0 ▲ Continue to the west.

GPS: N40°11.03' W121°42.65'

▼ 0.0 Continue to the east.
4.9 ▲ BR Track on left goes into Black Rock USFS Campground and Mill Creek Trail (4E10), which travels up and down the creek. Zero trip meter.

▼ 0.1 SO Cross over Mill Creek on curved wooden bridge. Black Rock is on the left. Entering state game refuge.
4.8 ▲ SO Cross over Mill Creek on curved wooden bridge. Black Rock is on the right. Leaving state game refuge.

▼ 0.4 SO Cross over creek on bridge.
4.5 ▲ SO Cross over creek on bridge.

▼ 0.5 SO Mill Creek Trailhead on right.
4.4 ▲ SO Mill Creek Trailhead on left.

GPS: N40°10.88' W121°42.77'

▼ 0.7 SO Cross over creek on bridge.
4.2 ▲ SO Cross over creek on bridge.

▼ 2.5 SO Cross over creek.
2.4 ▲ SO Cross over creek.

▼ 4.9 BR End of shelf road. Cedar Spring on left. Graded road on left is 27N08, spur to McCarthy Point Fire Lookout. Zero trip meter and bear right, remaining on 28N29 and following the sign to Deer Creek. Join the Lassen Trail.
0.0 ▲ Continue to the southwest. Entering Lassen National Forest. Cedar Spring on right. Start of shelf road.

GPS: N40°10.21' W121°39.93'

Spur to McCarthy Point Fire Lookout

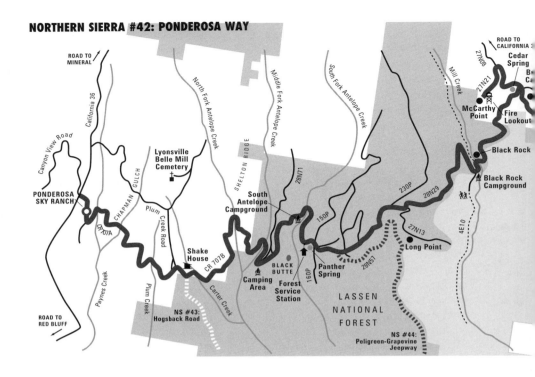

▼ 0.0   Turn north on 27N08, following the sign to The Narrows.

▼ 0.3 SO The Narrows.
       GPS: N40°10.45' W121°39.95'

▼ 0.4 SO Track on right.
▼ 0.7 SO Track on right.
▼ 1.2 TL Graded road continues straight ahead to California 32. Turn left onto 27N21, following marker for the lookout.
       GPS: N40°10.82' W121°39.38'

▼ 1.4 SO Track on left.
▼ 1.8 SO Track on right.
▼ 2.1 TL Turn left onto 740L3.
       GPS: N40°10.98' W121°40.27'

▼ 2.4   Locked gate. To reach the lookout, walk past the gate for a short distance to the sheds and parking area; then turn right and follow the narrow paved trail for 0.1 miles to the lookout.
       GPS: N40°11.05' W121°40.43'

Continuation of Main Trail

▼ 0.0   Continue to the south. Entering PG&E forest.

4.4 ▲ BL Graded road on right is 27N08, spur to McCarthy Point Fire Lookout. Zero trip meter and bear left, remaining on 28N29 and following the sign to Black Rock.
       GPS: N40°10.21' W121°39.93'

▼ 0.1 SO Track on left is 770L.
4.3 ▲ SO Track on right is 770L.
▼ 0.4 SO Track on right is 778L; then second track on right is 780L.
4.0 ▲ SO Track on left is 780L; then second track on left is 778L.
▼ 0.8 SO Bruff Camp on left at sign.
3.6 ▲ SO Bruff Camp on right at sign.
       GPS: N40°09.93' W121°40.51'

▼ 0.9 SO Track on left is 800L.
3.5 ▲ SO Track on right is 800L.
▼ 1.2 SO Track on right is 810L.
3.2 ▲ SO Track on left is 810L.
▼ 1.4 SO Track on right is 820L.
3.0 ▲ SO Track on left is 820L.
▼ 2.0 SO Track on right; then two tracks on left.

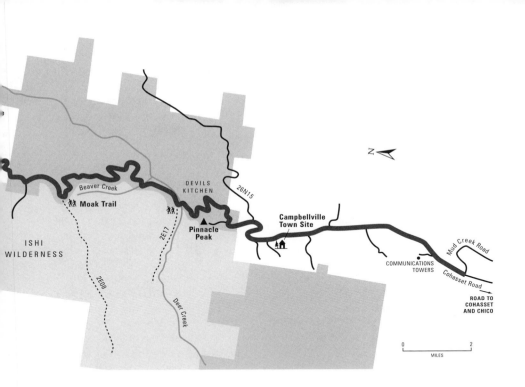

2.4 ▲	SO	Two tracks on right; then track on left.
▼ 2.3	SO	Track on right.
2.1 ▲	SO	Track on left.
▼ 2.7	BL	Two tracks on right and track straight ahead; then track on right.
1.7 ▲	BR	Track on left; then two tracks on left and track straight ahead.

GPS: N40°08.82′ W121°41.73′

▼ 3.2	SO	Track on right and track on left.
1.2 ▲	SO	Track on right and track on left.
▼ 3.4	SO	Track on left; then second track on left.
1.0 ▲	SO	Track on right; then second track on right.
▼ 3.5	SO	Track on right is 4500.
0.9 ▲	SO	Track on left is 4500.
▼ 4.4	BL	Three tracks on right at information boards. Zero trip meter. There is a Lassen Trail marker at this point. The Lassen Trail leaves the main route to the right.
0.0 ▲		Continue to the north.

GPS: N40°08.10′ W121°42.32′

▼ 0.0		Continue to the east.
8.8 ▲	BR	Three tracks on left at information boards. Zero trip meter. There is a Lassen Trail

marker at this point. The Lassen Trail now follows the main route.

▼ 0.7	SO	Re-entering Lassen National Forest. No sign.
8.1 ▲	SO	Entering PG&E-owned forest.
▼ 1.6	BL	Hiking trailhead on right for the Moak Trail (2E08), which enters the Ishi Wilderness. Start to descend shelf road.
7.2 ▲	BR	Hiking trailhead on left for the Moak Trail (2E08), which enters the Ishi Wilderness. End of shelf road.

GPS: N40°07.10′ W121°42.59′

▼ 3.5	SO	Viewpoint on right.
5.3 ▲	SO	Viewpoint on left.
▼ 7.3	SO	Cross through Beaver Creek.
1.5 ▲	SO	Cross through Beaver Creek.

GPS: N40°05.20′ W121°41.78′

▼ 7.7	SO	Track on left. End of shelf road.
1.1 ▲	SO	Track on right. Start of shelf road.
▼ 8.0	SO	Track on left.
0.8 ▲	SO	Track on right.
▼ 8.1	SO	Track on left.
0.7 ▲	SO	Track on right.
▼ 8.2	SO	Track on left.

0.6 ▲ SO Track on right.
▼ 8.6 SO Hiking trailhead on right is 2E17.
0.2 ▲ SO Hiking trailhead on left is 2E17.
GPS: N40°04.27′ W121°42.15′

▼ 8.8 SO Cross over Deer Creek on bridge. Zero trip meter at far end; then track on left.
0.0 ▲ Continue to the northeast and cross over Deer Creek on bridge. Entering state game refuge.
GPS: N40°04.23′ W121°42.21′

▼ 0.0 Continue to the southwest. Exiting state game refuge.
5.4 ▲ SO Track on right; then zero trip meter at the bridge over Deer Creek.
▼ 0.1 SO Track on right goes 0.1 miles to Devils Den Trail (2E09). Forest service information boards on right.
5.3 ▲ SO Track on left goes 0.1 miles to Devils Den Trail (2E09). Forest service information boards on left.
▼ 0.8 SO Cross over creek. Start of shelf road.
4.6 ▲ SO Cross over creek. End of shelf road.
▼ 1.1 SO Cross over creek.
4.3 ▲ SO Cross over creek.
▼ 1.5 SO Cross over creek.
3.9 ▲ SO Cross over creek.
▼ 1.7 SO Viewpoint on left over Devils Kitchen.
3.7 ▲ SO Viewpoint on right over Devils Kitchen.
GPS: N40°03.79′ W121°42.37′

▼ 2.4 SO Cross over creek.
3.0 ▲ SO Cross over creek.
▼ 4.3 SO Track on right to Pinnacle Peak. End of shelf road.
1.1 ▲ SO Track on left to Pinnacle Peak. Start of shelf road.
GPS: N40°02.96′ W121°42.66′

▼ 4.8 SO Exiting Lassen National Forest at sign.
0.6 ▲ SO Entering Lassen National Forest at sign.
GPS: N40°02.60′ W121°42.67′

▼ 5.4 SO Major 4-way intersection. Track on right is 260H, graded road on left is N Line (26N15). Zero trip meter.
0.0 ▲ Continue to the northeast.
GPS: N40°02.17′ W121°42.53′

▼ 0.0 Continue to the southwest on unmarked graded road 28N29. Two tracks on left are both 250H.
7.8 ▲ SO Two tracks on right are both 250H; then 4-way intersection. Track on left is 260H, graded road on right is N Line (26N15). Zero trip meter.
▼ 0.3 SO Track on left.
7.5 ▲ SO Track on right.
▼ 0.8 BL Track on right is 230H.
7.0 ▲ BR Track on left is 230H.
▼ 1.2 SO Track on right is 220H; then cleared area on left is the site of the Campbellville Fire Lookout.
6.6 ▲ SO Cleared area on right is the site of the Campbellville Fire Lookout; then track on left is 220H.
GPS: N40°02.09′ W121°43.07′

▼ 1.5 SO Track on right; then graded road on right at Campbellville—nothing remains.
6.3 ▲ SO Graded road on left at Campbellville—nothing remains; then track on left.
▼ 1.6 SO Track on right.
6.2 ▲ SO Track on left.
▼ 1.8 SO Track on left.
6.0 ▲ SO Track on right.
▼ 2.8 SO Two tracks on right.
5.0 ▲ SO Two tracks on left.
▼ 3.4 SO Track on right is 180H.
4.4 ▲ SO Track on left is 180H.
▼ 3.5 SO Track on left is 170H.
4.3 ▲ SO Track on right is 170H.
▼ 3.7 SO Track on right is 160H.
4.1 ▲ SO Track on left is 160H.
▼ 4.0 SO Track on left is 150H.
3.8 ▲ SO Track on right is 150H.
▼ 4.1 SO Track on left is 140H.
3.7 ▲ SO Track on right is 140H.
▼ 4.4 SO Track on left is 130H and track on right is 120H.
3.4 ▲ SO Track on right is 130H and track on left is 120H.
GPS: N39°59.37′ W121°42.10′

▼ 5.4 SO Track on right is 90H; then track on left is 80H.
2.4 ▲ SO Track on right is 80H; then track on left is 90H.
▼ 5.8 SO Track on right is 60H.

2.0 ▲	SO	Track on left is 60H.
▼ 6.6	SO	Track on right to communications towers.
1.2 ▲	SO	Track on left to communications towers.
▼ 7.4	SO	Road becomes paved. Entering Cohasset.
0.4 ▲	SO	Road turns to graded dirt.
▼ 7.8		Trail ends in Cohasset at the intersection with Mud Creek Road on the left. Continue straight ahead on paved Cohasset Road to exit to Chico and California 99.
0.0 ▲		To reach the start of the trail, take Cohasset Road north from California 99 in Chico for 16 miles. Trail commences on Cohasset Road in Cohasset, at the intersection of Mud Creek Road. Zero trip meter and proceed north on paved Cohasset Road.

GPS: N39°56.73' W121°43.28'

Hogsback Road

STARTING POINT California 99, 0.5 miles east of the intersection with California 36

FINISHING POINT Northern Sierra #42: Ponderosa Way, 8.2 miles south of California 36

TOTAL MILEAGE 22.9 miles

UNPAVED MILEAGE 22.4 miles

DRIVING TIME 2.5 hours

ELEVATION RANGE 300–3,200 feet

USUALLY OPEN April to November

BEST TIME TO TRAVEL Spring and fall

DIFFICULTY RATING 2

SCENIC RATING 9

REMOTENESS RATING +0

Special Attractions

■ Views into rugged Antelope Canyon.

■ Many pioneer sites along the way.

■ Can be combined with Northern Sierra #42: Ponderosa Way and Northern Sierra #44: Peligreen-Grapevine Jeepway to make a loop.

■ William B. Ide State Historic Park near the start of the trail.

History

The historic Hogsback Road commences in the old nut grove plantations outside Red Bluff, some 2.5 miles east of William and Susan Ide's property. Their picturesque adobe dwelling, dating back to the mid-1840s, sits on the western bank of the Sacramento River in the shade an enormous oak tree.

The Hogsback, for which this wagon road was named, was a challenge to cross before the introduction of basic horse-drawn graders. Before ascending the hogsback, try to imagine a stagecoach making its way to the Tuscan Springs Resort, approximately 4 miles north of today's route along the original stock trail.

A series of establishments, each more lavish than its predecessor, drew crowds seeking health and relaxation at the idyllic retreat. Settlers began taking over Tuscan Springs in 1854, when Dr. John Veach saw Indians enjoying the waters in a simple hut built above the springs. By the turn of the century, not an Indian was to be seen. Instead, an elaborate four-story hotel with all the attractions of a country club stood at the site. In the 1910s, the first automobile in Tehama County operated a shuttle service between Red Bluff and Tuscan Springs. In 1916, fire destroyed the resort, and efforts to rebuild continued into the late 1940s. Today, little remains of the resort.

Hogsback Road was formerly known as Belle Mill Road. In its time, loggers traveled the route to take advantage of the abundant timber in what is now Lassen National Forest.

Description

Hogsback Road begins just east of Red Bluff and climbs along the spine of Hogsback Ridge to join Northern Sierra #42: Ponderosa Way in Lassen National Forest. The historic route once led to the large, productive Belle Mill at Lyonsville. A flume once paralleled much of this route, but no traces of it remain.

Initially, the paved road serves as access to homes in the valley near Red Bluff. It quickly turns into a washboardy dirt road that climbs through private property to cross the Hogsback. Past the Hogsback, the trail crosses Mud Springs Plain through private, BLM, and Tehama State Wildlife Area lands. Most of the trail is clearly signed, but you should always make sure that you are on public lands before stopping or camping. The sparsely vegetated ridge top has fantastic views into the deep Antelope Creek Canyon, the wild and remote canyon region that enabled the Yahi called Ishi (see page 304) to remain undetected for so many years. The canyon is volcanic in origin, lined with rough, dark lava rock.

At Grecian Bend, the trail leaves Mud Springs Plain to travel across what locals once called Jack Rabbit Ridge. The whole area is marked on today's maps as Hogback Ridge.

The trail passes the north end of Northern Sierra #44: Peligreen-Grapevine Jeepway as it enters Lassen National Forest. Some excellent campsites tucked among large oaks have brilliant views over Antelope Creek. The trail briefly joins paved Plum Creek Road to finish at the intersection with Northern Sierra #42: Ponderosa Way. Turning right here allows you to loop back to Hogsback Road by following part of Ponderosa Way and then taking Northern Sierra #44: Peligreen-Grapevine Jeepway. A minimum of one full day should be allowed for the entire loop.

A point of interest close to the end of the trail is the Lyonsville-Belle Mill Cemetery, which can be found at GPS: N40°18.26' W121°44.59'. Many early settlers are buried in the Lyonsville-Belle Mill Cemetery, a quiet graveyard near the end of the trail.

The trail is 2-rated all the way, except for one 3-rated spot that requires high-clearance.

Current Road Information

Bureau of Land Management
Redding Field Office
355 Hemsted Drive
Redding, CA 96002
(530) 224-2100

Lassen National Forest
Almanor Ranger District
PO Box 767
Chester, CA 96020
(530) 258-2141

Map References

BLM   Red Bluff, Lake Almanor
USFS Lassen National Forest
USGS 1:24,000   Red Bluff East, Tuscan Springs, Dewitt Peak, Inskip Hill, Finley Butte
      1:100,000 Red Bluff, Lake Almanor
Maptech CD-ROM: Shasta Lake/Redding
Northern California Atlas & Gazetteer, p. 57
California Road & Recreation Atlas, pp. 58, 59

Route Directions

▼ 0.0   From California 99, on the east side of Red Bluff, 0.5 miles east of the intersection with California 36, zero trip meter and turn northwest on paved road at the sign for Hogsback Road (CR 774A). Remain on paved road for 1.5 miles.
4.1 ▲   Trail ends at T-intersection with California 99. Turn right for Red Bluff.
             GPS: N40°11.06' W122°10.51'

▼ 1.5   SO Road turns to graded dirt.
2.6 ▲   SO Road becomes paved.
▼ 1.7   SO Graded road on left to Tuscan Springs.
2.4 ▲   SO Graded road on right to Tuscan Springs.
▼ 2.2   SO Road on right through gate.
1.9 ▲   SO Road on left through gate.
▼ 3.7   SO Trail crosses the Hogback.
0.4 ▲   SO Trail crosses the Hogback.
▼ 4.1   SO Cattle guard. Zero trip meter.
0.0 ▲   Continue to the southwest.
             GPS: N40°12.79' W122°06.88'

▼ 0.0   Continue to the east. Track on right and track on left.
5.3 ▲   SO Track on right and track on left; then cattle guard. Zero trip meter.
▼ 0.3   SO Track on left to building.
5.0 ▲   SO Track on right to building.
▼ 0.5   SO Track on left and track on right.
4.8 ▲   SO Track on left and track on right.
▼ 1.8   SO Track on left through gate.
3.5 ▲   SO Track on right through gate.
▼ 2.1   SO Track on right.
3.2 ▲   SO Track on left.
▼ 2.3   SO Cattle guard.
3.0 ▲   SO Cattle guard.

▼ 4.6   SO Mud Spring on right. Stone remains on
              left and right were the site of Cone's
              Sheep Camp.

0.7 ▲   SO Mud Spring on left. Stone remains on
              left and right were the site of Cone's
              Sheep Camp.
              GPS: N40°13.19′ W122°01.74′

▼ 5.3   SO Cattle guard. Zero trip meter.

0.0 ▲   Continue to the southwest.
              GPS: N40°13.31′ W122°00.94′

▼ 0.0   Continue to the northeast.

5.9 ▲   SO Cattle guard. Zero trip meter.

▼ 0.6   SO Track on right.

5.3 ▲   SO Track on left.

▼ 1.2   SO Track on right; then track on left; then
              cattle guard.

4.7 ▲   SO Cattle guard; then track on right; then
              track on left.
              GPS: N40°13.74′ W121°59.70′

▼ 2.3   SO Corral on left.

3.6 ▲   SO Corral on right.

▼ 2.8   BL Grecian Bend. Track on right over
              cattle guard.

3.1 ▲   BR Grecian Bend. Track on left over
              cattle guard.
              GPS: N40°14.64′ W121°58.32′

▼ 4.1   SO Cattle guard.

1.8 ▲   SO Cattle guard.
              GPS: N40°15.52′ W121°57.82′

▼ 4.4   SO Track on left.

1.5 ▲   SO Track on right.
              GPS: N40°15.73′ W121°57.57′

▼ 4.6   SO Track on left at Thatcher's Rock Piles.

1.3 ▲   SO Track on right at Thatcher's Rock Piles.
              GPS: N40°15.83′ W121°57.36′

▼ 4.9   SO Cattle guard.

1.0 ▲   SO Cattle guard.

▼ 5.9   SO Cattle guard under major power line;
              then track on right. Zero trip meter.

0.0 ▲   Continue to the west.
              GPS: N40°16.00′ W121°55.87′

Rough sections of the Hogsback Road require 4WD

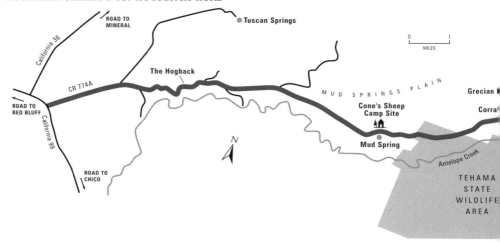

▼ 0.0   Continue to the east. Dam on left.

2.9 ▲   SO   Dam on right; then track on left; then cattle guard under major power line. Zero trip meter.

▼ 0.7   SO   Track on left.

2.2 ▲   SO   Track on right.

        GPS: N40°16.04′ W121°55.15′

▼ 1.0   SO   Track on right.

1.9 ▲   SO   Track on left.

▼ 1.1   SO   Cattle guard.

1.8 ▲   SO   Cattle guard.

▼ 1.9   SO   Track on left.

1.0 ▲   SO   Track on right.

▼ 2.0   SO   Cattle guard; then well-used track on left.

0.9 ▲   SO   Well-used track on right; then cattle guard.

        GPS: N40°16.25′ W121°53.60′

▼ 2.8   SO   Track on left at small cemetery enclosed by wire fence.

0.1 ▲   SO   Track on right at small cemetery enclosed by wire fence.

        GPS: N40°16.23′ W121°52.61′

▼ 2.9   SO   Well-used track on right is Northern Sierra #44: Peligreen-Grapevine Jeepway; then cattle guard. Entering Lassen National Forest at sign. Zero trip meter.

0.0 ▲   Continue to the southwest. Road is now designated CR 774A.

        GPS: N40°16.20′ W121°52.49′

▼ 0.0   Continue to the east. Track on left.

4.7 ▲   SO   Track on right; then cattle guard. Leaving Lassen National Forest. Well-used track on left is Northern Sierra #44: Peligreen-Grapevine Jeepway. Zero trip meter.

▼ 0.1   SO   Track on right.

4.6 ▲   SO   Track on left.

▼ 0.4   SO   Track on left.

4.3 ▲   SO   Track on right.

▼ 0.8   SO   Track on right.

3.9 ▲   SO   Track on left.

▼ 1.0   SO   Track on left.

3.7 ▲   SO   Track on right.

▼ 1.1   SO   Track on right is 28N69 around Finley Lake.

3.6 ▲   SO   Track on left is 28N69 around Finley Lake.

        GPS: N40°16.22′ W121°51.24′

▼ 1.3   SO   Track on left.

3.4 ▲   SO   Track on right.

▼ 1.9   SO   Graded road on left is 28N23 and track on right. This is High Trestle. Parking area for hiking trail to McClure Place and North Fork Antelope Creek.

2.8 ▲   SO   Graded road on right is 28N23 and track on left. This is High Trestle. Parking area for hiking trail to McClure Place and North Fork Antelope Creek.

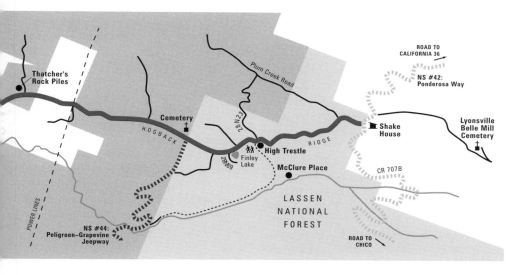

▼ 2.2 SO Track on right. Many tracks on right and left to campsites for the next 2 miles.
2.5 ▲ SO Track on left.
▼ 3.4 SO Cattle guard.
1.3 ▲ SO Cattle guard.
▼ 4.2 TR T-intersection with paved Plum Creek Road.
0.5 ▲ TL Paved Plum Creek Road continues straight ahead. Turn left onto graded dirt Hogsback Road. Many tracks on right and left to campsites for the next 2 miles.
       GPS: N40°17.79' W121°48.64'

▼ 4.7   Trail finishes at intersection with Northern Sierra #42: Ponderosa Way. Turn right to travel this trail to Chico; turn left to exit to California 36 and Mineral. Shake House (private property) is at the intersection.
0.0 ▲   Trail commences on Northern Sierra #42: Ponderosa Way, 8.2 miles south of California 36. Zero trip meter and turn southwest onto paved Plum Creek Road. Ponderosa Way heads southeast to Black Rock. Shake House (private property) is at the intersection.
       GPS: N40°17.87' W121°48.04'

NORTHERN SIERRA #44

Peligreen-Grapevine Jeepway

STARTING POINT Northern Sierra #42: Ponderosa Way, 1.3 miles south of Panther Spring Forest Service Station
FINISHING POINT Northern Sierra #43: Hogsback Road, 4.7 miles west of Northern Sierra #42: Ponderosa Way
TOTAL MILEAGE 19.8 miles
UNPAVED MILEAGE 19.8 miles
DRIVING TIME 5 hours
ELEVATION RANGE 1,400–3,900 feet
USUALLY OPEN April to November
BEST TIME TO TRAVEL Spring and fall
DIFFICULTY RATING 6
SCENIC RATING 10
REMOTE RATING: +1

Special Attractions

■ Moderate to difficult trail that can be driven in conjunction with Northern Sierra #43: Hogsback Road and Northern Sierra #42: Ponderosa Way.
■ Trail wraps around the Ishi Wilderness with many hiking access points.
■ Panoramic views of the volcanic region around Antelope Creek.

History

The harsh yet beautiful landscape through which this trail passes was home to the last members of the Yahi, a subgroup of the Yana tribe (see page 304). The Yahi occupied the eastern side of the Sacramento Valley and like the Nomlaki on the western side of the valley, they were losing land to settlers by the mid-1800s.

In the 1860s, territorial conflicts resulted in bloodshed on both sides. The Three Knolls Massacre of 1866 was one attempt by settlers to rid the valley of Indians. Dozens were killed; a few, including a mother and her six-year-old son, escaped. After the last massacre in 1871, the remaining Yahi took shelter in nearby mountains. Like hunted animals, they led a dangerous life on the run. They couldn't even have a fire because it would alert settlers who were determined to kill any survivors.

The Peligreen-Grapevine Jeepway passes north of Kingsley Cove, the scene of one of the last bloody massacres. In 1871, 30 members of the Yahi tribe were killed in a single day. Intermittent Indian sightings occurred over the next few years, though none were substantiated. Both settlers and army troops seemed satisfied they had killed the last of the Yahi.

In August 1911, a frail man was discovered in a slaughterhouse corral in Oroville, quite some distance to the south. After questioning through sign language, it was determined that he was a six-year-old boy who survived the Three Knolls Massacre of 1866. Given the name Ishi, meaning man in the Yahi language, he was called the last wild Indian. He and three members of his family had managed to survive for 40 years in hiding.

Description

Peligreen-Grapevine Jeepway follows sections of two OHV trails—the Peligreen Jeep Trail, which takes its name from Peligreen Place midway along the route, and the Grapevine Jeepway, which follows above Grapevine Canyon. The trail's 6 difficulty rating comes from several steep, loose-surface ascents and descents, which will test

Looking down toward Mill Creek from atop the ridge

The ford through the fast-flowing North Fork Antelope Creek has metal grating for traction

your tires' grip. Fist-size, rubbly volcanic rocks combined with smaller stones provide little traction.

The trail leaves Northern Sierra #42: Ponderosa Way through mixed conifer forest along a graded dirt road that quickly becomes a well-used formed trail. An alternate route to the one described below follows the sign for the Peligreen Jeep Trail at its first point of divergence, 1.4 miles from the start. This route travels down into the gully and climbs back up to rejoin the main trail near Peligreen Place; it is rougher than the main route, which travels around the hillside.

Much of this trail skirts the northern edge of the Ishi Wilderness, providing many wilderness access points for hikers. The Rancheria Trailhead is the first access point. From here, the Rancheria Trail drops swiftly, more than 1,000 feet in 2 miles, to join the Mill Creek Trail. Because it is so steep and strenuous, the Rancheria Trail is for experienced hikers only. The Mill Creek Trail is gentler and follows the creek west to Papes Place and east to other trails within the wilderness. Many swimming holes and fishing spots can be found along Mill Creek, as can small fossil shells.

The Ishi Wilderness in the southern Cascade foothills encompasses 41,000 acres of low-elevation wilderness. It has basalt outcroppings, caves, and pillar lava formations. Most of the ridges in the wilderness run east to west. The vegetation is a mixture. Chaparral covers the lower southern slopes, and white pines and oaks grow in the moister, higher areas. More than 90 percent of the wilderness was burned in the Campbell Fire of 1990; it is still recovering.

The Tehama deer herd, the largest migratory herd in California, winters in this area, much of which is a state wildlife refuge where hunting is prohibited. Other animals in the refuge include wild hogs, mountain lions, black bears, coyotes, and bobcats. The area provides nesting sites for raptors, turkeys, quails, and a number of songbirds. The region is also habitat for a large number of western diamondback rattlesnakes. Ticks and poison oak are also common.

The trail becomes rougher after it passes the site of Peligreen Place and starts to follow the Peligreen Jeep Trail. This section is slow going as it is littered with rough volcanic rocks and boulders. The trail runs along the ridge top and offers views south over Mill Creek, and west over the Sacramento Valley. The low scrub vegetation provides little shade, and it can get blisteringly hot in summer; spring and fall are the ideal times to travel this trail. You are likely to see other travelers in fall because the region is popular with deer hunters. It is very lightly used at other times of year.

A second wilderness access point for hikers is at Black Oak Grove, a large grove of mature black oaks on top of the ridge. The USFS map shows an undeveloped camping area here; there are no facilities, but it is possible to find a pleasant, shady campsite. Other camping areas along the trail often have fabulous views but are very exposed. Past Black Oak Grove, the trail is used less, but still well defined. Several steep loose slopes make traction a challenge. However, a carefully driven stock, high-clearance 4WD with good tires should be able to handle it.

At Wild Horse Corral, the trail turns right and follows the Grapevine Jeepway above Grapevine Canyon. Initially, the trail appears lightly used and narrower than the previous section of the Peligreen Jeep Trail. Moguls and uneven off-camber sections will tilt vehicles sideways and test wheel articulation. Once the trail enters the Tehama State Wildlife Area, the surface improves somewhat and the trail becomes easier. It drops down to join the graded road, which in turn drops down to cross through the North Fork of Antelope Creek. A second USFS camping area is north of the creek. This one has picnic tables, fire rings, a pit toilet, and several shady sites. It is located near Payne Place, another early homestead site where nothing remains. A hiking trail leads out from Payne Place to McClure Point and High Trestle.

The graded road finishes at the intersection with Northern Sierra #43: Hogsback Road. The trail should not be attempted in wet weather.

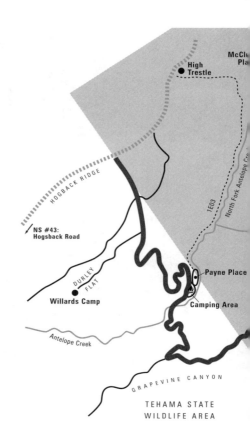

Current Road Information
Lassen National Forest
Almanor Ranger District
PO Box 767
Chester, CA 96020
(530) 258-2141

Map References
BLM   Lake Almanor
USFS   Lassen National Forest
USGS 1:24,000   Panther Spring, Dewitt
        Peak, Inskip Hill
        1:100,000 Lake Almanor
Maptech CD-ROM: Shasta Lake/Redding
Northern California Atlas & Gazetteer, p. 57
California Road & Recreation Atlas, p. 59
       (incomplete)
Other: Off Highway Vehicle Trails of the
       Almanor Ranger District; A Guide
       to the Ishi, Thousand Lakes, &
       Caribou Wilderness

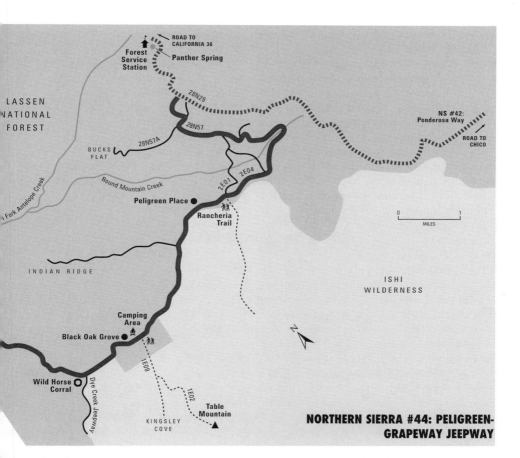

NORTHERN SIERRA #44: PELIGREEN-GRAPEWAY JEEPWAY

Route Directions

▼ 0.0   From Northern Sierra #42: Ponderosa
         Way, 20.2 miles south of California 36
         and 1.3 miles south of Panther Spring
         Forest Service Station, zero trip meter
         and turn southwest on graded dirt road
         28N57, following the sign for Peligreen
         Jeep Trail.
▲ 1.4   Trail ends at T-intersection with
         Northern Sierra #42: Ponderosa Way.
         Turn left for California 36 and Mineral;
         turn right for Chico.
         GPS: N40°14.07'W121°46.50'

▼ 0.1   SO   Track on right is 180P.
▲ 1.3   SO   Track on left is 180P.
▼ 0.5   SO   Track on left.
▲ 0.9   SO   Track on right.
▼ 0.7   BL   Track on right is 28N57A to Bucks
              Flat. Bear left; then track on left.

▲ 0.7   BR   Track on right; then track on left is
              28N57A to Bucks Flat. Follow the sign
              for Panther Spring.
              GPS: N40°13.73' W121°46.80'

▼ 0.9   SO   Track on left.
▲ 0.5   SO   Track on right.
▼ 1.2   SO   Track on right.
▲ 0.2   SO   Track on left.
▼ 1.4   SO   Track on right is Peligreen Jeep Trail,
              which goes 2 miles to the Rancheria
              Trailhead. Camping area on left. Zero
              trip meter.
▲ 0.0   Continue to the west.
              GPS: N40°13.31' W121°46.23'

▼ 0.0   Continue to the east.
▲ 3.1   SO   Track on left is Peligreen Jeep Trail,
              which goes 2 miles to the Rancheria
              Trailhead. Camping area on right. Zero
              trip meter.

▼ 0.4	SO	Track on left.		1.2 ▲	SO	Track on left.
2.7 ▲	SO	Track on right.		▼ 2.1	SO	Track on right.
▼ 1.3	SO	Cross over Round Mountain Creek.		1.0 ▲	SO	Track on left.
		Trail drops in standard and is now des-		▼ 2.3	SO	Track on right.
		ignated OHV Route 2E04.		0.8 ▲	SO	Track on left.
1.8 ▲	SO	Cross over Round Mountain Creek.		▼ 2.4	SO	Track on left.
		Trail improves in standard and is now		0.7 ▲	SO	Track on right.
		designated 28N57.		▼ 2.7	SO	Track on right.
		GPS: N40°12.89′ W121°45.16′		0.4 ▲	SO	Track on left.
				▼ 3.1	TL	Rancheria Trailhead on left provides
▼ 1.9	SO	Track on right.				hiking access to the Ishi Wilderness;

YANA AND THE MYSTERIOUS ISHI

The Yana were a small tribe in Northern California. They lived east of the Sacramento River, with volcanic Lassen Peak, which the tribe called Yana Wahganupa, as a prominent landmark. Together, the four subtribes of the Yana, each of which spoke a slightly different dialect, totaled about 1,500 individuals in the years prior to the gold rush. The small linguistic variations among the groups was further confused by differences in speech between males and females. Each sex spoke a distinct variation of their local dialect. During conversations between sexes, the female dialect was used.

Despite the diminutive size of the Yana people, they were feared as fighters. When salmon were scarce in their rivers, Yana warriors would raid Wintun villages to steal food and to capture women and children as slaves. Generally though, the tribe was able to subsist on resources found within its homeland. Wild raspberries and grapes grew abundantly, and acorns and salmon—staple foods for many Northern California Indians—were easily found in Yana territory.

The gold rush dramatically altered the tribe's way of life. American and European migrants came in droves to seize land the Yana considered theirs. The settlers killed or drove away deer and elk, game that the Indians depended on for survival. Runoff from mining operations polluted rivers, killing salmon and other fish. Livestock brought by the newcomers grazed on plants and acorns, further depleting Yana food supplies. When starving Indians raided mining camps, angry miners responded in force. At times, whole villages were wiped out, every resident either killed or captured.

Because Yana culture was destroyed within just a few decades, little was recorded about their way of life. Almost nothing is known of their religious beliefs. Narrative myths of gods manifested in the form of a rabbit, a squirrel, and a lizard survive today but their significance is not recorded. Some sexual taboos seem to have been observed by the Yana, but their exact nature is unknown. Certainly, a child born out of wedlock was considered socially inferior.

Though the destruction of Yana society as a whole is tragic, the story of its southernmost band, the Yahi, is even more so. Until 1911, the Yahi were thought to be extinct—victims of disease and settlers' aggression. After 45 years of hiding in the wilderness northeast of Oroville, the sole survivor of the band presented himself at a farmhouse. Ishi, as the man became known, spoke no English and knew only traditional Indian ways. He and a small group of Yahi had escaped a murderous raid on their camp during which most of the band had been killed. The survivors camped in the woods, hiding all traces of their existence, and

then track on right is the Peligreen Jeep Trail (OHV Route 2E01) rejoining. Follow sign to Black Oak Grove and zero trip meter.

0.0 ▲ Continue to the south onto 2E04. Rancheria Trailhead on right provides hiking access to the Ishi Wilderness.

GPS: N40°12.53′ W121°46.77′

▼ 0.0 Continue to the west, joining Peligreen Jeep Trail (OHV Route 2E01).

4.5 ▲ TR Peligreen Jeep Trail (OHV Route 2E01) leaves main route to the left at this point. Zero trip meter.

▼ 0.5 SO Site of Peligreen Place.
4.0 ▲ SO Site of Peligreen Place.

GPS: N40°12.58′ W121°47.34′

▼ 1.2 BL Track on right leads onto Indian Ridge.
3.3 ▲ BR Track on left leads onto Indian Ridge.

GPS: N40°12.30′ W121°48.02′

only occasionally coming out of hiding to steal food and supplies from ranches and mining settlements. When he became separated from the last of his companions, Ishi was forced out of hiding by hunger, although he probably expected to be killed when he did. Instead, he became the subject of great public and scientific interest

Known as the "last of the Yahi," Ishi was introduced to the American public in 1911. Ishi was born in about 1860. By this time, the Yahi—a subtribe of the Yana—had already seen their traditional life destroyed by settlers who rushed to their homeland in search of gold. Resistance against the settlers was met with harsh reprisal. The major Yahi village on Mill Creek was raided in 1863 and its residents massacred. Three years later, the surviving Yahi were cornered in a cave and slaughtered; only about a dozen escaped.

The small group survived in the mountains, living off the land, capturing game with the same weapons their ancestors had used for generations. Only occasionally did they raid ranches and mining camps for supplies. In 1908, the group—which now numbered only four—was sighted in Deer Creek Canyon. Ishi lost all his companions as they fled from their white discoverers.

Finally in August 1911, Ishi walked to the settlement of Oroville, where he was taken into custody by the sheriff. His appearance caused great interest among Californian ethnologists. He had no knowledge of modern customs or of the English language, and other Indians were also unable to communicate with him. Alfred Kroeber, an anthropologist in San Francisco, recognized Ishi as the sole survivor of the Yahi, until then thought to be extinct. Kroeber brought him to the anthropological museum of the University of California, Berkeley, where Ishi could be studied.

Ishi related his story to Kroeber, but refused to give his real name. Kroeber decided to call him Ishi, "man" in the Yahi language. Ishi had no desire to return to the wilderness. He slowly learned English and adopted modern clothing and habits. He showed anthropologists a variety of traditional skills, including how to make arrowheads, bows, and nets and how to catch deer and start a fire. All knowledge about Yahi mythology and culture comes from Ishi's recollections.

In 1916, Ishi died of tuberculosis. With him, the Yahi also died. Kroeber's wife, Theodora, later published a biography of Ishi, calling him "the last wild Indian of North America." Most of Ishi's body was cremated according to his wishes, but his heart was sent to the Smithsonian Institution in Washington. Recently, California Indians have requested that it be returned to them for proper burial.

▼ 1.4   SO Pass through fence line.
3.1 ▲   SO Pass through fence line.
▼ 2.1   SO Pass through fence line.
2.4 ▲   SO Pass through fence line.
▼ 3.1   SO Kingsley Cove Trail (1E09) and Table Mountain Trail (1E02) on left provide hiking access to the Ishi Wilderness. Undeveloped USFS camping area at Black Oak Grove on right.
1.4 ▲   SO Kingsley Cove Trail (1E09) and Table Mountain Trail (1E02) on right provide hiking access to the Ishi Wilderness. Undeveloped USFS camping area at Black Oak Grove on left.
        GPS: N40°11.48′ W121°49.49′

▼ 3.5   SO Pass through fence line.
1.0 ▲   SO Pass through fence line.
▼ 3.8   SO Pass through fence line.
0.7 ▲   SO Pass through fence line.
▼ 4.5   TR Wild Horse Corral. Track straight ahead is Dye Creek Jeepway. Zero trip meter and follow the sign for Grapevine Jeepway.
0.0 ▲   Continue to the northeast on Peligreen Jeep Trail.
        GPS: N40°11.42′ W121°50.79′

▼ 0.0   Continue to the northwest.
4.2 ▲   TL T-intersection at Wild Horse Corral. Track on right is Dye Creek Jeepway. Zero trip meter.
▼ 2.8   SO Cattle guard. Entering Tehama State Wildlife Area.
1.4 ▲   SO Cattle guard. Leaving Tehama State Wildlife Area.
        GPS: N40°13.02′ W121°52.47′

▼ 4.2   TR Intersection with graded road. Turn sharp right and zero trip meter.
0.0 ▲   Continue to the southeast.
        GPS: N40°13.35′ W121°53.82′

▼ 0.0   Continue to the east.
6.6 ▲   TL Zero trip meter and turn sharp left onto rough formed trail at unmarked intersection. Start to climb up the ridge.
▼ 2.0   SO Cross through Antelope Creek.
4.6 ▲   SO Cross through Antelope Creek.
        GPS: N40°13.91′ W121°53.08′

▼ 2.3   SO Track on right over cattle guard to undeveloped USFS camping area. Main trail starts to climb.
4.3 ▲   SO Second entrance to camping area on left. End of descent.
▼ 2.5   SO Second entrance to camping area. Track on right loops around the site of Payne Place. Hiking trail 1E03 to McClure Place and High Trestle leaves from the loop.
4.1 ▲   SO Track on left loops around the site of Payne Place. Hiking trail 1E03 to McClure Place and High Trestle leaves from the loop. Track on left to undeveloped USFS camping area.
        GPS: N40°14.07′ W121°52.66′

▼ 4.6   SO End of climb from river. Start to cross Durley Flat.
2.0 ▲   SO Leave Durley Flat and start to descend to river.
▼ 5.3   SO Track on left goes to the site of Willards Camp.
1.3 ▲   SO Track on right goes to the site of Willards Camp.
        GPS: N40°15.07′ W121°52.81′

▼ 5.7   SO Track on right.
0.9 ▲   SO Track on left.
▼ 5.8   SO Track on left and track on right; then cattle guard.
0.8 ▲   SO Cattle guard; then track on right and track on left.
▼ 6.6   Seasonal closure gate; then trail ends at T-intersection with Northern Sierra #43: Hogsback Road. Turn left to travel the trail to Red Bluff; turn right to exit to Northern Sierra #42: Ponderosa Way and California 36.
0.0 ▲   Trail commences on Northern Sierra #43: Hogsback Road, 4.7 miles west of Northern Sierra #42: Ponderosa Way. Zero trip meter and turn south on graded dirt road and pass through seasonal closure gate. Trail initially crosses Durley Flat.
        GPS: N40°16.20′ W121°52.49′

West Prospect Peak Trail

STARTING POINT California 44/89, 8.5 miles northeast of the northern entrance to Lassen Volcanic National Park
FINISHING POINT West Prospect Peak
TOTAL MILEAGE 11.1 miles (one-way)
UNPAVED MILEAGE 11.1 miles
DRIVING TIME 1 hour (one-way)
ELEVATION RANGE 4,800–8,000 feet
USUALLY OPEN May to November
BEST TIME TO TRAVEL May to November
DIFFICULTY RATING 1
SCENIC RATING 9
REMOTENESS RATING +0

Special Attractions
- Views of Lassen Peak and Chaos Crags.
- West Prospect Peak Fire Lookout.

History
The final climb to West Prospect Peak provides an excellent opportunity to observe a volcanic landscape. Between 1914 and 1921, Lassen Peak exploded in a series of eruptions. In 1915, locals witnessed a massive eruption that sent a 7-mile-high cloud of steam and ash into the stratosphere. A national park was established in 1916 to preserve the landscape resulting from this dramatic activity. Lassen Peak was then the most recently active volcano in the contiguous United States, a title it held until Washington's Mount St. Helens erupted in 1980. Varying degrees of recovery can be seen across this explosive landscape of lava beds, cinder cones, and steaming hot springs. Conifers are returning to some areas, and in some regions different kinds of trees have established themselves than were there prior to the eruptions. The cinder cones southeast of West Prospect Peak have seen little re-growth since the eruptions.

Approaching the base of West Prospect Peak

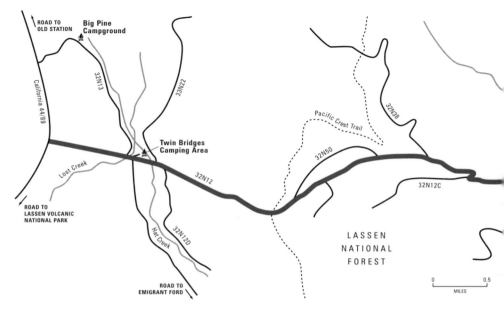

NORTHERN SIERRA #45: WEST PROSPECT PEAK TRAIL

Prospect Peak, a conical and slightly higher peak immediately southeast of West Prospect Peak, was the site of a fire lookout from 1912 to 1935. In 1935, the Civilian Conservation Corps constructed a 10-foot-tall enclosed structure just outside the national park boundary on West Prospect Peak. Today's tower, at an elevation of 8,172 feet, is still in service. The fire spotter can watch over an area of more than 200,000 acres, including Lassen National Forest to the north and Lassen Volcanic National Park to the south.

Description

This graded gravel road travels through Lassen National Forest and climbs to West Prospect Peak Fire Lookout. The trail leaves California 44/89 and travels past the site of Twin Bridges, a stopping point on the Nobles Trail. An undeveloped USFS camping area is at Twin Bridges, and there are some excellent backcountry campsites along Hat Creek on 32N13.

The main trail runs close to the northern boundary of Lassen Volcanic National Park. The park can be reached via the Pacific Crest National Scenic Trail, which crosses the vehicle trail and connects with hiking trails in the park, or via a couple of vehicle trails that stop at the park's boundary.

The trail climbs a shelf road toward the lookout; views over the surrounding area open up the higher you get. The lookout tower is manned during fire season and can be reached by climbing up a short flight of stairs. Visitors are welcome to admire the sweeping 360-degree view between 8:30 A.M. and 5:30 P.M. Mount Sugarloaf is a prominent symmetrical cone to the northwest, with the open area of Old Station at its base. Lassen Peak, Mount Loomis, and the Chaos Crags, among others, stand out to the southwest. The lookout has pointers to the main peaks around its interior walls. Hat Creek Rim is a prominent feature to the north.

Current Road Information

Lassen National Forest
Hat Creek Ranger District
43225 East Highway 299
Fall River Mills, CA 96028
(530) 336-5521

Map References

BLM   Burney
USFS   Lassen National Forest

Fire Lookout

West Prospect Peak

32N20

B O X

C A N Y O N

32N12B

32N12

32N13Y

LASSEN
VOLCANIC
NATIONAL PARK

USGS 1:24,000   West Prospect Peak,
Prospect Peak
1:100,000 Burney
Maptech CD-ROM: Shasta Lake/Redding
Northern California Atlas & Gazetteer, p. 48
California Road & Recreation Atlas, p. 53

Route Directions

▼ 0.0   From California 44/89, 8.5 miles northeast of the junction of California 89 and
California 44 and the northern entrance
to Lassen Volcanic National Park, zero
trip meter and turn east onto graded
dirt road 32N12, following the sign to
West Prospect Lookout.
GPS: N40°37.38′ W121°28.80′

▼ 0.2   SO   Cattle guard.
▼ 0.3   SO   Track on right.
▼ 0.4   SO   Track on right.
▼ 0.7   SO   Track on left is 32N13; then cross over
Lost Creek. Graded road on right goes
to Emigrant Ford; then track on left
goes into Twin Bridges undeveloped
USFS camping area. Nobles Trail on
left and right at this point.

GPS: N40°36.94′ W121°28.12′

▼ 0.9   SO   Cross over Hat Creek on bridge; then
track on left is 33N22. Camping area
at intersection.
▼ 1.0   SO   Track on right is 32N12D.
▼ 1.2   SO   Cattle guard.
▼ 1.6   SO   Track on left.
▼ 1.8   SO   Track on left.
▼ 2.1   SO   Pacific Crest Trail crosses main route;
then track on right.
GPS: N40°35.99′ W121°27.22′

▼ 2.3   SO   Track on left is 32N50.
GPS: N40°35.99′ W121°26.91′

▼ 2.6   SO   Track on right.
▼ 3.1   SO   Track on left is 32N50.
▼ 3.5   SO   Track on left is 32N38. Zero trip meter.
GPS: N40°35.76′ W121°25.51′

▼ 0.0   Continue to the southeast, following
sign to the lookout.
▼ 0.6   TL   Track straight ahead is 32N12C.

West Prospect Peak Fire Lookout, active since 1935

▼ 2.5 SO Track on right is 32N13Y.
   GPS: N40°34.24′ W121°24.10′

▼ 2.7 SO Track on right; then cross over creek.
▼ 3.1 SO Track on left is 32N12B.
▼ 4.0 SO Track on left.
▼ 4.6 SO View on left over a boulder field to Lassen Peak.
▼ 5.2 SO Track on left.
▼ 5.4 BR Track on left on right-hand bend is 32N20.
   GPS: N40°34.89′ W121°23.10′

▼ 6.5 SO Start of shelf road.
▼ 6.8 SO Track on right.
▼ 7.3 SO Track on left.
▼ 7.6   Trail ends at West Prospect Peak Fire Lookout.
   GPS: N40°35.65′ W121°22.71′

NORTHERN SIERRA #46

Hat Creek Rim Trail

STARTING POINT California 44, 2.7 miles east of California 89 and Old Station

FINISHING POINT Doty Road, 1.3 miles east of California 89

TOTAL MILEAGE 18.9 miles, plus 1.6-mile spur to the lookout site

UNPAVED MILEAGE 16.5 miles, plus 1.6-mile spur

DRIVING TIME 3 hours

ELEVATION RANGE 3,300–5,000 feet

USUALLY OPEN April to October

BEST TIME TO TRAVEL Dry weather

DIFFICULTY RATING 1

SCENIC RATING 8

REMOTENESS RATING +0

Special Attractions

■ Subway Cave.
■ Hat Creek Rim scenic overlook at the southern end of the trail.
■ Hang gliding launch pad at the northern end of the trail.
■ University of California Hat Creek Radio Observatory.

History

The name Hat Creek dates back to the mid-1850s. The name may come from the Achomawi word *hatiwiwi*, their name for Hat Creek. Another origin may be that a member of William H. Nobles' emigrant party dropped his hat in the stream.

The route runs close to a cutoff along the Nobles Trail, which ran below present-day California 44. Called the Yreka and Fort Crook Road, it branched due north from the main trail to Lockhart's Ferry via Government Well and was used by stagecoaches traveling between California and Oregon in 1856.

The Hat Creek Rim Fire Lookout, along the upper reaches of the rim, was destroyed in the 1987 Lost Fire. Lightning caused the fire and ultimately burned nearly 23,000 acres. All that remains of the old tower is the steel frame base.

One not-to-be-missed feature of this area is a short distance from the start of the trail. Subway Cave, a lava tube, formed less than 20,000 years ago when molten lava flowed out of a series of north–south fissures in the earth. Surface lava cooled and hardened, but lava below the surface continued to flow, eventually draining away to leave the tube. A marked trail runs through the cave and returns to the parking area aboveground. A reliable flashlight is essential because there is zero visibility inside the cave, and the floor is very rough. The temperature in the cave remains a constant 46 degrees Fahrenheit year-round, so you might want to bring along a jacket. Inside the cave, you can see hardened lava formations, chambers, and burst lava bubbles. Subway Cave is just off California 89, 0.5 miles north of the intersection of California 44 and California 89 at Old Station.

Description

The trail proper leaves California 44, 2.7 miles east of Old Station. The Hat Creek Rim scenic overlook, at the start of the trail, is an interpretive site that provides a panoramic view of the Hat Creek Valley and surrounding volcanic peaks. On a clear day, Mount Shasta is clearly visible to the northwest. Mud flows from the 1915 eruption of Lassen Peak poured into the

Hat Creek drainage. Snowmelt from Lassen Peak, Big Spring, and Rising River feed the stream, and it is regularly stocked with brook, brown, and rainbow trout in summer. Good fishing can be found near the southern end of the trail at Hat Creek Campground, Old Station Day-Use Area, and Cave Campground. The graded road heads north from the scenic overlook, following close to the geological fault of Hat Creek Rim. Nearly a million years ago, a block of the Earth's crust dropped 1,000 feet below the rim (Hat Creek Valley), leaving behind the fault scarp known as Hat Creek Rim.

The easy trail is generally suitable for passenger vehicles. One small loop near the start leaves the main graded road to travel closer to the rim; this section is rated 2 and is more suitable for high-clearance vehicles. If you do not wish to drive the loop, remain on graded road 34N34—the loop rejoins in 0.8 miles.

The trail stays back from the rim most of the way, but a spur leads to the site of the old fire lookout tower, now used for communications equipment and as an alternative launch site for hang gliders. This Back Launch was constructed in 1993 and is considered more difficult than the more popular Front Launch farther north along the trail. Back Launch should only be used by experienced pilots. The Pacific Crest National Scenic Trail runs past this launch site very close to the rim.

The Front Launch for hang gliders and paragliders is marked partway along the descent to Hat Creek Valley. For non-flyers, this is a wonderful viewpoint and picnic area, with the added bonus that you may be lucky enough to see hang gliders launching from the pad. The site has a reliable updraft in summer and is used from spring through to October. Northern Sierra #47: Murken Bench Trail loops off from the main trail and passes beside two landing sites at the base of the rim.

The road then becomes paved and passes the University of California Hat Creek Radio Observatory. Visitors are welcome on weekdays between 9:00 A.M. and 4:00 P.M. The facility houses the University of California at Berkeley's Radio Astronomy Laboratory.

The trail ends at a T-intersection with Doty Road, which you can take either way back to California 89.

Subway Cave, a lava tube

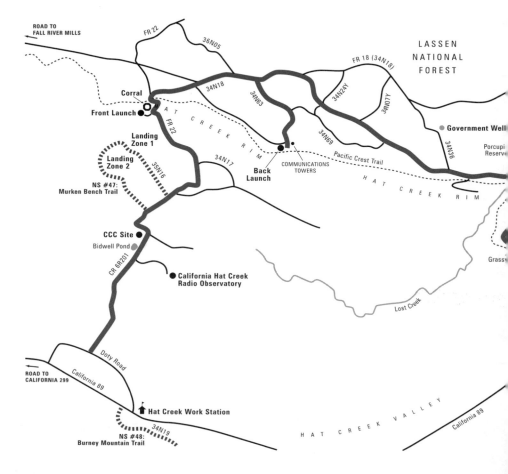

Current Road Information
Lassen National Forest
Hat Creek Ranger District
43225 East Highway 299
Fall River Mills, CA 96028
(530) 336-5521

Map References
BLM   Burney
USFS Lassen National Forest
USGS 1:24,000   Old Station, Murken
        Bench, Burney Mtn. East
        1:100,000 Burney
Maptech CD-ROM: Shasta Lake/Redding
Northern California Atlas & Gazetteer, p. 48
California Road & Recreation Atlas, p. 53

Route Directions

▼ 0.0   From California 44, 2.7 miles east of
         the intersection with California 89 at
         Old Station, zero trip meter and turn
         southwest, following the sign for the
         Hat Creek Rim scenic overlook.
         Immediately turn right onto graded
         road 34N34, following the sign for
         Plum Valley Reservoir. Paved road con-
         tinues ahead for another 0.2 miles to
         the Hat Creek Rim scenic overlook.

3.1 ▲   T-intersection with paved road. To the
         right goes 0.2 miles to the Hat Creek
         Rim scenic overlook. Turn left; then
         trail immediately ends at the T-inter-
         section with California 44. Turn left for
         Susanville; turn right for Old Station
         and California 89.

GPS: N40°41.91′ W121°23.97′

▼ 0.2   SO   Trails West marker for the Nobles Trail on right.

2.9 ▲   SO   Trails West marker for the Nobles Trail on left.

▼ 0.3   SO   Track on left.

2.8 ▲   SO   Track on right.

▼ 0.4   SO   Track on left to Pacific Crest Trailhead.

2.7 ▲   SO   Track on right to Pacific Crest Trailhead.

▼ 0.6   SO   Track on left; then second track on left is 34N34G.

2.5 ▲   SO   Track on right is 34N34G; then second track on right.

▼ 0.8   SO   Track on right is 33N15Y.

2.3 ▲   SO   Track on left is 33N15Y.

▼ 1.6   SO   Track on left is 34N34D.

1.5 ▲   SO   Track on right is 34N34D.

▼ 1.7   SO   Plum Valley Reservoir on right; then

track on right; then second track on right is 34N34E; then cattle guard.

1.4 ▲   SO   Cattle guard; then track on left is 34N34E; then second track on left; then Plum Valley Reservoir on left.
GPS: N40°43.30′ W121°23.78′

▼ 1.9   SO   Track on right.

1.2 ▲   SO   Track on left.

▼ 2.3   SO   Track on left.

0.8 ▲   SO   Track on right.

▼ 3.1   TL   4-way intersection. Graded road on right is 33N57. Graded road straight ahead is 34N34. Zero trip meter.

0.0 ▲   Continue to the southwest on 34N34.
GPS: N40°44.39′ W121°23.81′

▼ 0.0   Continue to the northwest on 34N34C.

3.7 ▲   TR   4-way intersection. Graded road straight ahead is 33N57. Graded road on right and left is 34N34. Zero trip meter.

▼ 0.4   BL   Track on right. Grassy Lake (dry) on right.

3.3 ▲   BR   Track on left. Grassy Lake (dry) on left.

▼ 1.2   SO   Track on left.

2.5 ▲   BL   Track on right.
GPS: N40°45.19′ W121°24.12′

▼ 1.7   BR   Track on left.

2.0 ▲   BL   Track on right.

▼ 1.9   TL   T-intersection with 34N34. Rejoin 34N34.

1.8 ▲   TR   Turn right onto unmarked formed trail 34N34B.
GPS: N40°45.02′ W121°23.46′

▼ 2.7   SO   Graded road on right is 34N09 to Porcupine Reservoir.

1.0 ▲   SO   Graded road on left is 34N09 to Porcupine Reservoir.
GPS: N40°45.48′ W121°22.80′

▼ 2.9   SO   Cross over Lost Creek; then cattle guard; then track on left.

0.8 ▲   SO   Track on right; then cattle guard; then cross over Lost Creek.

▼ 3.7   SO   Track on left drops 0.8 miles to Little Lake. Zero trip meter.

0.0 ▲   Continue to the southeast.
GPS: N40°46.10′ W121°23.53′

▼ 0.0   Continue to the north.

University of California Hat Creek Radio Observatory

4.2 ▲	SO	Track on right drops 0.8 miles to Little Lake. Zero trip meter.
▼ 0.4	SO	Track on right is 34N36 via Government Well.
3.8 ▲	SO	Track on left is 34N36 via Government Well.
▼ 1.5	SO	Track on left is 34N69.
2.7 ▲	SO	Track on right is 34N69.
		GPS: N40°47.39′ W121°23.75′

▼ 2.1	SO	Track on right is 34N07Y.
2.1 ▲	SO	Track on left is 34N07Y.
▼ 2.7	SO	Track on right and track on left are both 34N24Y.
1.5 ▲	SO	Track on left and track on right are both 34N24Y.
		GPS: N40°48.48′ W121°23.79′

▼ 3.3	TL	T-intersection with FR 18 (34N18). Follow sign to Fall River Mills.
0.9 ▲	TR	Turn right onto small graded road 34N34, following sign to Government Well.
		GPS: N40°48.94′ W121°23.48′

▼ 4.2	SO	Track on left is 34N63, spur to the old Hat Creek Rim Fire Lookout (now communications towers). Zero trip meter.

0.0 ▲		Continue to the southeast.
		GPS: N40°49.52′ W121°24.01′

Spur to the old Hat Creek Rim Fire Lookout

▼ 0.0		Proceed south on 34N63.
▼ 0.8	BR	Track on left is 34N69.
▼ 1.5	SO	Track on right.
▼ 1.6		Spur ends at communications towers (site of the old fire lookout) on the edge of Hat Creek Rim. Pacific Crest Trail runs along the rim, with the Back Launch a few steps along it to the north.
		GPS: N40°48.53′ W121°24.83′

Continuation of Main Trail

▼ 0.0		Continue to the northwest.
2.2 ▲	SO	Track on right is 34N63, spur to the old Hat Creek Rim Fire Lookout (now communications towers). Zero trip meter.
		GPS: N40°49.52′ W121°24.01′

▼ 0.2	SO	Track on left goes to Murken Bench Plantation; then cattle guard; then second track on left.

2.0 ▲	SO	Track on right; then cattle guard; then track on right goes to Murken Bench Plantation.
▼ 0.3	SO	Track on right is 36N05.
1.9 ▲	SO	Track on left is 36N05.
▼ 0.8	SO	Track on left.
1.4 ▲	SO	Track on right.
▼ 0.9	BL	Graded road on right goes to Sixmile Hill and Fall River Mills. Bear left on 34N18, following sign for California 89.
1.3 ▲	SO	Graded road on left goes to Sixmile Hill and Fall River Mills. Remain on 34N18.
		GPS: N40°50.17′ W121°24.60′

▼ 1.8	BL	Graded road on right goes to Bald Mountain Reservoir. Bear left, joining FR 22; then track on right.
0.4 ▲	BR	Track on left; then graded road on left goes to Bald Mountain Reservoir. Bear right onto 34N18, following sign to Bainbridge Reservoir.
		GPS: N40°50.68′ W121°25.35′

▼ 1.9	SO	Pacific Crest Trail crosses.
0.3 ▲	SO	Pacific Crest Trail crosses.
▼ 2.0	SO	Corral on right; then cattle guard. Start of shelf road descending from the rim.
0.2 ▲	SO	End of shelf road. Cattle guard; then corral on left.
▼ 2.2	SO	Track on right goes 0.1 miles to Front Launch and viewpoint. Zero trip meter.
0.0 ▲		Continue to the northeast.
		GPS: N40°50.52′ W121°25.55′

▼ 0.0		Continue to the southeast.
2.2 ▲	SO	Track on left goes 0.1 miles to Front Launch and viewpoint. Zero trip meter.
▼ 1.3	SO	Track on left is 34N17.
0.9 ▲	SO	Track on right is 34N17.
▼ 2.1	SO	Track on left.
0.1 ▲	SO	Track on right.
▼ 2.2	SO	Track on right over cattle guard is the start of Northern Sierra #47: Murken Bench Trail (35N16), also marked LZ-1 (Landing Zone 1). Zero trip meter.
0.0 ▲		Continue to the east.
		GPS: N40°49.66′ W121°26.80′

▼ 0.0		Continue to the west.
3.5 ▲	SO	Track on left over cattle guard is the end of Northern Sierra #47: Murken Bench Trail (35N16), also marked LZ-1 (Landing Zone 1). Zero trip meter.
▼ 0.4	SO	Track on right over cattle guard is the end of Northern Sierra #47: Murken Bench Trail, also marked LZ-2 (Landing Zone 2).
3.1 ▲	SO	Track on left over cattle guard is Northern Sierra #47: Murken Bench Trail, also marked LZ-2 (Landing Zone 2).
▼ 0.8	SO	Exposed basalt pillars on left.
2.7 ▲	SO	Exposed basalt pillars on right.
		GPS: N40°49.85′ W121°27.58′

▼ 1.1	TR	Road ahead into private property. Turn right onto paved road. Remain on paved CR 6R201 for the next 2.4 miles.
2.4 ▲	TL	T-intersection. Track on right goes into private property. Turn left onto FR 22 following the sign for Bainbridge Reservoir and hang glider launch. Road is now graded dirt.
		GPS: N40°49.61′ W121°27.58′

▼ 1.4	SO	Parking area on right at site of old Civilian Conservation Corps camp.
2.1 ▲	SO	Parking area on left at site of old Civilian Conservation Corps camp.
		GPS: N40°49.62′ W121°27.80′

▼ 1.5	SO	Bidwell Pond on right was put in by the Bidwell Ranch to provide water seepage to the valley.
2.0 ▲	SO	Bidwell Pond on left was put in by the Bidwell Ranch to provide water seepage to the valley.
▼ 1.7	SO	University of California Hat Creek Radio Observatory on left.
1.8 ▲	SO	University of California Hat Creek Radio Observatory on right.
▼ 3.5		Trail ends at T-intersection with Doty Road. Turn either right or left to exit to California 89.
0.0 ▲		Trail commences on Doty Road (6R200), 1.3 miles east of California 89. Zero trip meter and turn east on paved Bidwell Road, following sign to the Hat Creek Radio Observatory.
		GPS: N40°49.41′ W121°30.17′

Murken Bench Trail

STARTING POINT Northern Sierra #46: Hat
Creek Rim Trail, 3.5 miles from the
northern end

FINISHING POINT Northern Sierra #46: Hat
Creek Rim Trail, 3.1 miles from the
northern end

TOTAL MILEAGE 3 miles

UNPAVED MILEAGE 3 miles

DRIVING TIME 30 minutes

ELEVATION RANGE 3,500–3,600 feet

USUALLY OPEN Year-round

BEST TIME TO TRAVEL Dry weather

DIFFICULTY RATING 2

SCENIC RATING 8

REMOTENESS RATING +0

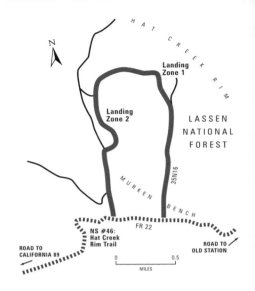

Special Attractions

■ Views along the face of Hat Creek Rim.

■ Chance to see hang gliders and paragliders
soaring above the rim.

■ Backcountry campsites in the open forest
below Hat Creek Rim.

History

The Atsugewi occupied the Murken Bench
and Hat Creek region prior to the arrival of explorers and settlers. They lived in nearby villages at Burney and Cassel, and along Hat
Creek in winter and moved to higher ground
around Lassen Peak in summer. Hat Creek
had salmon, pike, and trout; deer were abundant; and there were berries, seeds, and bas-
ketry materials. Atsugewi shamans visited the
nearby high mountains in search of spiritual
guidance.

John Work and a band of trappers crossed
Hat Creek just west of Murken Bench on two
occasions in the 1830s. The first was in November 1832 en route to the Sacramento Valley
from the British outpost at Fort Nez Perce in
what was then called Oregon Country. The second was on the return trip in August 1833. A
substantial number of the trappers became ill
while traveling in the Sacramento and San
Joaquin Valleys. Southbound trappers may have

unknowingly started an epidemic, which killed
thousands of Indians in the Sacramento Valley.
Those still alive were too weak to dispose of the
dead and a foul stench permeated the villages.
These Native Americans had no resistance to
the introduced disease thought to be malaria.
The Atsugewi people, however, fared better
than their neighbors. They continue to live in
the Hat Creek Valley.

Description

This short loop starts and finishes on Northern Sierra #46: Hat Creek Rim Trail and provides excellent views of the escarpment from
below. It is a formed trail, well used by hang
gliders and paragliders who land their crafts
at one of the two landing sites along the loop.
The launch site can be spotted on the rim by
looking for the wind cones.

The trail winds its way through pines, junipers, and open grassland. In wet weather,
the packed dirt trail is very muddy and may
be impassable. The first landing site is a short
distance off the main trail to the right. This is
the smaller of the two sites and is recommended for experienced pilots only. The second, more popular landing zone is at the apex
of the loop along an open grassland area on

Ponderosas at the foot of Hat Creek Rim

Landing Zone 2 at the foot of Hat Creek Rim

Murken Bench. Note that the northernmost part of this area is unmarked private property. If camping, keep to the trees at the southern end of the landing zone, away from the open area. This area offers excellent backcountry camping with views of Hat Creek Rim. Late afternoon and sunset are good times to see hang gliders.

Current Road Information
Lassen National Forest
Hat Creek Ranger District
43225 East Highway 299
Fall River Mills, CA 96028
(530) 336-5521

Map References
BLM   Burney
USFS Lassen National Forest
USGS 1:24,000 Murken Bench
        1:100,000 Burney
Maptech CD-ROM: Shasta Lake/Redding
Northern California Atlas & Gazetteer, p. 48
California Road & Recreation Atlas, p. 53

Route Directions

▼ 0.0   From Northern Sierra #46: Hat Creek Rim Trail, 3.5 miles from the northern

end, zero trip meter and turn north over cattle guard on 35N16, also marked LZ-1 (Landing Zone 1).

1.9 ▲   Trail ends at T-intersection with Northern Sierra #46: Hat Creek Rim Trail. Turn right for California 89; turn left to travel this trail to Old Station.
GPS: N40°49.66' W121°26.80'

▼ 0.9   SO Track on right to Landing Zone 1.
1.0 ▲   SO Track on left to Landing Zone 1.
             GPS: N40°50.36' W121°26.37'

▼ 1.6   SO Track on right.
0.3 ▲   SO Track on left.
▼ 1.9   SO Well-used, unmarked track on right. Zero trip meter.
0.0 ▲   Continue to the north toward the rim.
             GPS: N40°50.69' W121°26.97'

▼ 0.0   Continue to the south toward the hang gliding landing site.
1.1 ▲   BR Well-used, unmarked track on left. Zero trip meter.
▼ 0.3   SO Hang gliding landing site on left in open area of Murken Bench.
0.8 ▲   SO Hang gliding landing site on right in open area of Murken Bench.
             GPS: N40°50.43' W121°26.95'

▼ 0.5	SO	Track on right.
0.6 ▲	SO	Track on left.
▼ 0.6	SO	Track on right.
0.5 ▲	SO	Track on left.
▼ 0.9	SO	Track on right.
0.2 ▲	SO	Track on left.
▼ 1.1		Trail ends at T-intersection with Northern Sierra #46: Hat Creek Rim Trail. Turn right to return to California 89; turn left to travel the trail to Old Station.
0.0 ▲		Trail commences on Northern Sierra #46: Hat Creek Rim Trail, 3.1 miles from the northern end on California 89. Zero trip meter and turn north over cattle guard on formed dirt trail. There is a sign for LZ-2 (Landing Zone 2) on the gatepost.

GPS: N40°49.78′ W121°27.21′

NORTHERN SIERRA #48

Burney Mountain Trail

STARTING POINT California 89, 0.3 miles north of Hat Creek USFS Work Center
FINISHING POINT California 299, 0.9 miles west of Burney
TOTAL MILEAGE 22.2 miles, plus 2.5-mile spur to Cypress Trailhead and 8.5-mile spur to Burney Mountain Fire Lookout
UNPAVED MILEAGE 21.9 miles, plus spurs
DRIVING TIME 4 hours
ELEVATION RANGE 3,200–7,700 feet
USUALLY OPEN May to November
BEST TIME TO TRAVEL Dry weather
DIFFICULTY RATING 2
SCENIC RATING 9
REMOTENESS RATING +0

Special Attractions

- Panoramic views from Burney Mountain Fire Lookout.
- Upper Burney Creek Baker Cypress Grove.
- Hiking access to the Thousand Lakes Wilderness.

History

The last half of Burney Mountain Trail travels a section of the Tamarack Road, established in 1874. David B. "Kentuck" Branstetter pushed the trail through to connect the upper reaches of the Sacramento Valley with Burney. In time, the trail became a popular wagon route because it was not a toll road. The route left Redding via the Millville Plains and climbed northeast along Old Cow Creek to an overnight camp at Whitmore, a place once used as summer grazing pasture. In the 1890s, James Burton built a store at Whitmore, halfway between Redding and Burney, and offered accommodations at his nearby two-story house. By the early 1900s, a hotel and post office operated by the Sheridans were catching both passing and local trade, and an 80-foot-deep, hand-dug well provided a reliable supply of cool water.

The Tamarack Grade northeast of Whitmore was a long twisting climb and one of the worst sections of the trail. Quite often, drivers would hitch teams together to pull wagons up the steep grade. Going down the hill could be dangerous as well. Too much momentum and a teamster could lose his load and his life. Teamsters sometimes dragged a log behind their wagons to help control their downhill speed. On the far side of the Tamarack Grade, the trail was somewhat easier because it made a gentle descent all the way to Burney.

Burney Mountain (7,863 feet) can be seen clearly to the east as the trail descends toward Haynes Flat. The Burney Mountain Fire Lookout was built in 1934 and the present steel cabin was constructed in 1965.

Description

Burney Mountain rises west of the Hat Creek Valley, opposite the Hat Creek Rim. Like all the peaks in the region, it is a cinder cone. Burney Mountain, and other volcanic peaks in the vicinity, marks the southern extent of the Cascade Range.

The trail begins along a well-marked, graded forest road, heading west from California 89. It travels through Lassen National

View of Mount Shasta and the town of Burney from the lookout

Forest and sections of privately owned forest managed for timber harvesting. If you plan to camp along the trail, make sure that you are in the national forest.

The first spur leads to the Cypress Trailhead, a hiking trail into the Thousand Lakes Wilderness. The wilderness has many small lakes and volcanic and glacial features traversed by 22 miles of backcountry trails. The best time to hike here is from mid-June to mid-October. High peaks include Crater Peak (8,677 feet), Magee Peak (8,550), and Fredonyer Peak (8,054 feet).

The second spur winds up a long shelf road to the fire lookout on top of Burney Mountain. The shelf road is generally wide enough for two vehicles to pass each other, but it travels above a dizzyingly sheer drop of several hundred feet, so use care when passing. The trail crosses several boulder-strewn slopes before reaching the lookout tower, which is normally manned from late spring until October. Visitors are welcome to climb to the tower with permission from the lookout on duty. The climb is well worth it.

Mount Shasta dominates the skyline, rising to an elevation of 14,162 feet to the north. The town of Burney can be seen below in the valley. Lassen Peak (10,457 feet) is to the south and the Hat Creek Valley and Hat Creek Rim can be seen to the east. The gate below the tower is locked daily at 6 P.M. when the tower is manned. In addition, the trail is closed after hunting season. Hang gliders sometimes launch from Burney Mountain, but the winds are erratic, and the site is not as popular as the nearby Hat Creek Rim sites.

Another interesting feature along the trail is the grove of rare Baker cypresses. The trees grow up to 70 feet tall and are only found in 11 isolated groves in Northern California and southern Oregon. They grow on volcanic and serpentine soils at elevations between 3,500 and 7,000 feet. These trees can be recognized by their gray-green needles and small cones about an inch in diameter.

The trail ends on California 299 on the outskirts of Burney.

Current Road Information
Lassen National Forest
Hat Creek Ranger District
43225 East Highway 299
Fall River Mills, CA 96028
(530) 336-5521

Map References
BLM   Burney
USFS Lassen National Forest
USGS 1:24,000   Burney Mtn. East,
      Thousand Lakes Valley, Burney
      Mtn. West
      1:100,000 Burney
Maptech CD-ROM: Shasta Lake/Redding
Northern California Atlas & Gazetteer,
      pp. 47, 48
California Road & Recreation Atlas, p. 53
Other: Modoc Country USFS/BLM Map
      (incomplete); A Guide to the Ishi,
      Thousand Lakes, & Caribou
      Wilderness (incomplete)

Route Directions

▼ 0.0   From California 89, 0.3 miles north of Hat Creek USFS Work Station at Hat Creek, zero trip meter and turn west on graded dirt FR 26 (34N19), following the sign for Burney Springs and Burney Mountain Lookout.

4.8 ▲   Trail finishes at T-intersection with California 89 at Hat Creek USFS Work Station. Turn left for California 299; turn right for Old Station.
GPS: N40°48.57′ W121°30.77′

▼ 0.2   SO   Track on right; then second track on right is 34N19D.

4.6 ▲   SO   Track on left is 34N19D; then second track on left.

▼ 0.5   SO   Track on left is 34N44 for official vehicles only.

4.3 ▲   SO   Track on right is 34N44 for official vehicles only.

▼ 1.1   SO   Track on right.
3.7 ▲   SO   Track on left.
▼ 1.5   SO   Track on right.
3.3 ▲   SO   Track on left.

▼ 1.7   SO   Track on left and track on right.
3.1 ▲   SO   Track on left and track on right.
▼ 1.9   SO   Track on right.
2.9 ▲   SO   Track on left.
▼ 2.3   SO   Track on right.
2.5 ▲   SO   Track on left.
▼ 2.8   SO   Track on left; then track on right.
2.0 ▲   SO   Track on left; then track on right.

▼ 3.4   TR   Track on right is 34N19G; then 4-way intersection. Track straight ahead is 34N78A. Graded road on left goes to Tamarack Trailhead. Remain on FR 26, following the sign to Burney Spring; then track on left.

1.4 ▲   TL   Track on right; then 4-way intersection. Track on right is 34N78A. Graded road continues straight ahead to Tamarack Trailhead. Remain on FR 26, following the sign to California 89. Immediately track on left is 34N19G.
GPS: N40°46.75′ W121°32.16′

▼ 3.7   SO   Track on left.
1.1 ▲   SO   Track on right.
▼ 3.9   SO   Track on right.
0.9 ▲   SO   Track on left.
▼ 4.0   SO   Track on left.
0.8 ▲   SO   Track on right.
▼ 4.1   SO   Track on left.
0.7 ▲   SO   Track on right.
▼ 4.2   SO   Track on left.
0.6 ▲   SO   Track on right.
▼ 4.6   SO   Two tracks on left.
0.2 ▲   SO   Two tracks on right.

▼ 4.8   TL   4-way intersection. Track straight ahead is 35N35. Track on right is 34N77, which goes 1 mile to seasonal Cornaz Lake. Zero trip meter and follow sign to Burney Mountain Lookout.

0.0 ▲   Continue to the southeast on FR 26.
GPS: N40°47.55′ W121°33.38′

▼ 0.0   Continue to the west on FR 26.

2.8 ▲   TR   4-way intersection. Track on left is 35N35. Track straight ahead is 34N77, which goes 1 mile to the seasonal Cornaz Lake. Zero trip meter and follow the sign to California 89.

▼ 0.6   SO   Track on left; then track on right is 34N19A; then track on left.

2.2 ▲	SO	Track on right; then track on left is 34N19A; then track on right.
▼ 0.8	BR	Track on left.
2.0 ▲	SO	Track on right.

GPS: N40°47.16' W121°34.08'

▼ 1.4	SO	Track on left.
1.4 ▲	SO	Track on right.
▼ 1.6	SO	Track on left.
1.2 ▲	SO	Track on right.
▼ 1.7	SO	Track on left.
1.1 ▲	SO	Track on right.
▼ 1.8	SO	Track on right.
1.0 ▲	SO	Track on left.
▼ 2.2	SO	Track on left.
0.6 ▲	SO	Track on right.
▼ 2.8	TR	T-intersection. To the left is 34N69, spur to Cypress Trailhead. Zero trip meter and follow the sign to Burney Mountain Lookout.
0.0 ▲		Continue to the east on FR 26.

GPS: N40°46.24' W121°35.88'

Spur to Cypress Trailhead

▼ 0.0		Proceed southeast on 34N69, following the sign to Cypress Trailhead.
▼ 0.2	SO	Track on left.
▼ 1.2	SO	Track on left.
▼ 1.7	SO	Track on right.
▼ 2.0	SO	Track on left.
▼ 2.2	SO	Track on right.
▼ 2.3	SO	Track on right.
▼ 2.5		Spur ends at the Cypress Trailhead parking area. Hiking trail 3E03 goes up Eiler Gulch to Lake Eiler in the Thousand Lakes Wilderness.

GPS: N40°44.30' W121°36.41'

Continuation of Main Trail

▼ 0.0		Continue to the northwest on FR 26.
2.9 ▲	TL	Graded road straight ahead is 34N69, spur to Cypress Trailhead. Zero trip meter and follow the sign to California 89.

GPS: N40°46.24' W121°35.88'

▼ 0.1	SO	Track on right is 34N79.
2.8 ▲	SO	Track on left is 34N79.
▼ 0.6	SO	Track on left and track on right.

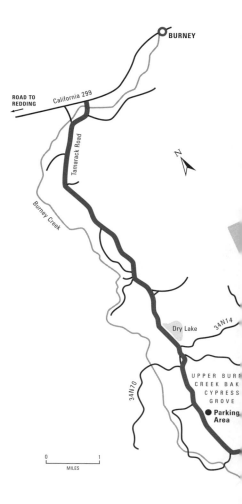

2.3 ▲	SO	Track on left and track on right.
▼ 1.1	SO	Track on right.
1.8 ▲	SO	Track on left.
▼ 1.5	SO	Burney Spring. Small track on left; then well-used track on left.
1.4 ▲	SO	Burney Spring. Well-used track on right; then small track on right.

GPS: N40°46.85' W121°37.28'

▼ 1.9	SO	Cattle guard.
1.0 ▲	SO	Cattle guard.
▼ 2.1	SO	Track on left.
0.8 ▲	SO	Track on right.
▼ 2.3	SO	Graded road on left is 34N22.
0.6 ▲	SO	Graded road on right is 34N22.

GPS: N40°46.79' W121°38.02'

NORTHERN SIERRA #48: BURNEY MOUNTAIN TRAIL

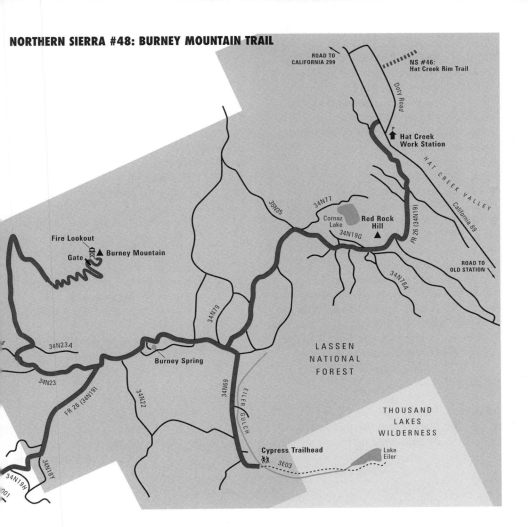

▼ 2.9 BL Graded road on right is 34N23, spur to Burney Mountain Fire Lookout. Zero trip meter and follow the sign to California 44.

0.0 ▲ Continue to the east on FR 26.

GPS: N40°46.82' W121°38.53'

Spur to Burney Mountain Fire Lookout

▼ 0.0 Proceed west on 34N23, following the sign to Burney Mountain Lookout.

▼ 0.5 SO Track on right.
▼ 1.0 SO Track on left.
▼ 1.2 SO Track on left.
▼ 1.7 TR Track straight ahead is 34N14. Zero trip meter and follow the sign to

Burney Mountain Lookout.

GPS: N40°47.49' W121°40.06'

▼ 0.0 Continue to the northwest, remaining on 34N23.

▼ 0.4 BL Track on right is 34N23A; then pass through seasonal closure gate.

▼ 2.0 SO Start of shelf road.
▼ 4.5 SO Game tank on right.
▼ 6.2 SO Gate. Closed at 6 p.m.

GPS: N40°48.48' W121°37.77'

▼ 6.8 Spur ends at Burney Mountain Fire Lookout (7,863 feet).

GPS: N40°48.42' W121°37.61'

Continuation of Main Trail

▼ 0.0   Continue to the southwest on FR 26.

3.3 ▲   BR   Graded road on left is 34N23, spur to Burney Mountain Fire Lookout. Zero trip meter and follow the sign to Cypress Trailhead.

         GPS: N40°46.82′ W121°38.53′

▼ 0.4   SO   Track on right.
2.9 ▲   SO   Track on left.
▼ 0.5   SO   Track on left.
2.8 ▲   SO   Track on right.
▼ 1.9   SO   Track on right.
1.4 ▲   SO   Track on left.
▼ 2.0   BR   Track on left is 34N18Y.
1.3 ▲   SO   Track on right is 34N18Y.

         GPS: N40°45.89′ W121°40.46′

▼ 2.2   SO   Leaving Lassen National Forest and entering Sierra Pacific Industries forest. No fires or camping past this point.
1.1 ▲   SO   Entering Lassen National Forest.
▼ 2.9   SO   Track on left is 34N19H.
0.4 ▲   SO   Track on right is 34N19H.
▼ 3.0   SO   Track on left.
0.3 ▲   SO   Track on right.
▼ 3.3   TR   T-intersection with graded road. Zero trip meter and follow the sign to Burney.
0.0 ▲   Continue to the northeast on FR 26 (34N19).

         GPS: N40°45.84′ W121°41.79′

Burney Mountain Fire Lookout

▼ 0.0   Continue to the northwest on CR 4M001.

8.4 ▲   TL   CR 4M001 continues straight ahead. Zero trip meter and follow the sign to Burney Mountain Lookout.

▼ 0.5   SO   Track on left.
7.9 ▲   SO   Track on right.
▼ 0.8   SO   Track on right.
7.6 ▲   SO   Track on left.
▼ 1.2   SO   Track on left.
7.2 ▲   SO   Track on right.
▼ 1.4   SO   Upper Burney Creek Baker Cypress Grove parking area on right, with a trail around a grove of rare Baker cypresses.
7.0 ▲   SO   Upper Burney Creek Baker Cypress Grove parking area on left, with a trail around a grove of rare Baker cypresses.

         GPS: N40°46.95′ 121°42.35′

▼ 1.7   SO   Track on left.
6.7 ▲   SO   Track on right.
▼ 1.9   SO   Track on left.
6.5 ▲   SO   Track on right.
▼ 2.1   SO   Track on left; then track on right.
6.3 ▲   SO   Track on left; then track on right.
▼ 2.4   SO   Track on left is 34N70; then track on left to corral.
6.0 ▲   SO   Track on right to corral; then track on right is 34N70.

         GPS: N40°47.82′ W121°42.30′

▼ 2.7   SO   Track on right; then track on left.
5.7 ▲   BR   Track on right; then track on left.
▼ 2.9   BL   Track on right.
5.5 ▲   SO   Track on left.
▼ 3.0   SO   Track on right is 34N14.
5.4 ▲   BR   Track on left is 34N14.

         GPS: N40°48.19′ W121°42.23′

▼ 3.4   SO   Track on left; then Dry Lake on right.
5.0 ▲   SO   Dry Lake on left; then track on right.
▼ 3.6   SO   Track on right.
4.8 ▲   SO   Track on left.
▼ 4.0   SO   Track on right.
4.4 ▲   SO   Track on left.
▼ 4.1   SO   Track on right.
4.3 ▲   SO   Track on left.

▼ 4.5   SO   Three tracks on left.
3.9 ▲   SO   Three tracks on right.
      GPS: N40°49.48′ W121°42.46′

▼ 4.9   SO   Track on right.
3.5 ▲   SO   Track on left.
▼ 5.3   SO   Track on left.
3.1 ▲   SO   Track on right.
▼ 5.4   SO   Track on right.
3.0 ▲   SO   Track on left.
▼ 5.5   SO   Track on right.
2.9 ▲   SO   Track on left.
▼ 5.7   SO   Track on left.
2.7 ▲   SO   Track on right.
▼ 6.4   SO   Track on left and track on right.
2.0 ▲   SO   Track on left and track on right.
▼ 6.7   SO   Track on left under power line.
1.7 ▲   SO   Track on right under power line.
▼ 6.8   SO   Track on right.
1.6 ▲   SO   Track on left.
▼ 7.2   SO   Track on left.
1.2 ▲   SO   Track on right.
▼ 7.3   SO   Track on left.
1.1 ▲   SO   Track on right.
▼ 7.5   SO   Track on right.
0.9 ▲   SO   Track on left.
▼ 7.8   BR   Graded road continues straight ahead. Bear right onto graded road.
0.6 ▲   SO   Graded road joins on right.
      GPS: N40°52.12′ W121°42.31′

▼ 8.0   SO   Track on right.
0.4 ▲   SO   Track on left.
▼ 8.1   SO   Track on right. Road is now paved. Remain on paved road until the end of the trail.
0.3 ▲   SO   Track on left. Road turns to graded dirt.
▼ 8.3   SO   Cross over Burney Creek on bridge.
0.1 ▲   SO   Cross over Burney Creek on bridge.
▼ 8.4   Trail ends at T-intersection with California 299. Turn left for Redding; turn right for Burney.
0.0 ▲   Trail commences on California 299, 0.9 miles west of Burney. Zero trip meter and turn south on paved Tamarack Road. Note that there is also a Tamarack Avenue on the edge of town, which is a different road.
      GPS: N40°52.38′ W121°41.79′

Popcorn Cave Trail

STARTING POINT   Cassel Fall River Road (CR 7R02), 3.7 miles south of Fall River Mills
FINISHING POINT   Little Valley Road (CR 404), 2.1 miles south of Pittville
TOTAL MILEAGE 11.1 miles
UNPAVED MILEAGE 9.1 miles
DRIVING TIME 1 hour
ELEVATION RANGE 3,300–4,000 feet
USUALLY OPEN April to November
BEST TIME TO TRAVEL April to November
DIFFICULTY RATING 1
SCENIC RATING 8
REMOTENESS RATING +0

Special Attractions

■ Easy trail through a volcanic region.
■ Volcanic landscape around Popcorn Cave and Big Cave.

Popcorn Cave Trail

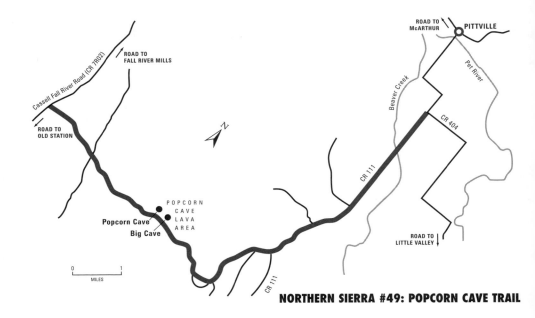

NORTHERN SIERRA #49: POPCORN CAVE TRAIL

History

Pittville, near the eastern end of this trail was established in 1873. The settlement's primary activity was agriculture. A post office was added in 1878, and the town was officially named Pittville (at a time when the river was still spelled Pitt). In 1871, William Henry Winter established a flourmill at the site that became Fall River Mills. A hamlet grew around the mill, and by 1886, the population was about 300. Businesses included two hotels, a blacksmith shop, three stores, two saloons, Winter's flourmill, and a door and sash factory.

The Lockhart Ferry was established at the junction of the Pit and Fall Rivers in 1856 and later relocated below the Fall River Falls, named when John C. Frémont passed through the vicinity in the 1840s.

Description

This graded cinder loop starts and finishes just off California 299 and travels through an arid volcanic region that is part of the Modoc Plateau. The trail passes stands of ponderosa pines, oaks, and manzanitas. It is a short, pleasant drive suitable for passenger vehicles in dry weather.

Midway around the loop, a short spur leads to a parking area alongside a volcanic boulder field. The large rocks are the site of Popcorn Cave and Big Cave. Although very hard to spot, it is fun to scramble over the rough boulders and explore the depressions and ridges of hardened lava.

The trail continues north of Bald Mountain to join CR 111, which wraps around to the north, joining CR 404 south of the small settlement of Pittville.

Current Road Information

Bureau of Land Management
Redding Field Office
355 Hemsted Drive
Redding, CA 96002
(530) 224-2100

Map References

BLM   Burney, McArthur
USFS   Lassen National Forest
USGS 1:24,000 Hogback Ridge, Coble
          Mtn., Pittville
          1:100,000 Burney, McArthur
Maptech CD-ROM: Shasta Lake/Redding;
          Shasta-Trinity/Modoc
Northern California Atlas & Gazetteer,
          pp. 38, 48
California Road & Recreation Atlas, p. 53
Other: Modoc Country USFS/BLM Map

Route Directions

▼ 0.0　　From California 299 in Fall River Mills, proceed south on CR 7R02, marked Main Street, and cross over the Pit River. Continue 3.7 miles south, remaining on Cassel Fall River Road. Zero trip meter and turn east on unmarked graded dirt road and cross over cattle guard. The trail is 0.1 miles south of Chaffey Court.

3.6 ▲　　Trail ends on Cassel Fall River Road (CR 7R02). Turn right for Fall River Mills; turn left for Old Station.
　　　　　GPS: N40°57.38′ W121°26.31′

▼ 0.2　SO　Track on right.
3.4 ▲　SO　Track on left.

▼ 0.3　SO　Track on left.
3.3 ▲　SO　Track on right.
▼ 0.5　SO　Track on left.
3.1 ▲　SO　Track on right.
▼ 0.6　SO　Track on right; then cattle guard; then track on left.
3.0 ▲　SO　Track on right; then cattle guard; then track on left.
▼ 0.9　SO　Track on left.
2.7 ▲　SO　Track on right.
▼ 1.1　SO　Track on right.
2.5 ▲　SO　Track on left.
▼ 1.4　SO　Track on left and track on right.
2.2 ▲　SO　Track on left and track on right.
▼ 2.6　SO　Cattle guard.
1.0 ▲　SO　Cattle guard.
　　　　GPS: N40°56.89′ W121°23.55′

Ponderosas, oaks, and rabbitbrush along the trail

▼ 3.6 SO Unmarked cinder track on left goes 0.3 miles to Popcorn Cave. Zero trip meter.

0.0 ▲ Continue to the west.

GPS: N40°56.87' W121°22.45'

▼ 0.0 Continue to the east.

3.1 ▲ SO Unmarked cinder track on right goes 0.3 miles to Popcorn Cave. Zero trip meter.

▼ 1.3 BL Track on right.

1.8 ▲ SO Track on left.

▼ 1.4 SO Cinder pit on right.

1.7 ▲ SO Cinder pit on left.

▼ 1.6 SO Graded road on right.

1.5 ▲ BR Graded road on left.

GPS: N40°56.53' W121°20.81'

▼ 1.7 SO Track on right.

1.4 ▲ SO Track on left.

▼ 1.8 SO Track on right.

1.3 ▲ SO Track on left.

▼ 1.9 SO Track on left.

1.2 ▲ SO Track on right.

▼ 2.1 SO Cattle guard.

1.0 ▲ SO Cattle guard.

▼ 2.3 SO Track on right.

0.8 ▲ SO Track on left.

▼ 2.8 SO Track on right.

0.3 ▲ SO Track on left.

▼ 3.0 SO Track on left.

0.1 ▲ SO Track on right.

▼ 3.1 TL Cattle guard; then T-intersection with CR 111. Zero trip meter.

0.1 ▲ Continue to the southwest.

GPS: N40°57.65' W121°20.07'

▼ 0.0 Continue to the northwest.

4.4 ▲ TR CR 111 continues straight ahead. Zero trip meter and turn right on unmarked graded road and cross cattle guard.

▼ 1.1 SO Track on left.

3.3 ▲ SO Track on right.

▼ 1.9 SO Track on left; then cattle guard.

2.5 ▲ SO Cattle guard; then track on right.

▼ 2.4 SO Road becomes paved. Remain on paved road for next 2 miles, ignoring turns to the left and right.

2.0 ▲ SO Road turns to graded dirt.

▼ 3.4 SO Cross over Beaver Creek on bridge.

1.0 ▲ SO Cross over Beaver Creek on bridge.

▼ 4.4 SO Road on right; then trail ends at intersection with Little Valley Road (CR 404). Continue straight ahead for McArthur; turn right for Little Valley.

0.0 ▲ Trail starts on Little Valley Road (CR 404) at the intersection with CR 111, 2.1 miles south of Pittville. Zero trip meter and turn south on CR 111. Remain on paved road for next 2 miles, ignoring turns to the left and right.

GPS: N41°01.37' W121°19.24'

Hayden Hill Trail

STARTING POINT Susanville Road (CR A2), 0.4 miles west of the intersection with California 139

FINISHING POINT California 139, 1.3 miles north of Willow Creek Campground

TOTAL MILEAGE 16.6 miles

UNPAVED MILEAGE 16.5 miles

DRIVING TIME 1.5 hours

ELEVATION RANGE 4,400–5,800 feet

USUALLY OPEN April to November

BEST TIME TO TRAVEL Dry weather

DIFFICULTY RATING 1

SCENIC RATING 7

REMOTENESS RATING +0

Special Attractions

■ Easy winding trail through Modoc National Forest.

■ Trail passes close to the historic site of Hayden Hill.

History

The site of Providence Mine, the first mine established at Hayden Hill, may have been accidentally discovered by prospectors from Yreka in search of the fabled Lost Cabin Mine in the fall of 1869. Another story is that clergymen staked the claim in 1870 while traveling north from Susanville to Adin. Regardless of which tale is true, the mines were well established by the end of 1870.

Heavily mined Hayden Hill

After J. W. Hayden and Seneca Lewis established the Providence Mine, a horde of prospectors followed. A mill was hauled to Hayden Hill from a failed mining operation at Hardin City, Nevada.

By April 1871, the Hayden post office opened; its name was later changed to Haydenhill. During the late 1870s a mini gold rush brought several hundred people to the area. Businesses, including a butcher shop, hotel, blacksmith, and saloon opened. The White Swan, Brush Hill, Golden Eagle, Juniper, Blue Bells, Idaho, Evening Star, and Vicuna Mines supported the town. The Lassen Mining Company owned many of the mines and operated a mill. More than $2 million worth of gold was extracted from the area around Hayden Hill between 1880 and 1911. The Hayden Hill Consolidated Mining Company continued small-scale mining for a few years after 1911.

Description

Hayden Hill Trail loops into Modoc National Forest, passing near the former gold mining settlement. The uneven, narrow road winds through semi-open forest and mead-ows, and passes some private property. The trail swings west to join the good, graded road that serves as access to mines around Hayden Hill. As you approach, the re-vegetated terraces of Hayden Hill stand out clearly to the south. There is no public access to the privately owned mines. In the past, rock hounds have found rhyolite around the old site of Hayden Hill.

The trail passes through a state game refuge—no firearms allowed—to finish on California 139, 13 miles south of Adin.

Current Road Information

Modoc National Forest
Big Valley Ranger District
PO Box 159
Adin, CA 96006
(530) 299-3215

Map References

BLM   Alturas, Eagle Lake
USFS Modoc National Forest
USGS 1:24,000   Letterbox Hill, Silva Flat
      Reservoir, Said Valley, Lane Reservoir
      1:100,000 Alturas, Eagle Lake

NORTHERN SIERRA #50: HAYDEN HILL TRAIL

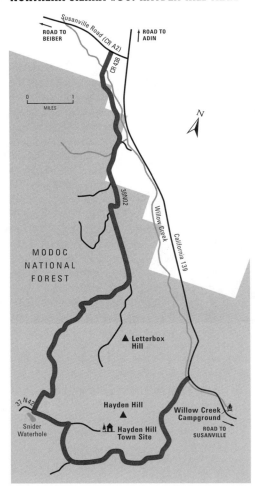

Maptech CD-ROM: Shasta-Trinity/
 Modoc; Shasta Lake/Redding
Northern California Atlas & Gazetteer,
 pp. 39, 40, 49, 50
California Road & Recreation Atlas, p. 54
Other: BLM Recreation Guide for
 Northeastern California and
 Northwestern Nevada

Route Directions

▼ 0.0   From Susanville Road (CR A2), 0.4
          miles west of California 139 and 11
          miles east of Beiber, zero trip meter
          and turn south on graded cinder

Armstrong Road (CR 438, 38N02).
5.5 ▲   Trail ends on Susanville Road (CR A2).
          Turn left for Beiber; turn right for
          California 139 and Adin.
          GPS: N41°06.83′ W120°55.65′

▼ 0.4   SO Cross over Willow Creek.
5.1 ▲   SO Cross over Willow Creek.
▼ 0.8   SO Cattle guard.
4.7 ▲   SO Cattle guard.
▼ 1.7   SO Track on right.
3.8 ▲   SO Track on left.
▼ 2.1   BR Track on left.
3.4 ▲   BL Track on right.
▼ 2.2   SO Cross through creek.
3.3 ▲   SO Cross through creek.
▼ 2.5   SO Cattle guard. Entering Modoc National
              Forest. Road is now designated
              38N02. Follow sign to Hayden Hill.
3.0 ▲   SO Leaving Modoc National Forest.
              Cattle guard.
          GPS: N41°04.91′ W120°54.73′

▼ 3.2   SO Track on right.
2.3 ▲   SO Track on left.
▼ 3.9   SO Track on right.
1.6 ▲   SO Track on left.
▼ 5.5   BR Track on left. Zero trip meter.
0.0 ▲   Continue to the northwest on 38N02.
          GPS: N41°02.64′ W120°53.33′

▼ 0.0   Continue to the south on 38N02.
4.5 ▲   BL Track on right. Zero trip meter.
▼ 0.5   SO Track on left.
4.0 ▲   SO Track on right.
▼ 0.8   SO Track on right.
3.7 ▲   SO Track on left.
▼ 3.7   SO Cattle guard.
0.8 ▲   SO Cattle guard.
          GPS: N41°00.04′ W120°54.15′

▼ 4.5   TL T-intersection with graded road 37N42.
              Zero trip meter and follow the sign to
              Hayden Hill. Snider Waterhole is
              straight ahead.
0.0 ▲   Continue to the north.
          GPS: N40°59.63′ W120°54.43′

▼ 0.0   Continue to the east.
6.6 ▲   TR Track straight ahead is 37N42 to

Summit Spring. Zero trip meter and turn right onto 38N02, following the sign to Adin. Snider Waterhole is to the left.

▼ 0.8   TR   Cattle guard; then turn right on major graded road and enter state game refuge. Track on left goes to Hayden Hill.

5.8 ▲   TL   Graded road continues straight ahead to Hayden Hill. Turn left over cattle guard onto unmarked graded road and enter Modoc National Forest.
            GPS: N40°59.67′ W120°53.52′

▼ 1.9   SO   Track on right.
4.7 ▲   SO   Track on left.
▼ 2.6   SO   Track on right.
4.0 ▲   SO   Track on left.
▼ 6.5   SO   Cattle guard. Road is now paved. Track on left.
0.1 ▲   SO   Track on right. Road turns to graded dirt. Cattle guard.

▼ 6.6   Cross over Willow Creek; then trail ends at T-intersection with California 139. Turn right for Eagle Lake and Susanville; turn left for Adin.

0.0 ▲   Trail commences on California 139, 1.3 miles north of Willow Creek USFS Campground, 13 miles south of Adin. Zero trip meter and turn south on paved road at the sign for Hayden Hill.
            GPS: N41°01.23′ W120°51.08′

NORTHERN SIERRA #51

Likely Mountain Trail

STARTING POINT   Ash Valley Road (CR 527), 9 miles west of Madeline
FINISHING POINT   US 395, 4.5 miles south of Likely
TOTAL MILEAGE   23.2 miles
UNPAVED MILEAGE   23.2 miles
DRIVING TIME   4 hours
ELEVATION RANGE   5,200–6,700 feet
USUALLY OPEN   May to November
BEST TIME TO TRAVEL   Dry weather
DIFFICULTY RATING   3
SCENIC RATING   8
REMOTENESS RATING   +0

Special Attractions

- Trail passes the sites of Portuguese and Fleming Sheep Camps.
- Panoramic views from Likely Fire Lookout.
- Mountain bike trail from US 395 to Likely Fire Lookout.
- Lightly traveled trail through a variety of forest and open landscapes.

History

Likely Mountain Trail follows a well-beaten path made by shepherds and their flocks in the vicinity of Sears Flat and Knox Mountain. The Fleming and Portuguese Sheep Camps were regular stops when flocks were moved. Sheep were introduced to the northeastern corner of California in the late 1860s. The animals could be herded for hundreds of miles across open range. By the end of the nineteenth century and into the next, large-scale sheep ranches came into conflict with cattle operations. Cattlemen thought sheep overgrazed the range. Intensive lobbying by cattlemen reduced the wide-ranging movement of sheep. Some herds came from Idaho to Madeline, the northernmost terminus on the Nevada-California-Oregon Railway.

Likely Fire Lookout

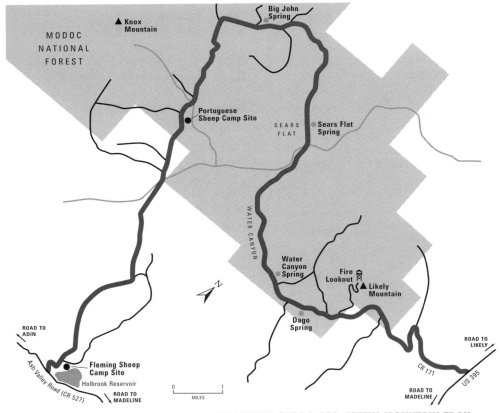

NORTHERN SIERRA #51: LIKELY MOUNTAIN TRAIL

National forest lands were established around the Warner Mountains in order to put a stop to sheep grazing. Some sheep owners bought small plots of land and moved their flocks from patch to patch, grazing as they went.

Description

Likely Mountain Trail leaves Ash Valley Road (CR 527) and travels a long arc through a mixture of vegetation to finish on US 395. The well-used formed trail leaves from the west side of Holbrook Reservoir near the site of Fleming Sheep Camp; little remains of the camp. The trail travels up the eastern side of Knox Mountain through a wide, rabbitbrush-covered valley and passes the site of Portuguese Sheep Camp, where only a collapsed wooden building remains. Wildlife that can typically be seen along this

trail includes blue grouse, golden mantle ground squirrels, chipmunks, black-tail deer, and occasionally mountain lions. After entering Modoc National Forest, the trail swings east around the top of the loop to pass Big John Spring, set among ponderosa pines. The many tracks in the area can make navigation a bit confusing, but generally the most-used trail is the correct one. The route leaves the forest to cross through sagebrush and junipers on Sears Flat.

The lumpy trail surface is formed all the way with embedded rocks. Although it makes for slow travel, it is not a difficult trail. After passing through Water Canyon, the trail climbs up to join the graded county road to the Likely Fire Lookout, an active fire lookout perched amid communications towers on Likely Mountain. The tower is manned from May to mid-October (depending on weather), and visitors are usually welcome to climb the steep stairway to the tower. Panoramic views include Tule Mountain directly to the east, Moon Lake to the southeast, and Nelson Corral Reservoir to the south. The trail across Sears Flat is visible to the northwest and the settlement of Likely is visible in the valley to the north. From the lookout tower, the trail follows the graded county road to finish on US 395.

Current Road Information
Bureau of Land Management
Eagle Lake Field Office
2950 Riverside Drive
Susanville, CA 96130
(530) 257-0456

Modoc National Forest
Big Valley Ranger District
PO Box 159
Adin, CA 96006
(530) 299-3215

A well and cattle trough remain at Portuguese Sheep Camp

Map References
BLM   Alturas
USFS Modoc National Forest
USGS 1:24,000   Ash Valley, Knox Mtn.,
        Likely
        1:100,000 Alturas
Maptech CD-ROM: Shasta-Trinity/Modoc
Northern California Atlas & Gazetteer, p. 40
California Road & Recreation Atlas, pp. 54,
        48 (incomplete)
Other: BLM Recreation Guide for
        Northeastern California and
        Northwestern Nevada (incomplete),;
        Modoc Country USFS/BLM Map

Route Directions

▼ 0.0   From Ash Valley Road (CR 527), 9
          miles west of Madeline and 23 miles
          east of Adin and California 139, 0.1
          miles west of Holbrook Reservoir, zero
          trip meter and turn northwest on
          unmarked graded dirt road. There is no
          directional sign pointing up the road,
          but there is a BLM sign giving direc-
          tions for Adin and Madeline.
6.1 ▲   Trail ends at T-intersection with Ash
          Valley Road (CR 527). Turn left for US
          395 and Madeline; turn right for
          California 139 and Adin.
          GPS: N41°04.62' W120°37.98'

▼ 0.5   SO Track on right.
5.6 ▲   SO Track on left.
▼ 2.1   SO Dam on left.
4.0 ▲   SO Dam on right.
▼ 2.2   SO Track on left.
3.9 ▲   SO Track on right.
▼ 3.0   SO Track on right.
3.1 ▲   SO Track on left.
          GPS: N41°06.88' W120°37.88'

▼ 3.5   SO Track on left.
2.6 ▲   SO Track on right.
▼ 4.9   SO Track on left.
1.2 ▲   SO Track on right.
▼ 5.1   SO Cross over creek.
1.0 ▲   SO Cross over creek.
▼ 5.3   SO Track on left.
0.8 ▲   SO Track on right.

Trail heading toward Likely Mountain

GPS: **N41°08.74′ W120°38.98′**

▼ 5.6   SO   Track on left.
0.5 ▲   SO   Track on right.
▼ 6.0   SO   Track on left.
0.1 ▲   SO   Track on right.
▼ 6.1   SO   Pass through fence line. Leaving National Resource Lands. Zero trip meter at sign.
0.0 ▲   Continue to the southeast.
GPS: **N41°09.35′ W120°39.35′**

▼ 0.0   Continue to the northwest.
2.7 ▲   SO   Pass through fence line. Entering National Resource Lands. Zero trip meter and follow sign for Ash Valley Road.
▼ 0.4   SO   Site of Portuguese Sheep Camp.
2.3 ▲   SO   Site of Portuguese Sheep Camp.
GPS: **N41°09.67′ W120°39.49′**

▼ 0.5   SO   Track on left opposite well.
2.2 ▲   SO   Track on right opposite well.
▼ 0.9   SO   Cross through wash; then track on left.
1.8 ▲   SO   Track on right; then cross through wash.

▼ 1.1   SO   Gate. Entering Modoc National Forest.
1.6 ▲   SO   Gate. Leaving Modoc National Forest.
GPS: **N41°10.22′ W120°39.61′**

▼ 2.1   SO   Gate.
0.6 ▲   SO   Gate.
▼ 2.2   SO   Track on left.
0.5 ▲   SO   Track on right.
▼ 2.7   BR   Trail continues straight ahead. Bear right onto unmarked, formed trail and zero trip meter.
0.0 ▲   Continue to the southwest.
GPS: **N41°11.43′ W120°40.30′**

▼ 0.0   Continue to the north.
2.6 ▲   SO   Track on right. Continue on unmarked formed trail and zero trip meter.
▼ 0.6   SO   Track on right.
2.0 ▲   SO   Track on left.
▼ 0.8   SO   Track on left.
1.8 ▲   SO   Track on right.
▼ 1.1   SO   Big John Spring on left.
1.5 ▲   SO   Big John Spring on right.
GPS: **N41°12.00′ W120°39.32′**

▼ 1.2   SO   Gate.
1.4 ▲   SO   Gate.
▼ 1.3   BL   Track on right.
1.3 ▲   BR   Track on left.
▼ 2.5   SO   Cross through wash.
0.1 ▲   SO   Cross through wash.
▼ 2.6   BR   Track on left. Zero trip meter and follow old sign to Likely Mountain and
Highway 395.
0.0 ▲   Continue to the west.

GPS: N41°12.25′ W120°37.90′

▼ 0.0   Continue to the southeast.
7.7 ▲   BL   Track on right. There is a directional
sign for Likely Mountain at the intersection pointing back the way you
have come. Zero trip meter.

▼ 0.1   SO   Cross through wash.
7.6 ▲   SO   Cross through wash.
▼ 1.4   SO   Gate.
6.3 ▲   SO   Gate.
▼ 1.6   SO   Cross through wash.
6.1 ▲   SO   Cross through wash.
▼ 1.7   SO   Water tank on left at Sears Flat Spring.
6.0 ▲   SO   Water tank on right at Sears Flat Spring.

GPS: N41°11.03′ W120°37.10′

▼ 2.2   SO   Cross through wash.
5.5 ▲   SO   Cross through wash.
▼ 2.7   SO   Cross through wash.
5.0 ▲   SO   Cross through wash.
▼ 3.3   SO   Gate; then cross through wash.
4.4 ▲   SO   Cross through wash; then gate.

GPS: N41°09.84′ W120°36.90′

▼ 3.5   SO   Cross through wash. Leaving Sears Flat.
4.2 ▲   SO   Entering Sears Flat. Cross through wash.
▼ 3.6   SO   Cross through wash.
4.1 ▲   SO   Cross through wash.
▼ 3.9   SO   Cross through wash.
3.8 ▲   SO   Cross through wash.
▼ 4.1   SO   Well-used track on right.
3.6 ▲   SO   Well-used track on left.

GPS: N41°09.25′ W120°36.69′

▼ 4.5   SO   Cross through wash. Trail enters Water
Canyon. Many wash crossings for the
next 1.5 miles.
3.2 ▲   SO   Cross through wash. Trail leaves Water
Canyon.

▼ 5.4   SO   Tank on left is supplied by Water
Canyon Spring.
2.3 ▲   SO   Tank on right is supplied by Water
Canyon Spring.

GPS: N41°08.53′ W120°35.65′

▼ 5.5   SO   Water Canyon Spring on left.
2.2 ▲   SO   Water Canyon Spring on right.

GPS: N41°08.52′ W120°35.56′

▼ 5.7   SO   Track on left across wash.
2.0 ▲   SO   Track on right across wash.

GPS: N41°08.40′ W120°35.29′

▼ 6.0   SO   Cross through wash.
1.7 ▲   SO   Cross through wash. Many wash
crossings for the next 1.5 miles.
▼ 6.1   SO   Tank on left.
1.6 ▲   SO   Tank on right.
▼ 6.2   SO   Tank on right.
1.5 ▲   SO   Tank on left.
▼ 6.3   BL   Unmarked track on right enters BLM land.
1.4 ▲   BR   Unmarked track on left enters BLM land.

GPS: N41°08.30′ W120°34.81′

▼ 6.6   SO   Dago Spring on right.
1.1 ▲   SO   Dago Spring on left.

GPS: N41°08.39′ W120°34.49′

▼ 7.3   SO   Track on left.
0.4 ▲   BL   Track on right.

GPS: N41°08.57′ W120°33.87′

▼ 7.4   SO   Tank on left; then gate; then track
on right.
0.3 ▲   SO   Track on left; then gate; then tank
on right.
▼ 7.7   TR   T-intersection with graded road. To the
left goes 1.3 miles to Likely Mountain.
Zero trip meter.
0.0 ▲   Continue to the southwest.

GPS: N41°08.75′ W120°33.55′

▼ 0.0   Continue to the northeast on CR 171.
4.1 ▲   TL   Graded road continues straight ahead for
1.3 miles to Likely Mountain. Zero trip
meter and follow the sign to Sears Flat.
▼ 1.0   SO   Track on right.
3.1 ▲   SO   Track on left.
▼ 2.5   SO   Track on left.

1.6 ▲	SO	Track on right.
▼ 2.7	SO	Track on right under power lines.
1.4 ▲	SO	Track on left under power lines.
▼ 3.7	SO	Track on right.
0.4 ▲	SO	Track on left.
▼ 3.9	SO	Cattle guard.
0.2 ▲	SO	Cattle guard.
▼ 4.0	SO	Track on left and track on right.
0.1 ▲	SO	Track on left and track on right.
▼ 4.1		Trail ends at T-intersection with US 395. Turn left for Likely and Alturas; turn right for Susanville.
0.0 ▲		Trail commences on US 395, 4.5 miles south of Likely and 0.3 miles south of Lassen County mile marker 137. Zero trip meter and turn southwest on unmarked graded dirt road.

GPS: N41°09.33' W120°30.45'

Buckhorn Backcountry Byway

STARTING POINT US 395 at Termo
FINISHING POINT Nevada 447, 30.5 miles southeast of Eagleville, CA
TOTAL MILEAGE 49.1 miles
UNPAVED MILEAGE 48.4 miles
DRIVING TIME 3 hours
ELEVATION RANGE 4,800–6,500 feet
USUALLY OPEN Year-round
BEST TIME TO TRAVEL Spring and fall
DIFFICULTY RATING 1
SCENIC RATING 8
REMOTENESS RATING +1

Special Attractions

■ Fishing and backcountry camping at small reservoirs along the trail.
■ Chance to see wild horses.
■ Remote byway suitable for passenger vehicles.

Description

The Buckhorn Backcountry Byway is one of a number of backcountry roads nationwide that have been designated for their remote and scenic qualities. The Buckhorn route travels past low hills, dry lakes, and country covered in sagebrush and rabbitbrush. The trail is well-graded, often graveled, for its entire length, and it is generally suitable for passenger vehicles. However, access to Buckhorn Reservoir and the Round Corral Wetlands requires a high-clearance vehicle. The trail is remote, and you are unlikely to see other travelers. There are many pleasant backcountry campsites along ridge tops, among junipers, and around the dry lakes. There are no developed campgrounds along the trail.

Initially, the trail passes through private land as it leaves US 395 and Termo, crosses Juniper Ridge, and descends to Coyote Flat. After joining the road from Ravendale, the route travels toward Buckhorn Canyon. Buckhorn Reservoir is a short distance from the main trail, and although listed on the BLM map as an angling spot, it is often dry in summer and fall. A second reservoir—Round Corral—is marked as wetlands but is also usually dry. Some good campsites at the reservoir are accessible by high-clearance 2WDs in dry weather only.

Continuing along the main route, the trail crosses into Nevada at dry Pilgrim Lake, before crossing a ridge and descending to the large, open dry area of Burnt Lake. This is a good place to spot the herds of wild horse that roam these ranges. Small bands of horses are often found around the lakes along the trail. Do not approach them! They are wild and easily spooked.

The trail drops down off the ridge to Cedar Canyon, passing beside some of the basalt pillars characteristic of this volcanic region. It finishes on Nevada 447, 37.5 miles northwest of Gerlach, Nevada, and 30.5 miles southeast of Eagleville, California.

Current Road Information

Bureau of Land Management
Eagle Lake Field Office
2950 Riverside Drive
Susanville, CA 96130
(530) 257-0456

Map References

BLM   Eagle Lake, Gerlach
USGS 1:24,000 Termo, Ravendale,
      Juniper Ridge, Dodge Reservoir,
      Observation Peak, Buckhorn Canyon,
      Buckhorn Lake, Hole in the Ground,
      Burnt Lake, Rye Patch Canyon
      1:100,000 Eagle Lake, Gerlach
Maptech CD-ROM: Shasta Lake/Redding
Northern California Atlas & Gazetteer, p. 51
Nevada Atlas & Gazetteer, p. 26
California Road & Recreation Atlas, p. 55
Other: BLM Recreation Guide for
      Northeastern California and
      Northwestern Nevada; Modoc
      Country USFS/BLM Map

Route Directions

▼ 0.0   From US 395 at Termo, zero trip meter
           and turn east on graveled Juniper

           Ridge Road (CR 508) and cross over
           railroad tracks.
10.9 ▲   Cross over railroad tracks; then trail
           ends on US 395 at Termo. Turn right
           for Alturas; turn left for Susanville.
           GPS: N40°51.99′ W120°27.57′

▼ 0.1   SO Cattle guard.
10.8 ▲ SO Cattle guard.
▼ 1.0   BR Road on left is Jones Road (CR 522).
9.9 ▲   BL Road on right is Jones Road (CR 522).
▼ 3.4   SO Graded road on right.
7.5 ▲   SO Graded road on left.
▼ 4.9   SO Graded road on right is Chicken Ranch
           Road (CR 505, but marked CR 502 on
           BLM map). Track on left. Continue
           straight ahead on CR 508. McDonald
           Peak is to the left.
6.0 ▲   SO Graded road on left is Chicken Ranch
           Road (CR 505, but marked CR 502 on
           BLM map). Track on right. Continue

The trail over Rodeo Flat near Buckhorn Canyon

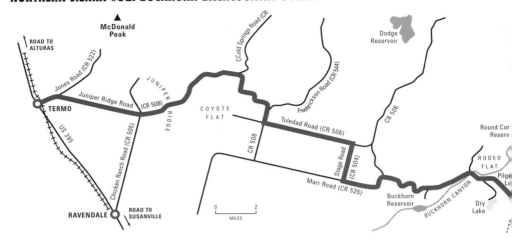

straight ahead on CR 508. McDonald
Peak is to the right.

GPS: N40°52.45' W120°21.86'

▼ 5.8   SO   Cresting Juniper Ridge—views east
to Coyote Flat.

5.1 ▲   SO   Cresting Juniper Ridge—views west
to Madeline Plains.

▼ 10.9   BR   Graded road on left is Cold Springs
Road (CR 515). Zero trip meter.

0.0 ▲   Continue to the west.

GPS: N40°55.08' W120°16.73'

Mustangs near Cedar Canyon

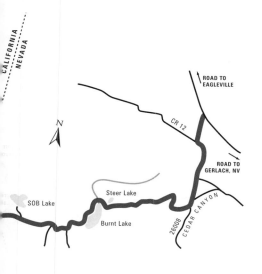

506). To the right goes to Dodge Reservoir. Zero trip meter.

▼ 1.9   TL   T-intersection with Marr Road (CR 526).

5.0 ▲   TR   Road continues ahead to Ravendale. Turn right onto Stage Road (CR 504).
     GPS: N40°51.62' W120°09.77'

▼ 4.1   BR   Track on left. Entering BLM land. Road is now marked as the Buckhorn Back Country Byway. Leaving Coyote Flat.

2.8 ▲   BL   Track on right. Leaving BLM land.

▼ 5.4   SO   Cattle guard.

1.5 ▲   SO   Cattle guard.

▼ 5.9   SO   Track on right.

1.0 ▲   SO   Track on left.

▼ 6.7   SO   Track on right.

0.2 ▲   SO   Track on left.

▼ 6.9   SO   Cross over creek; then small, unmarked sandy track on right goes 0.8 miles to Buckhorn Reservoir, which is visible down in the valley. Zero trip meter.

0.0 ▲   Continue to the west and cross over creek.
     GPS: N40°52.12' W120°05.02'

▼ 0.0   Continue to the northeast.

3.6 ▲   SO   Small, unmarked sandy track on left goes 0.8 miles to Buckhorn Reservoir, which is visible down in the valley. Zero trip meter.

▼ 0.9   SO   Two tracks on right to campsite.

2.7 ▲   SO   Two tracks on left to campsite.

▼ 1.1   SO   Track on left and track on right.

2.5 ▲   SO   Track on left and track on right.

▼ 2.3   SO   Track on left across Rodeo Flat. Buckhorn Canyon is to the right.

1.3 ▲   SO   Track on right across Rodeo Flat. Buckhorn Canyon is to the left.
     GPS: N40°53.20' W120°02.87'

▼ 3.0   SO   Track on right to Dry Lake.

0.6 ▲   SO   Track on left to Dry Lake.

▼ 3.6   SO   Unmarked formed track on left goes 0.5 miles to Round Corral Reservoir. Zero trip meter.

0.0 ▲   Continue to the northwest.
     GPS: N40°53.18' W120°01.46'

▼ 0.0   Continue to the southeast.

▼ 0.0   Continue to the southeast.

7.6 ▲   BL   Graded road on right is Cold Springs Road (CR 515). Zero trip meter.

▼ 2.5   SO   Graded road on left is Frederickson Road (CR 544). Road becomes paved.

7.1 ▲   SO   Graded road on right is Frederickson Road (CR 544). Road turns to graded dirt.
     GPS: N40°53.99' W120°14.96'

▼ 3.2   TL   4-way intersection. Paved Mail Route (CR 508) continues straight ahead. Track on right. Turn left onto graded dirt Tuledad Road (CR 506).

4.4 ▲   TR   4-way intersection. Track straight ahead. Paved road on left and right is Mail Route (CR 508). Turn right onto paved road.
     GPS: N40°53.33' W120°14.97'

▼ 5.2   SO   Cattle guard.

2.4 ▲   SO   Cattle guard.

▼ 7.6   TR   Cattle guard; then road ahead is the continuation of CR 506 to Dodge Reservoir. Zero trip meter.

0.0 ▲   Continue to the west and cross cattle guard.
     GPS: N40°53.37' W120°09.78'

▼ 0.0   Continue to the south on Stage Road (CR 504).

6.9 ▲   TL   T-intersection with Tuledad Road (CR

15.3 ▲ SO Unmarked formed track on right goes 0.5 miles to Round Corral Reservoir. Zero trip meter.

▼ 1.7 SO Track on right is 26029 and track on left. Entering Washoe County, Nevada, at sign. Pilgrim Lake on left; then track on right.

13.6 ▲ SO Track on left; then Pilgrim Lake on right. Entering Lassen County, California, at sign. Track on left is 26029 and track on right.

GPS: N40°52.30′ W119°59.89′

▼ 2.2 SO Cattle guard; then track on left to lake's edge.

13.1 ▲ SO Track on right to lake's edge; then cattle guard.

▼ 2.9 SO Cattle guard.

12.4 ▲ SO Cattle guard.

▼ 4.3 SO Track on left toward SOB Lake.

11.0 ▲ SO Track on right toward SOB Lake.

GPS: N40°52.89′ W119°57.10′

Basalt columns

▼ 5.8 SO Track on right.

9.5 ▲ SO Track on left.

▼ 6.8 SO Track on right.

8.5 ▲ SO Track on left.

▼ 7.8 SO Two tracks on right at the southern end of Burnt Lake.

7.5 ▲ SO Two tracks on left at the southern end of Burnt Lake.

GPS: N40°53.38′ W119°53.71′

▼ 9.2 SO Cross over outlet from Burnt Lake.

6.1 ▲ SO Cross over outlet from Burnt Lake.

▼ 9.5 SO Track on left to dry Steer Lake.

5.8 ▲ SO Track on right to dry Steer Lake.

▼ 12.0 SO Track on right.

3.3 ▲ SO Track on left.

▼ 13.5 SO Start of drop toward Cedar Canyon.

1.8 ▲ SO End of climb away from Cedar Canyon.

▼ 14.4 SO Track on right.

0.9 ▲ SO Track on left.

▼ 15.3 SO Well-used track on right is 26008. Zero trip meter.

0.0 ▲ Continue to the southwest, remaining on Buckhorn Road.

GPS: N40°55.15′ W119°48.09′

▼ 0.0 Continue to the north, remaining on Buckhorn Road.

4.8 ▲ BR Well-used track on left is 26008. Zero trip meter.

▼ 0.2 SO Track on right.

4.6 ▲ SO Track on left.

▼ 1.4 SO Track on right; then cattle guard.

3.4 ▲ SO Cattle guard; then track on left.

▼ 1.9 SO Track on right into private property; then cattle guard; then track on left.

2.9 ▲ SO Track on right; then cattle guard; then track on left into private property.

GPS: N40°56.84′ W119°48.10′

▼ 2.9 SO Two tracks on left.

1.9 ▲ SO Two tracks on right.

▼ 3.1 SO Track on left.

1.7 ▲ SO Track on right.

▼ 3.4 BR Graded road on left is CR 12. Small track on right.

1.4 ▲ BL Graded road on right is CR 12. Small track on left.

GPS: N40°58.02′ W119°48.66′

▼ 4.8	Trail ends at T-intersection with Nevada 447. Turn left for Eagleville, CA; turn right for Gerlach, NV
0.0 ▲	Trail commences on Nevada 447, 37.5 miles northwest of Gerlach, NV, and 30.5 miles southeast of Eagleville, CA. Zero trip meter and turn south onto graded dirt road, following the sign for Buckhorn Road and US 395. Round Mountain is opposite. **GPS: N40°59.23' W119°48.65'**

NORTHERN SIERRA #53

South Warner Mountains Trail

STARTING POINT Jess Valley Road (CR 64), 5.9 miles east of Likely and US 395

FINISHING POINT Surprise Valley Road (CR 1), 3 miles south of Eagleville

TOTAL MILEAGE 31.8 miles

UNPAVED MILEAGE 31.6 miles

DRIVING TIME 4 hours

ELEVATION RANGE 4,500–7,600 feet

USUALLY OPEN June to December

BEST TIME TO TRAVEL Dry weather

DIFFICULTY RATING 3

SCENIC RATING 9

REMOTENESS RATING +0

Special Attractions

- Aspen viewing in the fall.
- Fishing and camping at Blue Lake and West Valley Reservoir.
- Hiking and equestrian trails into the South Warner Wilderness.

History

The Warner Mountains were named for Captain William H. Warner, who was killed along with his guide in a surprise Indian attack on September 26, 1849. The attack occurred just north of Surprise Valley, beyond the northern end of the mountains that now bear his name. With the help of a few scouts, the captain was trying to find a safe route for emigrants to travel through the mountains.

The trail begins in the upper reaches of the Pit River in West Valley, just east of the town of Likely. In 1878, townsfolk from South Fork tried to establish a post office there. They submitted several names, but each one was rejected because a post office already existed with the name. When the fourth name was suggested, a member of the party thought that it was unlikely that this one would be accepted either. All present jumped on the name Likely, thinking surely such a name would be available. Likely was indeed accepted by post office authorities.

West Valley and Jess Valley were easier to name. Brothers Rollin and Herbert West purchased and amalgamated ranches in the valley in 1878, naming the region after themselves. Three years earlier, the Jess brothers, Archie and Jonathan, settled in the valley that now bears their name.

Settling lands in Pit River country was a dangerous venture for all concerned. Indians considered emigrants as invaders and their oxen as food. Newcomers discovered that their lives were in danger. Scattered incidents in the late 1840s and '50s brought about the establishment of Camp Hollenbush on the Fall River in 1857. A large cattle drive from Oregon to Nevada City passed through this region in August 1861, and Pit River Indians attacked it. A number of cowboys managed to escape, but the owners of the 800 head of cattle, Joseph and Samuel Evans, were killed in the fight. Two patrols of dragoons were dispatched from Camp Hollenbush, later renamed Fort Crook, to retrieve the cattle and punish the Indians. Fewer than 200 head of cattle were retrieved and several Pit River warriors were killed. One of the many skirmishes with the Indians occurred during a second patrol in West Valley, near the start of this trail.

Description

South Warner Mountains Trail runs south of the South Warner Wilderness, which covers much of the southern Warner Mountains. The trail crosses the range from west to east, past two very different lakes and a mixture of forests. It leaves Jess Valley Road east of Likely and immediately starts to climb into the range along a rough and lumpy formed trail. Side trails lead down to the edge of West Valley Reservoir, where there are campsites and fishing opportunities when water levels permit.

The trail travels around the north side of Parsnip Peak before passing along Parsnip Creek, which flows through lush green, aspen-fringed meadows. The creek crossing comes about a mile before the trail briefly intersects with paved Blue Lake Road. Blue Lake, a short distance farther down the paved road, has a USFS campground, a boat launch, and wheelchair fishing access. You can fish for rainbow and brown trout at the lake. A national recreation trail—the Blue Lake Trail—circles the 160-acre lake. Much of this area was burned by the Blue Fire of August 2001, which was caused by lightning strikes. Measures have been taken to prevent ash and eroded material from silting up the lake.

The trail leaves the paved road and rejoins a smaller, formed trail that travels through mixed conifer forest to the open Long Valley. Several aspens in the meadows southeast of Long Valley around Jenkins Spring have carvings made by Basque shepherds. A few flocks of sheep graze in the wilderness under a permit system. This section of the trail is particularly pretty in fall, when the many stands of aspens are resplendent in golden foliage.

At the north end of Long Valley, the trail passes near the Patterson USFS Guard Station, a small campground, and the Summit Trailhead. The Summit Trail begins here and runs the 27-mile length of the South Warner Wilderness, ending at the Pepperdine USFS Campground. It also connects with other trails within the wilderness area. The small campground near the guard station has a handful of sites tucked among the trees. Patterson is also an equestrian trailhead, with a corral for as many as 10 horses and a parking lot for trailers.

Wheelchair fishing access point on Blue Lake

The standard of the road increases from here, becoming a graded, lightly graveled road. It passes both ends of Northern Sierra #54: Bearcamp Flat Trail, a more difficult loop to the north. Some good backcountry campsites can be found around Homestead Flat near the start of the loop. The trail drops abruptly to Surprise Valley, descending more than 1,700 feet in the final few miles. It finishes on Surprise Valley Road on the edge of Lower Lake.

Current Road Information

Modoc National Forest
Warner Mountain Ranger District
PO Box 220
Cedarville, CA 96104
(530) 279-6116

Map References

BLM   Alturas
USFS   Modoc National Forest
USGS   1:24,000   Tule Mtn., Jess Valley,
          Emerson Peak, Snake Lake, Eagleville
          1:100,000 Alturas
Maptech CD-ROM: Shasta-Trinity/Modoc
Northern California Atlas & Gazetteer, p. 41
California Road & Recreation Atlas, p. 49
Other: Modoc Country USFS/BLM Map

Route Directions

▼ 0.0   From Jess Valley Road (CR 64), 5.9
           miles east of Likely and US 395, zero
           trip meter and turn southeast on grad-
           ed dirt road 39N19, following the sign
           to West Valley Reservoir and Blue Lake
           Campground.
2.4 ▲   Trail ends at T-intersection with Jess
           Valley Road (CR 64). Turn left for US
           395 and Likely; turn right for Jess
           Valley.
           GPS: N41°14.05' W120°23.80'

▼ 0.1   SO Track on left; then cross over South
            Fork Pit River on bridge. Seasonal
            closure gate; then track on right and
            track on left.
2.3 ▲   SO Track on left and track on right; then
            seasonal closure gate. Cross over

South Fork Pit River on bridge; then
track on right.
▼ 0.2   SO Track on left and track on right.
2.2 ▲   SO Track on left and track on right.
▼ 0.3   SO Track on left.
2.1 ▲   SO Track on right.
▼ 0.4   SO Gate.
2.0 ▲   SO Gate.
▼ 0.7   SO Track on right and track on left. Cross
            over ditch.
1.7 ▲   SO Cross over ditch. Track on right and
            track on left.
▼ 0.9   SO Track on left.
1.5 ▲   SO Track on right.
▼ 1.1   SO Unmarked track on right goes to West
            Valley Reservoir.
1.3 ▲   SO Unmarked track on left goes to West
            Valley Reservoir.
            GPS: N41°13.15' 120°23.64'

▼ 1.6   SO Track on right.
0.8 ▲   SO Track on left.
▼ 1.8   SO Cross through wash.
0.6 ▲   SO Cross through wash.
▼ 2.0   SO Track on left; then cattle guard.
0.4 ▲   SO Cattle guard; then track on right.
▼ 2.4   BL Unmarked track on right goes 0.4
            miles to West Valley Reservoir. Zero
            trip meter.
0.0 ▲   Continue to the north.
            GPS: N41°12.19' W120°22.96'

▼ 0.0   Continue to the east.
5.8 ▲   BR Unmarked track on left goes 0.4 miles
            to West Valley Reservoir. Zero trip
            meter.
▼ 0.7   SO Cross through wash.
5.1 ▲   SO Cross through wash.
▼ 0.8   SO Cross through wash.
5.0 ▲   SO Cross through wash.
▼ 1.4   SO Track on left. West Valley Spring on left.
4.4 ▲   SO Track on right. West Valley Spring on right.
            GPS: N41°12.03' W120°21.44'

▼ 1.6   SO Cross through wash.
4.2 ▲   SO Cross through wash.
▼ 2.2   SO Pass through fence line.
3.6 ▲   SO Pass through fence line.
▼ 3.2   SO Tank on left.
2.6 ▲   SO Tank on right.

▼ 3.4　SO　Track on right.
2.4 ▲　BR　Track on left.
　　　GPS: N41°11.04′ W120°20.12′

▼ 3.5　SO　Track on right toward Parsnip Mountain.
2.3 ▲　SO　Track on left toward Parsnip Mountain.
▼ 3.6　SO　Gate.
2.2 ▲　SO　Gate.
▼ 5.4　SO　Gate.
0.4 ▲　SO　Gate.
▼ 5.8　TL　T-intersection with 39N34. Parsnip Creek is straight ahead. Zero trip meter.
0.0 ▲　　　Continue to the north on unmarked formed trail.
　　　GPS: N41°10.07′ W120°17.74′

▼ 0.0　　　Continue to the east on graded road.
1.7 ▲　TR　Graded road continues straight ahead. Zero trip meter. Parsnip Creek is on the left.
▼ 0.3　SO　Track on right to meadows surrounding Parsnip Creek.
1.4 ▲　SO　Track on left to meadows surrounding Parsnip Creek.
▼ 0.6　TR　Cattle guard and seasonal closure gate; then small track on right; then T-intersection with paved CR 258. Turn right onto small formed track immediately before paved road.
1.1 ▲　TL　T-intersection with graded road immediately in front of paved CR 258, which is on the right. Turn left onto graded dirt 39N34; then small track on left. Cross cattle guard and seasonal closure gate.
　　　GPS: N41°10.03′ W120°17.06′

▼ 1.2　SO　Cross through creek.
0.5 ▲　SO　Cross through creek.
　　　GPS: N41°09.60′ W120°16.69′

▼ 1.4　SO　Track on left joins paved road.
0.3 ▲　SO　Track on right joins paved road.
▼ 1.5　TR　Join paved road 39N30 to Blue Lake.
0.2 ▲　TL　Turn off paved road onto small formed trail, which runs parallel to paved road along the fence line. This turn is hard to spot.
　　　GPS: N41°09.44′ W120°16.62′

▼ 1.7　TL　Small track on right. Turn left onto unmarked, graded CR 510. The turn is immediately before a cattle guard. The paved road continues straight ahead for 0.6 miles to Blue Lake. Zero trip meter.
0.0 ▲　　　Continue to the north.
　　　GPS: N41°09.29′ W120°16.60′

▼ 0.0　　　Continue to the southeast.
3.0 ▲　TR　T-intersection with paved Blue Lake Road (39N30). To the left goes 0.6 miles to Blue Lake. Small track straight ahead. Zero trip meter and turn right alongside paved road.
▼ 1.0　BR　Track on left to Parsnip Creek.
2.0 ▲　SO　Track on right to Parsnip Creek.
▼ 1.2　SO　Track on left to Parsnip Creek.
1.8 ▲　SO　Track on right to Parsnip Creek.
▼ 1.6　SO　Tank on left.
1.4 ▲　SO　Tank on right.
▼ 2.1　SO　Track on right.
0.9 ▼　SO　Track on left.
　　　GPS: N41°08.88′ W120°14.99′

▼ 2.3　TR　T-intersection with graded dirt road 39N12.
0.7 ▲　TL　Graded road continues ahead. Turn left onto unmarked formed trail CR 510, which leads downhill.
　　　GPS: N41°08.79′ W120°14.73′

▼ 2.4　SO　Cattle guard.
0.6 ▲　SO　Cattle guard.
▼ 3.0　TL　T-intersection with CR 511 (39N15). Corral on right. Zero trip meter.
0.0 ▲　　　Continue to the northwest on unmarked graded road 39N12.
　　　GPS: N41°08.19′ W120°14.38′

▼ 0.0　　　Continue to the north.
2.9 ▲　TR　Graded road continues straight ahead past corral. Zero trip meter.
▼ 0.3　SO　Track on right is 38N55.
2.6 ▲　SO　Track on left is 38N55.
▼ 1.2　SO　Track on right.
1.7 ▲　SO　Track on left.
▼ 2.9　TR　Corporation Meadow. Graded road straight ahead is 38N15. Zero trip meter and follow the sign to Patterson Guard Station.

Fording Parsnip Creek

0.0 ▲   Continue to the south on 39N15.
      GPS: N41°10.45′ W120°13.17′

▼ 0.0   Continue to the southeast.
4.4 ▲ TL Graded road straight ahead is 38N15. Zero trip meter and follow the sign for Madeline.

▼ 0.2 SO Two tracks on right and two tracks on left.
4.2 ▲ SO Two tracks on left and two tracks on right.

▼ 1.5 SO Track on right is 38N16.
2.9 ▲ SO Track on left is 38N16.

▼ 2.0 SO Cross over Mosquito Creek.
2.4 ▲ SO Cross over Mosquito Creek.

▼ 2.1 SO Track on left goes to East Creek Bridge. Follow the sign to Patterson Guard Station.
2.3 ▲ SO Track on right goes to East Creek Bridge. Follow the sign to Long Valley Road.
      GPS: N41°10.08′ W120°12.08′

▼ 2.7 SO Track on right is Mosquito Creek Loop Road (38N16).
1.7 ▲ SO Track on left is Mosquito Creek Loop Road (38N16).

▼ 3.2 SO Track on right.
1.2 ▲ SO Track on left.

▼ 4.0 SO Cross over creek.
0.4 ▲ SO Cross over creek.
      GPS: N41°11.21′ W120°11.31′

▼ 4.4 TR Corral on left at Patterson Meadow. FR 64 goes 0.3 miles ahead to Patterson USFS Campground, Patterson Guard Station, and Summit Trailhead. Zero trip meter and turn right onto FR 64, following the sign to CR 1.
0.0 ▲   Continue to the south.
      GPS: N41°11.62′ W120°11.37′

▼ 0.0   Continue to the east.
2.1 ▲ TL Patterson Meadow. FR 64 continues 0.3 miles to the right to Patterson USFS Campground, Patterson Guard

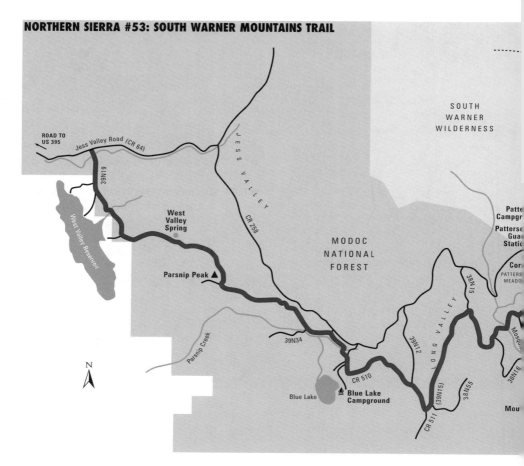

Station, and Summit Trail. Zero trip
meter and turn left onto 38N07, following sign to Corporation Meadow.

▼ 1.8   SO   Track on left to campsite; then cross
over East Creek.

0.3 ▲   SO   Cross over East Creek; then track on
right to campsite.

▼ 2.0   SO   Cattle guard.

0.1 ▲   SO   Cattle guard.

▼ 2.1   SO   Track on left is the western end of
Northern Sierra #54: Bearcamp Flat
Trail (39N11). Zero trip meter.

0.0 ▲   Continue to the west.

       GPS: N41°11.78' W120°09.52'

▼ 0.0   Continue to the southeast.

1.2 ▲   SO   Track on right is the western end of
Northern Sierra #54: Bearcamp Flat
Trail (39N11). Zero trip meter.

▼ 0.6   SO   Track on right goes to Buck Mountain Trail.

0.6 ▲   SO   Track on left goes to Buck Mountain Trail.

▼ 1.1   SO   Track on right goes to Camp One.

0.1 ▲   SO   Track on left goes to Camp One.

▼ 1.2   SO   Track on left is the eastern end of
Northern Sierra #54: Bearcamp Flat
Trail. Zero trip meter.

0.0 ▲   Continue to the west.

       GPS: N41°11.37' W120°08.47'

▼ 0.0   Continue to the east.

4.1 ▲   SO   Track on right is the eastern end of
Northern Sierra #54: Bearcamp Flat
Trail. Zero trip meter.

▼ 0.3   SO   Track on right.

3.8 ▲   SO   Track on left.

▼ 0.6   SO   Track on right; then start to descend to
Surprise Valley. Sworinger Reservoir is
visible below.

3.5 ▲   SO   End of climb from Surprise Valley.
Sworinger Reservoir is visible below.

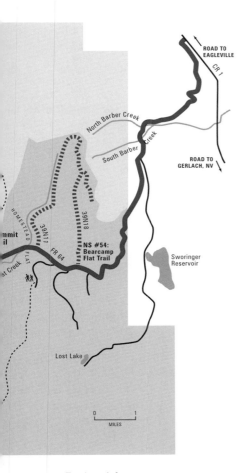

Track on left.
▼ 0.9 SO Track on left.
3.2 ▲ SO Track on right.
▼ 2.8 SO Cattle guard. Leaving Modoc National Forest.
1.3 ▲ SO Cattle guard. Entering Modoc National Forest.
GPS: N41°12.60' W120°06.88'

▼ 3.7 SO Unmarked track on right.
0.4 ▲ SO Unmarked track on left.
GPS: N41°13.39' W120°06.58'

▼ 4.1 SO Graded road on right goes to Lost Lake. Zero trip meter and follow the sign to Eagleville.
0.0 ▲ Continue to the south, remaining on FR 64.
GPS: N41°13.69' W120°06.65'

▼ 0.0 Continue to the north, remaining on FR 64.
4.2 ▲ BL Graded road on left goes to Lost Lake. Zero trip meter and follow the sign to Patterson Campground.
▼ 0.1 SO Cattle guard.
4.1 ▲ SO Cattle guard.
▼ 0.5 SO Cross over South Barber Creek.
3.7 ▲ SO Cross over South Barber Creek.
▼ 0.6 SO Track on left to private property.
3.6 ▲ SO Track on right to private property.
▼ 0.8 SO Cross over North Barber Creek; then track on left.
3.4 ▲ SO Track on right; then cross over North Barber Creek.
▼ 2.1 SO Track on left.
2.1 ▲ SO Track on right.
▼ 2.3 SO Track on right to viewpoint.
1.9 ▲ SO Track on left to viewpoint.
▼ 3.0 SO Track on left.
1.2 ▲ SO Track on right.
▼ 4.2 Track on left; then cattle guard; then trail ends at T-intersection with paved Surprise Valley Road (CR 1). Turn left for Eagleville; turn right for Gerlach, NV.
0.0 ▲ Trail commences on Surprise Valley Road (CR 1), 3 miles south of Eagleville. Zero trip meter and turn southwest on graded dirt road, marked CR 42. Cattle guard; then immediately track on right.
GPS: N41°16.32' W120°05.33'

NORTHERN SIERRA #54

Bearcamp Flat Trail

STARTING POINT Northern Sierra #53: South Warner Mountains Trail, 2.4 miles east of Patterson Guard Station
FINISHING POINT Northern Sierra #53: South Warner Mountains Trail, 3.6 miles east of Patterson Guard Station
TOTAL MILEAGE 7.1 miles, plus 1.2-mile spur to Horse Mountain
UNPAVED MILEAGE 7.1 miles, plus 1.2-mile spur
DRIVING TIME 1.5 hours

ELEVATION RANGE 7,300–8,500 feet
USUALLY OPEN May to October
BEST TIME TO TRAVEL Dry weather
DIFFICULTY RATING 5
SCENIC RATING 10
REMOTENESS RATING +0

Special Attractions

■ Aspen viewing in fall.
■ Panoramic views over Surprise Valley and the South Warner Wilderness.
■ Hiking access to the South Warner Wilderness via the Bear Camp Trail.

History

In the 1800s, Pit River Indians were living near the Pit River drainage when fur trappers and explorers first met them. Their tribal area spanned from Mount Shasta to the Warner Mountains, and Goose Lake to Lassen Peak. Several small bands with different dialects lived within this area. An eastern band upriver known as the Hammawi occupied a large area in the natural bowl of Bearcamp Flat, flanked by Emerson Peak and Horse Mountain. A rancheria was located to the south of the flat.

A flat such as Bearcamp was an important source of edible roots, sunflower seeds, grass seeds, and insects. The roots would be dug up during early summer and dried for use in winter. After drying, the sunflower and grass seeds were combined and often mashed into a cake-like form for cooking in an earthen oven. The Hammawi hunted deer, elk, mountain goats, antelope, and smaller animals. In general these people enjoyed a bountiful environment.

Settlers also reaped the benefits of this country. Cattle ranching and sheep herding were major activities in the northeastern corner of California, and Bearcamp Flat was ideal for summer grazing.

Basque sheepherders, like other emigrants, made their way to California during the gold rush. Instead of being miners, many turned to feeding miners and tended sheep in summer. Bearcamp Flat was a favorite Basque camp location, where the sheep could graze in somewhat of a natural corral. The sheepherders built a Basque style oven that can be seen near the start of this trail.

Description

This short loop trail starts and finishes on the longer Northern Sierra #53: South Warner Mountains Trail, which crosses the range from west to east. Bearcamp Flat Trail is rated a 5 for difficulty because of one loose moguled slope, and a long section of side slope that tilts vehicles toward the drop. Most of the trail is rated a 3 or 4 for difficulty because of the uneven formed surface and embedded rocks that can catch a vehicle's underbody.

The trail starts by traveling up the eastern side of Homestead Flat, where many pleasant campsites are situated among the trees. On the right-hand side of the trail, a short distance from the start, a keen eye will spot the old Basque oven at the edge of the woods. The trail gradually climbs through sagebrush and stands of aspens to the Bear Camp Trailhead. This hiking trail leads through the wilderness and connects to the Emerson Trail and the network of trails within the South Warner Wilderness.

The return portion of the loop travels high on Horse Mountain. A spur leads to a campsite and a breathtaking vista, with views north over the wilderness and east over Surprise Valley, Lower Lake, and into Nevada. It continues to a second viewpoint high on the mountain above Waterbox Canyon. The main route travels down the west side of the mountain, through more stands of aspens, to finish back on Northern Sierra #53: South Warner Mountains Trail.

This trail is particularly pretty in fall, when the turning leaves look like bright splashes of gold against the gray-green sagebrush.

Current Road Information

Modoc National Forest
Warner Mountain Ranger District
PO Box 220
Cedarville, CA 96104
(530) 279-6116

Map References

BLM Alturas
USFS Modoc National Forest
USGS 1:24,000 Emerson Peak
      1:100,000 Alturas
Maptech CD-ROM: Shasta-Trinity/Modoc
Northern California Atlas & Gazetteer, p. 41
California Road & Recreation Atlas, p. 49
      (incomplete)
Other: Modoc Country USFS/BLM Map

Route Directions

▼ 0.0   From Northern Sierra #53: South
          Warner Mountains Trail, 2.4 miles east
          of Patterson Guard Station, zero trip
          meter and turn northwest on formed
          trail 39N11, following the sign to
          Bearcamp Flat.
3.3 ▲   Trail ends back on Northern Sierra
          #53: South Warner Mountains Trail.
          Turn right for Patterson Guard Station;
          turn left for CR 1.

GPS: N41°11.78′ W120°09.52′

▼ 0.2 BR Track on left through fence line.
3.1 ▲ SO Track on right through fence line.
▼ 0.5 SO Track on right; then cross through
           wash.
2.8 ▲ SO Cross through wash; then track on left.
▼ 1.2 SO Spring on left.
2.1 ▲ SO Spring on right.

GPS: N41°12.60′ W120°09.50′

▼ 1.5 SO Track on right; then cross through
           wash.
1.8 ▲ SO Cross through wash; then track on left.
▼ 1.6 SO Cross through wash.
1.7 ▲ SO Cross through wash.
▼ 2.7 BR Track on left.
0.6 ▲ SO Track on right.

GPS: N41°13.75′ W120°08.92′

▼ 2.8 BL Track on right. Follow sign to Bear
           Camp Trail.
0.5 ▲ SO Track on left.

Cold Spring

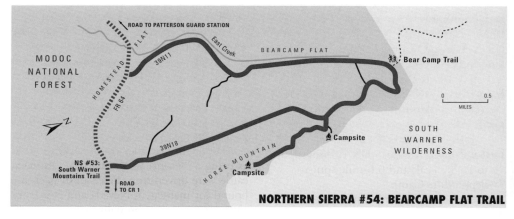

▼ 3.3   BR   Bear Camp Trailhead at information board. The hiking trail leads to the north. Zero trip meter.

0.0 ▲   Continue to the southwest.
GPS: N41°14.19' W120°08.66'

▼ 0.0   Continue to the east.

1.3 ▲   BL   Bear Camp Trailhead at information board. The hiking trail leads to the north. Zero trip meter.

▼ 0.3   TR   T-intersection.

1.0 ▲   TL   Track continues straight ahead.

▼ 0.5   TL   T-intersection.

0.8 ▲   TR   Track continues straight ahead.
GPS: N41°13.92' W120°08.55'

▼ 1.3   TR   Track straight ahead is the spur to the top of Horse Mountain. Zero trip meter.

0.0 ▲   Continue to the northwest.
GPS: N41°13.43' W120°08.24'

Spur to Horse Mountain

▼ 0.0   Continue to the east.

▼ 0.2   TR   Track on left goes 0.1 miles to viewpoint and campsite overlooking Surprise Valley.
GPS: N41°13.39' W120°08.16'

▼ 1.2   Spur ends at a viewpoint and campsite.
GPS: N41°12.66' W120°07.96'

Continuation of Main Trail

▼ 0.0   Continue to the southwest.

2.5 ▲   TL   T-intersection. Track on right is the spur to the top of Horse Mountain. Zero trip meter.
GPS: N41°13.43' W120°08.24'

▼ 0.7   SO   Spring on left.

1.8 ▲   SO   Spring on right.
GPS: N41°12.89' W120°08.49'

▼ 1.3   SO   Spring on left.

1.2 ▲   SO   Spring on right.
GPS: N41°12.37' W120°08.42'

▼ 1.5   SO   Track on right.

1.0 ▲   SO   Track on left.
GPS: N41°12.15' W120°08.42'

▼ 2.1   TL   T-intersection with graded road. To the right goes 0.7 miles to quarry.

0.4 ▲   TR   Graded road continues straight ahead for 0.7 miles to quarry. Turn right onto unmarked formed trail.
GPS: N41°11.64' W120°08.41'

▼ 2.5   Trail ends back on Northern Sierra #53: South Warner Mountains Trail. Turn right for Patterson Guard Station; turn left for CR 1.

0.0 ▲   Trail commences on Northern Sierra #53: South Warner Mountains Trail, 3.6 miles east of Patterson Guard Station. Zero trip meter and turn north on graded road 39N18.
GPS: N41°11.37' W120°08.47'

Payne Peak Trail

STARTING POINT Alpine Road (CR 58), 9.2 miles east of Alturas

FINISHING POINT Surprise Valley Road (CR 1), 3.5 miles south of Cedarville

TOTAL MILEAGE 22.1 miles, plus 1.3-mile spur to Payne Peak and 0.6-mile spur to Pepperdine Camp

UNPAVED MILEAGE 22.1 miles, plus spurs

DRIVING TIME 3 hours

ELEVATION RANGE 4,600–7,600 feet

USUALLY OPEN June to November

BEST TIME TO TRAVEL Dry weather

DIFFICULTY RATING 3

SCENIC RATING 9

REMOTENESS RATING +0

Special Attractions

■ Aspen viewing in fall.
■ Rockhounding for petrified wood in Granger Canyon.
■ Old hunting cabins at Pepperdine Camp.
■ Panoramic views from Payne Peak.

History

This trail provides a good opportunity to view the early wagon road through Cedar Pass (present-day California 299). From an elevation of 7,618 feet on Payne Peak, you can look down on the lower Cedar Pass (6,305 feet) and imagine how delighted settlers must have been to discover it. The route ran from Dorris Bridge (present-day Alturas) through the high Warner Mountains to Surprise Valley. Access to arable lands on the west side of Surprise Valley was highly sought after by early settlers. However, attacks by the Northern Paiute discouraged settlers moving into the valley.

Henry Talbert settled in the Cedarville area in 1864 when he built a log cabin at Deep Creek, just north of the exit point of this trail. Talbert sold out to James Townsend, who ran a store out of the cabin and catered to wagon trains. Indians killed Townsend in 1867. Two men from Red Bluff, J. H. Bonner and W. T. Cressler, saw an opportunity in this developing valley and relocated the cabin to Cedar Creek at the site of present-day Cedarville. Like Townsend, they catered to wagon trains and people camping by the creek before and after crossing Cedar Pass. The old trading post cabin has been preserved in Cedarville Park.

A road ran north from Cedar Creek up the valley to Fort Bidwell and south toward what would become Reno, Nevada. Early descriptions of life in the valley describe the foothills as being a "Utopia to stockraisers." Fattened cattle were driven from here, south to Reno, bound for markets in Nevada and San Francisco. As agriculture brought wealth to the region, Bonner and Cressler's business flourished. A daily stage ran from Reno to Cedarville, and up through Cedar Pass to Alturas. Stages also traveled north over Fandango Pass to Goose Lake. The fate of two cabins at Pepperdine Camp, reached by a spur on the Payne Peak Trail, is in doubt. Leases on the Hunting Cabin, built in 1930, and the Reid Cabin, built in 1948, were held through the forest service, but they expired in 2000.

Petrified wood chips on the exposed slopes of Granger Canyon

Description

Payne Peak rises directly south of Cedar Pass in the Warner Mountains. Although it is usually accessed along a graded road from Cedarville, there is a lesser known trail that links the towns of Alturas and Cedarville and avoids the traffic of California 299.

The trail leaves the paved county road east of Alturas and follows a graded dirt county road through private property before entering Modoc National Forest. Once in the forest, the formed winding trail gradually climbs into the Warner Mountains. A side trail branches south to the Dry Creek Trailhead, and the main trail continues to travel west beneath the looming bulk of the rugged Sheep Rock, which rises immediately to the north.

The trail joins major graded FR 31 and travels north around the southern slope of Payne Peak. A worthwhile spur leads through stands of curl-leaf mahoganies to 360-degree views from the top of the peak. The 3-rated climb is not difficult, but the surface is loose enough that 4-wheel-drive is preferred. There is a communications tower on top of the peak. The Warner Mountains extend to the north and south, with Bear Mountain immediately to the north. Warren Peak is the highest point visible to the south. To the east are Cedarville and the Surprise Valley. The edge of Goose Lake can be seen to the northwest and Mount Shasta and Alturas are prominent features to the west. Cedar Pass and California 299 are below the peak to the north.

A second short spur leads to Pepperdine Camp, Reid Cabin, and the start of the Summit Trail into the South Warner Wilderness. Pepperdine Trailhead, like the Pepperdine cabins, has corrals for horses and pack animals, as well as a five-site campground. From here, it is possible to hike through the wilderness and connect to the many hiking and equestrian trails leading to the Patterson Guard Station on Northern Sierra #53: South Warner Mountains Trail.

The main trail swings east and descends toward Granger Canyon, becoming smaller and traveling on an uneven formed surface that requires high-clearance 4WD. Gardner Canyon is one of the prettiest parts of the trail. Its creek flows year round and is edged with aspens and cottonwoods. A highlight for rockhounds is the petrified wood that can easily be found on exposed slopes of the canyon. The wood fragments are easy to spot because they are light bone-colored chips that stand out against the dark background material. You will need to climb up the slopes to see some of the finer specimens, but take care; the slope is very steep and the surface is very loose. It is extremely easy to lose your footing and risk an undignified swift descent or worse. Check with the forest office for current regulations before collecting.

The trail within the canyon is small. A flood in 1997 washed out much of it, and although it is passable, small landslides have deposited material across the trail, which has now become part of the surface. As you descend through the deep canyon, the surface gradually improves until the trail spills out onto the county road on the western side of Surprise Valley. The trail finishes at the intersection with CR 1, south of Cedarville.

In fall, aspens and cottonwoods give the trail a golden color. Aspens are normally at their peak color between mid-September and mid-October.

Current Road Information

Modoc National Forest
Warner Mountain Ranger District
PO Box 220
Cedarville, CA 96104
(530) 279-6116

Map References

BLM   Cedarville, Alturas
USFS   Modoc National Forest
USGS   1:24,000   Surprise Station, Payne
          Peak, Shields Creek, Warren Peak
          1:100,000 Cedarville, Alturas
Maptech CD-ROM: Shasta-Trinity/Modoc
Northern California Atlas & Gazetteer,
          pp. 30, 31, 41
California Road & Recreation Atlas, p. 49
Other: Modoc County USFS/BLM Map

Route Directions

▼ 0.0   From US 395 in Alturas, take CR 56 for 6.5 miles east; then turn left on Alpine Road (CR 58), following the sign for Cedar Pass. Proceed 2.7 miles and zero trip meter. Turn southeast on graded dirt CR 58B at the sign and cross cattle guard.

2.9 ▲   Cattle guard; then the trail ends at T-intersection with Alpine Road (CR 58). Turn left and travel 2.7 miles to CR 56. Turn right on CR 56 and travel an additional 6.5 miles to reach US 395 in Alturas.

GPS: N41°31.43′ W120°23.49′

▼ 0.5 SO CR 58C on left.
2.4 ▲ SO CR 58C on right.
▼ 0.9 SO Cattle guard.
2.0 ▲ SO Cattle guard.
▼ 1.4 TL Turn left, following the sign to Dry Creek Basin.
1.5 ▲ TR Track on left.
▼ 2.6 SO Entering Modoc National Forest at gate.
0.3 ▲ SO Leaving Modoc National Forest at gate.

GPS: N41°31.08′ W120°20.97′

▼ 2.9 SO Track on right goes 2 miles to the start of Dry Creek Trail and Lower Dry Creek. Zero trip meter and follow the sign to Upper Dry Creek Basin and Deep Creek.
0.0 ▲   Continue to the northwest.

GPS: N41°30.93′ W120°20.81′

▼ 0.0   Continue to the southeast.
4.0 ▲ SO Track on left goes 2 miles to the start of Dry Creek Trail and Lower Dry Creek. Zero trip meter.
▼ 0.6 SO Cross through creek.
3.4 ▲ SO Cross through creek.
▼ 1.1 SO Cross over creek.
2.9 ▲ SO Cross over creek.
▼ 1.3 SO Track on left.
2.7 ▲ SO Track on right.

GPS: N41°30.81′ W120°19.40′

▼ 1.5 SO Cross through Dry Creek; then gate— private property on left and right.
2.5 ▲ SO Gate—private property on left and right; then cross through Dry Creek.

▼ 1.6 SO Track on right is private.
2.4 ▲ SO Track on left is private.
▼ 1.8 SO Pass through fence line.
2.2 ▲ SO Pass through fence line.
▼ 1.9 SO Track on right.
2.1 ▲ SO Track on left.
▼ 2.2 SO Track on right.
1.8 ▲ SO Track on left.
▼ 2.5 SO Spring on left.
1.5 ▲ SO Spring on right.

GPS: N41°30.48′ W120°18.26′

▼ 2.6 SO Cross over creek.

Granger Canyon's fall colors

1.4 ▲	SO	Cross over creek.
▼ 2.8	SO	Track on right.
1.2 ▲	BR	Track on left.
		GPS: N41°30.40' W120°18.04'

▼ 4.0	TL	T-intersection with graded dirt road. Zero trip meter.
0.0 ▲		Continue to the west on 42N30.
		GPS: N41°30.30' W120°16.73'

▼ 0.0		Continue to the northwest on FR 31.
2.0 ▲	TR	FR 31 continues straight ahead. Zero trip meter and follow the sign to Dry Creek Basin.
▼ 0.6	SO	Track on right.
1.4 ▲	SO	Track on left.
▼ 0.9	SO	Cattle guard.
1.1 ▲	SO	Cattle guard.
▼ 1.1	SO	Track on left; then track on right.
0.9 ▲	SO	Track on left; then track on right.
▼ 1.2	SO	Track on right.
0.8 ▲	SO	Track on left.
▼ 1.3	SO	Track on right.
0.7 ▲	SO	Track on left.
▼ 1.6	SO	Track on right.
0.4 ▲	SO	Track on left.
▼ 2.0	TR	Track on left is 42N43, spur to Payne Peak. Zero trip meter.
0.0 ▲		Continue to the southeast on FR 31.
		GPS: N41°31.68' W120°16.89'

Spur to Payne Peak

▼ 0.0		Proceed northwest on 42N43.
▼ 0.2	SO	Track on left.
▼ 0.4	SO	Track on left and track on right.
▼ 0.5	TR	Track continues straight ahead through gate. Turn right before gate.
		GPS: N41°32.02' W120°16.86'

| ▼ 1.3 | | Spur ends at the communications towers on Payne Peak. |
| | | **GPS: N41°32.49' W120°16.57'** |

Continuation of Main Trail

▼ 0.0		Continue to the east on FR 31.
1.5 ▲	TL	Track on right is 42N43, spur to Payne Peak. Zero trip meter.
		GPS: N41°31.68' W120°16.89'

NORTHERN SIERRA #55: PAYNE PEAK TRAIL

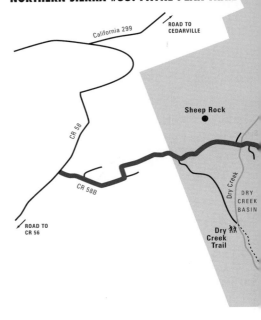

▼ 0.5	SO	Track on left.
1.0 ▲	SO	Track on right.
▼ 1.5	TR	Track on left is 42N31 to Cedarville. Zero trip meter.
0.0 ▲		Continue to the west, joining 42N31.
		GPS: N41°31.06' W120°15.55'

▼ 0.0		Continue to the southeast on 42N49.
5.4 ▲	TL	Track straight ahead is 42N31 to Cedarville. Zero trip meter and follow the sign to Deep Creek.
▼ 0.6	SO	Turnout on right.
4.8 ▲	SO	Turnout on left.
▼ 1.0	SO	Cross over South Deep Creek.
4.4 ▲	SO	Cross over South Deep Creek.
▼ 2.4	SO	Track on left.
3.0 ▲	SO	Track on right.
▼ 4.0	SO	Track on left is 42N02.
1.4 ▲	SO	Track on right is 42N02.
		GPS: N41°28.64' W120°14.79'

▼ 4.3	TL	Cattle guard; then turn left at T-intersection with FR 31.
1.1 ▲	TR	Turn right on unmarked, well-used trail and cross cattle guard.
		GPS: N41°28.41' W120°14.88'

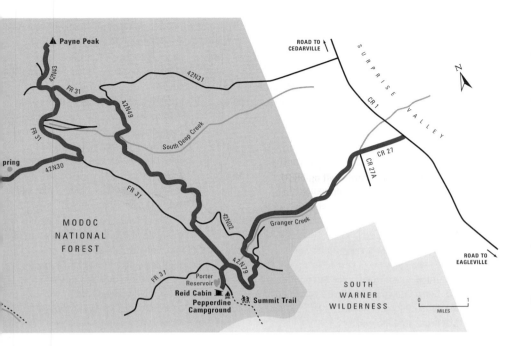

▼ 5.4   TL   FR 31 continues to the right and is the spur to Pepperdine Campground. Zero trip meter and turn left onto 42N79 following the sign to Granger Canyon. Small track straight ahead.

0.0 ▲   Continue to the north.

      GPS: N41°27.59' W120°14.43'

Spur To Pepperdine Camp

▼ 0.0   Proceed west on FR 31, following the sign to Pepperdine Campground.

▼ 0.2   TL   Turn left at the sign for Pepperdine Campground and Trailhead.

      GPS: N41°27.55' W120°14.64'

▼ 0.3   BR   Track on left goes 0.4 miles to Pepperdine Trailhead and USFS Campground.

▼ 0.6   Cross through creek; then spur ends at Pepperdine Campground and Reid Cabin.

      GPS: N41°27.20' W120°14.75'

Continuation of Main Trail

▼ 0.0   Continue to the east.

6.3 ▲   TR   Small track on left. Road ahead is FR 31 and is the spur to Pepperdine Campground. Zero trip meter and join FR 31, following the sign to Deep Creek Summit.

      GPS: N41°27.59' W120°14.43'

▼ 1.3   TL   Track on right. Bear left, remaining on main trail; then 4-way intersection. Track on right goes to Tom Lee Meadows—privately owned and closed to the public. Track straight ahead. Turn left, remaining on main trail.

5.0 ▲   TR   4-way intersection. Track on left. Track straight head goes to Tom Lee Meadows—privately owned and closed to the public. Turn right, remaining on main trail; then track on left.

      GPS: N41°27.42' W120°13.78'

▼ 1.6   SO   Cross over Granger Creek; then track on left.

4.7 ▲   SO   Track on right; then cross over Granger Creek.

▼ 1.7   SO   Track on left; then track on right.

4.6 ▲ SO Track on left; then track on right.
▼ 2.2 SO Cross through creek.

4.1 ▲ SO Cross through creek.
▼ 2.3 SO Cross over creek. Petrified wood can be found on the bare slopes on the left.

4.0 ▲ SO Cross over creek. Petrified wood can be found on the bare slopes on the right.

▼ 3.0 SO Cross through wash.

3.3 ▲ SO Cross through wash.

▼ 3.4 SO Cross through Granger Creek twice.

2.9 ▲ SO Cross through Granger Creek twice.
GPS: N41°28.02′ W120°12.47′

▼ 4.0 SO Cattle guard.

2.3 ▲ SO Cattle guard.
GPS: N41°28.21′ W120°11.89′

▼ 4.1 SO Track on left; then cross through wash.

2.2 ▲ SO Cross through wash; then track on right.

▼ 4.4 SO Cross through wash.

1.9 ▲ SO Cross through wash.

▼ 5.3 SO Track on right into private property.

1.0 ▲ BR Track on left into private property.

▼ 5.4 SO Cross through Granger Creek; then paved road on right is CR 27A. Continue on CR 27. Road becomes paved.

0.9 ▲ SO Road turns to graded dirt; then paved road on left is CR 27A. Cross through Granger Creek.
GPS: N41°28.73′ W120°10.56′

▼ 6.3   Trail ends at T-intersection with paved Surprise Valley Road (CR 1). Turn left for Cedarville; turn right for Eagleville.

0.0 ▲   Trail commences on paved Surprise Valley Road (CR 1), 3.5 miles south of the center of Cedarville, 0.6 miles south of Modoc County mile marker 26. Zero trip meter and turn west on paved road marked CR 27.
GPS: N41°28.72′ W120°09.48′

Selected Further Reading

Alt, David D., and Donald W. Hyndman. *Roadside Geology of Northern California*. Missoula, Mont.: Mountain Press Publishing Co., 1996.

———. *Roadside Geology of Northern and Central California*. Missoula, Mont.: Mountain Press Publishing Co., 2000.

AAA California, *Nevada Tour Book*, 2001.

Beck, Warren A., and Ynez D. Haase. *Historical Atlas of California*. Norman, Okla.: University of Oklahoma Press, 1974.

Bischoff, Matt C. *Touring California & Nevada Hot Springs*. Helena, Mont.: Falcon Publishing, Inc., 1997.

Boessenecker, John. *Gold Dust and Gunsmoke*. New York: John Wiley & Sons, Inc., 1999.

Braasch, Barbara. *California's Gold Rush*. Medina, Wash.: Johnston Associates International, 1996.

Bright, William. *1500 California Place Names, Their Origin and Meaning*. Berkeley, Calif.: University of California Press, 1998.

Broman, Mickey, and Russ Leadabrand. *California Ghost Town Trails*. Baldwin Park, Calif.: Gem Guides Book Company, 1981.

Browning, Peter. *Place Names of the Sierra Nevada*. Berkeley, Calif.: Wilderness Press, 1992.

———. *Day Trips: Roaming the Backroads of Northern California*. San Francisco: Chronicle Books, 1979.

DeDecker, Mary. *Mines of the Eastern Sierra*. Glendale, Calif.: La Siesta Press, 1993.

Deverell, William. *Railroad Crossing: Californians and the Railroad, 1850-1910*. Los Angeles: University of California Press, 1996.

Dunn, Jerry Camarillo, Jr. *National Geographic's Driving Guides to America: California and Nevada and Hawaii*. Washington, D.C.: The Book Division National Geographic Society. 1996.

Durham, David L. *Place-Names of California's Eastern Sierra, Including Death Valley*. Clovis, Calif.: Word Dancer Press, 2000.

———. *Place-Names of California's North Sacramento Valley*. Clovis, Calif.: Word Dancer Press, 2000.

———. *Place-Names of California's North San Joaquin Valley*. Clovis, Calif.: Word Dancer Press, 2000.

———. *Place-Names of Central California*. Clovis, Calif.: Word Dancer Press, 2000.

Fix, David, and Andy Bezener. *Birds of Northern California*. Renton, Wash.: Lone Pine Publishing, 2000.

Florin, Lambert. *Ghost Towns of The West*. New York: Promontory Press, 1993.

Gray, Mary Taylor. *Watchable Birds of California*. Missoula, Mont.: Mountain Press Publishing, 1999.

Grossi, Mark. *Longstreet Highroad Guide to the California Sierra Nevada*. Atlanta, Georgia: Longstreet Press Inc., 2000.

Gudde, Erwin G. *1000 California Place Names*. Berkeley, Calif.: University of California Press, 1959.

Harris, Edward D. *California Place Names*. Berkeley, Calif.: University of California Press, 1998.

Hart, James D. *A Companion to California*. New York: Oxford University Press, 1978.

Heizer, Robert F., ed. *The Destruction of California Indians*. Lincoln, Neb.: University of Nebraska Press, 1993.

Heizer, Robert F., and Albert B. Elasser. *The Natural World of the California Indians*. Berkeley, Calif.: University of California Press, 1980.

Hirschfelder, Arlene. *Native Americans*. New York: Dorling Kindersley Publishing, Inc., 2000.

Holliday, J.S. *Rush for Riches: Gold Fever and the Making of California*. Berkley, Calif.: University of California Press, 1999.

Holmes, Robert. *California's Best-Loved Driving Tours*. New York: Macmillan Travel, 1999.

Hoxie, Frederick E., ed. *Encyclopedia of North American Indians*. Boston: Houghton Mifflin Company, 1996.

Huegel, Tony. *Sierra Nevada Byways*. Idaho Falls, Idaho: The Post Company, 1997.

The Indians of California. Alexandria, Va.: Time-Life Books, 1994.

Johnston, Verna R. *California Forests and Woodlands*. Berkeley, Calif.: University of California Press, 1994.

Kavanagh, James, ed. *The Nature of California*. Helena, Mont.: Waterford Press Ltd., 1997.

Keyworth, C.L. *California Indians.*. New York: Checkmark Books, 1991.

Klein, James. *Where to Find Gold in Northern California*. Baldwin Park, Calif.: Gem Guides Book Company, 2000.

Kroeber, A. L. *Handbook of the Indians of California*. New York: Dover Publications, Inc., 1976.

Kyle, Douglas E. *Historic Spots in California*. Stanford, Calif.: Stanford University Press, 1990.

Lamar, Howard R., ed. *The New Encyclopedia of the American West*. New Haven, Conn.: Yale University Press. 1998.

Lewellyn, Harry. *Backroad Trips and Tips*. Costa Mesa, Calif.: Glovebox Publications, 1993.

Marinacci Barbara, and Rudy Marinacci. *California's Spanish Place*. Houston, Texas: Gulf Publishing Company, 1997.

Martin, Don, and Betty Martin. *California-Nevada Roads Less Traveled*. Henderson, Nevada: Pine Cone Press, Inc. 1999.

McFerrin, Linda Watanabe. *Best Places Northern*

California. Seattle, Wash.: Sasquatch Books, 2001.

McGlashan, C.F. *History of the Donner Party*. Stanford, Calif.: Stanford University Press, 1947.

Milner, Clyde A., II, Carol A. O'Conner, and Martha A. Sandweiss, eds. *The Oxford History of the American West*. Oxford: Oxford University Press, 1996.

Mitchell, James R. *Gem Trails of Northern California*. Baldwin Park, Calif.: Gem Guides Book Company, 1995.

Nadeau, Remi. *Ghost Towns & Mining Camps of California*. Santa Barbara, Calif.: Crest Publishers, 1999.

National Audubon Society Field Guide to North American Birds: Western Region. New York: Alfred A. Knopf, Inc., 1998.

Norris, Robert M., and Robert W. Webb. *Geology of California*. Santa Barbara: John Wiley & Sons, Inc., 1976.

North American Wildlife. New York: Readers Digest Association, Inc., 1982.

Oakeshott, Gordon B. *California's Changing Landscapes*. San Francisco: McGraw-Hill Book Company, 1978.

Paher, Stanley W. *Early Mining Days – California Gold Country: The Story Behind the Scenery*. KC Publications, Inc., 1996.

Patterson, Richard. *Historical Atlas of the Outlaw West*. Boulder, Colo.: Johnson Publishing Company, 1985.

Pearson, David W. *This Was Mining in the West*. Atglen, Penn.: Schiffer Publishing, 1996.

Pierce, L. Kingston. *America's Historic Trails with Tom Bodett*. San Francisco: KQED Books, 1997.

Powers, Stephen. *Tribes of California*. Berkeley and Los Angeles: University of California Press, 1976.

Roberts, George, and Jan Roberts. *Discover Historic California*. Baldwin Park, Calif.: Gem Guides Book Co., 1999.

Rolle, Andrew. *California: A History*. Wheeling, Ill.: Harlan Davidson, Inc., 1998.

Sagstetter, Beth, and Bill Sagstetter. *The Mining Camps Speak*. Denver: Benchmark Publishing, 1998.

Schoenherr, Allan A. *A Natural History of California*. Berkeley, Calif.: University of California Press, 1992.

Small, Arnold. *California Birds*. Vista, Calif.: IBIS Publishing Company, 1994.

Smith, Raymond M. *Ten Overnight Trips on the Backroads of Nevada & California*. Minden, Nevada: Mr. Raymond M. Smith, 1994.

Taylor, Colin F. *The Native Americans: The Indigenous People of North America*. London: Salamander Books Ltd., 2000.

Teie, William C. *4 Wheeler's Guide to the Rubicon Trail*. Rescue, Calif.: Deer Valley Press.

Thollander, Earl. *Earl Thollander's Back Roads of California*. Seattle, Wash.: Sasquatch Books, 1994.

Trafzer, Clifford E., and Joel R. Hyer, eds. *Exterminate Them!* East Lansing, Mich.: Michigan State University Press, 1999.

Varney, Philip. *Ghost Towns of Northern California*.

Stillwater, Minn.: Voyager Press, Inc., 2001.

Vinson, Brown, Henry Weston Jr., and Jerry Buzzell. *Handbook of California Birds*. Happy Camp, Calif.: Naturegraph Publishers, 1986.

Waldman, Carl. *Encyclopedia of Native American Tribes*. New York: Facts on File, 1988.

Wyman, David M. *Backroads of Northern California*. Stillwater, Minn.: Voyager Press, Inc., 2000.

Zauner, Lou, and Phyllis Zauner. *California Gold: Story of the Rush to Riches*. Sonoma, Calif.: Zanel Publications, 1997.

Selected Web sources

California Indians and their Reservations, http://infodome.sdsu.edu/research/guides/calindians/calinddict.shtml

Ghost Towns, http://www.ghosttowns.com

Gorp.com, http://www.gorp.com

Henness Pass Road, http://www.ncgold.com/Museums_Parks/syrp/henness.html

Lake Tahoe, http://www.tahoevacationguide.com/laketahoe.html

Lassen County Historical Landmarks, http://ceres.ca.gov/geo_area/counties/Lassen/landmarks.html

National Park Service, http://www.nps.gov/

U.S.D.A National Forest Service, Pacific Southwest Region, http://www.fs.fed.us/r5/index.shtml

U.S. Bureau of Land Managment, California, http://www.ca.blm.gov

About the Authors

Peter Massey grew up in the outback of Australia, where he acquired a life-long love of the backcountry. After retiring from a career in investment banking in 1986 at the age of thirty-five, he served as a director for a number of companies in the United States, the United Kingdom, and Australia. He moved to Colorado in 1993.

Jeanne Wilson was born and grew up in Maryland. After moving to New York City in 1980, she worked in advertising and public relations before moving to Colorado in 1993.

After traveling extensively in Australia, Europe, Asia, and Africa, the authors covered more than 80,000 miles touring the United States and the Australian outback between 1993 and 1997. This experience became the basis for creating the Backcountry Adventures and Trails guidebook series.

As the research team grew, a newcomer became a dedicated member of the Swagman team.

Angela Titus was born in Missouri and grew up in Virginia, where she attended the University of Virginia. She moved to Alabama and worked for *Southern Living Magazine* traveling, photographing, and writing about the southeastern U.S. She moved to Colorado in 2002.

Since research for the Backcountry Adventures and Trails guidebooks began, Peter, Jeanne, and Angela have traveled more than 75,000 miles throughout the western states.

Photo Credits

Unless otherwise indicated in the following list of acknowledgments (which is organized by page number), all photographs were taken by Bushducks—Maggie Pinder and Donald McGann.

31 California Historical Society, San Francisco; **103** Denver Public Library, Western History Collection; **179** California Historical Society, San Francisco; **261** (left, middle left, and right) Corel, (middle right) Don Baccus Photography.

Cover photography: Bushducks—Maggie Pinder and Donald McGann

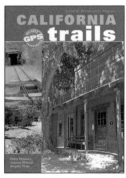

more
california trails
backroad guides

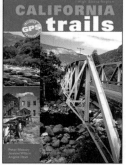

California Trails–Central Mountains

This guide is comprised of painstaking detail and descriptions for 52 trails located near the towns of Big Sur, Fresno, San Luis Obispo, Santa Barbara, Bakersfield, Mojave, and Maricopa. **ISBN-10, 1-930193-19-X; ISBN-13, 978-1-930193-19-2; Price $19.95**

California Trails–High Sierra

This guidebook navigates and describes 50 trails located near the towns of Fresno (north), Oakhurst, Lone Pine, Bishop, Bridgeport, Coulterville, Mariposa, and Mammoth Lakes. **ISBN-10, 1-930193-21-1; ISBN-13, 978-1-930193-21-5; Price $19.95**

California Trails–North Coast

This guide meticulously describes and rates 47 off-road routes located near the towns of Sacramento, Redding (west), Red Bluff, Clear Lake, McCloud, Mount Shasta, Yreka, Crescent City, and Fort Bidwell. **ISBN-10, 1-930193-22-X; ISBN-13, 978-1-930193-22-2; Price $19.95**

California Trails–South Coast

This field guide includes meticulous trail details for 50 trails located near the towns of Los Angeles, San Bernardino, San Diego, Salton Sea, Indio, Borrego Springs, Ocotillo and Palo Verde. **ISBN-10, 1-930193-24-6; ISBN-13, 978-1-930193-24-6; Price $19.95**

California Trails–Desert

This edition of our Trails series contains detailed trail information for 51 off-road routes located near the towns of Lone Pine (east), Panamint Springs, Death Valley area, Ridgecrest, Barstow, Baker and Blythe. **ISBN-10, 1-930193-20-3; ISBN-13, 978-1-930193-20-8; Price $19.95**

to order
call 800-660-5107 or
visit 4WDbooks.com

arizona trails
backroad guides

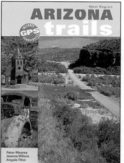

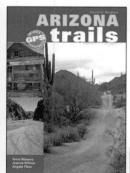

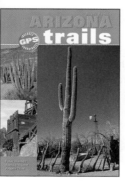

Arizona Trails–Northeast
This guidebook consists of meticulous details and directions for 47 trails located near the towns of Flagstaff, Williams, Prescott (northeast), Winslow, Fort Defiance and Window Rock. **ISBN-10, 1-930193-02-5; ISBN-13, 978-1-930193-02-4; Price $19.95**

Arizona Trails–West
This volume consists of comprehensive statistics and descriptions for 33 trails located near the towns of Bullhead City, Lake Havasu City, Parker, Kingman, Prescott (west), and Quartzsite (north). **ISBN-10, 1-930193-00-9; ISBN-13, 978-1-930193-00-0; Price $19.95**

Arizona Trails–Central
This field guide includes meticulous trail details for 44 off-road routes located near the towns of Phoenix, Wickenburg, Quartzsite (south), Payson, Superior, Globe and Yuma (north). **ISBN-10, 1-930193-01-7; ISBN-13, 978-1-930193-01-7; Price $19.95**

Arizona Trails–South
This handbook is composed of comprehensive statistics and descriptions for 33 trails located near the towns of Tucson, Douglas, Mammoth, Reddington, Stafford, Yuma (southeast), Ajo and Nogales. **ISBN-10, 1-930193-03-3; ISBN-13, 978-1-930193-03-1; Price $19.95**

utah trails
backroad guides

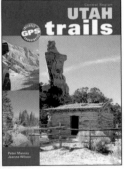

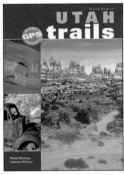

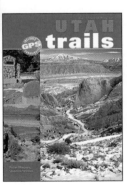

Utah Trails—Northern

This field guide includes meticulous trail details for 35 off-road routes near the towns of Vernal, Logan, Salt Lake City, Price, Wendover, Beaver, and Milford. **ISBN-10, 1-930139-30-0; ISBN-13, 978-1-930193-30-7; Price $16.95**

Utah Trails—Central

This volume is composed of comprehensive trail statistics for 34 trails near the towns of Green River, Richfield, Hanksville, Crescent Junction, and Castle Dale. **ISBN-10, 1-930193-31-9; ISBN-13, 978-1-930193-31-4; Price $16.95**

Utah Trails—Moab

This guidebook contains detailed trail information for 57 trails in and around Moab, Monticello, Canyonlands National Park, Arches National Park, Green River, Mexican Hat, Bluff, and Blanding. **ISBN-10, 1-930193-09-2; ISBN-13, 978-1-930193-09-3; Price $19.95**

Utah Trails—Southwest

This travel guide outlines detailed trail information for 49 off-road routes in the Four Corners region and around the towns of Escalante, St. George, Kanab, Boulder, Bryce Canyon, Hurricane, and Ticaboo. **ISBN-10, 1-930193-10-6; ISBN-13, 978-1-930193-10-9; Price $19.95**

to order
call 800-660-5107 or
visit 4WDbooks.com

4WDBOOKS.COM

colorado trails
backroad guides

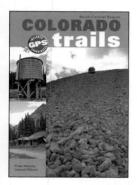

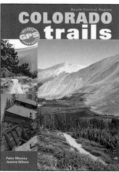

Colorado Trails–North-Central

This guidebook is composed of comprehensive statistics and descriptions of 28 trails, including 8 trails additional to those profiled in the Adventures Colorado book, around Breckenridge, Central City, Fraser, Dillon, Vail, Leadville, Georgetown, and Aspen. **ISBN-10, 1-930193-11-4; ISBN-13, 978-1-930193-11-6; Price $16.95**

Colorado Trails–South-Central

This edition of our Trails series includes meticulous trail details for 30 off-road routes located near the towns of Gunnison, Salida, Crested Butte, Buena Vista, Aspen, and the Sand Dunes National Monument. **ISBN-10, 1-930193-29-7; ISBN-13, 978-1-930193-29-1; Price $16.95**

Colorado Trails–Southwest

This field guide is comprised of painstaking details and descriptions for 31 trails, including 15 trails additional to those described in the Adventures Colorado book. Routes are located around Silverton, Ouray, Telluride, Durango, Lake City, and Montrose. **ISBN-10, 1-930193-32-7; ISBN-13, 978-1-930193-32-1; Price $16.95**

to order
call 800-660-5107 or
visit 4WDbooks.com

4WDBOOKS.COM

backcountry adventures
guides

Each book in the award-winning *Adventures* series listed below is a beautifully crafted, high-quality, sewn, 4-color guidebook. In addition to meticulously detailed backcountry trail directions and maps of every trail and region, extensive information on the history of towns, ghost towns, and regional history is included. The guides provide wildlife information and photographs to help readers identify the great variety of native birds, plants, and animals they are likely to see. This series appeals to everyone who enjoys the backcountry: campers, anglers, four-wheelers, hikers, mountain bikers, snowmobilers, amateur prospectors, sightseers, and more...

Backcountry Adventures Northern California

Backcountry Adventures Northern California takes readers along 2,653 miles of back roads from the rugged peaks of the Sierra Nevada, through volcanic regions of the Modoc Plateau, to majestic coastal redwood forests. Trail history comes to life through accounts of outlaws like Black Bart; explorers like Ewing Young and James Beckwourth; and the biggest mass migration in America's history—the Gold Rush. Contains 152 trails, 640 pages, and 679 photos.
ISBN-10, 1-930193-25-4; ISBN-13, 978-1-930193-25-3
Price, $39.95.

Backcountry Adventures Southern California

Backcountry Adventures Southern California provides 2,970 miles of routes that travel through the beautiful mountain regions of Big Sur, across the arid Mojave Desert, and straight into the heart of the aptly named Death Valley. Trail history comes alive through the accounts of Spanish missionaries; eager prospectors looking to cash in during California's gold rush; and legends of lost mines. Contains 153 trails, 640 pages, and 645 photos.
ISBN-10, 1-930193-26-2; ISBN-13, 978-1-930193-26-0
Price, $39.95.

backcountry adventures
guides

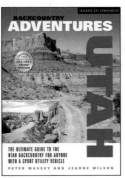

Backcountry Adventures Utah

Backcountry Adventures Utah navigates 3,721 miles through the spectacular Canyonlands region, to the top of the Uinta Range, across vast salt flats, and along trails unchanged since the riders of the Pony Express sped from station to station and daring young outlaws wreaked havoc on newly established stage lines, railroads, and frontier towns. Trail history comes to life through the accounts of outlaws like Butch Cassidy; explorers and mountain men; and early Mormon settlers. Contains 175 trails, 544 pages, and 532 photos.
ISBN-10, 1-930193-27-0; ISBN-13, 978-1-930193-27-7
Price, $39.95.

Backcountry Adventures Arizona

Backcountry Adventures Arizona guides readers along 2,671 miles of the state's most remote and scenic back roads, from the lowlands of the Yuma Desert to the high plains of the Kaibab Plateau. Trail history is colorized through the accounts of Indian warriors like Cochise and Geronimo; trailblazers; and the famous lawman Wyatt Earp. Contains 157 trails, 576 pages, and 524 photos.
ISBN-10, 1-930193-28-9; ISBN-13, 978-1-930193-28-4
Price, $39.95.

4WD Adventures Colorado

4WD Adventures Colorado takes readers to the Crystal River or over America's highest pass road, Mosquito Pass. This book identifies numerous lost ghost towns that speckle Colorado's mountains. Trail history is brought to life through the accounts of sheriffs and gunslingers like Bat Masterson and Doc Holliday; millionaires like Horace Tabor; and American Indian warriors like Chief Ouray. ains 71 trails, 232 pages, and 209 photos.
ISBN 0-9665675-5-2.
Price, $29.95.

to order
call 800-660-5107 or
visit 4WDbooks.com

4WD BOOKS.COM

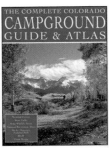

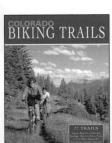

other
colorado outdoors
guides

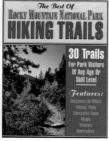

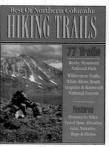

Colorado's Guide to Hunting

Colorado's backcountry is habitat for all sorts of game animals. The guide contains land regulations, permits needed, detailed directions and maps for the best places to hunt. **ISBN 0-930657-42-X; Price $14.95**

Best of Northern Colorado Hiking Trails

Contains 77 trails from short, easy day hikes to difficult backpacking adventures. The book covers Arapaho, Roosevelt, White River, and Routt National Forests. It includes directions, maps, trail length, elevation gains, and difficulty. **ISBN 0-930657-18-7; Price $12.95**

Best of Western Colorado Hiking Trails

Contains 50 trails from short, easy day hikes to difficult backpacking adventures. The book covers White River and Gunnison National Forests. It includes directions, maps, trail length, elevation gains, and difficulty. **ISBN 0-930657-17-9; Price $9.95**

Best of Rocky Mountain National Park Hiking Trails

Contains 30 trails for hikers of all skill levels from short, easy hikes to more difficult trails. It includes camping information, estimated hiking time, trail narratives, directions, maps, trail length, elevation gains, and difficulty. **ISBN 0-930657-39-X; Price $9.95**

Colorado Lakes & Reservoirs: Fishing and Boating Guide

Colorado is home to hundreds of natural and man-made lakes. This book provides information about 150 of them. Included are driving directions, maps, fishing regulations, lake size, fish species, boating ramps, camping facilities, and contact information. **ISBN 0-930657-00-4; Price $14.95**

to order
call 800-660-5107 or
visit 4WDbooks.com